Making Men Moral

The American Social Experience

SERIES

James Kirby Martin

GENERAL EDITOR

Paula S. Fass, Steven H. Mintz,
Carl Prince, James W. Reed & Peter N. Stearns

EDITORS

1. *The March to the Sea and Beyond: Sherman's Troops in the Savannah and Carolinas Campaigns*
JOSEPH T. GLATTHAAR

2. *Childbearing in American Society: 1650–1850*
CATHERINE M. SCHOLTEN

3. *The Origins of Behaviorism: American Psychology, 1870–1920*
JOHN M. O'DONNELL

4. *New York City Cartmen, 1667–1850*
GRAHAM RUSSELL HODGES

5. *From Equal Suffrage to Equal Rights: Alice Paul and the National Woman's Party, 1910–1928*
CHRISTINE A. LUNARDINI

6. *Mr. Jefferson's Army: Political and Social Reform of the Military Establishment, 1801–1809*
THEODORE J. CRACKEL

7. *"A Peculiar People": Slave Religion and Community-Culture among the Gullahs*
MARGARET WASHINGTON CREEL

8. *"A Mixed Multitude": The Struggle for Toleration in Colonial Pennsylvania*
SALLY SCHWARTZ

9. *Women, Work, and Fertility, 1900–1986*
SUSAN HOUSEHOLDER VAN HORN

10. *Liberty, Virtue, and Progress: Northerners and Their War for the Union*
EARL J. HESS

11. *Lewis M. Terman: Pioneer in Psychological Testing*
HENRY L. MINTON

12. Schools as Sorters: Lewis M. Terman, Applied Psychology, and the Intelligence Testing Movement, 1890–1930
PAUL DAVIS CHAPMAN

13. Free Love: Marriage and Middle-Class Radicalism in America, 1825–1860
JOHN C. SPURLOCK

14. Jealousy: The Evolution of an Emotion in American History
PETER N. STEARNS

15. The Nurturing Neighborhood: The Brownsville Boys Club and Jewish Community in Urban America, 1940–1990
GERALD SORIN

16. War in America to 1775: Before Yankee Doodle
JOHN MORGAN DEDERER

17. An American Vision: Far Western Landscape and National Culture, 1820–1920
ANNE FARRAR HYDE

18. Frederick Law Olmsted: The Passion of a Public Artist
MELVIN KALFUS

19. Medical Malpractice in Nineteenth-Century America: Origins and Legacy
KENNETH ALLEN DE VILLE

20. Dancing in Chains: The Youth of William Dean Howells
RODNEY D. OLSEN

21. Breaking the Bonds: Marital Discord in Pennsylvania, 1730–1830
MERRIL D. SMITH

22. In the Web of Class: Delinquents and Reformers in Boston, 1810s–1930s
ERIC C. SCHNEIDER

23. Army of Manifest Destiny: The American Soldier in the Mexican War, 1846–1848
JAMES M. MCCAFFREY

24. The Dutch-American Farm
DAVID STEVEN COHEN

25. Independent Intellectuals in the United States, 1910–1945
STEVEN BIEL

26. The Modern Christmas in America: A Cultural History of Gift Giving
WILLIAM B. WAITS

27. *The First Sexual Revolution: The Emergence of Male Heterosexuality in Modern America*
KEVIN WHITE

28. *Bad Habits: Drinking, Smoking, Taking Drugs, Gambling, Sexual Misbehavior, and Swearing in American History*
JOHN C. BURNHAM

29. *General Richard Montgomery and the American Revolution: From Redcoat to Rebel*
HAL T. SHELTON

30. *From Congregation Town to Industrial City: Culture and Social Change in a Southern Community*
MICHAEL SHIRLEY

31. *The Social Dynamics of Progressive Reform: Atlantic City, 1854–1920*
MARTIN PAULSSON

32. *America Goes to War: A Social History of the Continental Army*
CHARLES PATRICK NEIMEYER

33. *American Women and the Repeal of Prohibition*
KENNETH D. ROSE

34. *Making Men Moral: Social Engineering during the Great War*
NANCY K. BRISTOW

35. *Tituba, Reluctant Witch of Salem: Devilish Indians and Puritan Fantasies*
ELAINE G. BRESLAW

Making Men Moral

Social Engineering during the Great War

Nancy K. Bristow

NEW YORK UNIVERSITY PRESS
New York and London

NEW YORK UNIVERSITY PRESS
New York and London

Library of Congress Cataloging-in-Publication Data

Bristow, Nancy K.
Making men moral : social engineering during the great war / Nancy K. Bristow.
p. cm.—(The American social experience series ; 34)
Includes bibliographical references and index.
Contents: "An invisible armor" : the progressive social vision and World War One—"Full-orbed moral manhood" : cultural nationalism and the creation of new men and women—Reformers between two worlds : the battle against tradition and working-class modernism—Building a national community : the complexities of gender—Repression and resistance : African Americans and the progressives' national community—The end of the crusade : demobilization and the legacy of the CTCA.
ISBN 0-8147-1220-7 (acid-free paper)
1. Soldiers—United States—Conduct of life. 2. United States. Commission on Training Camp Activities. 3. Social reformers—United States—History—20th century. 4. Military bases—Social aspects—United States. 5. World War, 1914-1918—Social aspects—United States. I. Title. II. Series.
UH630.B75 1996
355.1'33—dc20 95-32501
CIP

Manufactured in the United States of America

10 9 8 7 6 5 4 3 2 1

To my parents, with love and appreciation.

Contents

List of Illustrations

All photographs appear as a group following page 112.

Preface

Just a few days after the United States entered the First World War in April 1917, President Woodrow Wilson created a new federal agency, the Commission on Training Camp Activities (CTCA), and charged it with responsibility for protecting the newly mobilized American soldiers from the ravages of venereal disease. Over the course of the war this commission acquired substantial support from the Wilson administration and employed its financial and human resources to intervene considerably in the daily lives of soldiers and civilians across the United States.

Though appointed to prevent unnecessary manpower losses, the personnel of the CTCA always anticipated a much larger role for themselves. True to the progressive tradition from which they emerged, these reformers combined their concern for military efficiency with broader social and cultural goals. Americans had long viewed soldiers as social pariahs and their encampments as unsavory influences. With progressives commanding the war effort, however, this traditional affront to standards of decency was no longer acceptable. Fears of soldier immorality conflated easily with reformers' concerns about the cultural influence of others they viewed as marginal Americans. Eager to combat what they understood as looming social chaos, progressives in the commission envisioned the remaking of the soldiers' training environment as the first step in a more complete transformation of American culture. Beginning with the troops and their civilian neighbors, the progressives planned to use education, recreation, and repression to create crusaders worthy of the American cause and capable of sustaining the campaign for national uplift after the war.

In pursuing these plans during the war the CTCA reflected a broader tendency evident among progressive reformers. Many members of the progressive movement saw in the war a new opportunity to pursue reforms on the home front and anticipated taking advantage of the fluid environment of wartime to further their domestic reform agendas. Adapting to the changed circumstances of war, the reformers reasoned, Americans would more readily accept reforms identified with the war effort. This book illuminates the social and cultural vision one group of reformers brought to their work during World War One, as well as the way their programs operated in the real world of camp and community. It investigates both the actions of the progressive reformers and the reactions of the soldiers and civilians who were their primary targets, focusing on the Commission on Training Camp Activities.[1]

This work, though, is about much more than the administration of a federal program. Representative of the broad reforming impulse known as the progressive movement, the CTCA constitutes a useful example of progressivism at the height of its power. *Making Men Moral* uses both the reformers' theoretical ideal and the reality of their attempted application of that ideal to investigate the contours of the cultural contests of the early twentieth century, the place of reformers in those confrontations, and the role of the war in influencing both of these.

Attempting to remake American culture in their own white, urban, middle-class image, the CTCA reformers cultivated and ultimately enforced a form of cultural nationalism. Their norms, they hoped, would become national standards, replacing the multitude of American cultures with a homogeneous one. Articulating a comprehensive social vision in a rapidly changing society, the CTCA reformers embodied a single perspective in a dynamic competition that confronted specific issues of gender, class, and race relations, as well as broader issues of national identity. The context of war added both an apparent urgency and a heightened stridency to these debates. A society mobilizing for war, reformers maintained, could not afford to be flexible in delineating acceptable behavior.

Preoccupied with social stability, the reformers focused on reshaping social roles, defining anew constructions of manhood and womanhood. In promulgating these new ideals, the reformers' preexisting notions about gender, class, and racial identities profoundly influenced their actions. Though progressives realized the importance of class, race, ethnicity, and region in shaping an individual's cultural affiliations, they never planned to embrace many of the cultures with which their programs competed. Claiming to arbitrate existing cultural conflicts, the reformers did so without questioning their own assumptions and with no intention of altering the essential status structures of the nation.

In their efforts to establish national norms, reformers contended with Americans who did not share their views and who refused to toe their cultural line. While the war granted the CTCA progressives temporary rhetorical claim to patriotism and Americanism and placed those who opposed the CTCA in the unenviable position of defending themselves against charges of disloyalty and repression, the resultant power was nevertheless insufficient to undermine individuals' social and cultural customs based on regional, racial, ethnic, and class identities. At war's end, progressives involved with the CTCA found themselves isolated from the mainstream of American culture and alienated from many of their former allies in the progressive movement.

The book begins with an introductory chapter that outlines traditional fears of soldier immorality and the progressive response to those fears represented in the creation of the Commission on Training Camp Activities. Chapter 2 examines the masculine and feminine ideals that shaped the commission's programs and explains the role of the reformers' social identities in shaping them.

Chapter 3 moves us from the progressives' drawing boards to the training camps and civilian communities of war-time America, where the CTCA established its programs. This chapter considers the CTCA's attempts to counteract the competing influences of the urban working class and cultural traditionalists and the contradictions that resulted between the commission's expressed purposes and their methods. Chapter 4 continues the exploration of these contradictions, investigating the complexities of gender and class evident in the CTCA's work with women. The place of African Americans in the CTCA's national community is the topic of chapter 5; here is found the strongest example of resistance to these contradictions and to the reformers' cultural nationalism. The final chapter considers the CTCA during the demobilization period, exploring both the commission's efforts to retain support for its programs and the responses of soldiers and civilians to demobilization circumstances. The book ends with an epilogue, which attempts to suggest significant parallels between the commission's world and our own.

The reforming impulse has always been strong in the United States. It is difficult to generalize about this impulse, which has taken countless forms over the course of American history. Reform has been at its best when it has promoted equality, justice, and fairness. Yet the reforming impulse has promoted inequality as commonly as it has equality, injustice as commonly as justice, and discrimination as commonly as fairness.

Reformers in the CTCA seemed to promise all that is best in American reform as they identified themselves with democracy and equality, and yet the programs they produced too often contradicted these expressed ideals and highlighted the more coercive side of the reforming impulse. The failure of the CTCA reformers to meet their lofty goals, though, should not cause us to discount their sincerity or encourage us to dismiss them as hypocrites. Indeed, it is the combination of their sincerity and their failure that makes these reformers of such compelling interest. The CTCA's struggles during and after the war illuminate the contested quality of American culture in the early twentieth century, the nature of progressivism and the progressive alliance, and the fate of both of these in the Great War.

Acknowledgments

There are few things in life more elusive than historical truth. Yet over the years of working on this project, one truth has become eminently clear to me—that this book would never have reached completion without the valuable assistance and support of many institutions, colleagues, friends, and family members.

The University of California at Berkeley provided funds that aided in the researching and writing of the dissertation on which this book is based. The University of Puget Sound provided travel funding and a junior sabbatical, which permitted me the time and resources to complete the project. Both of these institutions, as well as Wabash College, also granted me funding to attend conferences where I was able to share my early efforts on this work. I would like to thank the commentators and chairpersons at those conferences for their invaluable suggestions, which have informed my thinking on many subjects included here. In particular, I would like to express appreciation to Beth Bailey, Gerald D. Nash, Richard Polenberg, Julie Liss, Alan Dawley, Mark C. Carnes, and Wilbur R. Miller, as well as to participants at the Northwest Women's Studies Association conference in 1991, the Northwest American Studies Association conference in 1991, and the Society for the Interdisciplinary Study of Social Imagery conference in 1992.

I also owe an enormous debt to the staffs of several libraries, including the staffs in the Central Reading Room, the Still Picture Branch, and the Motion Picture, Sound and Video Branch of the National Archives in Washington, D.C., as well as the staffs at the Suitland, Maryland, branch of the National Archives, the Library of Congress, Princeton University's Seeley G. Mudd Library, the Ayer Public Library in Ayer, Massachusetts, and the Social Welfare History Archives at the University of Minnesota. I would like to offer special thanks to the archivists at the U.S. Army Military History Institute and to George Challou, Michael Knapp, and Mitch Yockelson in the Military Records Branch of the National Archives for their expertise and assistance in helping me make my way through the mazes of their archives. I am also especially indebted to the librarians at the University of California at Berkeley and at the University of Puget Sound, particularly those in the interlibrary loan departments.

A number of teachers have influenced my academic life through their teaching, their encouragement, and the example of their scholarly ability, and to all of them I wish to express my appreciation and my tremendous respect. At Colorado College George Drake, William Hochman, and Susan Ashley helped me discover my interest in the peoples of the past and gave me examples of teaching excellence to which I will always aspire. At the University of California James Kettner provided essential support and significant instruction that helped me to survive the early years of my graduate career. I owe special thanks to the members of my dissertation committee at Berkeley—Paula Fass, Lawrence Levine, and Norman Jacobson—who served with the good humor, patience, and wisdom every graduate student dreams of finding in his or her committee. Their advice and criticism improved my dissertation immensely, while their support maintained my morale. At the same time they have provided me with examples of scholarly and teaching excellence that I will long seek to emulate in my own work. Paula Fass, who chaired my dissertation committee, offered insightful comments on content and style that carried my work far beyond where I could have taken it alone. Equally importantly, her unwavering support allowed me to continue moving forward when my own tendency was to stop. For all of this I would like to thank her.

Colleagues have provided me with important intellectual insight and supportive friendship over the last several years. The members of my dissertation group at Berkeley assisted me while this book was still a dissertation. The members of this group were many and constantly changing, but I would like to thank especially Steve Aron, Michael Bess, Bill Deverell, Anne Hyde, Lynn Johnson, Sherry Katz, Kathy Kudlick, Maura O'Connor, Mary Odem, Tip Ragan, Gerda Ray, Lucy Salyer,

Jeff Wasserstrum, and Glennys Young. Colleagues at Wabash College, especially Peter Frederick, helped me make the transition from student to professor. Colleagues at the University of Puget Sound have provided me with a rich and supportive intellectual environment in which I continue to grow as a teacher and a scholar.

There are others without whose help this manuscript might never have reached completion. In particular I would like to thank Ruthanne Weinstein for editing assistance on early drafts, Gordon Jackson for his help with my endnotes and with countless other matters of uncertainty, Becky Dorocak for her mastery of charts and computers, and Florence Phillippi for her continual provision of assistance in all aspects of my academic work. I would also like to thank Niko Pfund, editor-in-chief at New York University Press, for his enthusiastic support of my project, for his willingness to offer suggestions on a very preliminary draft, for his significant insights on my work, and for his wonderful guidance through the entire publishing process.

Friends have helped me with this work in ways less tangible but no less significant. I would like to thank my friends from Sierra Designs, who for several of the years of my graduate career provided me with a refuge. Other friends, in particular Rob Shaeffer, Margaret Moulton, Bob Petersen, Ellen Grossman, Ruthanne Weinstein, and Eddie Rankin, have provided me with wonderful friendships, remarkable understanding, and limitless encouragement.

My family, too, has contributed a great deal to the project and deserve my thanks for all they have done. John and Vivian Bristow, May Ott, and Fred Moore provided me with my own history and provided role models I continue to emulate. Jim Bristow, Gwen Fyfe, John, and Elizabeth have been friends and supporters of mine on this project and in all other aspects of my life. Mike Bristow and Karen England, in addition to being friends, have served as important examples of the value of pursuing those things you love. Kasmine has provided her own special kind of assistance, while Sally has been my constant reminder that there is more to life than note cards, computers, and the study of the past.

My parents, to whom I have dedicated this book, have provided support—emotional, intellectual, and financial—without which it would never have been started. Their love, their generosity, their belief in me, and their enthusiasm for my work are beyond value. They have taught me to pursue my dreams and have provided me with the support to make that possible. My appreciation for all of this and my respect and admiration for both of them reach beyond what can be expressed here.

Finally, I would like to thank Gordon Jackson. His enthusiasm for understanding the past and his commitment to the value of education are infectious and have helped me to remember why I do what I do. He has never wavered in his support for my work; I literally could not have completed this book without his help, which took countless forms over the last several years. I appreciate his friendship and his support more than I will ever be able to articulate. He has made our house a home, and I thank him for everything.

Many of the strengths of the work that follows are the result of the assistance I have received from those listed above. Of course, only I am responsible for its shortcomings.

C H A P T E R   O N E

"An Invisible Armor": The Progressive Social Vision and World War One

> In a few days the young men from many homes will enter camps where they will receive their training for service in the war. Should they fall in battle their friends and parents will doubtless feel that they died in a worthy cause. But it is not the thought of battle that saddens the homes as much as the fear of what might happen in the camps at home. . . . Millions of parents and friends Mr. President are looking to you to protect their young men from worse than death.
>
> —Galen Morton of Beardstown, Illinois, to President Wilson, 29 August 1917

In the months following the United States declaration of war in World War One, President Woodrow Wilson and Secretary of War Newton D. Baker received a deluge of correspondence from anxious citizens like Galen Morton,[1] Americans concerned about the well-being of the men and boys destined to become America's fighting force. The hazards these petitioners feared were not the risks of the battlefield but those of the training camp, the immoral influences popularly associated with military encampments and their surrounding communities. Letters, telegrams, and petitions poured in from every region of the country, pleading with the commander-in-chief and his assistant to intercede and protect American youths from what correspondents feared would be a morally debilitating training camp environment. Though accepting the possibility of an honorable death in battle, citizens refused to tolerate the moral destruction of their sons and husbands as a reasonable military risk. As a mother from Oregon declared, "We are willing to sacrifice our boys, if need be, to die to make men free, but we rebel and protest against their being returned to us ruined in body and ideals. I know that I voice the sentiment of every pure woman in my state—yes, and the whole country."[2]

Most correspondents pointed to alcohol and illicit sexual relations as the primary scourges of the training camps. A petition from the Ministerial Association and Christian Endeavor Convention meeting in Fowler, Illinois, asserted:

> We . . . respectfully petition you to help keep our boys clean; not only from the ravages of the liquor traffic, but the scarlot *[sic]* woman as well. We have sincerely given you our best and we sincerely trust you will not only use them, but protect them from these foes that are more deadly than the armies of Europe, inasmuch as they destroy both soul and body.[3]

For many Americans the ravages of immorality associated with the training camps loomed more dangerously than the weapons of the enemy and were more damaging and more permanent in their consequences. Urging that soldiers be prevented from drinking alcohol, one woman lamented:

> In response to your call we have surrendered to your absolute control our hearts *[sic]* absolute dearest treasures—our sons. If their precious bodies that have cost us so dear should be torn to shreds by german shot and shells we will try to live on in the hope of meeting them again in the blessed Country of happy reunïons. But Mr. President, if the hell-holes that infest their training camps should trip up their unwary feet and they be returned to us besotted degenerate wrecks of their former selves cursed with that hell-born craving for alcohol we can have no such hope.[4]

This mother's willingness to accept even the most violent death of her child clearly reflected both her belief in an afterlife and her conviction that an honorable death would be more tolerable than a dishonorable life. Similarly, a widowed mother pleaded that her only son be kept from "lewd women," explaining, "I am willing to sacrifice much for my country. I would give up my own life willingly, or what is dearer than that, I will offer up my boy, if necessary. But I am not willing to give up his honor or his immortal soul."[5] Although acquiescent in sacrificing much for their nation in wartime, many civilians recoiled in horror from the perceived consequences of sending a relative to the training camps.

"You Will Smell Hell Here": The Historical Image of the Soldier and the Training Camp

Images of the military encampment as a corrupt and immoral environment were not new in 1917, but were based on a long history. Camps and their inhabitants had often represented important departures from contemporary standards of decency. In army camps during the War for Independence American soldiers strained their claims to "revolutionary virtue" as they "embraced military vices."[6] Desertion, theft, fighting, and profanity all plagued the Continental Army, and alcohol use, though acceptable in moderation to the revolutionary generation, became excessive, only exacerbating existing discipline problems.[7]

Military encampments of the Civil War did little to change Americans' views of training camps. In both the Confederate and the Union camps soldiers exhibited a rejection of moral conventions that shocked many Americans. In his study of the Confederate soldier, Bell Irvin Wiley observes, "Objective study of soldiers' letters and diaries makes inescapable the conclusion that all the evils usually associated with barrack and camp life flourished in the Confederate Army."[8] Those evils included Sabbath breaking, gambling, drinking, theft, and illicit sexual relations, and they were equally prevalent among the Union troops.[9] In the popular mind soldiering and immorality became closely linked; Americans of the Civil War generation came to view the troop encampments as breeding grounds for wickedness. As one Confederate soldier told his wife, "Dont *[sic]* never come here as long as you can ceep *[sic]* away for you will smell hell here."[10]

The military garrisons on the western frontier only reaffirmed this association of military life with moral decay. Though the military establishment maintained that it discouraged prostitution in both the garrisons and neighboring towns, vice was widespread, accepted, and sometimes encouraged by military leaders.[11] These frontier posts confirmed the reputations of military encampments as breeding grounds of immorality and fostered what historian Anne M. Butler describes as the "entrenchment of institutionalized vice."[12]

In 1917 Americans did not have to hark back to the distant past to find evidence that military training camps could be dangerously immoral places. They needed only to recall the previous year, when American troops served in camps on the Mexican border. Time and again letters and petitions to the president referred uneasily to the conditions in those camps. One woman from Woodstock, Illinois, pleaded with the president "that the scandalous and dreadful things that happened on the border last year 'may never be repeated.' "[13] Another reported: "One of the boys of our town said he had never heard of as much debauchery as he saw while down at the Mexican border. Mothers who have always reared their boys in purity become very much disheartened when they know of these conditions."[14] In the spring of 1917 the calls for troops were overshadowed for many by the memory of those conditions, a specter of innocent American boys overwhelmed by the forces of alcohol, sex, and immorality.[15]

In past wars the government had tolerated these conditions. In World War One, however, concerned citizens found a federal government that shared their revulsion at the training camps and their determination that in this war things would be different. As Americans mobilized for war in the spring of 1917, the nation's war effort was led by a president and a secretary of war who strongly identified with the reform agendas of progressivism and were committed to cleaning up the training camps.

"The Social Possibilities of War": The Emergence of the Commission on Training Camp Activities

Secretary of War Newton D. Baker had come to the War Department in March 1916 with established progressive credentials. He had served as both city solicitor and mayor in Cleveland. Though initially skeptical of the advantages of federal activism, during his time as mayor Baker worked to accomplish important reforms in his city through local action. Advocating municipal use of the initiative, referendum, and recall, and favoring public ownership of utilities, Baker sought to democratize and rationalize urban politics. At the same time Baker also developed a deep interest in the "social problems raised by the growth of a great urban industrial center."[16] Committed to improving the recreational environment of Cleveland's urban residents as one step in coping with those social problems, Baker worked to remove unsavory dance halls and campaigned to replace them with more wholesome parks and playgrounds.[17]

Baker approached the problems of the military as a reformer. Distrustful of the military establishment and antimilitarist in his convictions, Baker viewed the military with the eyes of an outsider.[18] This perspective, combined with his experiences in Cleveland reform, made possible Baker's innovative approach to the problem of the training camp.

The conflict on the Mexican border in 1916 introduced Baker to the realities of training camp life. Conditions among American troops on the Mexican border initially duplicated the debauchery of camps of the past; alcohol abuse, prostitution, and venereal disease were rampant. In July 1916 reformers affiliated with the American Social Hygiene Association, an organization dedicated to sexual purity and sexual health, visited Baker in Washington to complain about conditions on the border.[19] Sensitive to these reformers' worries, Baker engaged an investigator to conduct a survey of conditions in the camps, selecting the noted urban reformer Raymond B. Fosdick for the job.

Though Fosdick had been involved with the social settlement movement and had served as a city official in New York, he was best known for investigations of the European and American police systems, which he had conducted under the auspices of John D. Rockefeller's Bureau of Social Hygiene.[20] In these studies Fosdick had found the quality of the European police, as well as public respect for the police, in sharp contrast to the American example, where police had little sense of professionalism and maintained neither the respect nor the trust of the populace. In the United States, Fosdick lamented, "the average police force sinks in its rut, while crime and violence flourish."[21] With the publication of these reports Fosdick gained national recognition as a muckraker and reformer.

In his investigation of several cities and towns along the border, Fosdick found precisely the conditions Baker and the social hygiene reformers had feared—camps surrounded by brothels and saloons, soldiers physically ill with venereal disease and morally corrupted by alcohol and prostitution, and local governments generally unconcerned about the conditions. Outlining the flourishing trade in bodies and bottles along the border, Fosdick's report in August 1916 acknowledged that "in all these cities the maxim that prostitution follows an army is fully substantiated." Complicating the situation still further, he continued, "there are numerous saloons in most if not all towns and villages where the troops are encamped."[22] Though the situation varied from camp to camp, it also appeared that military officers not only allowed, but sometimes encouraged, the immorality.[23]

On the basis of his findings Fosdick outlined a plan to clean up the border camps and towns. He encouraged the secretary of war to use public condemnation and repression of alcohol and prostitution, as well as the substitution of other opportunities for recreation, to eliminate the men's attraction to the illicit trades.[24]

Baker's resulting demands for tighter restrictions on soldier life were marginally successful in improving what he defined as the moral conditions of camp life along the border. Yet the work with soldiers on the Mexican border was limited in important ways.[25] Baker relied primarily on repression and discipline and did not develop the constructive recreational program Fosdick recommended. Further, the American action itself was short-lived, was confined to a small and isolated geographic area, and involved only a modest number of troops. As a result, any changes in army life affected only a handful of Americans.

American entry into World War One, however, presented reformers with a dramatically changed circumstance. Following the outbreak of war in Europe in 1914, American progressives tangled with one another, and sometimes with themselves, as they sought to resolve the tension between the reforming impulse and the seemingly irresistible pull of the war.[26] In the months following American entry, progressives continued to disagree on the appropriate relationship between reforming forces and the war. Although much of the opposition to the war came from reformers, with public figures such as Jane Addams and Robert LaFollette leading the way, by April 1917 the prowar forces owned equal claim to the progressive banner.[27] Determined to apply progressive principles to the American war effort, reformers like President Wilson and Secretary of War Baker defined the war in progressive terms and sought to use it to progressive ends.

On 2 April 1917, in a grave tone commensurate with the "solemn and even tragical character" of his request, Woodrow Wilson asked the United States Congress for a declaration of war against the Imperial German Government. In his speech Wilson emphasized the selflessness of American motivations and urged the Congress and the people of the United States to commit themselves to a war to free the people of Europe. "The world must be made safe for democracy," he declared. "We have no selfish ends to serve. . . . We are but one of the champions of the rights of mankind. We shall be satisfied when those rights have been made as secure as the faith and the freedom of nations can make them."[28] As the historian David Kennedy suggests, the president, preparing Americans for war, urged them to understand the war as "a war for democracy, a war to end war, a war to protect liberalism, a war against militarism, a war to redeem barbarous Europe, a crusade." Translating the war into progressive terms, the president provided many reformers with the justification they needed to support the military effort.[29]

If the war was to be a crusade in the international sphere, for many progressives it was to be a war full of "social possibilities" at home, the culmination of the progressive crusade against domestic enemies.[30] Rooseveltian progressives embraced the war for the strengthening effect the martial spirit would bring to American society. Progressives such as Herbert Croly and Walter Lippmann of the *New Republic* welcomed the conflict for the unifying and uplifting effect it would have "in the realm of the spirit."[31] Social justice reformers, too, saw in the war an opportunity to bring "to a climax" their efforts for reform.[32] The war for democracy in the world would be fought on the home front as well, a continuation of the long progressive struggle, with new and grander possibilities for success.[33]

In this context Fosdick's recommendations for the remaking of soldier life gained new stature and the full support of the War Department and the oval office. On 2 April 1917, the day of the president's war message to Congress, Baker urged Wilson to realize the regained importance of the lessons learned on the Mexican border.[34] With President Wilson describing the American involvement as a battle for the betterment of mankind, Fosdick's vision of a new military environment dovetailed with Wilson's description of the purposes of the war. Enlisted to bear arms for the United States in the international crusade, American troops became the target of an important domestic reform program. Unlike any army ever before assembled, the American troops were to be kept physically healthy *and* morally pure, free of the traditional degradation of training camp culture. Announcing this intention, President Wilson declared, "The Federal Government has pledged its word that as far as care and vigilance can accomplish the result, the men committed to its charge will be returned to the homes and communities that so generously gave them with no scars except those won in honorable conflict."[35]

On 17 April 1917, less than two weeks after the formal declaration of war against Germany, the War Department established a new federal agency, the Commission on Training Camp Activities (CTCA), and charged it with responsibility for fulfilling the president's pledge. Baker asked Raymond Fosdick to assume the chairmanship of the commission.[36]

In its initial stages the commission established both in-camp and community recreation programs designed to replace the less savory attractions of the saloon and whorehouse with more wholesome pastimes. Carefully selected recreation, reformers hoped, could be used to teach both soldiers and civilians sound leisure habits. The commission also organized social hygiene education programs for both soldiers and civilians, which encouraged both groups to accept the importance of sexual purity and their own responsibility in promoting it. Finally, though the War Department hoped the lessons taught through recreation and sex education would make further efforts unnecessary, the commission provided additional weaponry for the battle against venereal disease in a program of chemical prophylaxis, and for the struggle against alcohol and vice more generally in a program of law enforcement and repression.[37]

The CTCA was a classically progressive federal agency. Both the secretary of war and the chairman of the commission were established reformers, identified with progressivism. As they articulated the commission's purposes and developed its programs, they reflected again and again their commitment to the broader progressive movement.

It is this connection to progressivism that grants the CTCA much of its historical significance. An exploration of the CTCA allows us to move beyond generalizations about progressivism into a specific study of that historical phenomenon, offering us the opportunity to understand it much more completely. Though never entirely unified, progressive reformers nevertheless wielded notable power in the first two decades of the twentieth century. The CTCA illustrates both the tensions resulting from the complexity of progressivism and the overarching social vision that nevertheless defined the progressive movement's primary impact on its society.

The Progressive Social Vision: Morality, Social Justice, and Efficiency

What exactly was progressivism? In the simplest terms it was a reform movement that began in the 1890s, dominated the American political scene between 1900 and 1918, and then faded from view in the following decade.[38] Beginning in the 1890s, reformers who would term themselves progressives began organizing to combat the consequences of industrialization. Although convinced of the fundamental soundness and superiority of the American political and economic systems, progressives found that industrialization and the resulting urbanization and immigration had created a multitude of new problems in their society. Eternally optimistic, however, progressives were certain of their ability to cope with the changes while maintaining the integrity of their democratic, capitalist society. Aware of the immensity of their task, progressives hoped to use governmental power to surmount the new problems America faced.

These general characteristics defined the progressives, but one must be cautious about too simple or too concise a definition of progressivism; progressivism itself was never simple. Representing Americans from all classes, sexes, races, and regions, the progressive movement is best understood not as a traditional movement, but rather as a series of "shifting coalitions" among reformers sharing certain essential beliefs but often varying in their particular concerns and priorities.[39]

Indeed, its diversity was an important feature of the progressive movement. Progressives shared the broad assumptions outlined above—a belief in capitalism and democracy, a concern about the dangers posed to both systems by industrialization and its consequences, and a confident optimism about their ability to use the government to remake America—but they also had a marked tendency to disagree on particulars. The outbreak of war, for instance, prompted several different responses among the progressives. In their understandings of the nature of society's problems, too, progressives often disagreed with one another. As a result progressives sometimes differed in the goals they set; often their varying agendas prevented them from working together. Even when progressives formed powerful coalitions with one another, the coalitions rarely included all progressive reformers.

Accepting the notion that progressives were not all alike and that the movement consisted of little more than shifting coalitions based in overlapping goals and political expediency, one can nevertheless identify dominant strains within the progressive movement, defining concerns shared by sufficient numbers of progressives to constitute a powerful force within the movement. These dominating concerns gave much of the tone and direction to progressivism.

Moralism appeared as perhaps the most common and most distinct goal of the progressives.[40] For many reformers morality lay at the center of their purpose. They hoped to return Americans to the moral standards they believed were the foundation of their nation's greatness. Detecting corruption in politics, the rise of a plutocracy and an underclass in the economy, and a general descent into degeneracy in the social sphere, these progressives hoped through a restoration of nineteenth-century values to return the United States to its former position as moral leader in the world. Identifying with an older America, these progressives often blamed the victims of industrialization—the urban poor and immigrants—for the social and political ills they abhorred. As a result they often advocated programs that today seem regressive, even repressive. Immigration restriction and prohibition, for instance, were two legacies of moral crusades in the progressive era.

Another common concern among progressives involved the declining quality of many Americans' lives. Working for what they termed social justice, some reformers pointed to many of the same social and economic ills the moralists noted, but they were more willing to blame industrialization and urbanization, rather than its victims, for the dreadful condition of modern America. This is not to suggest, however, that social justice reformers did not sometimes adopt a moralizing, condescending attitude toward those victims. Seeking primarily to alleviate suffering and return opportunity to the people of the United States, social justice reformers enlisted old and new strategies alike. Muckrakers, for instance, employing a modern version of the jeremiad, adopted an age-old approach to the problem of social ills. Seeking legislation to limit working hours and establish workers' compensation, on the other hand, social justice reformers experimented with new techniques for bringing about social and economic change.

A third group of reformers, emphasizing efficiency, agreed that industrialization had brought new problems to the United States, but they believed that the problems of the modern world required modern solutions. These reformers looked to industrialization itself for ideas on how best to adapt to the new conditions. Seeking to eliminate waste and accepting specialization, these progressives advocated new systems of local government, of organizing the economy, even of organizing leisure. They called for government by experts in the city management plan, hoping to remove the corruption of the city bosses. They believed economic centralization could heighten efficiency industry wide, and they looked to scientific management to tighten the operation of individual plants. Emphasizing efficiency rather than morality, they called for social hygiene education to prevent leisure-time activities from crippling the health of the nation. A broad and multifaceted group, the efficiency reformers sought to address the waste and corruption of the industrial age through new, usually scientific strategies.[41]

The relationship among these three dominant elements of the progressive coalition was always complex; though sometimes overlapping, at other times their work brought progressives into conflict. Both within the movement and within individual progressives, progressivism remained an often shifting collection of priorities and goals.

"An Invisible Armor": Progressives and the Soldier

All three of the dominant strains of progressivism were evident in the work of the CTCA. As the government began to publicize their work for the soldiers, discussions of the program's purposes varied widely in their emphases but always reflected an underlying preoccupation with efficiency, morality, and/or social justice. While all three of these goals had their foundations in progressivism, their relationship was not always complementary.

Official explanations of the CTCA's importance placed a high value on efficiency and stressed again and again the role the commission could play in helping to create and preserve military efficiency in particular. Of primary concern in maintaining efficiency was the problem of disease, most specifically venereal disease. According to rumors during the war, the Austrian army alone had lost the service of as many as one and one-half million men, or sixty-seven divisions, to venereal disease. Aware of the incredible military cost of this disease among European armies, and aware too of their own experiences on the Mexican border, American leaders hoped to stymie this seemingly unnecessary drain on their manpower by eliminating venereal disease among the troops.[42]

The efficiency forces claimed the prospect of military victory as justification for their concerns. An efficient army, they claimed, was a winning army. As Edward F. Allen, who published a book about the commission during the war, explained in 1918, "There is one big purpose behind it all: *to win the war.* . . . To make the men fit for fighting, and after, to bring them back from war as fine and as clean as they went, is just plain efficiency."[43] Raymond Fosdick made a nearly identical statement: "To make men fit for fighting—and after—is just plain efficiency plus."[44] These appeals to the military importance of efficiency appeared most frequently as the justification for the efforts of the commission.[45]

The commission, the War Department as a whole, and the commander-in-chief himself, however, never suggested that efficiency was the only concern of the Commission on Training Camp Activities. The reformers always understood that their goals reached beyond the simple elimination of manpower losses toward the loftier purpose of moral uplift. The CTCA promised Americans that their troops would return home not the besotted and diseased veterans of former wars, but healthier and more wholesome than when they left. The war would serve to make the soldiers into better men, as the crusading impulse turned its attention to the morals of the American troops. As Edward F. Allen asserted regarding the appointment of the commission, "It marked the beginning of an epoch. For the first time in history a government looked beyond the machinery of fighting to the personal and moral welfare of the fighters."[46] Noting that "there are things that soldiers can bring home that are worse than wounds," Secretary of War Baker promised to train the soldiers in a new moralism.[47] Through the CTCA the administration would ensure that the pure and chaste youth of the nation would be protected, their moral state even improved, and that the perilous environment of the old training camps would be replaced by a healthful environment conducive to moral and physical growth. "We are sending into this contest Americans of culture and high ideals—worthy of the cause they are going to defend," the secretary of war maintained in October 1917.[48] In the army men would no longer learn debauchery and dissipation. Instead, soldiers would learn morality and idealism to prepare them for their role in the regeneration of the world.

While moralists certainly headed the campaign for soldier purity, their concern with the training camp environment easily translated into a humanitarian regard for the quality of soldier life. Alongside the efficiency and morality enthusiasts, the CTCA also harnessed social justice energies. When soldiers reported for duty, the commission pointed out, they left behind all that was familiar. To compensate for the loss of the home environment and usual pastimes, social relations with family and friends had all too often been replaced by the immoral and hazardous ties to the barkeep and the prostitute. The commission contended that an effort to reestablish some form of normal social ties for the soldiers could help to eliminate the attraction of these less savory relationships. This would humanize the camp environment, granting the soldiers some of the comforts of home, family, and friends. Raymond Fosdick explained,

> When one considers that the hundreds of thousands of men who began pouring into the army and navy camps had been suddenly wrenched loose from all their familiar social contacts of families, friends, clubs, schools, theatres, athletics, libraries, etc., to enter the bewildering military environment, the need of some rationalizing force becomes apparent if there is to be that *sine qua non* of fighting efficiency—contentment.[49]

Providing the troops with these familiar social outlets would improve army morale, and contented soldiers would in turn be more moral, more healthy, and more efficient soldiers, liberated from the allure of the bar and the whorehouse.

It is important to note that though Fosdick promoted a humanized environment for the troops, he nevertheless emphasized the value to efficiency these happier soldiers represented. Frequently the words of the commission demonstrated this sort of intertwining of purposes. Secretary of War Baker, advocating programs to improve morale, justified them as an element of the program to ensure army efficiency. He explained in a speech to recreation workers:

> Napoleon said that in war, morale is to force as three to one. Everybody in this room, everybody in this nation, wants us to win this war. Now we want to win it with our strength and our strength is a basis of four parts; one of them is our force, according to Napoleon, the other three are our morale, according to Napoleon. You gentlemen are in part the manufacturers of morale for the nation. You are, therefore, contributors to the manufacture of three-fourths of the aggregate of the nation's natural strength with which we go into this enterprise.[50]

It is not coincidental that both Baker and Fosdick emphasized the importance of efficiency in their statements. Though their words described a profitable overlapping of goals in these instances, they also illustrated the potential for tension between the various progressive forces within the

CTCA. Mirroring the stresses in the broader progressive movement, the CTCA always contained reformers disparate in their priorities and competing for power within the agency. Although much of the time the various goals complemented one another within the commission's work, when conflicts arose, efficiency and the elimination of disease always preceded other priorities.

Efficiency loomed preeminent and wielded significantly more power than concerns for morality and social justice in the day-to-day workings of the commission, but a fourth goal seemed to unite many CTCA reformers in a common purpose, even as it enhanced the importance of their potential disagreements. Through the work of the CTCA many reformers envisioned a program for the remaking of American culture, which would begin with the fighting men and then expand to include their civilian neighbors. Embracing what I will term *cultural nationalism*, these reformers hoped to use the fluid circumstances of wartime to create a single national culture, based in the progressive social vision.

Essentially optimistic, and firm believers in the malleability of individuals, progressives were environmentalists, committed to the notions that surroundings shaped the individual and that, given the proper circumstances and sufficient education, a person could overcome most limitations.[51] In its response to the soldier problem the CTCA embraced these basic assumptions and the method they implied. Noting his determination to remake the training environment, the chairman of the CTCA declared, "The President and Secretary Baker determined that new social conditions must be created in connection with the military environment; camp life must be made wholesome and attractive."[52] As Fosdick's words suggest, the commission intended to go further than simply eliminating the dangers of the old training camp. The influence of environment not only encouraged reformers to suppress unsavory settings, but also permitted reformers to use corrected surroundings for positive purposes. Secretary of War Baker explained, "It was determined that so far as these training camps in this country were concerned they should be wholesome and stimulating and that the young men trained in them should have the opportunity to progress and learn."[53] The camps would cease to be a drag on society and would become instead a setting for the uplift of their residents.

This uplift would take the shape of training in new social values and cultural habits, what Secretary of War Baker termed an "invisible armor." Describing the traditional problem of the soldier, he warned,

"These boys are going to France. They are going to face conditions that we do not like to talk about, that we do not like to think about." He outlined his plan for dealing with those conditions:

> I want them to have an invisible armor to take with them. I want them to have an armor made up of a set of social habits replacing those of their homes and communities, a set of social habits and a state of social mind born in the training camps, a new soldier state of mind, so that when they get overseas and are removed from the reach of our comforting and restraining and helpful hand, they will have gotten such a set of habits as will constitute a moral and intellectual armor for their protection overseas.[54]

Rather than shielding the soldiers through a series of external protections, the CTCA would train the soldiers to accept new internal restraints.

Detailing the nature of the armor in a speech to recreation workers charged with its construction, Baker referred to "the invisible suit which you are making" and described it as "this attitude of mind, this state of consciousness, this *esprit de corps* which will not tolerate anything unwholesome, this brand of righteousness . . . this pride that they ought to have in being American soldiers and representing the highest ethical type of a modern civilization."[55] The adoption of a particular way of thinking—about themselves, about their habits, and about the nation—would protect the soldiers from the dangers posed to their physical and moral health.

From the beginning the reformers understood the broad social utility of this effort. Retraining the troops to a new set of values, the reformers would return them after their service better Americans than when they departed for camp.[56] Newton D. Baker announced in a speech to the National Conference on War Camp Recreation Service in October 1917, "Now when this is all over . . . our soldiers will come back to us better citizens, not merely for the patriotic heroism in which they have been engaged, but because of this lesson of social values which they will have learned."[57]

Given the shape of the CTCA's programs, too, these lessons in social values would reach beyond the classroom of the cantonment and into the nation's cities and towns. He explained, "This work is going to contribute not only to the strength of the army, making it vigorous and sound physically, mentally and morally, but it is going to advance the solution of that vexing and perplexing and troublesome city question which has for so many years hung heavy on the conscience of our country."[58]

How, precisely, would the CTCA work this miracle of social change? Enlisted to work with the CTCA, communities across the country would be exposed to the reform vision of the progressives, gaining new insights into both their duties and their potential. Baker continued,

> Each city in this country will have gotten, I think, a greater start toward a realization of the community responsibility for the lives of people who live in it, and near it, and a higher realization of the value of these experiences which we are putting into operation, and a stronger sense of its own greatness, by what it has done for the stranger within its gates, than it has ever had before.[59]

The broad meaning of this uplift was clear. At a time when many Americans feared the nation's diversity would weaken the war effort, the CTCA allayed those worries with promises that the shared values soldiers learned in the training camps would help to mold the nation into a more uniform and unified whole. Describing the postwar promise of the CTCA's programs, Baker declared,

> When the war is over, and our boys come back, and our cities have strengthened themselves by their cooperation, and we have throughout the country the common feeling that we all helped and shared the pride of having participated in this great undertaking and achievement, then we will find that . . . American public opinion has been strengthened and made more wholesome and comprehending, that America is truly a more united people, and that it understands itself better than it ever did in its history.[60]

This hope—for the creation of a new nation, united by common aspirations based in common values—represented the culmination of the aspirations of the CTCA reformers.

Progressivism had emerged, at least in part, out of the sense of disorder and chaos experienced by many middle-class Americans as their nation and its citizens changed. In the wake of industrialization the nation diversified, and the hope of a homogeneous people, never fulfilled, seemed to many Americans to grow ever more distant. The war, and the programs of the CTCA, seemed to offer new hope. As men and women, soldiers and civilians, pulled together to improve themselves and their nation, adherence to common values would eliminate the competing loyalties and the parochialism that divided Americans along lines of class, race, ethnicity, region, and religion. Out of the war effort would emerge a new American citizen, loyal first and foremost to the nation and united with other citizens through shared values.

The success of cultural nationalism, in the eyes of the CTCA reformers, rested in the cultivation of the proper social vision, the proper set of values, among this diverse population. It would be the responsibility of the progressives in the CTCA to define and then develop this "new soldier state of mind." Of course, as they went to establish a new soldier culture, and ultimately a new national culture, it was to their own values that the reformers turned. As the historian John C. Burnham explained regarding progressives more generally, "About the crucial question of precisely who should manipulate the environment and who should decide which manipulations were desirable, the progressive leaders had no doubts or hesitations: they would."[61]

The reformers' confident assumption of their ability to shape the future of American culture, however, ignored the chasms of difference that often separated them from other Americans and sometimes separated them from one another. A closer look at the CTCA's work confirms the importance of the reformers' social identity in shaping their program and also suggests the multitude of conflicts that program engendered. As the progressives in the War Department set out to remake American culture in the midst of heated cultural competition, their perceptions and hence their actions were constantly affected by their status as white, urban, middle-class, native-born Americans. On the basis of powerful assumptions about other Americans, the reformers celebrated the superiority of their own habits and values while castigating the cultural alternatives posed by those others. At the same time, though the reformers might agree on the importance of creating a homogeneous society based in progressive values, they frequently disagreed on the precise nature of those values. While the CTCA would articulate a clear vision for American culture, in doing so it would soon alienate members of its own movement.

The CTCA reformers began their efforts to mold Americans and American culture in the training camps, as they attempted to inculcate a new and shared vision of manhood among the men in uniform. In the programs they developed to create these new crusaders, the reformers revealed both their highest hopes and their worst fears for their society, hopes and fears inextricably tied to their social identities.

CHAPTER TWO

"Full-Orbed Moral Manhood": Cultural Nationalism and the Creation of New Men and Women

> The eyes of all the world will be upon you, because you are in some special sense the soldiers of freedom. Let it be your pride, therefore, to show all men everywhere not only what good soldiers you are, but also what good men you are, keeping yourselves fit and straight in everything and pure and clean through and through. Let us set for ourselves a standard so high, that it will be a glory to live up to it and then let us live up to it and add a new laurel to the crown of America.
>
> —President Wilson to the American troops

In 1918, in a published communication to the American fighting men, President Woodrow Wilson relied on the imagery of a crusade in urging the soldiers to adopt new moral guidelines.[1] Engaged in a battle for freedom, the troops were "undertaking a great duty," a duty that extended beyond the traditional martial responsibilities. The soldiers' behavior would be "watched with the deepest interest and with the deepest solicitude," not only by friends and family, "but by the whole nation besides."[2] These observers, Wilson intimated, would measure the troops by their military successes and, as importantly, by their ability to embody a new definition of manliness.

This was not mere rhetoric on the part of the president. Describing the training of American troops for war, Wilson openly acknowledged the attention to masculinity embodied by the programs of the Commission on Training Camp Activities:

> The career to which we are calling our young men in the defense of democracy must be made an asset to them, not only in strengthened and more virile bodies as a result of physical training, not only in minds deepened and enriched by participation in a great heroic enterprise, but in the enhanced spiritual values which come from a life lived well and wholesomely. I do not believe it an exaggeration to say that no army ever before assembled has had more conscientious and painstaking thought given to the protection and stimulation of its mental, moral and physical manhood.[3]

From the beginning the CTCA had as its primary official charge the prevention of venereal disease among the American troops. All of its programs—social hygiene education, recreation, law enforcement, and prophylaxis—addressed this responsibility directly. At the same time the reformers in the CTCA always maintained the broader opportunities for social change embodied in their programs. Charged with responsibility for the physical health of the men in uniform, the reformers chose to fulfill this responsibility through the construction of a new American fighting man, worthy of the crusading role Wilson had assigned him. In shaping programs capable of creating this crusader, the reformers displayed their commitment to a particular understanding of manhood and their resolve to promote that vision among the men in uniform.

"You Must Be Worthy Champions": New Standards of Manhood

A number of mutually reinforcing characteristics constituted the "mental, moral and physical manhood" promoted by the CTCA. Perhaps in sharpest contrast with the traditional image of the soldier, the CTCA's man in uniform would aspire to sexual purity. In his appeal to the troops Woodrow Wilson suggested the link between sexual purity and masculinity by urging the soldiers to keep themselves "fit and straight in everything and pure and clean through and through."[4] In all of its programs the CTCA sought to assert this new male standard, linking it to the troops' responsibility as soldiers. As one CTCA pamphlet articulated this connection:

> You are going to fight for the spirit of young girlhood raped and ravished in Belgium by a brutal soldiery. You are going to fight for it in this country, too, where you yourselves are its protectors, so that it may never need to submit to the same insults and injuries. But in order to fight for so sacred a cause you must be worthy champions. You must keep your bodies clean and your hearts pure. It would never do for the avengers of women's wrongs to profit by the degradation and debasement of womanhood.[5]

The reformers encouraged soldiers to view sexual abstinence as proper, even manly, seeking, in the historian Allan Brandt's words, "to define a new male sex role—powerful yet pure, virile yet virginal."[6] An editorial in the YMCA's camp newspaper highlighted this connection between purity and masculinity:

> Has it ever been put that way to you, young soldier, that in order to fight for your country you have to be good enough to stand in the ranks and live with decent men? For the American army is not made up of dissolute boys who have wasted their substance in riotous living. . . . Let this thought be before you always, there is a depth so low in which it is possible to be so degraded that you cannot even die for your country. Keep out of the mire.[7]

The men's moral manhood would be reinforced by a second masculine behavior, self-control, and the reformers in the CTCA often emphasized this connection. The pamphlet *Keeping Fit to Fight*, distributed by the CTCA to the men in uniform, suggested:

> Will-power and courage go together. A venereal disease contracted after deliberate exposure through intercourse with a prostitute, is as much of a disgrace as showing the white feather. . . . Every man can by self-control restrain the indulgence of those imprudent and reckless impulses that so often lead men astray, and he who thus resists is a better soldier and a better man than the man of weaker will who allows his bodily appetites to rule him.[8]

The reformers' new man exhibited a powerful self-control that allowed him to protect his purity. Those who did not embrace this self-control demonstrated weakness, not strength, and failed as soldiers and as men.

Sexual purity and self-control would contribute to another aspect of the soldiers' masculinity, a powerful virility exemplified by physical prowess. Promoting Wilson's "physical manhood," the CTCA worked hard to develop physical fitness among the men in uniform. One publicist for the CTCA exclaimed, "Never before in the history of this country have so large a number of men engaged in athletics; never before has its physical welfare received such a stimulus. . . . Men are learning to get bumped, and not to mind it."[9] Noting the connection between this physical development and the notion of manhood, the chairman of the commission commented in a published article in 1918, "Educational and recreative athletics seemed vital in the development of the whole man."[10] This focus on men's bodies, in turn, reinforced the importance of purity and self-control, providing a physical rationale for the moral and mental standards.

As these first three standards focused men's attention on the consequences of their behavior in their own lives, other masculine standards outlined the troops' new responsibilities to others. Alongside male purity, the CTCA encouraged the troops to understand the importance of a corresponding female purity and their role in protecting it. One CTCA pamphlet explained to the troops:

> The public demands clean records of the men it chooses to honor. Our people have a right to ask that the soldier shall set an example of self-respect and self-control for young men and boys, and keep up the clean reputation of our army. Our country has a right to ask that women be honored and protected as the sisters, wives, and future mothers of the race we are fighting for—whether these women be American or of any other nationality.[11]

The single sexual standard, the CTCA hoped, would foster the opportunity for men and women to meet as social equals. Articulating this vision, Edward F. Allen, who published a book-length study of the commission with the help of its chairman, explained: "America is the land where women are partners, not chattels. In carrying this atmosphere of chivalry toward women into the training camps of the army and navy, the Government is fostering one of the basic principles of a well-ordered democracy—the sanctity of the home."[12] To truly fulfill the role of woman's partner, Allen suggested, men had to respect not only women, but also their shared households. In another discussion Allen noted, "Home is coming to have a new significance to these men in the camps. They are learning how much they like pink."[13] Though the CTCA certainly adhered to the cult of masculinity, at the same time the commission complemented its physical approach to manliness with a concern for the interior man. In "learning how much they like pink" men would gain a fuller appreciation of women and the home and join with them as equal partners in the domestic pursuits.[14]

Men's commitment to a new equality with women conflated easily with the final standard of manhood outlined by the reformers, a new commitment to social responsibility. The CTCA used the men's sense of duty as soldiers to encourage among them a broad notion of responsibility that could, in turn, be used to foster particular behaviors. This tendency is particularly evident in the reformers' discussions of sexual purity. The pamphlet *Keeping Fit to Fight* cautioned the soldiers: "If you go with a prostitute, you endanger your country because you risk your health, and perhaps your life. You lessen the man-power of your company and throw extra burdens on your comrades. You are a moral shirker."[15] In order to discourage illicit sex, the CTCA urged the men to embrace a sense of obligation to their fellow soldiers and to the nation.

To some extent this emphasis on duty derived naturally from the men's role as soldiers. At the most basic level soldiers serve their nations, performing the most dangerous services on behalf of their government and in defense of other citizens. The CTCA simply urged the troops to define their responsibilities as soldiers more broadly, encouraging them to understand their adherence to the standards of morality, self-control, physical strength, and sexual equality as one part of their duty as men in uniform.

Yet the CTCA also described social responsibilities that reached beyond the soldier identities of the men in uniform. For instance, the soldiers had duties as sons, fathers, and husbands to protect their families from the ravages of venereal disease and moral dissipation. A series of posters produced by the CTCA made this responsibility clear. One poster reminded soldiers of their duty to their family's honor. In this poster a soldier faces his father in front of a white picket fence. The text states simply: "Remember—Your Father. Your Dad gave YOU the best there was in *him*. He expects you to make good. Don't splash mud on his name."[16] Another poster reminded soldiers of their responsibility to their unborn children. Picturing a blond, curly-haired child with a bow in her hair, it urged: "Remember—Your Future Children—Give 'em a chance. Don't start 'em out with a mortgage on body or mind."[17] The soldier's sense of social responsibility extended beyond his role as a soldier to his role as a father, a son, a husband, a brother, and ultimately a citizen. It applied, in the simplest terms, to his role as a man. Sexually pure, self-controlled, physically fit, and ready to accept women as equal partners, the CTCA's new man also stood ready to shoulder broad responsibilities to others.

Degeneration and Feminization: Historical Roots of the New Man

This was not the first time that Americans had concerned themselves with the issue of manhood or attempted to shape their society's understanding of the proper construction of masculinity.[18] As reformers attempted to cultivate a new image of manhood in 1917, they continued a long process of defining and redefining the cultural meaning of maleness—masculinity or manhood—which stretched back centuries.[19] While some historians have described a "crisis" in American understandings of masculinity in the decades preceding World War One, these debates only continued a lengthy and often anxious public conversation about maleness that has been an almost constant feature of American culture since its inception.[20] To be sure, Americans *were* involved in heated debates about the meaning of manhood during this period. To understand these discussions and the place of the CTCA reformers within them, however, requires an appreciation of the evolution of masculine standards over the preceding century.

In the several decades before the Civil War, the gradual infusion of industrialization and the growth of the market economy had a profound impact on the ways Americans understood masculinity. As production became specialized and left the household, men's and women's work, as well as masculine and feminine roles, grew further apart. Middle-class Americans developed the ideology of *separate spheres*, in which the public and private spheres divided rigidly, and sex roles were sharply defined. According to this doctrine the home became the moral bulwark against a changing outside world, and women became the guardians of both the home and the family in a role defined by a "cult of domesticity."[21]

At the same time, the public sphere became an exclusively male domain in which men defended their families' interests in the increasingly competitive worlds of economics and politics. This new role demanded a redefinition of manhood, reflected in a shift from "communal manhood" to "self-made manhood." Increasingly, Americans measured masculinity by a man's performance in the economy rather than in his household or in the community; economic power replaced "public usefulness" as a measure of manliness. Independence, individualism, competitiveness, even selfishness were viewed as manly traits.[22]

Though this vision carried substantial cultural weight in the middle decades of the nineteenth century, its claim as the sole measure of masculinity was always complicated by political, regional, and class differences. Among middle-class men in the North, for instance, individuals defined manhood differently based on their political affiliations. Many white, middle-class abolitionists, for instance, adopted an intensely emotional form of fraternity, which diverged from the dominant definition of manhood.[23] In the South, though separate spheres existed, masculinity was defined significantly less by economic behaviors than by recreational behaviors, by a man's participation in a male culture defined by physical aggressiveness and at least in part by its difference from the broadly accepted evangelical culture of the South. Most southern men experienced a tension between these two cultures, but they found their manliness in a more sinful recreational life rather than in their economic life.[24] Similarly, and perhaps most importantly, working-class men defined manhood according to standards very different from those of their northern, middle-class counterparts. Unable to establish their economic independence, working-class men, like southern men, emphasized recreation as a sphere of masculine affirmation and chose physical rather than economic definitions of power and dominance.[25]

Ultimately, then, early- and mid-nineteenth-century notions of manhood were distinct not for any one shared understanding, but rather for the multiplicity of understandings evident among the American population. In the years spanning the turn of the century, though, this pattern began to change as middle-class reformers sought to assert a single definition of manhood. Basing their manly image in their own experiences and values, these reformers hoped to apply their standards to all Americans, especially those with different backgrounds and cultural understandings. In articulating this definition, reformers revealed concerns about the rapid economic, social, and cultural changes taking place in the nation and the impact of these changes on both working-class and middle-class men. The CTCA reformers are a prime example of this effort to remake

American manhood according to a single, shared definition of masculinity.

The rapid redefinition of manhood in the nineteenth century seemed to many in the middle class to pose a threat to the nation's moral and ethical fiber. Before the end of the century many middle-class Americans preached self-control as a check on what they viewed as men's unbridled passions. Visualizing an ethical system individualized like other aspects of a man's role, this self-control included mastery of one's sexual urges. Though accepting the notion that men had a natural and powerful sexual urge, moralists in the middle class urged men to master that urge.[26]

The articulation by many middle-class men of a standard of self-mastery and sexual purity coexisted with a reality of masculine behaviors that often failed to conform to the ideal. The arena of sexual values contained a conflict between two versions of masculinity, one an idealized notion of self-control, the other a practical acceptance of what was understood as man's natural animal instincts.[27] Despite an ideal of male purity, even many in the middle class accepted men's sexual transgressions as unavoidable, and some even linked sexual adventuring to the positive male attribute of aggressiveness.

This attitude, the reformers maintained, was especially prevalent among working-class men.[28] By definition propertyless, or nearly so, working-class men were never able to define their maleness on the basis of economic independence and dominance. Rather than abandon notions of masculinity, however, working-class men redefined maleness in the wake of industrialization to emphasize those aspects of manhood still accessible to them. Threatened in their role as workers and thereby weakened in their authority in the household, working-class men turned to recreation as a primary sphere for masculine affirmation.[29]

Late in the nineteenth century, workers in industry claimed a gradually increasing portion of the day for their own, time that they used in the pursuit of leisure activities.[30] As a result of this increase in free time, members of the working class, both men and women, developed their own distinct leisure patterns, different from those of the middle and upper classes.[31] It was here that working-class men found a new avenue for masculine validation in recreational patterns emphasizing saloon-based sociability, sexual prowess, and physical strength.[32] Sexually lascivious and frighteningly uncontrolled according to middle-class reformers, the working-class male represented a corrupted version of manhood demanding reform. Preaching sexual self-mastery, the CTCA would initiate this uplift.

Concern over the moral state of the working-class male prompted the reformers' attention to sexual purity and self-control, but in addition fears regarding the feminization of the middle-class male encouraged their focus on the soldiers' physicality. According to reformers, middle-class men had been enduring powerful forces of feminization over the latter half of the nineteenth century in both the economic and the social spheres.

Changes in the work lives of middle-class men had made more difficult the development of masculine traits. Industrialization and the bureaucratization of the American economy led to a dramatic increase in the numbers of men working in white collar positions.[33] Between 1870 and 1910 the number of technicians, professionals, and clerical, retail, and government workers grew from 756,000 to 5.6 million.[34] Put another way, the number of salaried and nonpropertied workers increased eight times in this period and grew from 33 percent to 66 percent of the middle class. By 1910 20 percent of the male labor force was white collar.[35] More and more middle-class men worked in offices, under the supervision of a superior, with the profits of their labor taking on an increasingly intangible quality.

Though the growth of industrialization had prompted the redefinition of manhood by its new economic standards, over the course of the century further development of the industrial system made the acquisition of manly status increasingly difficult. The opportunity for independent success or for exceptional success declined continually as men found themselves working for others in jobs with only limited potential for upward mobility. In the modern business a glass ceiling based in education and personal background increasingly separated clerks from their superiors and blocked progress up the corporate ladder.[36] This situation conflicted with middle-class men's expectations regarding their own masculinity. As the historian Jeffrey P. Hantover explains, "The dependency, sedentariness, and even security of these middle-class positions clashed with the active mastery, independence, self-reliance, competitiveness, creativity, and risk-taking central to the traditional male ideal."[37] Forced to endure these changes, middle-class men found their primary route to manhood blocked by economic reality.

Many at the time worried about the feminization of the middle-class man. Dependent on a corporation for his daily bread, forced to answer passively to his superiors in the workplace, engaged in inactive, indoor work that yielded no concrete product, and having little chance of escaping this situation, a middle-class man's work life increasingly reflected characteristics traditionally associated with the lives of women.

Reacting to the forces of feminization represented by changes in male work, middle-class men sought out new ways to confirm their masculinity. A new mania for sports resulted. In the closing decades of the nineteenth century, athletics rose to a new importance in the lives of American men, providing a training ground not only for men's muscles, but also for their manhood.[38] Athletics offered white collar workers the opportunity to regain the physical dominance lost in the law office and the clerk's cubicle.

Concerns over middle-class men's masculinity were not limited, however, to those changes taking place in men's work lives. The rise of dead-end white collar jobs and the belief in the resulting feminizing consequences might not have been felt so keenly if they had not been accompanied by women's increasing incursion into spheres previously the exclusive domain of men. In the nineteenth century middle-class manhood found its basis in men's dominant economic and political role; a middle-class man knew he was a man because he represented his household in the public realm. In the late nineteenth century, however, women increasingly entered the public sphere in both economic and political guises. In each case they seemed to threaten men's preeminence in their traditional sphere, thereby undercutting men's masculinity still further.

In the closing decades of the nineteenth century, rising numbers of women entered the world of paid labor. By 1890 almost one in five women over sixteen were active in the work force. Most female workers were lower-class, generally unmarried, young, immigrant women.[39] Though the increase was most notable among lower-class women, middle-class men employed in white collar jobs nevertheless found their previously male domain, the office, invaded by women. In 1870 women had constituted only 3 percent of clerical workers. By 1910 that figure had grown to 35 percent.[40] Between 1890 and 1920 alone, the number of women among white collar workers tripled.[41] For men already feeling threatened by changes in their work life, the infusion of women coworkers enhanced their fears. Further, the environment of the office itself was altered by the arrival of women, taking on a more feminized atmosphere.[42] Though the economic threat posed to middle-class men by working women was limited, the cultural threat was potent: it called into question traditional roles and the separation of spheres.[43]

As unmarried middle-class women joined working-class women in seeking work outside the home, the shock of women in the workplace was matched by the shock of their departure from the household. In the last decades of the nineteenth century the first generation of college-educated women posed an additional threat to middle-class gender roles. Almost half of these women never married, and those who did married later, raising smaller families than other middle-class women.[44] Career women—independent, unmarried, and self-supporting—seemed to pose a direct threat to traditions of female domesticity and male preeminence in the public sphere.

Finally, female infiltration of the political sphere further threatened middle-class notions of masculinity. Throughout the nineteenth century women raised a growing public voice in an effort to shape a society that matched their moral sensibilities. Beginning with social reform movements such as abolitionism and temperance, women increasingly sought political power to facilitate their reform efforts. Though most women justified their entry into the public sphere according to the most traditional understandings of women's roles, their actions nevertheless ended men's sole occupation of the public sphere and blocked another route to male affirmation.[45]

Reformers concerned for middle-class manhood had two options for dealing with this evolution of women's roles. On the one hand they could attempt to drive women from the worlds of paid employment and politics. Given the political and social reality of women's rising public role and the importance of women in the progressive movement, this option was never a viable one for the CTCA reformers. Far easier, with greater potential for success, was to redefine the manly relationship with women in such a way as to incorporate recent changes in the relationship. Arguing that real men maintained a partnership *with* women, rather than a dominance *over* women, the CTCA provided both middle-class and working-class men with a route to masculine validation that allowed for the changing behaviors of women.

In doing so the reformers reflected society's growing acceptance of women's public roles as well as changes in marriage and the home.[46] By the end of the nineteenth century Americans largely embraced companionate notions of marriage, perceiving the marital union as emotional, rather than simply economic. Increasingly, both men and women understood marriage as a joining of romantic partners in a relationship fulfilling to both.[47] The CTCA's promotion of partnership among men and women reflected this new understanding of the marital relationship.

It also reflected the growing acceptance of what the historian Margaret Marsh terms "masculine domesticity." In the late nineteenth and early twentieth centuries middle-class men increasingly considered their home and family lives an important part of their manliness. In addition to the cult of masculinity, defined by the rising attention to physical prowess and exemplified by the rise of athletics, Marsh maintains that a new role model, the "contented suburban father," contended for men's allegiance at the turn of the century.[48]

The CTCA's efforts at defining new relations between the sexes confirm Marsh's conclusions. Determined to establish a new social equality between men and women, the CTCA preached a new domestic partnership alongside the shared sexual standard. Men would expand their responsibilities into the private realm in a complementary reflection of women's movement into the public sphere. This new encouragement of the domestic among men may seem to contradict the reformers' preoccupation with manliness and mastery.[49] For reformers in the CTCA, however, this apparent conflict was easily resolved if one put the proper interpretation on the relations between men and women.

Even as the CTCA articulated a vision of equality and partnership, the notion of chivalry and its attendant assumptions of women's dependence surfaced in its ideology.[50] Indeed, the reformers continually referred to men's responsibility for the protection of women as one aspect of their role as soldiers and used this reasoning to advocate manly behaviors. The need to protect women, the commission urged, should encourage men to strive for self-control. Men would share a single sexual standard with women, creating a new equality and partnership. At the same time women would remain dependent upon men for their own purity and sexual safety. Despite some rhetoric to the contrary, the power dynamic between men and women remained unchanged, and men's masculinity was reinforced, not threatened, by their new interest in family and home.[51] The redefinition of manliness to incorporate new domestic responsibilities provided middle-class men with an accessible route to masculinity that mirrored their new social reality and eliminated its apparently feminizing tendency.

Worried about the feminization of middle-class men, reformers faced their own struggle with the masculine image. In a society devoted to individualism and competition, preoccupation with social reform hardly earned one the mantle of masculinity. Like the Social Gospelers before them, male reformers in the progressive movement redefined manhood, and their work, so as to confirm their own masculinity and its connection to their work as reformers.[52] Preaching the soldiers' broad social responsibilities, the CTCA reformers maintained the manly quality of social activism. Reform became chivalrous, a duty to be carried out using masculine methods and described in masculine terms.[53] In this context the blustering figure and "manly" rhetoric of reformers like Teddy Roosevelt encouraged Americans to believe that one could be a reformer without threatening one's masculinity. Indeed, for middle-class men reform become one route to masculine affirmation.[54]

CTCA reformers sought to inculcate precisely this attitude among the men in uniform. Selected to serve their country, the soldiers would prove their masculinity by fighting for a noble cause and by doing so according to certain principles. This articulation of the troops' social responsibility served to reinforce all other aspects of the CTCA's standards for manhood by suggesting that the troops needed not only to serve well as soldiers, but also to serve well as men and to understand their masculinity in terms delineated by the CTCA.

"This Is a Man-to-Man Talk": Social Hygiene Education and Chemical Prophylaxis

The commission used several avenues of action to ensure production of these new men. In 1917 Joseph H. Odell traveled to the training camps to observe the conditions there. In a series of articles in *Outlook* and later in a collected volume entitled *The New Spirit of the New Army*, Odell outlined what he viewed as the remarkable transformation in army life taking place in the training camps. He exclaimed,

> As the result of visits to several camps and cantonments I got the impression that there was a veritable conspiracy of positively good forces, a kind of confederacy of sanely moral agencies, to present to the world, not only a

> victorious fighting machine, but to create an order of healthy, clean, intelligent, and full-orbed moral manhood such as this country would never have had if the degeneracy of Germany had not forced us into the war.[55]

This "conspiracy of positively good forces" included, first and foremost, education and recreation programs designed to inculcate proper habits and values among the men in uniform. Though the CTCA's work would include a substantial law enforcement program, discussed in chapter 4, the CTCA progressives always emphasized the importance of their positive programs. As Secretary of War Baker anticipated, "Our progress, our substantial and tremendous progress, is going to be along the line of healthy and wholesome and stimulating and strengthening substitutes as counterweights to temptation."[56] It was the building of the secretary of war's invisible armor, his new set of social habits, that the commission viewed as its primary goal, for it was here that the commission could make a contribution to the society that would outlast the war—the creation of a new and better man. In the social hygiene education and recreation programs the reformers could define and then create this man.

The reformers began their efforts to create Odell's "healthy, clean, intelligent, and full-orbed moral manhood" with social hygiene education, a program that addressed the commission's official responsibility for the prevention of venereal disease while also promoting its very particular image of manhood. Facing the practical problem of military efficiency, the CTCA hoped to promote soldier health through practical sex education. "This is a man-to-man talk, straight from the shoulder without gloves. It calls a spade a spade without camouflage," the CTCA's social hygiene pamphlet, *Keeping Fit to Fight*, began. Directed specifically at the men in uniform, the pamphlet reflected the commission's determination to educate the men to the dangers of venereal disease through frank discussions of scientific fact in order to preserve their health for service.[57] An instruction manual for company commanders urged those educating the men to "emphasize the individual responsibility of each soldier for avoiding sexual intercourse" and recommended further, "Self control, the seeking of clean recreation, avoidance of sexual intercourse as a matter of good citizenship and good sense . . . are among the points which need to be driven home in every practicable way." And still further, "Don't forget that the strong man can control himself and avoid having sexual intercourse . . . because it is not best for the service or himself."[58]

This preaching would have the important effect of preventing disease among the troops. Walter C. Clarke, the head of the CTCA's social hygiene education program for soldiers, maintained, "The desideratum is that every man should have sane and practical information regarding the nature of venereal diseases, how they are contracted and how they may be avoided." Suggesting the success of this effort, he continued, "Our army is making the lowest record for venereal disease that has been made in its history and, what is more significant, the lowest of any mobilized army of the present day in the world."[59] Properly educated, the CTCA believed, the men in uniform could be dissuaded from engaging in illicit sexual relations and, in turn, could be preserved as members of the fighting force.

The CTCA's education program hoped to do more than simply discourage illicit sexual relations, however. In the process of influencing the men to avoid promiscuous sex, the commission also sought to convince them to understand this new behavior as part of a moral code and to perceive this moralism as manly. The moral message is obvious in the materials produced by the Social Hygiene Division. One soldier described a lecture he had attended at Camp Hancock:

> His speech was wonderful and I learned a lesson, which I hope I never will forget. It was a picture he drew before us in our minds of men who were terribly wounded. Not by shells or bayonets but by the young man's greatest sin, disease. He pictured how these men wanted to die, couldn't face home, with a body wrecked of manhood. . . . Then the picture of the wounded and crippled who were proud of their wounds. Why? Because they were inflicted in honorable battle.[60]

Though wounds caused in battle had the same military cost, the CTCA posed them as respectable alongside the morally egregious wounds of sexual promiscuity. Battle scars, reflecting honorable service, were manly, while wounds incurred through sex left a man robbed of his masculinity. Combining this kind of message with complete information about venereal disease, the CTCA hoped to eliminate infection while also teaching a new, morally based definition of manliness.

The message of moral masculinity and self-control was similarly clear in the CTCA's first full-length movie, *Fit to Fight*, produced for the men in uniform. In the film, five draftees react to the temptations of illicit sex with five different responses, ranging from one soldier's rejection of the temptations of the flesh to another doughboy's visit to a prostitute. Not surprisingly, those soldiers who engage in sexual relations suffer the consequences—disease and disgrace. Those who heed the teachings of the social hygiene education program, on the other hand, survive their brush with evil and gain the chance to serve as heroes overseas. One soldier narrowly escapes disease by an intelligent visit to the prophylactic station following an encounter with a prostitute, reminding the soldiers of the practical means available to help them avoid venereal disease, should their moral backbone prove too brittle. This same soldier, initially unconcerned with the issue of morality, is eventually convinced by a cleaner soldier to take a moral stance against sex, illustrating the commission's hope that prophylaxis would be only a stopover on the road to sexual purity.[61]

In developing a program with this blend of pragmatism and moralism, the CTCA reflected its ties to the social hygiene movement that developed in the decades before the war. The prewar years had witnessed the growth of a sizable social hygiene education movement in the United States, dramatic in its numerical strength and in its willingness to discuss issues of sexuality openly. In the late nineteenth and early twentieth centuries, scientists discovered important information about the causes and consequences of venereal diseases, illnesses crippling in their effects in these pre-penicillin years. Progressive physicians increasingly viewed venereal disease as a threat to the social order in the peril it posed to the family and sought ways to educate the public about the danger. Hoping to break the "conspiracy of silence," which encouraged the spread of the diseases, the physician Prince Morrow organized the American Society for Sanitary and Moral Prophylaxis in 1905 as an educational clearinghouse.[62]

Though the social hygiene forces appear quite modern in their openness, in reality their work constituted a complex mixture of nineteenth-century moralism and the rising twentieth-century attachment to science and reason.[63] Throughout its work the CTCA reflected the duality of the social hygiene movement. In the operation of its program the CTCA enrolled the aid of the American Social Hygiene Association, a coalition of social hygiene reformers and the leading promoter of sex hygiene education in the United States, as well as the Young Men's Christian Association, the social welfare organization of the evangelical protestant churches. The collaboration of these two groups provided a constant tension within the commission's work between reformers committed first and foremost to efficiency and those most devoted to morality.

The Social Hygiene Division of the CTCA adopted the most modern and scientific responses to the educational task that were available. Lectures, based on a standardized syllabus produced by the surgeon general, were delivered to soldiers by selected civilian physicians. Stereomotorgraphs or slides provided a visual accompaniment to other aspects of the education program. The official pamphlet, *Keeping Fit to Fight*, reached the hands of all enlisted men, introducing many soldiers to sex education for the first time. Placards exhibited around the cantonments dealt with "sex hygiene and venereal disease in plain outspoken language, illustrated with effective drawings, anatomical diagrams and photographs."[64] Demonstrating its willingness to use even the newest, untried means available to battle venereal disease, the commission produced the first movies made by a United States government agency; they were part of the effort to "tell convincingly the story of venereal disease and the Government's program against it."[65] Shocking to many Americans unused to the open discussion of sexual matters, the CTCA's program embraced any educational methods available to promote the concept of sexual abstinence and the soldiers' responsibility for their sexual condition.

The commission also developed a chemical prophylaxis program for soldiers who engaged in sexual relations. The prophylaxis program was essentially an early treatment of venereal infection given to the soldier as soon after contact as possible (preferably within three hours), which dramatically lessened the likelihood of the soldier contracting a disease. Making failure to obtain a prophylaxis treatment after sexual contact a court-martial offense, the army hoped to ensure that soldiers participated in the prophylaxis program.[66]

The promotion of open discussions of sexual matters was thought to encourage sexual abstinence and the promotion of a moral understanding of sexuality, but the development of a prophylaxis program seemed to contradict these purposes directly in its ability to remove the consequences of illicit sexual relations.[67] In some ways, however, chemical prophylaxis was a logical addition to the social hygiene program. While emphasizing the value of education and environment, many progressives were advocates of science and modern methods, as well as efficiency. To lessen the chance of disease among the men in uniform through prophylaxis made sense as it contributed to the central purpose of the CTCA, the protection of the troops' health. Contradictory to the moral elements of the CTCA position and offensive to many traditional moralists, chemical prophylaxis nevertheless could play an essential role in reducing venereal infection among the soldiers. The existence of the chemical prophylaxis program represented the CTCA's realistic acceptance of the impossibility of completely controlling the behavior of soldiers and civilians. Charged with the prevention of venereal disease, the reformers clearly felt compelled to employ all available methods in fulfilling that responsibility.

At the same time, the CTCA did not hesitate to suggest the status of prophylaxis in the constellation of programs they were developing. Aware that the prophylaxis program might suggest to some soldiers a new freedom in sexual activities, the American Social Hygiene Association (ASHA), affiliated with the CTCA, urged that soldiers be informed of the limited usefulness of the program. Further, the prophylaxis stations themselves were to serve as the final outpost of education and advice designed to convert the soldiers to the commission's new sexual standards. One ASHA pamphlet advised:

> The prophylactic station should be utilized as a place for personal advice and education against future exposure, and should be conducted as an early treatment dispensary. Any spirit of levity or condoning sexual promiscuity should be discouraged, and obscene stories or objectionable conduct should be rigidly repressed. The men assigned as officers in charge of these stations should be mature and with the personality and force of character calculated to gain the confidence and respect of the men applying for treatment.[68]

Conscious of the contradiction between its efforts to condemn illicit sex and its provision of protection for those who engaged in it, the CTCA and its allies sought to disguise the prophylaxis program in the garb of their broader educational effort and its attendant moralism.

"Leisure Time Is the Bugbear of the Man Away from Home": Recreation for the Man in Uniform

Through the lessons of the social hygiene education program the reformers attempted to instill new standards of manhood—purity and self-control—to replace those that they feared had created the working-class beast. The reformers realized, however, that it would take more than lessons in social hygiene to remake the working class. The acceptance of chemical prophylaxis was one concession to this reality; the development of the recreation program was another. Aware of the role of leisure activities in defining working-class masculinity, the reformers turned to recreational reform to complement the efforts of the social hygiene education program. This same recreation program would also offer reformers the opportunity to revitalize middle-class men.

The CTCA realized it could not develop this program without assistance, and it soon enlisted the help of several civilian organizations. Shortly after its own inception, the commission voted to recognize officially the Young Men's Christian Association (YMCA) as its first civilian partner in the recreation program.[69] Having served the government in this capacity on the Mexican border before the war, the YMCA was well prepared for the work and seemed an obvious choice for affiliation with the CTCA.[70]

Though eager to have the YMCA's assistance, the commission realized the need to limit the number of organizations cooperating in the official CTCA program. Countless organizations clamored for inclusion, and the CTCA could not admit all of them to the training camps.[71] Accordingly, the commission adopted a plan granting the status of official affiliation to only a few organizations; the commission encouraged all other groups to participate in the various patriotic roles available to them in the civilian communities. This gave the commission the opportunity to pick and choose among petitioners and to select only those organizations well suited, in the CTCA's eyes, to an official position in the CTCA programs.

The CTCA eventually granted seven organizations the status of official affiliated organizations, including the YMCA, the Knights of Columbus, the Jewish Welfare Board, the American Library Association, the Young Women's Christian Association, the Salvation Army, and the War Camp Community Service.[72] The first five of these organizations did the majority of their work inside the camps, assisting in the provision of on-base recreation. The War Camp Community Service, established in 1917 to serve with the CTCA but born of the American Playground and Recreation Association, coordinated the community recreation program. The Salvation Army generally did not participate in the recreation program but assisted families of men in the service and cared for soldiers traveling in the United States.

Fosdick envisioned the CTCA as a sort of clearinghouse for the civilian agencies that would serve the soldiers in the training camps. The role of the commission would be to coordinate the efforts of the various groups aiding the soldiers and thereby prevent the waste and inefficiency of several competing organizations operating uncontrolled. Pursuing a balanced and efficient war effort, the CTCA hoped to rationalize the participation of those organizations. At the same time, the coordination of activities by the CTCA would allow the commission to maintain control of the content and character of the program both inside and outside of the camp gates.[73]

In adopting a program of recreational reform the CTCA again relied on the work of activists in the prewar era. In the years before the war a group of reformers organized in response to what they understood as the dangers posed by industrialization and urbanization, in particular the problems created by the rise of working-class recreational alternatives. Members of what became known as the playground and recreation movement used play as an instrument of social reform. Reflecting the preoccupation with environment, these reformers hoped to use properly composed recreation to remake urban dwellers into better citizens, more moral in attitude and more respectable in behavior.[74]

The character of that recreation was crucially important.[75] These reformers saw in the leisure habits of the working class a regressive development in what ought to be, indeed needed to be, pure and healthful.[76] Prompted to action by these concerns, progressive reformers placed great faith in their ability to reshape the urban environment.[77] Reformers would use structured play spaces and supervised recreation for a number of social and cultural purposes that reached far beyond the simple provision of recreation for inner-city dwellers. Parks, playgrounds, and supervised recreation would restore play to its purer forms and allow it again to serve the socializing functions needed to maintain moral order in the cities.[78] At the same time regaining control of the urban world would allow old-stock, middle-class reformers to reestablish their cultural predominance.[79]

Members of the CTCA shared the determination to remake recreation into a training ground for middle-class culture. Through recreation the reformers could familiarize the predominantly working-class soldiers with the uplifting cultural habits and social values of the middle class, thus eliminating the dangers posed by working-class forms of recreation. Carefully planned recreation could also revitalize the middle-class man, replacing the threat of feminization with training in masculinity.

Working with their civilian allies, the CTCA reformers developed a multifaceted in-camp program that included everything from athletics to education, from social clubs to group sings, from Liberty Theatres to libraries. While always acknowledging the importance of military preparation in the shaping of their recreational work, the reformers also used their recreational work to further their cultural goal—the creation of properly masculine men.

The reformers began their recreation work with an athletic program. Coordinated by the CTCA, and placing an athletic director in every camp, this program made athletic instruction and competition a part of every soldier's camp life.[80] The program included training in all of the major American sports—football, baseball, basketball, soccer, boxing, and track and field events—as well as calisthenics and less structured games such as medicine ball and tag.

The reformers maintained the direct military usefulness of this involvement in athletics. One proponent of athletics argued that "the value of work of this sort cannot be overestimated" and pointed to both the narrow and broad applications of the men's athletic training. In some cases sports taught skills directly transferable to the battlefield. For instance, "the science of boxing" was reputed to be "intimately related to the business of bayonet-fighting." Noting that "nearly every blow and position [in boxing] has its counterpart in bayoneting," the CTCA insisted that the soldiers' boxing work would one day "be the means of saving their lives."[81]

Beyond the specific skills it developed, boxing, like other athletic activities, also promoted physical and mental characteristics vital to successful soldiering. Edward F. Allen explained:

> The big contribution of boxing to military training is to develop in men the willingness and ability to fight at close range. Its purpose is to teach soldiers to give and take punishment. There is close relation in the qualities required for boxing and bayonet fighting. Both require agility of body, quickness of eye, good balance, and control in giving a punch or thrust, and an aggressive fighting spirit that breaks down or weakens defense, and makes openings for an effective "finish."[82]

In general, reformers explained, recreational athletics could be used to develop the physical stamina, strength, and good health vital to a man at the front. Describing a game called "swat-tag," Allen queried, "What does this simple game do for the man?" and answered, "It develops an extreme physical alertness." He continued, "There are plenty of games of this sort that, besides promoting good feeling, develop self-control, agility, mental alertness, and initiative, all bases on which to build military efficiency."[83]

In the reformers' testimony regarding the athletic program, one can note clearly the overlap between the military and the cultural usefulness of their recreation program. On the one hand, athletics trained the bodies and minds of men in ways that developed their military skills, as the final comment above suggests; on the other hand this same training also served the cultural purposes of the reformers, cultivating "manly" characteristics and proper social behaviors.

For starters, athletics kept the bodies and minds of the soldiers actively engaged in constructive activities, providing a distraction from the less savory entertainment available to them. On the Mexican border, according to the reformers, "there was nowhere to go for any sort of decent diversion" when the soldiers finished a day of training, "and so, when they had any free time, many naturally gravitated to the saloons and partook of their unchallenged hospitality." Given this, the reformers concluded, "The great need was for something wholesome to compete with the only forms of diversion to which the men had access."[84] Athletics provided this healthy distraction. Indeed, the CTCA expected that all of its recreational programs would serve as healthful diversions for the troops.

In addition to simply distracting the soldiers, however, recreation could also teach valuable social and cultural lessons. For middle-class men, athletics might help them combat the tendency to feminization so evident in the civilian world. As one observer cheered regarding the CTCA's athletic program, "Narrow-chested clerks are making 3-base hits on the same base-ball teams with college athletes, and lean-visaged philosophers are learning how to use their fists. The book-keeper and the street-car motorman come to grips on the foot-ball gridiron."[85] Sports, it seemed, might make middle-class males men again.

Athletics might also provide an antidote to the degeneracy of the working-class man, encouraging his reformation and uplift. Again and again reformers noted the importance of boxing and other athletic endeavors in teaching the soldiers self-control, a characteristic vital in the soldiers' struggle for sexual purity.[86] In addition, participation in athletic events would encourage new cultural habits among working-class men that could permanently replace their formerly degenerate behaviors. In the end, the reformers hoped, the gridiron and boxing ring would replace the whorehouse and saloon in the recreational lives of working-class troops and reinforce their adherence to the new and healthful recreational patterns of middle-class men.

Other aspects of the recreation program would complement the work of the athletic program, cultivating habits and values while also promoting the men's military fitness. Certainly the CTCA's education program did so. The educational work included lessons in "English, French, spelling, reading, writing and primary arithmetic," as well as vocational training and classes in history and geography relevant to an understanding of the war. To the reformers the military role of this program was clear. For instance, to function as a soldier a man needed to read and write English. Yet many soldiers arrived in camp unable to do these things.[87]

As they taught the soldiers to read and write, the reformers also manipulated the lessons to include important cultural training. At the simplest level the classes taught soldiers basic habits of the urban middle class. Lessons in the *Camp Reader for American Soldiers*, for example, emphasized the value of showers and shaving, toothbrushes and fully chewed food.[88] Other readings taught more sophisticated lessons, stressing, for instance, the progressive social values that underlay the commission's preaching on manhood. Encouraging the veneration of women and decrying the evil of vice, these readings promoted the values of purity, self-control, and the manly relationship to women.[89]

Still further, beginning English classes inculcated a particular interpretation of the nation and of the war. Though the first central text of English classes, *The Roberts Series*, taught soldiers basic military language, the second, as Edward F. Allen described it, "Teaches not only the rudiments of reading and writing, but ideals as well. . . . In the book are reflected camp life and the ideals of a democracy, and it will help to preserve both on a high place." The classes themselves would reinforce these ideals. As Allen explained further, "For instance, he [the instructor] will ask the class to say in concert such sentences as : 'I am a soldier of America'; 'I am fighting for democracy'; 'democracy is the rule of the people.' The individual members repeat the phrases. Thus our new citizens learn both the language of the country and the meaning of its privileges."[90] As teaching the troops to read strengthened their soldiering, it also provided the reformers with the opportunity to acculturate those soldiers into the nation's mainstream.

The cultural education that troops received in their lesson books would be reinforced in other aspects of the recreation program. Soldier clubhouses, built and operated by the Young Men's Christian Association, the Jewish Welfare Board, and the Knights of Columbus, provided the troops with an informal atmosphere inside the camps. Here they could escape the watchful eye of superiors and rest comfortably on non–military issue furniture. The setting for many of the educational courses, the huts also housed libraries, playing cards, victrolas, stationery, and writing desks, and they hosted religious meetings and a variety of entertainments.[91]

Like the other forms of recreation, the soldier clubs served the needs of the CTCA by providing a promising distraction from soldier life. As Edward F. Allen explained:

> Leisure time is the bugbear of the man away from home. A successful traveling man told me that if it were not for Sunday, his work would be one hundred per cent. congenial. A soldier's predicament is even more of a problem, for with no more leisure time than the average man, he is much more restricted in his choice of diversions. Too often he has been in the position described by the popular song "All Dressed Up and No Place to Go." Within the camp of to-day, however, this conditions does not obtain. The fighting man may go to his club.[92]

Beyond simple diversion, however, these clubs also continued the education of the men in uniform. Allen suggested further, "They are more than 'places to go'; they combine a definite interest with a distinct personality." This personality was distinctly middle class and urban. Allen concluded:

> Many of these men are enjoying for the first time the intimate association and comradeship of club life. They have come from farms and from isolated villages in which there are no such advantages, and they will return to their homes with a broadened horizon and a set of social habits from whose influence they can never escape. This is one of the first indications of the

> socially constructive side of the work done by the many branches of the Commissions.[93]

Indeed, not only the farm boy but the slum dweller and the immigrant would experience the comforts of the social club for the first time in the camps. Already committed to the healthful pastimes of the playing field, these men would learn to relax after the game in a social club, far removed from the dangers of the whorehouse and the saloon.

The social clubs were useful not only for this training in habits, but also for the values they inspired. The clubs "promote democracy and they also effectively bridge the gulf that lies between the recruit and his environment," the CTCA explained. Here the troops could develop "that intangible 'spirit of the army,'" the belief in their cause, which was to make the American soldier special in this war.[94] This same "spirit," based in a belief in the nation and reinforced by cultural unity, was further fostered through singing.

The CTCA purported to attempt to make singing as popular with the troops as sports, encouraging group singing throughout the soldiers' daily routine. The singing program included group sings whenever large numbers of men were called together, as well as singing on the march, competitions between regiments and between companies, and the formation of quartets, glee clubs, and choruses. Singing, like the athletic program, was always understood by the reformers to have a military purpose in addition to its recreative and socializing roles. One YMCA secretary wrote to his compatriots, "Let us not cease to drive home to the men in our camps that we are not teaching them songs just for the fun of it or to pass the time away, but because *singing helps to win the war.*"[95] Singing, reformers maintained, gave men "a strong back, chest, and lungs . . . a throat less liable to infection . . . [and] increased circulation," which helped to clear nasal cavities, while strengthening and preserving the soldiers' voices. Further, singing contributed to men's "memory," powers of "observation," "initiative," "definiteness," "concentration," "accuracy," and the ability to make the "punctual attack and action."[96] In addition to strengthening the soldiers' bodies and minds, singing performed much the same purpose as other forms of recreation, allowing the men to forget their weariness and the drudgery and dullness of military life, thereby contributing to morale and good discipline.[97]

Singing also offered the CTCA another opportunity to socialize the troops. Through singing the reformers could cultivate patriotism. The commission produced two song books, *Songs for Soldiers and Sailors*, and the *Official Army Song Book*, which allowed the commission to standardize and control the soldiers' singing. The *Official Army Song Book* included primarily hymns such as "Onward, Christian Soldiers," traditional American folk songs heralding the pioneer past such as "There's a Long, Long Trail," patriotic standards such as "America, the Beautiful," and songs of the allies such as "God Save the King." (For a complete list of songs in the *Official Army Song Book* see Appendix A.) Christianity, traditionalism, patriotism, and an identification with the allies—all important ingredients of a healthy Americanism—could be cultivated through singing.[98] Edward F. Allen declared: "Patriotism is no hollow thing. It wins battles. And the music, be it instrumental or vocal, that awakens it and feeds it is scarcely less potent than high explosives."[99]

Familiarity with these songs would also help to integrate many Americans into a national culture. Through singing, the CTCA could acquaint rural and immigrant Americans with the popular tunes of the progressives' cultural mainstream, tunes heralding the nation and its heritage. If on the one hand this encouraged patriotism, on the other hand it also promoted a homogenization of American culture and an identification with a national community. In the camps, the CTCA contended, "the imagination of American youth was finding itself and fusing itself by all the laws of silent alchemy into the great soul of America."[100] Here in the camps, it seemed, the youth of America would lose its troublesome diversity and emerge with a new Americanism capable of strengthening the nation both militarily and culturally, both in war and in peace.

In creating this new American the CTCA boldly maintained that "paternalism is a stranger to this work."[101] Ironically, in the reformers' determination to remake the troops in their own image, a passion for social control and a correspondingly deep paternalism are clearly discernible. The reformers' commitment to democracy, stated and restated throughout the recreation program, was always subordinate to their devotion to social stability, defined by cultural homogeneity and dependent upon the soldiers' acceptance of urban, middle-class culture.

Although the reformers' attempts to control the troops were often subtle, at other times their control was more explicit, as well as more repressive. The entertainment program, provided both in the soldier clubs and in special buildings dubbed Liberty Theaters, exemplifies this tendency. Promising entertainment every night and asserting the supreme importance of the accessibility of entertainment, the commission also demanded that programs be safe and uplifting.[102] The National Board of Review cooperated with the CTCA's War Camp Motion Picture Committee in selecting and censoring movies for screening in the Liberty Theaters.[103] After viewing films, the commission released bulletins listing approved films by "character" as well as by name. The commission emphasized the importance of allowing soldiers to view only those films appearing on the lists.[104] By inspecting the films shown to soldiers, the CTCA intended to allow soldiers to view only those films that would be uplifting. (For an example of a bulletin listing approved films, see Appendix B.) Responsibility for control of the character of all other shows fell to the Military Entertainment Committee.[105]

Similarly, to ensure that the proper visions of the nation and of the war were developed through their programs, the CTCA kept a tight rein on the camp libraries. The American Library Association raised the money to build camp libraries, conducted book drives and fund-raising drives to supply those libraries with reading material, and staffed those libraries with professional librarians.[106] As part of their work libraries maintained careful censorship of their stacks.[107] Prohibited works included pro-German titles such as J. O'd. Bennett's *Germany's Just Cause* and Friedrich Wilhelm Von Frantzius' *Germans as Exponents of Culture.* Pacifist works such as Norman Thomas's *The Conquest of War* and David Starr Jordan's *War and Waste*, as well as leftist works such as Henri Barbusse's *Under Fire* and Leon Trotsky's *The Bolsheviki and World Peace*, were also considered dangerous literature. Books critical of the Allies such as *The Disgrace of Democracy: Open Letter to President Woodrow Wilson*, by Kelly Miller, and Seumas McManus's *Ireland's Cause* also faced banning.[108] (For a list of banned books, see Appendix C.)

At times this censorship reached ridiculous extremes. In mid-1918 *Popular Science* magazine was banned from camp libraries because of a fear that German spies might discover "technical secrets" there.[109] The censorship program revealed a great deal of nervousness, even panic, regarding the soldiers' ability to discriminate between American and un-American reading matter. The libraries were to build patriotism and better Americans, but they would do this through a carefully guarded collection of books, magazines, and pamphlets. As with other forms of entertainment for the soldiers, the libraries would offer them recreation, but it would offer recreation carefully circumscribed to make it suitable for crusaders. Though vocal about the importance of the positive efforts to remake the men, the CTCA relied on repression in the form of censorship as a critical feature of those positive efforts, revealing the close link between constructive and coercive work characteristic of many progressive programs.[110]

This same close relationship between positive and repressive programs was evident in the CTCA's work with women. Though the CTCA initiated its work with the soldiers and emphasized its efforts to inculcate proper habits and values among the men in uniform, from the beginning the reformers developed programs targeting women and therein articulated standards of behavior for women that complemented those posited for men. In these programs, too, the reformers combined entertainment with education and accepted social control and repression as constructive methods in the development of the ideal citizen.

Variations on True Womanhood: A New Feminine Ideal

Just as men's lives had changed as a result of the industrial revolution, women's lives also underwent dramatic transformations during the nineteenth century. In response to these changes middle-class Americans developed ideas about womanhood complementary to their tenets of manhood. As the CTCA reformers cultivated a new image of masculinity, implicit in this construction were suggestions about the nature of woman's role that maintained important aspects of traditional standards of femininity while adapting those standards to a changing society.

In the nineteenth century, when definitions of manhood shifted to meet the needs of an industrializing society and began to emphasize individualism, competition, and achievement, definitions of womanhood increasingly served to protect traditional societal values. The vision of "true womanhood" embraced by middle-class Americans in the early years of industrialization emphasized women's role as guardians of society's morality.[111] As middle-class men's and women's spheres diverged in the wake of industrialization, women became the keepers of society's homes and the values associated with those homes.

Women would protect the society's moral values through their piety, their purity, their domesticity, and their submissiveness. Piety served as the core of a woman's character, providing her with the guidance to fulfill her other charges. Purity, specifically sexual purity, was also vital to a true woman. Any woman stepping outside the bounds of propriety was seen as unnaturally depraved. Although many Americans hoped that men might share these first two characteristics, it was widely accepted that circumstances, as well as their natural tendencies, made this unlikely. The final two characteristics of true womanhood, submission and domesticity, demonstrated even more clearly the separation between men's and women's roles. While men struggled in the public world of politics and economics, women were destined to be the caretakers of the home, perfecting the domestic arts. Men were heralded for dominance and power, women for their ability to submit to men. This did not mean that women were lesser than men, contemporaries maintained, but rather that the natural order of things required a male head of household and a female helpmate.[112]

Certainly the notion of true womanhood did not describe every woman's life. And yet this gender norm wielded immense cultural power, even over those women outside its bounds. Working-class women often left the home to join their husbands in the earning of the family's income. Slave women were often forced to abandon both purity and domesticity by the command of the slave owner. Yet the ideals of the true woman circumscribed these women's lives, influencing middle-class interpretations of them. For instance, seeing women's paid labor as outside their accepted sphere, the middle class easily undervalued this labor. At the same time slave women, prevented from fulfilling the charges of womanhood, were often perceived by middle-class Americans as outside the pale of womanhood and exempt from the privilege of protection that designation promised.[113]

Over the course of the nineteenth century middle-class women modified true womanhood in a variety of ways, and yet the cultural power of this gender norm persisted.[114] Engaging in movements for social reform, many women defended their excursions into the public sphere on the basis of their natural purity and their domestic responsibility to defend the morality of the society.[115] Though some reform-minded women questioned the notions of domesticity and submission from an essentially feminist perspective, calling for public roles on the basis of their humanity rather than their femininity, such women were a minority, even among activists.

The CTCA reformers combined both traditional and modern notions about womanhood in shaping their feminine ideal. Their definition of what a woman ought to be and how she might fulfill her responsibilities as a woman often expanded, or even transcended, nineteenth-century notions of womanhood. But as reformers redefined womanhood they proved markedly reliant upon old understandings of woman's nature and woman's natural roles in their justifications for those redefinitions. Determined to promote a vision of womanhood that complemented their vision of manhood, the reformers seemed to worry less about the consistency of their notions about womanhood and more about whether the woman they were championing could, and would, support her man.

In their most important revision of true womanhood, the reformers rejected the notion that the only proper role for a woman was a private, domestic one. Throughout the war the CTCA advocated important public responsibilities for both women and girls. Over the course of the nineteenth century, even as middle-class men's and women's roles diverged, women were making inroads into the traditional male sphere of public life. Defining their domestic role broadly, by the early twentieth century many middle-class women justified involvement in social reform movements, even politics, on the basis of their position as guardian of home and family.[116] In the context of war this logic gained new power, and with the participation of prominent female reformers in the formative stages of the CTCA's work it was easy for the commission to accept, even encourage, the role of women as active public servants, even social reformers. In the process the CTCA encouraged the transformation of middle-class understandings of female domesticity.

Throughout the war the CTCA favored women's broad participation in the war effort and their specific involvement with the work of the commission. For instance, a pamphlet entitled *To Girls in Wartime—A Message from the American Government* began, "Have you seen any girls who think that when they have cried a little and waved their handkerchiefs and wished the boys good luck, their part in the war is all over? That kind of a girl is a slacker, isn't she?"[117] As this quotation suggests, in the context of the war the commission intimated that those women and girls who did *not* become involved in the war effort, *on the CTCA's terms*, were slackers, just as men who disobeyed the tenets of official manhood were.

Though the pamphlet began with a broad appeal for girls' participation in war work, its bulk was devoted to encouraging women to participate in the struggle against illicit sex and venereal disease, demonstrating the reformers' continued attachment to the image of women as moral guardians. Noting the ways girls might contribute to the war effort through war work, the leaflet continued, "The Government asks one more service of you. This leaflet will tell you about it." After laying out information about venereal diseases, the pamphlet explained, "Girls who are infected without knowing it, who think they must 'give the soldier or sailor anything he wants,' are really helping to spread venereal diseases to the soldiers and sailors." Stressing the role every girl could play, it concluded, "Help any girls you know not to 'lose their heads.' Help all the girls and boys you know to keep straight and have a good time in the decent sense of those words."[118] While granting women an important public role during the war, then, the reformers often understood the importance of women's role primarily in moral terms.

This understanding was reinforced by the reformers' continued attachment to the notion of woman as the natural moral superior of man. The head of the CTCA's community work, Joseph Lee, insisted that "the effect of the society of good women is wholly good, that one of the best influences in our lives is the desire to merit their esteem, and that the strongest influence for purity in the life of a young man is the hope of being some day worthy of the love of a good woman."[119] Men, he seemed to suggest, did not naturally aspire to goodness, but they might be prompted to do so through exposure to upstanding women.

In fact the CTCA hoped to harness these aspirations in the creation of their new men. Describing the role of the community work of the CTCA embodied in the programs of the War Camp Community Service, Lee maintained further, "Our soldiers are going across the sea where we can no longer control their environment. It is the duty of the women of America, as the Secretary of War has said, to make for them an invisible armor which shall protect them wherever they may go."[120] Anticipating the removal of American men from the moral guardianship of American women, the reformers hoped that these women might train the soldiers to internalize certain moral guidelines—in particular a pledge to sexual purity—before their departure. Women might have a public role in the war, but this role only carried their traditional role of moral guardian of the family into the public sphere where they might influence the millions of men in uniform.

The reformers also continued to understand women's public role in terms of their natural domesticity, assigning them responsibilities in keeping with their "natural" roles as mothers. Within the commission itself women worked most commonly as "protective workers" and as hostesses in YWCA Hostess Houses. In cities and towns throughout the country the CTCA employed protective workers, social workers assigned to patrol the streets and rescue young women straying into sexually promiscuous behaviors. Acting as surrogate mothers on the street, the protective workers were encouraged to "follow and warn young girls apparently in danger" and later to befriend them, taking whatever measures necessary to protect the girls from sexual danger.[121] In small towns it was even hoped that the protective workers might know the girls they met in the streets and would "get in touch with these girls and take them home to their mothers."[122]

In their other common role within the commission's work women participated as matrons of the YWCA's Hostess Houses, buildings inside the camps intended to provide a safe meeting place for soldiers and civilian women. Providing what the CTCA understood as a feminine refuge within the male environment of the training camp, the houses offered the comforts and casualness of home, provided meals by the thousands to soldiers and their friends, housed women in emergencies, and in a pinch sometimes served as the scene for weddings.[123]

As matrons of the Hostess Houses women could exert their feminine influence through both moral uplift and the re-creation of the home setting. Edward F. Allen explained the potential for moral guardianship as he quoted a young soldier's response to the Hostess House and its keepers: "I guess a lot of us would be awful reckless if it wa'n't for you people,' a young soldier stopped at the desk to say on his way out. 'You've kep' some of us out of the guard house."[124] Soldiers theoretically understood this moral pressure as motherly, reminiscent of the homes they left behind. As one soldier reportedly explained, "If we get too free, one of the Hostesses happens along and says: 'Not so much noise, please, boys.' We settle right down—it sounds so like mother!"[125]

Thus, although the CTCA encouraged women's participation in the war effort, it defined that participation according to traditional notions both of woman's domestic responsibility and of her natural moral superiority. Interestingly, the commission's encouragement of women's public responsibilities during the war was almost entirely free of any appeal to women's piety. As they asked women to take on war-time duties, and even as they advocated this participation in traditional moral and domestic terms, they did so without an emphasis on women's religiosity. It was this aspect of traditional true womanhood that the reformers most obviously discarded. By the early twentieth century, it seems, women's moral responsibilities had been largely secularized. This is not to suggest that many women did not understand their roles in religious terms, or that many in the society did not continue to view piety as an important aspect of femininity. Rather, it suggests the reformers' largely secular ideal for their society, an ideal based in urban, middle-class experience.

The CTCA redefined womanhood, modernizing it in the expansion of domesticity and in the departure from piety, while maintaining links to true womanhood in the continued reliance on images of women in their traditional roles as the defenders of domesticity and morality. The meaning of these images, though, had been altered by changes in the definition of manhood. Although women remained the superior custodians of morals and the primary domestic figures, the reformers encouraged men to understand their own duty in these spheres, embodied in the aspirations to purity and to a domestic partnership with women.

In this sense, then, the reformers attempted to define womanhood in terms that established woman's social importance not only through her difference from men, but also increasingly through the responsibilities she shared with men. Nineteenth-century true womanhood had always maintained that women had an importance comparable to men's, but it did so while emphasizing both the differences between men and women and women's natural subservience to men. The CTCA attempted to establish a new definition of womanhood based in shared responsibilities and partnership. Submission, theoretically, would be replaced by mutual respect and equality. The reformers' notions of womanhood would complement men's new roles, maintaining security through a continued attachment to tradition, while flexing to embrace society's changes and war-time needs.

"Builders in the Final and Higher Civilization": Cultural Nationalism and the New American

The reformers hoped that the development of manhood and womanhood among Americans would create a new and better citizenry, united in their shared social values and motivated by the same high national aspirations. Joseph H. Odell, the *Outlook* magazine contributor, described his view of the importance of the soldiers' training in manhood, suggesting:

> When I began my investigation of the camps my proclaimed aim was to discover, not what kind of soldiers Uncle Sam would send to France, but what kind of men Uncle Sam would send back to their homes and communities after the war is over. I have discovered both; for in making better men we are making finer soldiers, and in making efficient soldiers we are producing a higher type of men—healthier physically, broader mentally and nobler spiritually. If Germany should crumble before these men can get into action, if we have lavished billions of dollars to train men for battles they will never fight, yet the money has been well spent and I consider it the best investment in citizenship the country could have made.[126]

A CTCA representative in Little Rock shared Odell's perceptions. Explaining the public utility of the commission's creation of new men and women, he wrote, "Clean living, manhood and womanhood is the standard for which democracy is striving, a standard that spells civic efficiency and good citizenship."[127]

The nature of this "investment in citizenship," of this new "civic efficiency and good citizenship," was specific in character and included the development of a new set of ideals among Americans. As Edward F. Allen exclaimed,

> After the smoke of battle has cleared, when there shall be peace with honor and justice, there will come the great process of readjustment. The men will be mustered out and returned to their former tasks. Those who are spared—and may they be many!—will be better citizens than they were before they went in. They will have graduated from "the larger university." They will have learned the meaning of concerted effort, obedience, loyalty, cheerfulness, courage and generosity. They will come back with a new set of ideals, as men who have been tried by fire and found good metal.[128]

Joseph H. Odell concurred, noting, "Many who had never known the impelling force of a great motive or the alluring spell of a high ideal have found both in the purpose and spirit of the new army."[129] Through their experience in the military America's troops would gain a new social vision, a heightened idealism, born in the programs of the CTCA.

Not only the soldiers would be affected by the commission's work. Civilians, too, would find themselves acculturated to a "new set of ideals." Speaking to a conference of war recreation workers in October 1917, Secretary of War Baker suggested that while many people would prefer the role of soldier, some would have to remain behind, and in this self-sacrificing role they would actually be no less heroic. He explained,

> If you will impress upon the people of your communities, I think they will respond, and they will feel, not perhaps the spiritual exaltation that comes from carrying the flags, but they will feel that they are really builders in the final and higher civilization, the civilization of justice and opportunity, and of high thinking and high doing which we pray is to be the permanent state of civilized man after this terrible visitation and tragic calamity has passed.[130]

Describing its work as an "epoch-making movement," one progress report of the CTCA's community program explained, "History is being made in this the first year of America's share in the world's war, not only on the battle fields of France but in the cities of America which are preparing the way for a new democracy."[131] In the training camps and their neighboring communities the commission would rebuild the nation, using the combined strength of men and women remade in the image of the reformers themselves.

Here, then, was one social possibility of the war: the creation of a nation of good citizens, men and women aspiring to standards of behavior established by the progressives' definitions of manhood and womanhood. The benefit to be gained by the nation in this transformation would be twofold. First, as already suggested, the physical and moral state of the nation would be improved on the level of the individual because of men's and women's aspirations to higher standards of behavior. In addition the nation itself would be uplifted as men and women shared a sense of common goals for the nation and a sense of public duty to ensure that those goals were fulfilled. Expression of new definitions of masculinity and femininity and the attempted national application of those standards would tend toward the development of a community national in its scope. In the new American community men and women, aspiring to the same standards of behavior, would become members of the national community, moving beyond the bonds of loyalty to class groupings, ethnic and racial groupings, region, and religion, which the reformers knew imperiled the success of their work. As Maj. Granville Fortescue pronounced in an article on the new National Army camps, "When the benefits that come to the nation through the creation of the National Army are ultimately catalogued, the fact that it has welded the country into a homogeneous society, seeking the same national ends and animated by the same national ideals, will overtop all other advantages."[132] Sharing urban, white, middle-class values, Americans would constitute a unified people, united by their understanding of their roles as men and women and as Americans.

Though broadly successful in establishing their programs in the training camps and civilian communities of the nation, the reformers were considerably less successful in creating the crusaders of the national community they envisaged. Devoted to their own white, urban, middle-class vision, the reformers clung tenaciously to their assumptions regarding anyone outside their cultural group. As they entered the real world of training camps and communities the CTCA reformers stressed social stability over their commitment to democracy and equality. Unwilling to accept the diversity of the American population and unable to see beyond their own cultural standards, the reformers only encouraged resistance to the pressures of cultural nationalism.

CHAPTER THREE

Reformers between Two Worlds: The Battle against Tradition and Working-Class Modernism

> We are surrounding the people of this country with an entirely new population, a population which is not integrated with its life, a great mass of people who are encamped on the borders of a town or a city and are wholly foreign to the local feeling and sentiments of the community. Now that presents a very grave problem in dealing with human beings. It presents several problems. The first of them is: What are those soldiers going to do to the towns, and what are the towns going to do to the soldiers?
>
> —Secretary of War Baker, 23 October 1917

In September 1917 nearly 19,000 men reported for training at the new National Army installation opening at Camp Lewis, seventeen miles south of Tacoma, Washington, a midsized city with a population approaching 100,000. These troops were only the lead men in a parade of soldiers that would eventually expand the camp population to 44,000 by June 1918. Ray F. Carter, a CTCA representative in Tacoma, acknowledged his own uneasiness about the arrival of the new troops, as Secretary of War Baker had done in a more general way.[1] "Frankly, I am uneasy," Carter began, "Tacoma has nothing to offer a man. Perhaps I should say that its facilities are simply swamped." Carter understood the task the enormous influx of troops implied for reformers in that locale. "We are facing a big problem in this city. What is before us is nothing less than the pretty complete reorganization of the community life on a new basis. To absorb 50,000 men into a city of this size with all the conflicting elements of an American city is a difficult and delicate matter." Yet Carter, with the usual confidence of the progressives, asserted the conviction that he, and Tacoma, could meet this test. "I believe it can be done in time," he concluded, "by patient application and ingenuity."[2]

The situation in Tacoma in the fall of 1917 was not unique. Thirty-two major military installations, including sixteen new National Guard camps, and sixteen new National Army cantonments opened their gates that fall and admitted a stream of recruits new to army life. Some placed near major metropolitan areas and others stationed in rural outposts, the camps' impact on local life was always sizable. (For details on camp locations see Appendix D.) As New Yorkers took up residence in Spartanburg, South Carolina, and Mississippians traveled to Kansas and Illinois, soldiers and civilians, new arrivals and locals, faced each other across a chasm of cultural difference.

Despite the magnitude of the soldier "problem," however, the reformers of the CTCA fully expected to control the behavior of both the soldiers and their civilian counterparts through the combined efforts of their constructive and repressive work. Recreation and social hygiene education inside the camps would create new men, ready to shoulder the burdens of the nation's international campaign. Complementary recreation and education programs for civilian women would create worthy helpmates for the troops. A carefully controlled community recreation program would allow these men and women to meet in the most desirable and safe circumstances. And when all else failed, the strictest enforcement of the law would contain any resistance to the reformers' efforts. As they moved from the ideal world of drawing boards and committee meetings to the real world of training camps and civilian communities, the reformers firmly maintained their optimism regarding their ability to build a nation of crusaders.

This faith appeared rewarded by the reformers' rapid successes. Though facing some initial skepticism, both inside the camps and in neighboring communities the CTCA established broad social hygiene education programs and vast recreational programs that matched their progressive designs. Dramatically successful in establishing its programs, the CTCA entered the lives of Americans, rich and poor, black and white, in cities and towns, in the North and the South, and attempted to use its programs to transform a diverse nation into a united community, peopled by crusaders sharing common attitudes and behaviors.

In its description of the ideal man, the ideal woman, and the ideal community, the CTCA suggested sweeping changes in the nature of American society, particularly in the shape of its status structures. Its rhetoric described the elimination of traditional social hierarchies and their replacement by a new commitment to the values of equality and justice. In this context the CTCA promised a new democratization in class relations and a new equality between men and women. Further, promoting a vision of a new national community, the reformers depicted an inclusive and united nation, composed of the variety of people calling themselves Americans.

Rather than developing a new culture that integrated the habits and values of the diverse American population, however, the reformers cultivated an exclusive and ultimately repressive community reflecting only their own cultural beliefs and social habits. Preoccupied with social stability, the CTCA's programs fostered a continued acceptance of traditional social roles based in hierarchical social relations, even while it dismissed local traditions and showed little willingness to incorporate other cultural visions into the work.

Determined to reshape American values, the reformers placed themselves between what they viewed as two destructive forces in American culture—archaic traditionalism and the corruption of the urban working class. In its own way each of these forces stood in the way of the construction of the reformers' new nation. Their treatment of these two cultural alternatives showed the reformers' keen determination to reshape the nation in their own image and to take those measures necessary to ensure their success. Though the reformers emphasized the constructive nature of their programs, particularly the recreational and educational work, the programs always included an important element of control, even repression, which became increasingly prevalent as individuals resisted the commission and rejected its vision.

"You Have Contributed to Their Amusement and Entertainment": Establishing the In-Camp Programs

Inside the camp gates the CTCA established programs designed to remake the military man. In what was perhaps the commission's most remarkable success, it rapidly established a social hygiene program for soldiers that brought modern sex education to thousands and possibly millions of soldiers for the first time. Printing and distributing pamphlets, organizing lectures, displaying informational placards, producing and showing feature length movies advocating chastity and educating soldiers about the risks of venereal disease, the CTCA built and operated a social hygiene education program more extensive and affecting more Americans than anything that had preceded it. In one week in May 1918 Walter Clarke, the head of the CTCA's social hygiene education program for soldiers, reported that 28,960 men had heard social hygiene lectures, 30,200 had received pamphlets, and eighteen films were circulating. But these figures were almost disappointing in light of the figures of the previous week, when 66,314 soldiers had attended social hygiene lectures and 177,050 had been given pamphlets.[3]

The reformers' resounding success in establishing the social hygiene education program was matched by their triumph in building a new, in-camp recreation program. Athletics thrived under the CTCA's guidance. Soldiers competed among themselves on the individual and the company levels and on the divisional and the camp levels. They also competed against local civilians. Events ranged from football and baseball contests to games of leapfrog and tag. Every training camp newspaper printed long lists, some of events planned for the future, others reporting the outcomes of competitions already conducted.[4]

Singing, too, became a regular feature of camp life, with camp song leaders integrating group singing into many aspects of the training day. Soldiers sang on the march, at meals, and in the Liberty Theaters. According to the CTCA, as many as ten to fifteen thousand men gathered for mass sings on special occasions.[5]

Libraries sprang up in all of the camps, under the supervision of the American Library Association. Most were open fourteen hours a day, held more than twenty-five thousand volumes, and subscribed to thirty-eight publications, in addition to the thirteen magazines received gratis from the publishers. The libraries offered the soldiers seven-day circulation and operated in most cases on an honor system without fines.[6]

Through the Liberty Theaters and the affiliated organization huts the commission offered the soldiers an extensive entertainment schedule. The commission eventually succeeded in building a theater in each National Army camp and erecting a tent in each National Guard camp. Each auditorium presented an extensive entertainment bill, ranging from vaudeville shows, plays, movies, and athletic events to lectures on the war effort and group sings.[7] The YMCA, the Knights of Columbus, and the Jewish Welfare Board all built soldiers' clubs in the camps, and many of their buildings also included auditoriums of sorts. Soldiers came to these auditoriums both as performers and as spectators, and the events seemed constant and ever changing. Here the affiliates sponsored a regular schedule of "amateur vaudeville entertainments, Bible classes, movie shows, basketball games, song services and sparring matches."[8] Special events such as evangelical revivals, dances, and parties supplemented the regular program.[9]

Statistics illustrate the vastness of the affiliates' work. According to John S. Tichenor of the YMCA, 1,236 movies were shown in Y huts throughout the United States in one week. Measured in miles, Y hut projectors were playing 750 miles of movies every seven days.[10] In the six months from September 1917 to February 1918, the eleven Y huts at Camp Sherman had 5,336,626 soldier visitors, who wrote 4,548,509 letters on Y stationery. In those same six months, almost 500,000 soldiers attended the Camp Sherman huts' entertainments, and 200,000 men attended 915 religious meetings.[11] By September 1918 sixty-one Hostess Houses were also operating, under YWCA auspices, and twenty-five others were scheduled for construction.[12]

As the CTCA entered the military stronghold of the training camps, its initial reception was often a mixed one. To some military personnel the programs of the CTCA seemed civilian meddling at best, dangerous interference at worst. The commission's social hygiene program, for instance, met some resistance. As William Zinsser, head of the Social Hygiene Division's Section on Men's Work, declared about one of these foes, "I can see that the Major General . . . was out of sympathy with the Commission's program, who like so many of the officers think the work of the Commission is all 'tommy-rot.' I wish I could collar some of those guys someday and tell them where they 'get off'."[13] Yet this obstinacy was minimal. In general the military seemed to accept the value of the social hygiene education program; they integrated it into the training program.[14]

Though some commanding generals also expressed initial reservations about the recreation program, this apprehension quickly dissipated, replaced by a broad acceptance, sometimes even appreciation, of the work of the commission and its representatives. One district director for the CTCA observed:

> In my second trip over the Southeastern District I found a great improvement in the attitude of Commanding Officers of camps toward the Commission and its activities. Officers who only tolerated me because they had to in January, were very friendly in March, and in many cases urged me to obtain for their camps activities which heretofore they had refused to accept.[15]

The opinion of E. F. Glenn, commanding general of Fort Benjamin Harrison, expressed in a letter to one representative of the commission, reflected the military establishment's growing support of the recreation program: "I am taking advantage of this occasion to express to you my very sincere appreciation of the splendid work that your Bureau is doing for this Camp," he explained. "You have contributed to . . . [the soldiers'] amusement and entertainment in the form of athletics and private entertainments of various sorts, and have stood generally for a healthy moral tone in everything that you have touched."[16]

The Hostess Houses had seemed particularly suspect initially. The CTCA reported that even this skepticism was quickly forgotten once the houses opened. In fact, the commission suggested, they often "received indignant letters from commanding officers who say they have been discriminated against" because they had not yet received their YWCA outpost.[17]

The military's acceptance of the CTCA programs may well have been influenced by the commission's determination in pressing for their programs and by the remarkable speed and resounding success with which the reformers made those programs a reality in camps across the country. Inside the camp gates the CTCA operated within a closed system, a tightly controlled environment acknowledged by its inhabitants to be entirely under governmental control. The commission's effectiveness in actualizing its vision inside the camp gates was thus not particularly surprising. In the cities and towns surrounding the camps, though, the CTCA faced a less regulated environment, inhabited by the diversity of the American population.

A "Revolution in the Routine of Our Daily Affairs": Establishing the Community Programs

As the first round of draftees for the new National Army reached their training camps in the fall of 1917, civilians in surrounding cities and towns greeted their arrival with a mixture of excitement and trepidation. Community leaders generally welcomed their locale's selection as a training camp site. Though military camps had traditional reputations as hellholes of vice and dissipation, their additional reputation as moneymakers for local business made them a much-sought-after acquisition in the late spring of 1917. Led by businessmen and local political leaders, communities vied for selection as training camp sites for the new National Army and the newly mobilized National Guard. In Pierce County, Washington, the eventual home of Camp Lewis, residents voted in favor of a $2 million county expenditure for improvements for the American Lake camp site in an effort to attract a training camp.[18] Fort Worth, Texas, offered to supply all of the necessary land for a training camp free of charge as an inducement to its selection as a camp site.[19] In Little Rock, Arkansas, a local newspaper credited local officials and businessmen with the acquisition of Camp Pike, heralding the "capture" of a camp, and cautioned citizens about the risk of losing the camp as one Virginia community had.[20] Fiscal considerations clearly prompted this nationwide competition for the training camps. Even Joseph H. Odell, author of *The New Spirit of the New Army*, a collection of articles dedicated to painting a promising picture of morality and good cheer in the camps and communities, admitted that cities originally sought the cantonments out of hopes for monetary gain.[21]

Economic benefits were often used to dispel fears about what a training camp might mean for the city or town. One editorial in the *Stanford Palo Alto News* admitted concerns about hosting a training camp, noting:

> There are certainly two sides to the question of the desirability of a big soldiers' camp here from this community's point of view. There is no doubt that its presence would mean a tremendous boost for the business of the city, which would lead to permanent benefit. On the other hand in such a large body of soldiers . . . there would doubtless be a considerable number whose presence would be a cause for uneasiness.

Yet the paper went on to concede, "The certain benefits that will follow having the camp here very clearly far outweigh the possible inconveniences, which can be obviated by proper supervision, anyhow."[22] The general manager of the Little Rock Board of Commerce, George Firmin, took a similar tack, suggesting: "So now you ask what advantage is the army stationed at Little Rock going to be to this community. I will answer by asking what advantage is Little Rock going to take of its opportunity to improve her condition by reason of securing the army?" Firmin made clear that the advantages of which he spoke were business-related.[23] The economic benefits of a camp located close outside the city limits were obvious and unlimited. As one headline in San Diego exclaimed, "Expect Business Here to Double within Two Months; Tax Resources."[24]

Despite the economic value, civilians in the training camp communities often worried about the consequences of their selection as a cantonment site. Retaining traditional perceptions of the soldier, civilians in prospective training camp communities worried that a camp would threaten, even compromise, the moral and physical well-being of their women and girls. In Palo Alto, California, for instance, trustees of Stanford University worried about the army's plans to use a piece of land only one-half mile from the campus; they objected on the basis of the four hundred to five hundred women living on the campus.[25]

It may well be that concern for their community's well-being contributed to civilians' cooperation with the CTCA's community programs. Eager to mitigate the harmful effects of the arrival of the troops, citizens were open to CTCA suggestions that could help protect their hometowns. One Fort Worth newspaper admitted that the arrival of the troops would bring a "revolution in the routine of our daily affairs" and noted that failure to confront this fact would lead to social chaos. "There is no use of blinking the fact that the bringing of 30,000 young men to a community the size of Fort Worth will upset the routine of social life generally," it asserted. "If they are left to find enjoyment as best they might, if no conventional manner is provided in which they may meet our girls socially," it warned, "confusion and worse will result in many cases and in no case will the social situation be as desirable as it will be under the systemitized *[sic]* method which the war department has provided for." It was the careful provision of recreation, with the orchestrated meeting of boys and girls in clean and wholesome leisure, that could best prevent disaster. "The girls of Fort Worth must meet them [the soldiers] then, but THEY MUST MEET THEM IN THE CONVENTIONAL WAYS PROVIDED BY MEN AND WOMEN WHO HAVE THEIR INTERESTS AT HEART."[26] Nervous about the social impact of the soldiers, this newspaper editor urged cooperation with the War Department's recreation programs.

The profit motive, too, encouraged many civilians in the local communities to cooperate at least superficially with the CTCA and its community counterpart, the War Camp Community Service (WCCS). From the beginning Secretary of War Baker made clear the seriousness of his intentions to control the training camps' surroundings by suggesting that any community failing to abide by the War Department's strictures would lose its cantonment. Citizens in training camp communities heeded this warning. The head of the WCCS fund committee in Little Rock asserted in February 1918:

> Little Rock is going to raise the $30,000 asked for by the War and Navy departments for the War Camp Community Service, for it is not going to imperil Camp Pike or incur the displeasure of the authorities in Washington. It cannot afford to do so, even if it demands the raising of ten times this amount. . . . Failure in this might be disastrous for Little Rock.[27]

Although failure might not have been disastrous for all of Little Rock, business interests certainly viewed it in this way. The Little Rock WCCS committee, according to its chairman, was "composed of Little Rock's most successful business and professional men," and it maintained an office in the Board of Commerce building. Having brought the camp to Little Rock in pursuit of a financial bonanza, businessmen had no intention of losing the camp. To retain it, they cooperated with the CTCA and the WCCS.[28] An editorial in the *Fort Worth Star-Telegram* explained from a similar perspective:

> It has been demonstrated that Fort Worth can accomplish things when she acts about it in downright earnest. There is now a growing conviction that the success in landing the camps and the manner in which we have gone about meeting the new conditions, are simply the beginning of a new era in the city's growth. . . . let us strive to realize the two things we have referred to above: First, our increased RESPONSIBILITIES. Second, our new OPPORTUNITIES.[29]

Driven by the twin engines of patriotism and self-interest, communities worked with the CTCA to develop recreation programs for the soldiers stationed nearby. In major metropolises, smaller cities, towns, and rural hamlets, the forces of the WCCS mobilized citizens in the service of the visiting soldiers with remarkable success. Communities provided the facilities for recreation, building swimming pools and comfort stations, drinking fountains and soldier clubs. Churches, fraternal orders, and other civilian organizations cultivated ties to their own members and coordinated vast recreation programs, including dances, male-only get-togethers termed *smokers*, auto rides, picnics, parades, and pageants, which brought soldiers into close social contact with local civilians. Commercial entrepreneurs opened additional movie houses, and vaudeville shows and serious theater competed with the new medium of film for the patronage of the men in uniform. Families invited soldiers home for dinner, accepting the soldiers as their own. Fulfilling the designs of the progressive reformers, local governments, civic and fraternal organizations, and individuals rallied to provide soldiers with wholesome recreation that integrated the men in uniform into the social life of the community.[30]

In many instances progress was rapid. Heralding Little Rock's achievements, one WCCS progress report exclaimed, "Little Rock, another of the pioneer camp cities, began in May to blaze a trail in War Camp Community Service. . . . A program of activities began immediately."[31] Other communities followed this example. The end result of communities' activism was often an extensive organizational superstructure and a broad and far-reaching recreational program.[32]

In larger cities such as Little Rock, Houston, Atlanta, or Des Moines, existing recreational facilities and civilian organizations simplified the recreational mobilization. City parks, civic auditoriums, fraternal clubhouses, movie theaters, restaurants, and hotels provided WCCS representatives with recreational spaces. Fraternal organizations, churches, women's organizations, and reform groups provided them with citizens eager to assist in developing healthful amusement for the soldiers. In these cases the WCCS could quickly organize what it considered appropriate recreation for the men.

The more difficult, and often remarkable, transformation came in the smaller cities and towns. The experience in Hattiesburg, Mississippi, home of Camp Shelby, is emblematic of the broader experience of the CTCA in the smaller training camp communities. Camp Shelby, the National Guard cantonment for the 38th Division, lay just eleven miles south of Hattiesburg, a small city of fifteen thousand people.[33] A WCCS report on Hattiesburg in November 1917 judged, "This city is small, narrow and dirty. The only comfort station found is a vile place in the only hotel. This city needs a community secretary as no city ever needed one before; but the man who is assigned here should have a halo for being willing to stay here."[34] With only two movie theaters, no dance establishments, and several pool halls, Hattiesburg was viewed by WCCS representatives as a recreational wasteland, a community sorely lacking any facilities for the type of leisure prescribed by the commission and also lacking the human resources for program development.[35]

Initial progress in Hattiesburg was slow. In January 1918 a district director for the WCCS complained, "Community work not effective. The town is rotten,—the townspeople are sore. No good buildings except churches for a crowd of men. Only one soldiers' club in town and that unattractive. Nothing for men to do in town on Sunday except church."[36] The shortage of facilities slowed the work, requiring fundraising and building programs to develop the physical resources necessary for the WCCS's plans.[37]

Despite a sluggish start, though, the eventual transformation of Hattiesburg was impressive. By March 1918 the WCCS could point to a program of home entertainment being coordinated by the churches, which also offered socials and Saturday night suppers. Four clubs, including one for soldiers of the Jewish faith, were operating, and the city had installed comfort stations and drinking fountains. The local YMCA and two other fraternal orders had opened their doors to soldiers, and all fraternal orders had contacted their members in the camp.[38] A published report on Hattiesburg in March 1918 suggested that WCCS efforts "resulted in the development of an active program," a program operating "with a splendid spirit of hospitality." By May 1918 the program had expanded still further, including Sunday entertainment with addresses, concerts, social gatherings and refreshments, the continued involvement of churches and fraternal organizations, hospital visits, parties at the YWCA, and big league baseball events.[39] Hattiesburg, it seems, had met the expectations of the progressive reformers, creating a broad-based public recreation program that matched the CTCA's blueprints in every detail.

The reformers were similarly successful in creating the final component of their constructive programs, a social hygiene education program for civilians. According to the reformers, the threat to moral and physical health posed by illicit sex was shared by all Americans. In shaping an education program to protect civilians from this danger, though, the reformers' preoccupation with an efficient war effort and with protecting the men in uniform from disease remained clear. Early in the war the CTCA discovered that many of the soldiers were reporting to camp already infected with venereal disease. As the war and the CTCA program progressed, it became increasingly obvious that soldiers first entering the army, rather than those already in the camps, were the central source of venereal cases among the troops, forcing the reformers to integrate civilian men into their social hygiene education plans. Concerned not so much with the well-being of civilian men, but with the health of soon-to-be soldiers, the CTCA constructed a civilian education program targeting civilian males.[40]

The CTCA's education program also targeted civilian women, but again the overriding concern for the health of the men in uniform was evident. Whether venereal disease originated among troops or among civilian men, the CTCA contended, the disease was contracted from women. As one article in the soldier press explained, "In preventing this interchange of infection from soldier to civilian and civilian to soldier, we are again confronted with the problem that to better protect the soldiers' health we must safeguard the civilians."[41]

Only the "industrial army" among civilians warranted protection without regard to their relationship to the men in uniform. Defining the war effort broadly, the CTCA sought to suggest that industry could no more afford to lose personnel through venereal disease than could the army. As Katherine B. Davis of the CTCA asserted, "It is just as vital to success that our industrial army be fit as that our army in the field should be ready to fight. . . . We must bring to our industrial armies some knowledge of the menace of disease."[42] Concerned with efficiency, the reformers developed a civilian social hygiene education program designed to protect both military and industrial troops from venereal disease.

Mirroring the efforts with the soldiers, the civilian education program employed multiple methods to reach the American population with its message of sexual purity. Pamphlets such as *V.D.—U. Boat No. 13!* and *Smash the Line* targeted the civilian population as a whole, whereas more directed pamphlets such as *To Girls in Wartime—A Message from the American Government* and a second feature length film, *The End of the Road*, targeted young women and girls specifically. Traveling exhibits and lecturers, too, spread the CTCA's social hygiene message throughout the population.[43]

With remarkable rapidity soldiers and civilians alike found their camps and communities changed by the programs of the CTCA. Social hygiene education introduced explicit materials, unheard of in the years before the war, detailing the causes and consequences of venereal disease. In-camp and community recreation programs transformed the leisure activities of soldiers and civilians alike and clearly delineated proper and improper entertainment.

"We Have Been Not a Little Troubled by the Attitude of the Churches": The CTCA against Tradition

Despite its enormous success in establishing its programs, the CTCA never operated unopposed. Early in the war members of the commission recognized that there were Americans who saw in its programs a frightening tendency to immorality and looseness. Advocates of a traditional moral system once dominant in the country, these traditionalists saw in dancing and in certain other aspects of the CTCA program, particularly movies and Sunday recreation, a dangerous threat to the moral well-being of their communities and of the American troops. Institutionalized particularly in many southern churches, and representing the attitude of many rural Americans, this viewpoint criticized aspects of the CTCA program while sharing its interest in protecting the morality of soldiers and civilians.

Here the CTCA faced opponents who might under other circumstances have been allies. These Americans were, like the CTCA, concerned with morality. Conceivably members of the progressive movement, these moralists split with their colleagues when the commission's moral guidelines conflicted with their own. In the elimination of this friction the CTCA wielded substantial federal influence to ensure that the local cultural preferences, theoretically respected by the reformers, would conform to the purposes of the CTCA.

Pastors often attacked the WCCS's dance program with vehemence. An article in the soldiers' *Pass-in Review* of Camp Bowie in Fort Worth offered a series of rules for dancing, suggesting that there was a movement under way in town to have dancing halted.[44] A letter to Raymond Fosdick written at the request of the district representative of the CTCA made the roots of that movement clear. As Samuel B. Murray explained to Fosdick:

> Questions of personal conduct, which in my judgment are purely individual matters, are made of great religious importance in this section. The question of the dance, the theatre and card playing and even the moving picture show are looked upon as deciding factors in ones *[sic]* religious experience. I find that the ministers, who hold these different amusements to be particularly sinful, are rather antagonistic to every effort made to provide the boys with a sane and normal life.

Murray blamed the resistance of the ministers on their "spirit of religious intolerance and narrowness," as well as their interest in "denominational development."[45] Fosdick, in his reply, agreed with Murray's basic assessment of the resistance among the southern churches, noting, "We have been not a little troubled by the attitude of the churches in the South in their opposition to our work, and your diagnosis of the situation agrees with mine exactly."[46]

Although the southern churches were the most consistent opponents of the WCCS dances, opposition was not limited to that region. In Tacoma, Washington, Ray F. Carter, executive secretary of the local WCCS and the CTCA representative, complained of the resistance of even the YMCA and the YWCA to dances, pronouncing, "The YWCA says far be it from us to arrange for a dance; the YMCA holds up its hands in horror of the idea; all the uplifters in the town say the dance is taboo; and yet the soldier wants to dance, and if he does not get the chance to dance he is pretty sore about the deprivation."[47] The traditional American morality of the nineteenth century was alive and well in pockets throughout the United States, particularly among the Protestant churches and their members, and thereby among the CTCA's affiliated organizations.

From the beginning the CTCA publicly conceded to local preferences regarding soldier recreation. The CTCA and the WCCS would not force communities to offer amusements that broke local cultural taboos.[48] As Joseph Lee suggested regarding the provision of dances for soldiers, "We are careful not to go further in this matter in any particular locality than public opinion will sanction."[49] Though often professing their concern for local tradition, however, the CTCA and the WCCS inevitably asserted their own position, confident of its rectitude, and strove to shape each local situation to match the progressive ideal.[50]

This tendency was seen most clearly in the CTCA's response to opponents of Sunday recreation. While only a small minority of Americans opposed WCCS efforts to establish dances for the soldiers, many more openly resisted what they considered the desecration of the Sabbath represented by the CTCA's provision of entertainment for the soldiers on Sunday. The sanctity of the Sabbath had once been a widely accepted doctrine of Protestant Americans. In the late nineteenth and early twentieth centuries the decline in Americans' work hours and the rise of organized leisure activities had come to compete with, and even to overshadow, the traditional Sunday.[51] Though during the closing decades of the nineteenth century the Sabbatarians struggled to reassert the dominance of the old-style Sabbath, much of the country had abandoned it by 1920, using Sunday as an opportunity to enjoy the growing availability of commercial amusements.[52] Northerners moved away from the traditional Sabbath quickly, but forces in the south proceeded more slowly. Led by the Protestant clergy, many southern citizens resisted the WCCS policy of promoting Sunday entertainments.

A public statement of the WCCS policy regarding Sunday recreation demonstrates both the CTCA's awareness of the likely opposition of certain communities to entertainment on Sunday and its determination, nevertheless, to provide recreation for soldiers on the Sabbath:

> The problem of providing recreation for the soldier on Sunday, in some camps the only day on which he has leisure time, has been a perplexing one. This is particularly true of those parts of the country where Sunday has always been strictly observed and in the small town as contrasted with the city which offers greater facilities for Sunday entertainment. In a number of states laws forbid the opening of motion picture houses on Sunday and popular sentiment is against such action. Whatever the feeling, however, on the part of individual communities or people regarding Sabbath observance, it is the consensus of opinion that some form of wholesome recreation must be provided for the men in uniform on Sunday which is universally the lonesome day for one away from home.[53]

The CTCA based its arguments in favor of Sunday recreation on the greater danger posed to morality by neglecting the soldiers on Sunday. Fosdick responded to one concerned southerner:

> The blind tiger and the prostitute have no scruples about the Sabbath. The bottle with its promise of good-fellowship and the woman with open arms and itching palms draw men of the draft age seven days in the week, and

> do their worst in those hours when men, with nothing to do and no place to go, walk the streets with only their thoughts for company. . . . To leave these hours empty is to play into the hands of the illicit liquor seller, the woman of the streets, and all who prey upon the idle brain.[54]

For members of the CTCA the risks posed by these evils were far more dangerous than the desecration of the Sabbath.[55]

Realizing that its program would conflict with local tradition in many instances, the national handbook of the WCCS cautioned local workers from forcing a preconceived plan of recreation on a resistant community, suggesting, "The problem of Sunday recreation, unless rightly handled, may sometimes cause difficulty. The community organizer ought not to go into a community with any definite policy which he wishes to urge with regard to Sunday recreation." Yet this warning did not mean to suggest that local workers should bend to the unreasonable forces of reaction in the communities. The handbook continued, "If he is tactful and wise he will not attempt to go too far against the best conviction of the real community leaders, though it may in some instances be necessary to take a stand against narrow reactionaries. Clergymen ought not to be asked to decide the issue and should not be put on record."[56]

Similarly, in its relations with those "reactionaries" the CTCA often suggested its essential respect for those traditions as an introduction to pleas for cooperation. Fosdick explained to a reverend from East Point, Georgia, in March 1918, "I appreciate as much as any one the reasons, physical and religious, which lie at the basis of the principle of Sabbath observance, and we have no wish to destroy the barriers which usage and custom have sanctioned." But ultimately the CTCA demanded adherence to its progressive vision of the proper use of Sunday:

> At the same time, in the face of this great emergency, where we are striving by every means at our command to guard large bodies of troops against the unhealthy influences and cruder forms of temptation too often associated with their leisure hours, I feel that we shall be compelled to resort to many expedients which, under ordinary circumstances might never be thought of. In other words, I believe that legitimate forms of clean amusement and recreation should be encouraged on Sunday for the soldiers in Atlanta.[57]

To the CTCA the Sunday prohibitions seemed an unfortunate holdover from an earlier age. Responding to a letter regarding the prohibition of Sunday baseball in New York, Raymond Fosdick professed in September 1918:

> Personally, it does not seem to me that there can be any possible argument on the question and I find myself very much in sympathy with the manner in which my friend Edgrin sized up the situation when he said that the present law prohibiting Sunday baseball belongs to the age when scolding wives were ducked in the horse pond.[58]

Only the hopelessly outdated, Fosdick seemed to suggest, would forbid athletic competitions on Sunday.

Hoping to gain the voluntary compliance of communities on the Sunday issue, the CTCA appealed to the patriotism and civic pride of communities, intimating that any truly American community would understand the CTCA position and agree with it. Fosdick wrote to the city manager of Beaufort, South Carolina, "I am confident that the people of your community are fully conscious of this emergency situation and will not fail to provide for these obvious needs."[59] As in all of its programs the CTCA sought to cultivate a popular association between its work and the war cause.

Determined to create some form of amusement for the soldiers on Sunday, the CTCA provoked widespread protest in many southern cities and towns. An editorial in the *Arkansas Methodist* demonstrated the essential position of the Sabbatarians. "The craving for Sunday amusements is akin to the craving for drink and drugs," it noted, "and the one is no more legitimately entitled to gratification than is another."[60] To these Christians Sunday amusements were blatantly sinful, and the needs of war could not justify such transgressions. One congregation from Beeville, Texas, wrote to Secretary of War Baker:

> We respectfully protest against the use of the Sabbath as a day of amusement in all sorts of sports, athletic contests and theatrical entertainments at our army training camps. We sympathize with the boys' needs for recreation and entertainment, but we do not believe that such things are suitable for our soldier boys, any more than for private citizens, on the sabbath day. We do not believe that it is consistent with our prayers of blessing upon our boys, and our cause to flaunt a desecrated sabbath before the world at the same time. We, therefore, plead that as our soldiers go to war, they may go with reverence for God, and with clean hands.[61]

Adopting the rhetoric of the War Department, these citizens concluded, "We affirm that our boys, raised in our southland, have been taught to regard the sabbath as a holy day. We insist that our country should do all things possible to return our boys to us better and not worse, than when they went forth to fight for their country."[62]

Loosening of the strictures regarding the Sabbath stood for a much broader social degeneration for these citizens. An editorial from the *Arkansas Methodist* stated the case of the Sabbatarians clearly: "The encroachment upon the proper observance of the sabbath, such as Sunday mails, travel, the newspaper and simple and apparently harmless recreations have insidiously and impreceptibly *[sic]* affected our life so that ideals have become obscured and standards impaired."[63] Sabbatarians worried that Sunday entertainments were only the first evidence of an evil that would bring the total degeneration of their society and so hesitated to allow this initial corruption.[64] Given the earnestness of their beliefs, it is not surprising that Sabbatarians challenged the efforts of local WCCS committees to organize Sunday recreation in their communities.

Though in some cities and towns Sabbatarians were certainly the minority, in many others they commanded a majority opinion, backed by the force of state or local law. Particularly in the South, but in many northern communities as well, WCCS organizers encountered resistance as they set out to establish their recreation programs for the soldiers. In Hattiesburg, Mississippi, Sunday amusements met staunch popular resistance. As one report stated,

> The biggest problem which the Hattiesburg committee is facing is that of arranging to care for the men on Sunday afternoons. Owing to the attitude of the ministers and some of the prominent laymen, the activities that are now put on on Sunday afternoon are of such a religious nature that they do not appeal to . . . a certain class of the soldiers. Any move to open the theaters on Sunday, meets with a most violent opposition on the part of 90% of the community.[65]

Sunday concerts were opposed by "some of the strictest of the local people." The mayor stepped in to enforce the law when a motion picture was shown as part of a Sunday program.[66] In Beaufort, South Carolina, local ordinance prevented the opening of drug stores and fruit stands on Sundays, "and there is some little objection to revoking it."[67] In Anniston, Alabama, ministers opposed the WCCS program, and in Augusta,

Georgia, local ministers overturned a resolution passed by the city council permitting Sunday motion pictures. Demonstrating that concern for the Sabbath was not limited to the South, ministers in New London, Connecticut, opposed the opening of Sunday movies, while in Chillicothe, Ohio, "The Ministerial Alliance is attempting to have the motion picture houses closed on Sunday." Ohio law prohibited Sunday movies.[68]

These examples were not isolated cases. Yet the CTCA, backed by the patriotic fervor of wartime and ready to accuse opponents of slackerism, reshaped local culture to close approximations of the CTCA vision. Sometimes compromising, but never conceding, the CTCA threw its weight behind the modernizing forces of American communities and brought defeat to the traditionalists.

The experience of the CTCA in Little Rock, Arkansas, is illustrative of the cultural struggle that took place in many communities over the issue of Sunday recreation. In Arkansas state law forbade labor on Sundays, except in works of "necessity, comfort or charity."[69] This law made the Sunday opening of any commercial amusements in Little Rock illegal, complicating the position of the CTCA from the start. In June 1917 the mayor of Little Rock called in police to close three moving picture houses that were operating, in violation of the law, as a part of the Little Rock and Argenta CTCA program of free Sunday amusements for the soldiers. On 1 July Louis Rosenbaum, manager of the Princess Theatre, was arrested for violation of the law prohibiting Sunday labor. The plight of the movie houses became symbolic of the broader question regarding Sabbath observance. Citizens of Little Rock divided on the questions of the legitimacy of the Sunday laws, the propriety of any amusement for the soldiers on Sundays, and the specific question of the morality of Sunday movies.

Sunday entertainment was fundamental to the entire community program. CTCA representatives argued that movies, if free, did not violate any of the laws regarding Sabbath observance. The counsel for the defense of Louis Rosenbaum argued, "The provision of wholesome recreation for the soldiers on their one day of leisure is a factor contributing to the moral welfare of the city, and as such should be permitted under a liberal interpretation of the word 'necessity' in the old statute."[70] In accepting the camp, the CTCA reasoned, Little Rock had promised that the city would provide recreation for the soldiers. Sunday amusements were an important part of that pledge.[71]

The CTCA was not acting alone in Little Rock, but had staunch support for its policies from many citizens, a support voiced clearly and repeatedly by one local paper, the *Arkansas Democrat*. Agreeing wholeheartedly with the CTCA, the newspaper argued, "Sunday morning the soldiers should go to church, but Sunday afternoon they must have some kind of recreation and amusement of a wholesome kind provided for them; otherwise they will provide their own amusement of a kind that may not be for the best interests of the soldiers or of the community."[72]

Eager to associate themselves and the CTCA with law and order, the *Democrat* argued, "The *Arkansas Democrat* believes in law enforcement and it believes thoroughly in a proper observance of the Sabbath day, but neither of these would have been compromised by free moving pictures for the soldiers, as was planned by the Federation on Training Camp Activities."[73]

The newspaper and the CTCA were joined in their cause by the mayor of Argenta, or North Little Rock. Only a narrow interpretation of the law, the mayor argued, could cause Little Rock to neglect the needs of the soldiers on Sunday.

> Even were the action in question a technical violation of the law, which I feel sure it is not, I should rather be guilty of such a mistake than the larger one of being a factor in shaping such conditions as would be conducive to the lowering of the physical and moral tone of the men who have given up all for their country. Those who allow narrowness to guide their actions in these unusual times certainly are such factors.[74]

Here was the CTCA's position clearly stated by an ally—the traditionalists endangered the soldiers by refusing to acknowledge the reality of modern conditions. Failing to allow for healthful Sunday amusements, the traditionalists would drive the troops into the arms of the enemy, the purveyors of illicit recreation.

Aware that the strength of their opponents rested in the churches and their leaders in the Ministerial Alliance, those favoring recreation hoped to convince Little Rock residents that their position, too, fostered church support.[75] Not only that, recreation advocates suggested, but their position was the more public spirited as well. The patriotic response to the new situation brought on by the arrival of troops was full support for the federal program. "It is not only in the interest of good morals and law enforcement, to have moving pictures or other forms of innocent amusement for the soldiers on Sunday," the *Democrat* pointed out, "but it is also a matter of patriotism, for by seeing that the leisure time of the men is properly occupied the efficiency of the army is promoted."[76]

The allies of the CTCA dismissed their opponents in Little Rock as narrow-minded people unable to understand the situation at hand. According to the newspaper, a crowd of "old and bald-headed" churchmen, far removed from their youth, were denying the young men in the camps—"strong, virile types of manhood"—proper amusements. "The unusual emergency must be met, both from a patriotic and a community viewpoint, as a human situation that pulsates with a vitality that must be reckoned with," the paper maintained. Rather than protecting the town with Sunday restrictions, the paper asserted, the Ministerial Alliance was endangering the welfare of soldiers and civilians alike.[77]

Further, the *Democrat* suggested, these foes of Sunday recreation were sorely out of touch with popular culture in Little Rock. Responding to accusations of the Ministerial Alliance that movies would "blight" the soldier boys, the *Democrat* could only respond, "If it is 'blighting' to go to moving pictures, then the great majority of the people of Little Rock and Argenta are terribly blighted, for they go nearly every night."[78] Hoping to show the weakness and desperation of their opponents, the *Democrat* accused them of falsely linking movies to the reintroduction of the red-light district.[79]

While Mayor Pixley of Argenta, or North Little Rock, supported the CTCA position, Mayor Taylor of Little Rock, staunchly supported by the Ministerial Alliance, condemned the attempts of the CTCA to provide Sunday movies. According to the *Arkansas Methodist*, the official organ of the Little Rock and Arkansas conferences,

> It has not been demonstrated that man must have Sunday excitements. The demand comes largely from those who find their imperatives in perverted passions and appetites, and who have never seen or refuse to see the divine and spiritual elements in humanity. . . . No one today with any sense of propriety can imagine Jesus going on Sunday excursions, patronizing restaurants and drink and cigar stands, or frequenting Sunday dances or games or shows.[80]

Dances and movies, particularly on Sundays, were "pernicious and alluring." Dances attracted immoral persons and permitted improprieties, "which often lead to moral ruin." "It is also understood," Sabbatarians argued, "that movies have lowered sex standards, that they give unusual opportunities for forming improper acquaintances, and that the violation of the Holy Sabbath still further breaks down the restraints of conscience. It will be a reproach if the dances and 'movies' are the chief recreations offered to our soldiers by our city."[81]

While not suggesting that movies would lead to the reopening of the red-light district, the Ministerial Alliance did link those favoring the district with those favoring Sunday movies. Sam H. Campbell, president of the alliance, wrote Secretary of War Baker and described the unsuccessful efforts of "certain parties" to get the red-light district reopened in Little Rock. Defeated by the moral forces, Campbell suggested:

> The next step they take to try to prize the lid off is through the opening of the Sunday movies. Now I do not mean to say that all who stand for the opening of the Sunday movies stand for the other evils, but I do mean to say that all who stand for a wide open town, stand for the opening of the movies on Sunday, and they claim that it is in the interest of the soldier, all of which is not true, we have had too many political fights here not to know the gang.[82]

Not only were Sunday movies immoral, the alliance argued, but they were also illegal. As Sam H. Campbell suggested in a letter to the chairman of the CTCA, "If it is an improper act for some one to try to interfere with the selective draft law, after it has become a law, why it is not an improper act for some one to try to over ride a State law, after it has been placed upon the statute books?"[83] Reminding Fosdick of the law in Arkansas prohibiting Sunday movies, Campbell suggested the Ministerial Alliance would not oppose movies in the cantonments, but that it could not consider allowing them in Little Rock.

This was not to suggest, the alliance argued, that it did not understand the need to provide for the soldiers' needs. It was anxious to help with the soldiers and had already spent a great deal of time and energy providing basket dinners on Sundays and entertainments on Saturday nights and Sunday afternoons. It was not recreation, but *immoral* recreation that the alliance claimed it resisted. To do otherwise was to court disaster.

> We cannot stand idly by and see all this good work torn down, and evil influences thrown around our children and others simply because we are at

> war. If we go on our knees and pray for victory to come to our arms how can we hope to be heard by the God of heaven if we set aside His Holy Law, and desecrate His Holy Sabbath?[84]

Ultimately the Alliance came to blame the CTCA representative directly for the conflict raging in Little Rock. Their accusations make clear the Sabbatarians' view of themselves as a group besieged by the elites of Little Rock and their outsider allies. According to S. E. Ryan of the Methodist Episcopal Church, the CTCA in Little Rock had been organized by men who did not appreciate the importance of the religious forces of the city. Failing to consult with the Federation of Churches, the CTCA proceeded to emphasize "a series of dances for which the Churches could not stand for one minute." Ryan complained that in its organization the CTCA had allied with the wrong forces in town, failing to associate with the churches and choosing instead the morally questionable Chamber of Commerce. Ryan complained:

> I want to say frankly that it has been unfortunate that when the work of the Commission of Training Camp Activities was organized here the gentlemen who did so did not seem to think any person here was worth consulting except the body of men who are known as the Chamber of Commerce. The religious forces of the city were not taken into the plans, and had no chance to assist in any way in planning for the good of the soldiers who were coming among us. Saying nothing at all about the moral character of that body. I am only speaking the sober fact when I say that there are a good many in the organization who do not have the Christian idea of the Sabbath day, and other matters that I could mention.[85]

The ministers maintained that they were not seeking their own recognition but simply sought an opportunity to participate in the recreation program. As Ryan concluded, "All we ask is that the religious forces of the community be given a chance to do something, instead of being asked to help put across a programme that is to our mind decidedly unchristian."[86]

The proponents of this program, according to the Ministerial Alliance, were "the officious social set of our city," Myron Kessner, the original CTCA representative in Little Rock, and "Kessner's pal on the Sunday moving picture show business, the editorial writer of the Arkansas Democrat."[87] The *Arkansas Democrat* agreed with this assessment, adding "an overwhelming majority of the Rotary club" to the CTCA alliance.[88]

Although to the promovie forces this list seemed to include the leading citizens of the community, to those opposing the movies these forces included outsiders and elites unfamiliar with the traditions and the needs of Little Rock. An editorial in the *Baptist Advance* judged:

> Kessner, according to the dailies, is getting high praise for his work here in Little Rock from authorities in Washington. A big element of the best people of Little Rock are willing for the Washington authorities to take this little Jew that is trying to force Sunday picture shows and Saturday night dances on our people, to Washington or the moon or somewhere else than here and keep him forever. If he keeps up his present program we predict a big petition will go on in this city for his removal. It ought to go now. These outside forces must not dominate the morals of our city. Washington should praise the religious forces of the city, and not Kessner and his crowd.[89]

At issue, in the eyes of the Sabbatarians, was the identification of the leading citizens of Little Rock. Were they the members of the Chamber of Commerce and the Rotary Club, assisted by outsiders from Washington, or were they the traditional leaders, the ministers of the Protestant churches? Finding their definition of culture assaulted by the CTCA representative, the Ministerial Alliance and its allies lashed out at Myron Kessner of the CTCA. As a regional and religious outsider, Kessner seemed to the Alliance the perfect symbol of the insidious enemy of Little Rock's morality, its culture, and its traditions.

In the end the CTCA removed Kessner from his position in Little Rock, transferring him to Atlanta. Correspondence between Fosdick of the CTCA and H. S. Braucher, executive secretary of the WCCS, suggests that Kessner had been an unfortunate choice for the WCCS work in Little Rock, due not to his ethnicity or his position as an outsider but to his inability to work well with the various forces in a community sorely split by cultural issues.[90] Yet this change in local leadership did not change the purposes of the CTCA; it only smoothed its road to the cultural control of Little Rock.

As in most training camp cities, the CTCA ultimately gained the program it desired. With Kessner gone and Sunday movies removed from their program, the CTCA soon reached a compromise with the church forces. The compromise signaled a triumph for the Sabbatarians, and yet ultimately the CTCA and its allies in Little Rock may well have gained the greater victory. While conceding on Sunday movies in Little Rock, the CTCA gained a broad recreation program and the cooperation of the churches. A report on the Sunday issue in February 1918 noted, "We have a closed town on Sundays but we are giving splendid musical and literary programs at the theaters down town every Sunday afternoon. . . . We have solved the difficult problem of Sunday amusement and will continue to furnish entertainment regularly down town for the soldiers who visit us on that day."[91] Ministers participated in the Sunday shows as speakers on nonreligious subjects, and one early opponent of the WCCS work suggested regarding that work,

> I can see very clearly that your work is one of prevention, by employing the leisure time of the soldiers in a clean, wholesome manner, while our work should be one of redemption. You are reaching the boys in a manner that no other agency in the city has been able to do, and while, of course, as a minister, I cannot endorse dancing, yet if it has to be, it is far better to have it conducted in a well regulated manner such as you have succeeded in doing here.[92]

Using tact and persuasion the CTCA convinced church leaders in Little Rock to support their program for Sunday amusements. Removing movies from their program, the CTCA gained a broader victory by forcing their opponents to compromise on an issue they had previously considered incontrovertible.

To the CTCA the churches fighting their Sunday programs failed to understand the value of the WCCS work. Maintaining a different cultural and social vision, the conservative churches were easily dismissed as misguided. As Fosdick expressed this in March 1918, "The trouble with the churches is that they have no clear social vision." Further, "We are memorialized by clergymen and ministerial associations all over the country who are overlooking larger issues of social welfare in their concern for the minutiae of the law."[93] Entering a preexisting cultural conflict in Little Rock, the CTCA organized a compromise allowing for wholesome, moral recreation on Sundays. Although legislation prohibiting Sunday movies remained in force, progressives in the CTCA significantly weakened cultural sanctions against Sunday amusements, aiding those forces competing with the traditional Protestant Sabbath.[94] Determined to create a specific environment in the training camp communities, the CTCA overruled local cultural preferences in favor of their own social and cultural vision, a vision clearly connected to the reformers' status as urban, middle-class Americans.

"There Is a Great Crowd Not Taken Care Of": The Complexities of Class

The reformers hoped to eliminate the regressive forces of tradition in their recreation of American culture. They were motivated in this effort by their fears of the traditionalists' role in fostering the corrupt forces of modernism, represented by the dangerous class of urban dwellers, the working class. The traditionalists were problematic in part because of their unwillingness to move forward, their unwillingness to see in the war an opportunity for positive social change. But they were more significantly dangerous because of the encouragement they gave to the forces of degenerative social change. Refusing to accept the CTCA's uplifted version of modern culture, traditionalists worked against their own purposes, driving Americans to a corrupted modernism by denying them a respectable alternative.

It was this corrupted modernism, represented by the urban working class, that most obviously drew the attention of the commission reformers. The reformers targeted working-class recreation as especially problematic. Here they were even more aggressive than in their work with the traditionalists, demonstrating a determination not to temper, but to eliminate, the consequences of this cultural alternative. The WCCS always maintained its support of entertainment that served all soldiers equally, regardless of their class background. Yet the WCCS program often promoted class-segregated recreation, confounding the process of leveling that it theoretically favored. Further, in targeting working-class recreation for eradication, the CTCA frequently eliminated working-class men and women from their programs as well, thereby reinforcing preexisting hierarchies of class and status among soldiers and civilians alike.

Many progressives hoped that military service would serve a homogenizing role in an American society increasingly divided by ethnic and economic differences. One description of the transformation under way among the men at Camp Upton suggested, "They represent thousands of Izzies, Witzers, Johnnies, Mikes and Tonies in Camp Upton who are doing their level best to make themselves over into good soldiers for their Uncle Sam. Upton is the great Melting Pot."[95] The WCCS planned to encourage this development, bringing together soldiers and civilians of different social and economic backgrounds and ensuring that the enlisted man, regardless of his socioeconomic background, received ample recreational opportunity.

At the same time the CTCA sought to maintain strict control over this recreation by the careful repression of unsavory working-class recreation as well as the encouragement of proper entertainment opportunities. The WCCS had no intention of allowing sponsored amusements to degenerate into undesirable forms, and it acted quickly and aggressively to curtail the misbehavior of participants in the recreation program. In the process the reformers targeted working-class habits and working-class individuals for reform.

The WCCS always promoted the "proper" way for an activity to be engaged in, ways that would ensure the virtuous behavior of participants. Campfires, marshmallow roasts, and beach parties, for instance, would be held only on moonlit nights or with sufficient light from lanterns and fires.[96] The WCCS had no objections to commercial motion picture houses, but it encouraged local citizens to establish committees to "see that motion picture theatres are maintaining high standards."[97]

It was dancing, though, that the WCCS acted most diligently to control. Promoting familiarity and physical contact, dancing was especially popular with working-class youths. To the middle-class reformers, however, dancing posed a particularly dangerous situation for the soldiers. A WCCS pamphlet entitled *Dances—How to Conduct Them*, asserted:

> Dancing is one of the most popular forms of recreation today. . . . Once set aside for the privileged few, dancing now extends an invitation to all. As far as opportunity goes, it is on every hand. But in this very opportunity is danger. Frequently dancing makes appeal to neither beauty of form nor of sound, but does make its appeal to the vulgar and sensual-minded.[98]

Striving to promote purity and self-control, the reformers found in dance a real threat to their definitions of both manhood and womanhood. Elmore M. McKee of the Sanitary Corps described the danger posed by the public dances of Ayer, Massachusetts: "Many girls came in from out of town, mill workers. The respectable girls of Ayer do not attend. Most of the soldiers seemed anxious to dance with but one girl and to 'spoon' with her as much as possible. . . . The girls were not of the hardened prostitute type, but merely weak ignorant mill girls." The hazard represented by these working-class girls was obvious. The report continued, "The dance furnished the chance for the soldiers, and girls to make engagements for Saturday and Sunday. Ultimately I believe this dance will thus increase the venereal rate, and should be stopped."[99] Here was the reformers' worst fear realized—uncontrolled public dances attended by working-class girls ready to encourage the men in uniform to abandon their self-control and their purity.

Unlike their conservative opponents, though, progressives in the WCCS felt sure of their ability to control dancing. They believed they could allow it to fulfill its role as "a direct and beautiful self-expression of the spirit of youth and joy" without its becoming a danger to the well-being of its participants.[100] Unwilling to allow the corruption of the men in uniform to persist in Ayer, or in any civilian community, the CTCA stepped in.

Public dance halls had long been a concern of reformers; recall that Newton D. Baker had spearheaded efforts to control dance halls during his tenure as mayor of Cleveland. In 1917 and 1918 dance halls came under scrutiny by local WCCS committees, which attempted to control the dance halls through selective licensing in some cases and through direct supervision and chaperonage in others. Official policy encouraged these controls. Though the exclusion of prostitutes and other undesirables was beyond the purview of the WCCS, more subtle means of control were not.[101]

Requiring licenses for dance halls allowed the reformers to force out of business lower-class, and in their minds therefore unsavory, dance establishments. In Palo Alto the city council passed an amendment stating that each dance held in the city required a permit. As one Palo Alto newspaper described the meaning of this law, "It amounts to a practical prohibition of public dance halls and dance platforms, since a separate permit must be procured for each dance given."[102] In Louisville the local WCCS committee sought to control the licensing of public dance halls by raising the fee so steeply "that only the better class dance halls can afford to pay it."[103]

Licensed dance halls often faced supervision by local CTCA representatives. The dance halls that obtained licenses in Louisville, for instance, came under the supervision of the WCCS committee, leading to chaperonage of all dances and instruction in proper dance forms.[104] In Des Moines the supervision of dance halls by the WCCS led to tight restrictions on dance and music forms. As the *Camp Dodger*, the soldier newspaper for Camp Dodge, reported in June 1918:

> No more bunny hugs or moonlight waltzes at public dance halls in Des Moines. The ban put on public dance hall fancy dancing last Spring continues in effect, the municipal committee on dance halls decided Tuesday. Jazz music must be toned down. Chaperones chosen from the federation of women's clubs will be appointed to serve each week. A matron will be employed at the Owl, Moon and Circle halls.[105]

In other cases the WCCS developed its own dance halls, providing progressives with the opportunity to completely control the dance environment. In Ayer, Massachusetts, the local WCCS stepped in to host dances to help discourage attendance at the public dances mentioned above.[106] As one report suggested, "The purpose of the dances is to give men who desire to dance the desire to do so under absolutely desirable conditions."[107] To attain these conditions the WCCS enforced strict rules of propriety inside the dance halls. Careful supervision of the dances by chaperones, as well as careful regulation of dress, lighting, music, and dance styles and positions allowed the WCCS to mitigate the dangers of dance.[108] Girls were to wear "afternoon gowns. Bright colors preferable. No transparent waists or low cut evening gowns." Halls were to be well lit, and only the approved dance position, which required a woman to place her left hand on the arm of her partner, rather than on his shoulder or back, was to be permitted.[109] In Des Moines the War Recreation Board stepped in to teach soldiers to dance, ensuring their adherence to approved dance forms.[110] The Boston WCCS committee produced a pamphlet, *Dances—How to Conduct Them*, with step-by-step instructions on how to host the ideal dance. The pamphlet included suggestions for every aspect of the dance, from required attire to proper music types. Music would be of a "steady, unvarying tempo avoiding confusion following the sudden acceleration or moderation of time." Orchestras would "avoid too much ragtime with uneven accent."[111] Determined to protect the men in uniform from unhealthy influences, the reformers cleaned up dancing by eliminating dance halls and dance forms of working-class origin.

The reformers took their efforts one step further, often working to eliminate women of working-class origins from the soldiers' dance environment as well. The executive secretary of the CTCA, explaining commission policy, noted, "It is . . . within the province of the War Camp Community Service organizers to help in a constructive way in making the commercial dance halls in any city maintain higher standards through helping to secure matrons or helping to bring in women *of a better class* who would be glad to try to help the soldiers in their social life."[112] In many instances women attending the dances were specifically invited, and only "the right sort of girls," who met WCCS standards, were to be included.[113] When Little Rock, Arkansas, threw a community dance for the soldiers, the chairman of the CTCA heralded its popularity but noted, "In the future, however, invitations will be issued to certain contingents."[114] In Des Moines "patriotic women's clubs of the city" provided partners for the soldiers, and in Ayer and surrounding villages "representative women in each town . . . [were] responsible for securing ten girls whom she could vouch for and would chaperone when necessary."[115] Given the reformers' view of Ayer's "ignorant mill girls," it is unlikely that they gained many invitations. The implications were clear—the WCCS would allow only girls with unreproachable morals to attend their dances, and in the context of the reformers' belief regarding working-class girls, they were not likely to be on the guest list.[116]

Hoping to reshape soldiers' leisure habits, the reformers attempted to eliminate working-class recreational forms and even working-class women from the soldiers' recreational landscape. Theoretically, though, the reformers worked to replace what the soldiers lost with new leisure opportunities, such as their sanitized dances, which would amuse the troops while teaching them new ways to do things. Important in all of this was the assumption that these new entertainments would serve all soldiers equally, providing recreation for troops of all socioeconomic backgrounds and preventing any potential discrimination the loss of working-class recreational opportunities might create.

The soldier clubs, built in the communities as a home base for all soldiers, particularly the enlisted men, symbolized the WCCS program as a whole for the progressives. Here they were most successful in cultivating the classless recreation they espoused. In the club, one publicist for the WCCS explained, "There is a place for every soldier and his friends and relatives, whether they come from a fashionable residential district of a large city or from a cabin in a gully back in the Ohio mountains."[117] Though the club "would be too expensive for most of its guests if it were operated for profit," through the planning of the WCCS and the generosity of local civilians, community clubs provided a recreational opportunity for soldiers from all walks of life. As the publicist described the hypothetical guests of the Camp Sherman Community House,

> They would be carrying all sizes of pocket-books. There would be D.D.s., Ph.Ds., LL.Ds., high school freshmen, and folks who six months previously had never heard there was a war in Europe. There would be simple country folk, prosperous Ford-owning farmers, presidents of banks in towns of less than a thousand population, persons whose names appear on the social registers of the largest cities, and millionaire manufacturers.[118]

In cities and towns across the country, citizens provided soldier clubs, granting men of every class a recreational center in town.

Similarly, the WCCS encouraged communities to plan citywide entertainment such as street dances or pageants and parades that produced the intermingling of troops and civilians of all strata, encouraging the progressive ideal of military service as a democratizing, homogenizing agency. Yet in this type of celebration the lowly private of poor background could not always compete with his wealthier bunk-mate. Reporting on a street dance in Houston, the Camp Logan *Reveille* heralded the dance as a "big success" and "a grand affair." Yet the paper could also suggest, "Private Dubb may not have been as popular as his squad mate who wore a pinch-back trenchy coat and a white stetson hat, but some of the girls took pity on the lonesome kids who were in regulation uniform and gave them a dance once in a while."[119]

One CTCA report from Nogales, Arizona, outlined a related problem, the civilian preference for officers, and complained that the CTCA generally had done nothing to counteract it. According to the report it was common for officers to shun any woman known to befriend an enlisted man, even if they had met through her soldier brother. Further, "The officers usurp everything. The officers are entertained, the community ladies are more or less intimidated and are made to feel that they can not afford to have anything to do with a private. Now I have not read one word in the many bulletins which I have received relative to this problem, yet in many ways this question is the big problem."[120] In Nogales, and in other communities as well, civilians often displayed a preference for the officer at the expense of the enlisted man.

Within the camps the CTCA was guilty of this same elitism. Inside the Liberty Theatres, for instance, special seating was reserved for officers, allowing officers to arrive minutes before a show and gain entry, while soldiers often waited for lengthy periods, only to be denied admission altogether. Indeed, at times soldiers would be removed from seats to provide space for officers, and at other times spaces reserved for officers would remain empty and unused.[121] Though sworn to ignore differences of class in the provision of recreation, the WCCS did not always fulfill this promise. In fact, the progressives' own cultural preferences tended to skew the recreation program. Cultivating middle-class leisure forms in an effort to convert soldiers and civilians to the progressive social vision, the WCCS placed an inordinate emphasis on recreation that ultimately segregated soldiers and civilians by class and status.

From the beginning the CTCA favored the involvement of fraternal orders and social clubs in its programs, counting on these organizations to foster respectable recreation among the troops by cultivating contacts with their members in the training camps. Across the nation the WCCS was successful in enlisting the aid of these groups, which opened their doors to their members inside the camps and provided organized recreation such as smokers and dances.[122] The WCCS believed the role of fraternal orders and private clubs to be a crucial one. While offering safe entertainment, the fraternal orders' and social clubs' most important role may have been to cultivate the social ties the WCCS believed fundamental to happiness and to moral behavior. One article on the WCCS program suggested, "Next to the relationships of home, church and the circle of friends and acquaintances among whom a man moves and finds his social life, there is probably nothing the loss of which is so keenly felt by the man in camp as are club and fraternal relationships."[123] Participation in the local fraternal order or social club undoubtedly offered soldier members a sense of belonging similar to that they had cherished in their home town.[124] By asking these various organizations to reach out to their own members in the camps, the WCCS relied on membership loyalty and the bonds of brotherhood to assure their success.

Yet the incorporation of these organizations into the WCCS program rested on false assumptions about the socioeconomic background of the average doughboy. Imagining the man in uniform as an urban, middle-class American, the WCCS placed inordinate emphasis upon the importance of fraternities and social clubs in the recreational life of the soldiers. As the historian Weldon B. Durham asserts, "The camp reformers anticipated an homogeneous camp population of urbane and literate bourgeoisie, but such a population never materialized. Programs designed to replicate aspects of the social climate of middle-class America were simply not congruent with the social experiences of the conscripted soldier."[125] It seems likely that, in fact, the CTCA did not misunderstand the leisure habits of the soldiers but knew them and hoped to change them by introducing lower-class and rural soldiers to fraternal orders and social clubs. Yet the exclusiveness of those organizations limited their usefulness for most enlisted men. The WCCS maintained that these organizations offered recreation to those having no claim on them, as well as to their own members.[126] Yet evidence suggests that in many cases these offers were made only to those soldiers who would likely have been members under other circumstances.

This is most clearly true with the social clubs.[127] Many social clubs participated in the WCCS programs, but most generally reached out only to men of their own stature in the community. Clubs usually limited their contacts to officers or to men with club memberships elsewhere. In Tacoma, for instance, local clubs offered their privileges to officers "at a nominal cost," while the Commercial Club "issued cards to every officer in camp."[128] In Alexandria, Louisiana, the local country club offered the use of their golf links to the officers of Camp Beauregard.[129] In another instance the Houston Country Club extended membership to all officers and to all enlisted men who belonged to a country club back at home.[130] Among the enlisted men such soldiers would have been few.

As a result the provision of recreation on the basis of one's membership in fraternal orders, college fraternities, and social clubs broadened the likelihood that some soldiers would be left unprovided for, falling through the cracks of a recreation program based on membership in middle- and upper-class societies and clubs. Part of the WCCS program involved the registering of each soldier on a card that would list all of the soldier's religious and fraternal affiliations. On the basis of this census the San Antonio CTCA discovered "a large miscellaneous group of men who had neither church, fraternal nor union affiliations."[131] In this case a committee formed with the express purpose of caring for these soldiers. In another instance a report regarding the Sunday problem in Macon, Georgia, outlined the available recreation on Sundays and concluded, "But with all that there is a great crowd not taken care of and nothing for them to do. This applies particularly to the men of the low social strata of whom there are very, very, many in the camp. They are particularly hard to reach."[132] Relying on fraternal orders and social clubs to entertain their own members, the WCCS neglected the needs of many poorer and rural-born troops.

In addition to these organizations, with their preexisting constituency in the camps, the WCCS enlisted the aid of several other organizations, the character of which implies a great deal about the cultural preferences of the CTCA progressives. The WCCS Handbook listed organizations with whom workers might cultivate contacts, organizations that had already proven themselves useful allies in the WCCS cause. They included, first of all, other organizations deeply involved with the war effort, such as the Red Cross and the Woman's Branch of the Council of Defense, the YMCA, and the YWCA. The WCCS also listed groups whose activities neatly fit the need for soldier recreation, such as the Drama League of America. In addition the WCCS included organizations whose work would help ensure only healthful relations between soldiers and civilians, such as the National Travelers' Aid Society. Women's organizations, which would foster respectable entertainment while performing tasks appropriate to their members' gender, were also recruited. The WCCS also encouraged its workers to enlist the aid of organizations that stood for conservative patriotic Americanism, such as the Boy Scouts of America and the Daughters of the American Revolution. Finally, contacts among the economic and social leaders of each community through the Rotary Clubs and the chambers of commerce were actively cultivated.[133] Eager to offer only "respectable" amusement for the soldiers, and deeply immersed in the progressive social vision, the WCCS sought links with organizations whose work would fit this vision. These organizations rallied to the WCCS cause, promoting precisely the types of recreational activities the WCCS envisioned.[134]

The implications of this program as it operated on the local level were immense. In appealing to many organizations to work specifically with their own members, the WCCS did not threaten class or cultural boundaries within the local communities. Fraternal brothers worked for fraternal brothers, upper-class social clubs entertained officers and enlisted men of appropriately high class, Catholics found amusement for Catholics, and Italians planned social contacts for Italians.

One bulletin from the WCCS suggested a purposeful component to this segregation by class and ethnicity. Describing three enemies of the WCCS program, this bulletin suggested that the sentimental must be counted among those. It explained,

> They flock around the impressionable youth in uniform, persuade him that he is a hero, gush or cry over him as an idea, not as a person, thrust upon him service and material which he should pay for and upset his social ideas by throwing him into intimate contact with men and women of higher or lower social plane. A good woman can spoil a man almost as quickly as a bad one. For a woman of higher social cast to convince him by her patronage and adoration that he is a hero will be very hard on his wife and mother when he gets back home.[135]

Recreational involvement of soldiers with civilians of a higher class was thus deemed inappropriate, leading to problems for the soldier with heightened social aspirations.[136]

Though the WCCS did not purposefully encourage civilians to discriminate against enlisted men, the layout of their community program, with its emphasis on middle-class recreation and on civilians taking care of their own kind, ultimately led to discrimination and to the continuation of status based on class and related criteria. The WCCS did indeed provide recreational opportunities for all soldiers, but it did little to discourage, and likely encouraged, recreational opportunities provided on the basis of class and ethnicity. This shortcoming of the WCCS was exhibited most blatantly, and most disturbingly, in its provision of a separate and unequal recreation program for African American soldiers, the subject of chapter 5.

The Contradictions of Social Control

The CTCA was broadly successful in establishing its education and recreation programs in the training camps and neighboring civilian communities. As these programs became a reality for soldiers and civilians, the meaning of the reformers' community vision became sharpened, exhibiting characteristics less noticeable in the idealized imagery of public statements. Committed to particular definitions of manhood and womanhood and to the behavioral standards these definitions suggested, and at the same time operating from a very particular social and cultural perspective, the results of the reformers' efforts often contradicted their established purposes. Because they were profoundly influenced by their urban, middle-class identities, the reformers built a community both hierarchical and exclusive in nature.

While claiming to downplay class distinctions, the CTCA programs frequently discriminated against, and sometimes excluded altogether, working-class soldiers and civilians. Targeting the elimination of all vestiges of working-class culture, the CTCA tacitly demanded that lower-class people abandon their class identity in order to participate in the recreation program. Further, often assuming the inability of working-class citizens, especially women, to escape their class background, the CTCA's recreation programs often barred these individuals entirely because of the reformers' assumptions about working-class immorality. In the CTCA's recreational world the middle and upper classes retained their privileged status.

Further, while seeking to integrate all Americans into its community, the CTCA was rigid in its exclusion of American cultures different from its own. Not only working-class culture, but also more traditional aspects of American culture, were dismissed by the reformers for the threat they posed to the cultural vision of the progressives. If working-class culture was dangerously immoral, the religious traditions of many southern and rural Americans were ridiculously old-fashioned. Though purporting to respect local customs, the CTCA insisted that communities adopt the progressive program. When faced with resistance, the CTCA was unyielding in its determination to gain compliance, expecting not only individuals but towns, cities, even regions, to remake their cultures to match the designs of the reformers. Entering cultural competitions that preexisted the war, the CTCA threw its federal weight behind the forces of urban, middle-class culture, at the expense of local cultural preferences.

In many cases the consequence of the reformers' actions was a limited adjustment in local cultural traditions. In Little Rock, for instance, residents accepted Sunday recreation for the first time in modern memory and altered their moral standards to incorporate that change. Though an important shift, on the level of the individual the consequences of that change were perhaps not sizable.

In other cases the consequences of the reformers' activities were more dramatic, because more individualized. For many working-class Americans the CTCA's work enhanced their exclusion from the cultural mainstream, as the CTCA reinforced existing status structures and minimized mixing among soldiers and civilians of different classes and different social and cultural groupings.

For others the consequences of the CTCA's work would make an even greater impact, as the reformers moved from subtle social control through recreation and education into more straightforward control and repression through law enforcement. An investigation of the reformers' treatment of women in the practical application of their programs illustrates the reformers' willingness to use repression when faced by continued resistance to their programs and the power of their reliance on traditional images of womanhood in shaping that repression. Mired in the oldest notions of woman's nature, the reformers failed to support their own imagery of new womanhood and reflected again the importance of their cultural identities in shaping the application of their programs.

CHAPTER FOUR

Building a National Community: The Complexities of Gender

> At the moment the papers devote much attention to the effort to safeguard the young conscripts against predatory country girls. Around every camp, it appears, a "moral zone" is to be established, and it is apparently the intention to bar out from it every woman who cannot produce evidence that she has no desire to lead the soldiers astray. No enterprise, of course, could be more fantastically impossible of execution. . . . a great many innocent women will be abominably persecuted, and those who are not innocent will simply be scattered, and so made the more difficult to keep in order, and the more pertinacious and enterprising, and the more dangerous.
>
> —H. L. Mencken, September 1917

In 1918 the War Department released a feature length film entitled *The End of the Road*.[1] Targeting women and girls and set in war-time America, the film follows the story of two childhood friends, Vera and Mary. The mood and the purpose of the film are established by an introductory statement that suggests: "Two Roads There Are in Life. One reaches upward toward the Land of Perfect Love. The other reaches down into the Dark Valley of Despair where the sun never shines." In the film Mary follows this upward road, accepting advice and education on sexual matters from her mother and leading a life of abstinence.[2] Vera, on the other hand, takes up with "a hard worker in a nonessential industry—the sowing of wild oats." By the end of the film Vera has traversed the downward path and suffers from venereal disease and public disgrace, while Mary, always on the upward path, has won the love of a respectable doctor engaged in war work. The moral of the film was obvious—happiness in life depended on one's sexual purity. As the heroine in the film suggests, "I know . . . how hard it is to think of consequences now, when we're young. . . . unless we do we shan't find happiness at the end of the road." In its selection of imagery, though, the film conveyed a second social message. Women, it suggested, were of two types. Once they were on their chosen road, even the counsel of wise and well-meaning friends could do little to alter their course.

This dichotomized image of female sexuality permeated the CTCA's programs. "Remember THE FOLKS AT HOME," a poster distributed in army training camps urged, "Go back to them physically fit and morally clean. Don't allow a whore to smirch your record." Picturing the reformers' version of the perfect family—a loving mother, a pretty wife, a handsome brother, and a rosy-cheeked child—this poster juxtaposed the pure woman and the threat of the whore.[3] In educational pamphlets and placards, in films and lectures, the CTCA portrayed women as virginal maidens or hardened prostitutes.

At times the reformers' images of women left room for a greater complexity. Mary, heroine of *The End of the Road*, tries to educate and uplift her friend Vera, suggesting the potential for female redemption. But Vera's fate proves unalterable, and Mary's ascent to the "Land of Perfect Love" is directly contrasted to Vera's descent to disease and disgrace. In the reformers' programs, too, early acknowledgment of women who defied neat categorization as either pure or profligate soon gave way to narrow policies that admitted no behavioral middle ground. Women, in the eyes of most CTCA reformers, were either morally pure or a sexual disaster waiting to happen.

Demanding that men rise to the sexual standard to which women had long been held, many reformers saw in the single standard an important impetus toward social equality for women. The reformers' programs, however, based on the oldest images of female sexuality, did little to establish a new understanding of sexuality capable of upsetting the traditional gender hierarchy. These traditional female archetypes had long served to support the sexual double standard and did so again in the federal programs of the CTCA. In their positive programs of social hygiene education and recreation, reformers assigned certifiably pure women their traditional roles as moral and domestic guardians, and in the process they relegated women to positions of subservience and submission. Alternatively, in the law enforcement program the reformers aggressively repressed women they viewed as unnaturally corrupt, punishing women for moral transgressions, or even the appearance of moral transgressions, while forgiving the sins of men. Unable to envision a truly new woman, the reformers reverted to the oldest categorization of women and reinforced the traditional gender hierarchy.

"Upward Toward the Land of Perfect Love": Women in the Positive Programs of the CTCA

Submission, in addition to morality, piety, and domesticity, constituted the final component of nineteenth-century true womanhood. The CTCA never advocated submissiveness per se. In the advocacy of women's public roles, for instance, the reformers rejected passivity and submission for women. Though the CTCA acknowledged women as autonomous, active individuals in the rhetoric of its work, however, it tended nevertheless to rely on images of women's submission in the development of its positive programs of recreation and education. Emphasizing women's moral and domestic capacities, the reformers granted women an important role as uplifters. In the process, however, they inadvertently reinforced the notion of women's subservience, defining women almost exclusively in terms of their relationship to men. The CTCA earmarked components of its education and recreation programs for women, yet in each case the preoccupation of the programs remained the mental, moral, and physical well-being of men.

This tendency was not necessarily obvious in the commission's social hygiene education work. Here the reformers seemed sincerely concerned with the health of both groups and advocated the responsibility of both men and women in maintaining the nation's sexual health. Again, the film *The End of the Road* proves instructive. With an openness notable in its time, venereal disease was graphically depicted as a cruel and crippling result of foolishness and ignorance, a disease that women were empowered to avoid through education. The film also declared explicitly the new standards to which men were to be held. As the doctor in the film suggested, "If young men could only know what a harvest their wives and children may reap from their sowing of wild oats." Men, like women, were to resist the temptations of illicit sex and thereby prevent the personal and social consequences of that misbehavior. The rewards for abstinence were great—health, happiness, love, and success. The punishments for foolishness were equally great—illness, poverty, insanity, disgrace, and even death. Men, as well as women, would reap the rewards or suffer the punishments depending on their behavior. The film depicted women as independent actors, capable of controlling their own sexual destinies, while it also acknowledged men's shared responsibility for sexual health. In the character of Mary the film depicted a self-reliant, educated, and socially active woman as heroine, apparently dismissing the traditional approbation of female submissiveness and passivity.

On closer examination, though, the film also sent subtle messages that confirmed the continued force of the image of the subservient woman. A strong female character, Mary is nevertheless cast as a nurse to soldiers and is shown assisting an even more powerful male doctor. The film's happy ending relies on Mary's winning the love of that doctor, rejecting her autonomy for the bonds of love and marriage. Though depicted favorably, Mary is generally defined by her connection to men. Although the CTCA sincerely attempted to protect women's health and targeted them directly through its social hygiene education program for civilian women, even here the tendency to understand women in terms of their value to men remained.

In its recreation programs the CTCA asserted this tendency even more obviously, continually subverting women's interests to those of men and defining women's roles exclusively in the context of their relationship to the men in uniform. In both their programs for girls and their community recreation programs for both sexes the reformers subtly, and sometimes not so subtly, reinforced the notion of women's submission.

As a counterpart to the CTCA's in-camp recreation program for soldiers, the reformers developed recreation for local women and girls, designed to produce the same distraction from the more risky meetings of soldiers and civilians. The recreation program for girls involved "the formation of girls' clubs, the enrollment of girls in patriotic leagues and the utilization of churches, settlements, social centres, public schools and other resources of the community in increasing activities among girls." Through these various forms of recreation the girls' program would occupy the time and energy of the young women and girls, providing them with "wholesome recreation."[4]

In addition to keeping the girls occupied, the program helped to keep the girls physically removed from the soldiers. Raymond Fosdick explained:

> A second field of activity which I can suggest would be in regard to the younger girls of seventeen or eighteen, who are apt to be thrown off their balance by the sight of uniforms and brass buttons. I think there is a big work that can be done in keeping them in check. They should be kept away from camps, and as far as possible away from the soldiers. If your organization could do anything along this line, I am sure it would be fruitful of results.[5]

"Keeping them in check," it seemed, was an important social purpose for recreation programs for girls to fulfill.

Finally, it was hoped that while the girls stayed occupied, they would busy themselves with useful war work, participating in "expert housekeeping, gardening, hospital and Red Cross work, hygiene and athletics."[6] Special sex-segregated recreation, then, would busy the minds and bodies of girls with healthy, socially useful activities and in the process cultivate the "high social standard and a high ideal of the part that the women of America are called upon to play in their relation to our soldiers."[7] Properly trained in these standards and ideals, local girls would be ready to play the stabilizing and uplifting role in the soldiers' lives that the CTCA envisaged. The reformers believed young women would benefit from this training, but in the explication of their goals the reformers' preoccupation with the well-being of the soldiers is obvious, as is their assumption that women's primary role would be their service to those men.

This assumption was even more pronounced in the community recreation program, which sought to bring the soldiers and civilians together in carefully coordinated and controlled meetings. The CTCA had hoped that the work of the War Camp Community Service (WCCS), its community recreation branch, would ensure cordial yet healthful relations between soldiers and civilian women, relations that would encourage the development of manhood and womanhood among these citizens. In the pursuit of this broad goal, the WCCS programs often led to the blatant objectification of women, a development counter to the reformers' expressed goal of equality.

Assigning women to gender specific roles, the WCCS often dealt with women and girls less as people than as recreational commodities to be dispensed to the soldiers. One soldier's description of his own experience in acquiring the commodity reflects this tendency. A soldier at Camp Wadsworth, helping to plan his company's dance, realized the soldiers' desperate need for dance partners. He wrote, "It occurred to me that in order to make this affair a success we must have young ladies present." The problem, it seemed, would be to locate those ladies. Lunching at a Red Cross canteen, the soldier noted the nice look of the cashier and so approached her with his problem. He gained her agreement for the provision of a light lunch that evening, and at that time he saw his opportunity. "Here was my chance to tell my troubles and I did. Why, that is easy, I was told, and how many young ladies would you want? I was too stricken to reply."[8] While offering her aid in true WCCS spirit, the Red Cross volunteer revealed the essential attitude of the WCCS toward local girls. They were one of the local recreational resources, to be allotted to the soldiers as needed.

An article on the soldiers' relationship with women noted the same use of females, while also providing certain criteria for the women's suitability for this role. "The War Camp Community Service has had a list of more than three thousand girls who were ready to answer any call to a dance. All of the girls were personally selected, two things being required to make them come up to the standard set by the organization—morality and comeliness."[9] Targeted as playthings for the men in uniform, women were also required to fulfill certain traditional feminine standards in order to play the role.

Such treatment of women led naturally to their objectification. The soldier press sometimes encouraged this attitude. Running an article announcing a letter-writing program, the *Camp Dodger*, the troop paper at Camp Dodge, suggested that ten thousand girls had already signed up to adopt the soldiers. The paper noted, "All a lonesome Camp Dodge soldier need do is drop a line to The Editor of the Camp Dodger and his name will be sent to one of these ten thousand girls. He may even specify whether he prefers a blonde or a brunette."[10] Though the managing editor of the Minneapolis paper cosponsoring the letter-writing campaign wrote a letter attempting to clarify the serious nature of the program and refuting the idea that soldiers could select correspondents by appearance, the *Camp Dodger*'s initial offer appealed to the men in uniform and reinforced the role of women as recreational merchandise.[11]

Feeling themselves entitled to the attentions of the local women, soldiers could be presumptuous, even condescending, in their approaches to these women. Describing his designs to attend a dance at Kansas State Agricultural College, one soldier admitted, "Because we wanted to attend the dance, [we] called up a sorority house and very brazenly told them that we were a bunch of K.A.'s from Missouri and that we wanted them to give us four dates for the dance." Reinforcing these attitudes, the sorority provided the men with the dates they sought.[12]

This is not to suggest that all soldiers treated local women with a lack of respect or that soldiers and local girls did not often establish friendly relations that were mutually rewarding. Soldiers often wrote in praise of the local women and in appreciation for the treatment they received. At times relationships between soldiers and local women resulted in marriages.[13] Nonetheless, it remains true that the structure of the WCCS program not only supported traditional gender roles, but also cultivated a sense of the importance of men and the relative unimportance of women.

For many women their subservient position was reinforced by their status as members of the working class. Treated as recreational objects, women often found their value determined by their class background. An article in the Camp Logan *Reveille*, a fantasy interview with St. Valentine, while decrying the attitude of male superiority, also suggested its prevalence. In the process the article also indicated the important role played by a woman's socioeconomic position. Describing the devotion of the girls and the ways in which it was "quite spoiling the boys," St. Valentine jested, "I sent a two-fisted, double-jointed, red-headed, freckly-faced, husky-voiced soldier letters, valentines and devotions from half a score of browns, brunettes and Titian-tints today and, do you know, he phoned to ask if there is nothing doing in the way of ash-blondes this Valentine's day. He was quite snappy about it, too." The reason for this demanding attitude, according to St. Valentine, lay in the soldiers' great desirability. "You see," he explained, "we have only 1,700,000 soldiers and there are 10,000,000 marriageable girls in the country." Due to this shortage of soldiers, according to St. Valentine, the soldiers had become very picky about girls and demonstrated interest only in the beautiful and the well-to-do. He elaborated, "Some of them bar anything less than admitted beauty and an income of $10,000 in her own right." And further, "Cigar and cigarette makers, even when good-looking, are not wanted. Good lookers who are good dressers and who can pay for their own clothes and throw in a battle-grey roadster and a bungalow on the side are in demand. I find there is not much of a market for others."[14] Describing the girls like market goods, the *Reveille* clearly indicated a class element in the soldiers' process of selection.

Although this article was a humor piece, the attitudes it described were surprisingly common. Another soldier, Howard Walker, noted that the infusion of 30,000 soldiers into the small community of Chillicothe, Ohio, had glutted the market of eligible males, but he described his personal successes with the women and suggested to his brother, "I have forgotten all about Clara Fick. I have to *[sic]* many nice friends to let a common girl like her bother me. She hasn't very much education as you probably know, and she writes her letters with pencil which I detest."[15]

Subverting women's interests in their preoccupation with the well-being of the troops, the CTCA encouraged the objectification of women evident in Howard Walker's letter. The CTCA enlisted those women it believed sufficiently pure in the programs for the uplift of the soldiers. In the process, however, the reformers undercut their own attempt to create a new relationship between men and women based in shared interests, shared values, and a new equality. In their law enforcement program the reformers' subversion of their vision of women's equality was even more profound, and again it was based in an ancient stereotype of woman's nature.

"Into the Dark Valley of Despair": The Battle against the Red-Light Districts

Though members of the CTCA maintained that the constructive programs of supervised recreation and social hygiene education for soldiers and civilians were the heart and soul of the CTCA design, the reformers had always accepted the complementary need for a coercive program.[16] Section 13 of the Draft Act of 1917 gave the secretary of war the power to "do everything by him deemed necessary" to prevent the establishment of places of prostitution "within such distance as he may deem needful" of all training camps.[17] Using this power, the president and the secretary of war established "moral zones" around the training camps in which prostitution was prohibited. The Commission on Training Camp Activities, in addition to all of its constructive work for education and recreation, also coordinated the program for the enforcement of the moral zones.

The CTCA began its battle against what it considered immoral sexual behavior with an attack on prostitution, the most blatant and clear-cut threat. The reformers focused on the red-light district, where organized prostitution, "flaunting its invitation to vicious indulgence resulting in disease and impairment of efficiency," operated openly.[18]

In the early twentieth century restricted districts still flourished in cities and towns across the country. Many Americans favored segregated prostitution, considering it the best way to handle a "necessary evil." This attitude had its roots in Victorian constructions of sexuality, which accepted men's sexual desires while viewing them as essentially immoral. According to this view, prostitution served the valued cultural role of providing men with defiled women with whom to satisfy their depraved urges. Prostitution protected pure women from this debasement and preserved the sanctity of the home.[19]

In the context of war some advocates argued further that segregated prostitution might help to control venereal disease. Concerned with the problem of rampant disease, one citizen explained to Secretary of War Baker, "If a few houses were permitted under police surveillance & medical examination this condition could be practically eliminated. Nature will assert itself—and if the men cannot see women under the proper medicinal conditions here suggested they will take risks on the so called street walkers & suffer results."[20]

The restricted districts, though, did not operate unopposed. In its battle to close them the CTCA found ready allies in the antiprostitution movement, which had its roots in the social purity movement of the nineteenth century. Beginning in the 1860s and 1870s, reformers had attacked not only the segregated district but also the justifications for the districts. The social purity movement was based on the concept of "civilized morality," a moral framework developed in the Jacksonian era. This moral model denied the physical or psychological necessity of men's sexual activity and rested the progress of civilized society on men's ability to control their baser instincts. The social purity crusade argued for an end to the sexual double standard and for lifting urban men to the moral level occupied by women. The social purity movement was never a fully unified movement; it consisted rather of an alliance of groups united by their shared fears regarding the moral degeneration of American society.[21] As a result these reformers pursued a range of solutions, including "moral education, child rearing theories, sex education programs, organizations for the protection of women travelers and workers, vocational education, social hygiene, and especially, the abolition of prostitution" in their attempts to put American society back on a moral foundation.[22]

The sexual standards defined by the social purity movement, as well as the fear that these standards were losing their hold over American society, found expression in the proliferation of white slave narratives after 1909 and in the resultant vice commissions that sprang up in cities across the nation.[23] The white slave narratives, tales of the conspiratorial abduction of pure womanhood into the grips of the prostitution establishment, granted social purists a way to understand prostitution that reaffirmed the validity of their fears and of their prescriptions. Suggesting that women participated in prostitution unwillingly, the narratives highlighted the continued morality of women, the consequences of men's uncontrolled sex instinct, and the need for the repression of prostitution.[24]

Born of the same anxieties that produced the white slave narratives, the early-twentieth century vice commissions engaged in professional investigations of the character and social costs of vice in American cities. In their reports the commissions emphasized the continuing high costs of organized prostitution, noting the ties between alcohol and prostitution, the problems of corruption and graft related to the establishment of commercialized prostitution in the cities, the debilitating effects of prostitution on the American family, its tremendous success as a business, and its obvious antagonism to civilized morality. Based on this assessment the commissions called for the repression, not the regulation, of prostitution. Having neglected to investigate the social and economic roots of prostitution, the commissions believed in their ability to eliminate it.[25]

By 1917 the antiprostitution movement had attracted allies from a variety of sources. Like the earlier social purity movement, the antiprostitution movement was a loose coalition of reformers. Though united against prostitution, members of the antiprostitution movement, like other progressives, often brought with them varying, even conflicting, agendas. Social purity reformers, for instance, viewed prostitution as a symptom of deep decline in the nation. Feminists, on the other hand, fought prostitution as part of the struggle for women's emancipation. Other social justice reformers saw the eradication of prostitution as one element in the effort to cure the social ills of the city. In some cities antiprostitution served as a weapon in local struggles against the urban boss. Other reformers, physicians for instance, opposed prostitution for its role in spreading venereal disease. Because of these differences the CTCA's allies in the antiprostitution crusade found varying degrees of success over the course of the war.[26]

Initially, though, the antiprostitution forces celebrated the arrival of a new federal ally, the CTCA. As Raymond Fosdick articulated the CTCA's condemnations of prostitution, he reiterated the views of other antiprostitution reformers. Voicing concerns for army efficiency, Fosdick maintained that segregation never segregated entirely, but instead worked to publicize prostitution. Venereal disease, he maintained, could never be eliminated if the districts continued. Assigned to protect the American troops from venereal disease primarily for reasons of health and efficiency, Fosdick, like his antiprostitution allies, could not accept the segregated districts.

As in all of the CTCA's programs, Fosdick and the commission were interested in more than just the soldiers' physical health and military efficiency; they understood the role they might play in broader social and cultural terms. In addition to these practical condemnations of segregation, Fosdick and the CTCA always maintained the important social and psychological costs of prostitution.[27] "An even more important thing to be realized," one postwar account noted, "was that this problem was not a purely medical one." It continued:

> As one expert put it: "The transmission of the disease itself is only part of the problem. From the social point of view the question is not only one of the effect of venereal disease upon the social body, serious as that is. The more far-reaching evil is the state of mind and character which lies back of it. The greatest evil to society results from the shattered ideals, lowered standards, sensualized minds, and perverted practices which are brought into home life and society by these men who represent in large measure the cream of the young manhood of the nation. To safeguard the home and society against these basic evils, we must not only abolish venereal disease, but minimize, so far as possible, prostitution itself."[28]

Exhibiting the eternal progressive faith in legislation, the commission planned to rely on the strict enforcement of section 13 of the Draft Act in its attack on prostitution. The CTCA assumed an active role in the local enforcement of this law. As the first step the CTCA hired investigators to document the existence and extent of the social evil. The CTCA employed its own field agents and also cooperated with investigators of the Department of Justice, the Intelligence Department of the Army, the local provost guards, and members of local antivice organizations. Groups such as the Committee of Fourteen of New York, the Committee of Fifteen of Chicago, the Watch and Ward Society of New England, and the Bureau of Social Hygiene of New York, as well as the National American Social Hygiene Association, were anxious to cooperate with the CTCA, glad to find their campaign suddenly supported by federal power. At the same time the CTCA found in these organizations individuals well acquainted with local vice and liquor conditions and anxious to work for their eradication.[29]

The CTCA also encouraged communities to pass strict antivice legislation. In some communities this required only the rewording and strengthening of local regulations. In other cases the CTCA asked communities to establish as illegal behavior that had been at least passively tolerated in the past. Eager to facilitate the adoption of new laws, and determined to gain laws sufficiently strict to constitute real tools in the struggle against prostitution, the CTCA eventually printed a collection of standard laws that communities could use as models in writing their own legislation.[30]

Armed with federal and local legislation, as well as with detailed evidence of criminal misbehavior gathered by their corps of investigators, the CTCA insisted upon strict law enforcement by local police agencies. As Raymond Fosdick suggested, "Prostitution cannot be repressed nor venereal disease controlled by the passage of laws alone, however well conceived the laws may be. Constant enforcement of law must be maintained in order that even a measure of success may be attained."[31]

In its attempts to eradicate the red-light districts from American cities, the CTCA achieved rapid and resounding success. Many city officials, county officers, and governors wrote Fosdick or Baker with assurances of their willingness to cooperate and of their intentions to ensure that their city, county, or state met the War Department's standards.[32] More importantly, several training camp communities shut their red-light districts as soon as the War Department's demands were made clear. Deming, New Mexico, the home of Camp Cody, expressed "a willingness to do anything and everything for the good of the soldiers." When a YMCA representative urged that Deming close its red-light district, the city trustees immediately passed an ordinance for that purpose.[33] As early as October 1917 the CTCA was able to boast the closure of red-light districts in nineteen cities.[34]

Not all urban establishments, nor all citizens, however, supported the CTCA's plans for the enforcement of the new federal moral zones. In many cases red-light districts were an integral part of the city, viewed as necessary and profitable by many citizens. Public servants, too, often profited from prostitution and were reluctant to eliminate this lucrative trade.[35]

Even under these circumstances cities and towns often responded to CTCA demands. Louisville, Kentucky, home of Camp Taylor, closed a popular vice district, though many residents, including the mayor, favored its continued presence. The district, though never established by law, had long been countenanced in that city. A vice commission in 1915 had advocated a number of measures intended to bring about its eventual closure. Rules prohibiting music and liquor in the houses, the entry of new prostitutes into the district, and girls moving from house to house, as well as the closure of all houses outside the district were intended to make possible the closure of the segregated district in two years. When the War Department chose Louisville as a training camp site in 1917, however, the district remained in operation.[36]

An advocate of regulated prostitution, Mayor John H. Buschemeyer sent Secretary of War Baker a statement of his opinion about the role of segregated vice in Louisville. "I do not deem it proper, practical nor advisable in my humble judgement," he asserted, "to close these houses and disseminate these women through the orderly self-respecting and decent people and neighborhoods of the community, but realize that with strict surveillance we can control them absolutely with our police power, believing that regulation is the best method of handling this vast and aged problem."[37]

Although hoping to keep the district open, Buschemeyer was also eager to let the federal government know that it would receive the city's "heartiest cooperation." With the announcement of the moral zones in July 1917, Louisville immediately accepted the closure of its red-light district, seemingly without a struggle. The *Louisville Courier-Journal*, which in June had referred to the vice commission's attempt to facilitate the district's closure as "an impractical reform" and "unobtainable," quickly reordered its thinking, now opposing the "holders of the complacent 'men-will-be-men' theory—advocates of a standard immorality for men—of morality for women."[38] Though believing that laws alone could not end prostitution, the paper called for an extensive education plan to lead the soldiers away from vice.[39] On 16 August 1917 the Board of Public Safety issued orders for the police to close up the district permanently on 1 September. In the interim the War Department called for curfew laws for girls to help in the fight against vice. A mass meeting of four hundred citizens unanimously endorsed efforts to cooperate with the War Department.[40]

Though an occasional voice still called for regulation of prostitution rather than the elimination of the district, on the first day of September the Louisville vice district closed as planned.[41] On that day, though, the *Courier-Journal* reported the ambivalence of many. "It was not a joyful round of 'one last night,' of celebrating that marked the 'breaking up of the tenderloin,' as every one had anticipated," it suggested, "but one marked with sadness and gloom. The police on the beat, the saloonkeepers around the corner, the hot tamale man hated each for his own particular reason to see them go. There was no jeering. There was no rejoicing."[42] Hinting at the well-established intimacy between some men of Louisville and the women of the district, the paper implied another reason for the melancholy mood.[43] Despite its popularity, however, proponents of the district could not compete with the War Department's request for the expulsion of vice from Louisville.

Why did cities such as Deming and Louisville respond so eagerly to the directions of the War Department and the CTCA? In its attempts to enforce the antivice legislation, the CTCA was aided by two important factors—its federal power to enforce the law and the financial attractiveness of the camps. Early in the war Secretary of War Baker made clear his intention to remove to a more wholesome environment any training camp threatened by what he viewed as immoral and unhealthy conditions.[44] Backed by the power of the War Department, CTCA representatives always retained the threat of camp removal as a weapon to be used against recalcitrant local establishments.[45]

In some communities, however, powerful members of the community staunchly opposed the War Department's schemes and fought feverishly to retain their districts. In New Orleans, for instance, the deep entrenchment of the vice district in the economic structure of the city sparked more serious and more powerful resistance to the CTCA's efforts to eradicate vice. Early in the war the CTCA's jurisdiction over New Orleans, which housed no National Army troops, was somewhat uncertain. Yet its world-famous red-light district, Storyville, proved an irresistible target for the CTCA. Using the navy post there as justification, in August 1917 Bascom Johnson, chief of law enforcement for the CTCA, traveled to New Orleans to survey conditions and concluded that the district should be closed. When he met with the mayor to ask him to comply with the moral zone rulings, the mayor expressed in emphatic terms his belief that the closure of Storyville would produce a decline in health conditions, scattering vice throughout the city and leaving the police understaffed and unable to control it. Rather than complying with Johnson's request, the mayor took the bold approach of attempting to argue his case with Josephus Daniels, the secretary of the navy, and the president. The mayor traveled to Washington in early September to plead his case, but he failed to gain an interview with either the secretary of the navy or the president.[46]

An investigative report of 25 September 1917 reconfirmed the CTCA's worst suspicions. According to the report, conditions in New Orleans were "horrible" and "intolerable from every point of view," and the investigator urged that the cleanup of New Orleans begin with closure of the segregated district. The day before this report was issued, Josephus Daniels had asked the governor of Louisiana to use state power to close the district in New Orleans. Although Daniels had only questionable authority to call for the closure of the district at this date, the issue of jurisdiction was soon resolved in favor of Daniels and the CTCA when, on 6 October, Congress included the navy within the provisions of section 13 of the Draft Act.[47]

Perhaps seeing his defeat as inevitable, Mayor Martin Behrman of New Orleans had introduced into the city council on 2 October an ordinance abolishing the restricted district. On 9 October the council adopted the ordinance, but under protest. On 12 November 1917 the district closed forever, but it did so without the support of many of the local officials. In New Orleans as in Louisville, the district had its mourners.[48]

The CTCA had reason to proclaim its success in this first part of its antivice crusade, the battle against the red-lights. By May 1918 the number of closed districts had grown to 70, with 45 of these in nonmilitary communities. The annual report of the CTCA for 1918 claimed 110 closed districts, with 35 within the federally restricted zones and another 75 outside the districts but closed, nevertheless, because of action by the commission.[49]

The CTCA's handling of the case of New Orleans, and these statistics, reveal certain characteristics of the CTCA law enforcement program. In its pursuance of jurisdiction over New Orleans and other non–training camp cities, one can note the CTCA's broadening scope of action. Though originally intended to protect troops in the thirty-two new Army training camps, the CTCA gradually extended its domain. Determined to protect the soldiers, but also eager to improve the moral conditions of the entire nation, the CTCA defined ever more broadly the geographic area targeted by its programs.

In its ability to close famous and popular red-light districts such as those in New Orleans and Louisville, the CTCA also demonstrated the impact of the war on the antiprostitution forces. With sexual morality and health closely linked to the war cause in the popular mind, the antivice forces gained new stature, as well as the support and the power of the federal government.[50]

There was no question in the minds of reformers that their efforts to close the red-lights were a great success. One CTCA investigator and later head of the Section on Vice and Liquor Control did not hesitate to herald this success. "Even that Gibraltar of commercialized vice, notorious not only on this continent but abroad, the New Orleans district, which comprised twenty-four solid blocks given over to human degradation and lust and housing six to eight hundred women, has gone down with the rest," proclaimed George J. Anderson. The meaning of this success, and others, was clear. Anderson continued:

> As a result of these successes it may be stated that there is not now in the United States a red light district within the effective radius of any military establishment. More than that, the district itself has become an anachronism in American life, and the so-called segregation policy has been to all intents and purposes laid away in its burial shroud. Such is the victory of moral and military efficiency over the most brazen expression and dangerous form of commercialized vice.[51]

The chairman of the CTCA concurred.[52] In the closure of the districts the reformers had achieved a victory of moral and military import.

Yet these hopeful pronouncements about the red-light districts evaded a troublesome realization among the progressives of the CTCA. As the districts closed up across the nation, it became ever clearer that the closure of the districts did not put an end to prostitution in the training camp communities. Not only had vice always existed outside the districts, but closure of the districts seemed only to spread it more widely through communities. Finding new locations to pursue their trade, and finding new tactics for evading detection, the purveyors of prostitution and their customers remained plentiful.

"The Same Old Kind of Vice": Prostitution outside the Districts

From the beginning the CTCA had understood that prostitution existed outside the districts. Most obviously, communities without districts nevertheless often had vice problems. Little Rock, Arkansas, the site of Camp Pike, for instance, had closed its district in 1915. Yet a report on conditions there in August 1917 reported "a floating population of approximately 600 prostitutes."[53] In Atlanta, Georgia, home of Camp Gordon, though soldiers viewed the city as "a slow town," the CTCA assumed this distinction was rooted in a comparison to cities with districts. A report from "P.K." expressed the conviction that vice, nevertheless, was alive and well in Atlanta: " 'Outward decency' is very apparent in Atlanta," the report began. It continued: "The vice that exists centers principally about the streets and the hotels. The hotels I visited are nothing more than open houses of prostitution. They cater to vice, legitimate trade is not sought and, in some cases, even discouraged for the reason that it is less profitable."[54] Chillicothe, Ohio, too, located near Camp Sherman, though free of a district, had a reputation "as being the nearest to hell of any town in the State of Ohio, as regards its morals."[55] Although many communities in 1917 had never had restricted districts or had recently closed their districts, the CTCA was well aware that few communities had no vice trade.

Early in the war the closure of a district often meant the wholesale expulsion or departure of its residents not only from the district, but from the town or city itself. When Hattiesburg, Mississippi, home of Camp Shelby, closed its district, city officials drove the prostitutes from town, with assurances that their return would prompt shadowing by the secret service.[56] Similarly, when San Antonio, home of Camp Travis, closed its district, a veritable migration of women took place. As Bascom Johnson described it: "Many of the girls have left town. Mr. Needham . . . tells me that he has watched the outgoing trains and has himself seen not less than 500 leave in the last ten days." Though this certainly emptied San Antonio of prostitutes, the implications for surrounding cities and towns were distressing. Johnson continued, "I am also running down the statement attributed to an official at New Braunfells *[sic]* (a little town North East of here about 20 miles) that that town has had a large and sudden increase in its prostitute population."[57] Closing the districts cleaned up cities such as Hattiesburg and San Antonio, but often at the expense of surrounding locales.

In the case of San Antonio, women left town to find a new and safer place to work. In other cases, women remained in town, altering their style of solicitation to adapt to changed conditions. A letter to Secretary of War Baker from a citizen of East Waco, Texas, a community near Fort MacArthur but located outside the moral zone, suggested the problem created by prostitutes evicted from the districts. "Will you kindly give us the following information?" the letter queried. "Where the women of the 'Read *[sic]* Light District' who were removed from the reservation district by an order of the Government settle down in our resident communities and open up the same old kind of vice, and being visited by U.S. Soldiers in Uniform from night to night as well as many other men, and where the local officers do not take hold and stop same what shall we do?"[58] Though forced to relocate, prostitutes often emerged from the dismantled districts determined to continue in the trade.

A report on the closing of the red-light district in Louisville highlighted this determination. According to the report, whereas some planned to find new jobs, to return home, or to marry, a number of women expressed their preference to remain prostitutes. Noting that most of these women had entered prostitution willingly, the report suggested that roughly one-third of the district's prostitutes planned to stay in the trade if possible. Given these women's possible reluctance to call attention to their future actions, the actual proportion was likely even higher. As the report noted of the response from one house, "All Want to remain as they are, Absolutely and will remain if possible."[59] On the day following the district's closure an article in the *Louisville Courier-Journal* noted this same tendency, describing women's intentions to continue the trade outside the defunct district: "Not all the women who departed from the Tenderloin last night seemed to be victims of misfortune. There were many, still young and retaining marks of beauty, who were asking if it were still possible to carry on their profession. Many of them announced that they would test the law to the extent of getting arrested once." And further, "Most of the young ones were care-free and only cursed their luck, soldiers, cantonment and the Vice Commission, and announced that they would 'stick it out' on the streets in competition with others."[60]

In order to "stick it out" on the streets successfully, prostitutes resorted to new methods of solicitation to evade the tightening laws prohibiting their profession. As the letter from East Waco suggested, many moved into residential areas. In Little Rock, Arkansas, which had no district or open houses of prostitution, prostitutes operated as streetwalkers or out of cheap lodging houses and hotels. Prostitutes also continued to solicit in cafes and saloons.[61] In Hattiesburg, Mississippi, the district and all houses of prostitution were closed and vacated by 15 August 1917, but a report in December 1917 suggested, "The clandestine prostitutes seem to have been neglected by the city police." In this case, the primary problem involved the use of taxicabs for transportation into the country, with cabbies often serving as solicitors of business.[62] Forced out of the districts, prostitutes pursued their trade in new locations—lodging houses, dance halls, cafes, hotels, the streets, and the countryside.

Though the Hattiesburg report noted that the police had largely overlooked clandestine prostitution in their suppression of vice, the report did not suggest that this was intentional, but rather that the police had so far failed to address the problem, perhaps not understanding its significance. In other cities, too, the local police seemed to the CTCA incapable of fulfilling their now crucial role. A report on Battle Creek, Michigan, home of Camp Custer, complained: "Plain clothes men are willing to cooperate in this work. However, the new problems seem quite beyond their capacity. They seem somewhat indifferent and lax." And further, "The local Police cannot be depended upon for any work which requires initiative and resourcefulness."[63]

In still other cases the CTCA faced what it considered an even more difficult problem—intentional negligence on the part of local police or local officials, not unlike that initially displayed in New Orleans. In Philadelphia conditions totally anathema to the CTCA persisted as late as March 1918. "Our city government is incompetent, and we have reason to believe it is corrupt," Imogen Oakley wrote Secretary of War Baker. "Saloons sell liquor to enlisted men; gambling is tolerated; and prostitution is unchecked."[64] Similarly, in Bridgeport, Connecticut, hopes for cleaning the city seemed dim. "J.S." reported in February 1918, "Bridgeport's effort at keeping their town clean is doomed to failure for the good reason that the police not only appear to be lazy, but also mingle freely with the underworld element in a friendly manner."[65]

A final example, that of Alexandria, Louisiana, demonstrates how all of these factors—the continued interest of prostitutes in following their trade, their willingness to relocate when necessary, the development of more clandestine forms of prostitution, and the continued involvement of police or local officials in protecting vice—caused the CTCA to understand prostitution as a continuing, potentially worsening problem, despite the commission's success with the red-light districts.

When Camp Beauregard was established five miles outside of Alexandria, one report referred to it as "an overgrown country village." The town had thirty saloons, a red-light district, two dance halls, and three moving-picture houses.[66] A report in August 1917 described the general conditions in Alexandria:

> Alexandria is a wet town but the Mayor has recently ordered the saloons closed at 9:30 P.M. which doubtless has been generally obeyed. Within five minutes' walk from the heart of the city is a short wooden bridge which leads into the red-light district. Large electrical signs display the names of the "madams" and one would think they were entering a seashore resort. I understand there are about twenty houses there from the lowest type to real expensive ones.[67]

In his preliminary report on Alexandria, Bascom Johnson commented on "the generally reputed low standard of morals among many married women" in Alexandria and his impression "that the whole moral tone of the town was lower than that of any city I have visited except New Orleans." Johnson blamed the proximity of New Orleans, as well as the "downward pull of legalized vice" and "the easy going attitude of the French population" for the shameful conditions in Alexandria.[68] Alexandria, it seemed, was in need of a major cleanup.

To initiate its antivice work in Alexandria, the CTCA began by urging the town to close its red-light district and outlaw prostitution, which the community did on 15 September 1917 with just ten days preparation. As many other communities did, Alexandria hoped to rid itself of prostitution by closing the segregated district and chasing its residents out of town. In this case the CTCA investigator was optimistic, suggesting, "Here, at any rate, one seemed to have found a place where segregation had actually segregated."[69] With vice truly segregated, reformers hoped closure of the district would eliminate all vice from the city.

Initial reports supported this hope. By late September CTCA workers were able to report progress in the vice situation. A report of 22 September noted, "Not only was the district closed but apparently a thorough job of expulsion was done. All the previous week, the girls had been leaving in groups, sometimes as high as ten at a time." The report noted in addition, "Everywhere I found the accustomed sources of such information genuinely bewildered as to where to turn for a 'supply'; and this in a manner that would not have existed *[sic]* if they had been developing even the rudiments of a business outside the district before the closing."[70]

Yet Alexandria's vice problems were not solved. In November the report of Lt. Thomas Larremore of the Sanitary Corps, working with the CTCA, again suggested a vice problem. Regarding prostitution, he wrote, "The situation is fair at best and another week's investigation may bring me to the conclusion that it is poor." Though the district remained closed, dark, and deserted, streetwalkers had carried prostitution into the streets of the town, and automobile prostitution was carrying it into the countryside. Throughout December reports continued to note the problems of bootlegging and clandestine prostitution.[71] To make matters worse, Larremore found resentful city officials unwilling to admit that their community had a vice problem.[72]

Though the local officials became more cooperative, the vice situation remained troubling.[73] A report in April 1918 complained:

> No great agitation under way to clean up tho' Police are still nibbling. . . . There seems no determined effort being made to rid Alexandria of "home town girls." Friday night, standing with the desk Sergeant of Police watching Cloud's saloon, a pair of "the type" passed and the sergeant told me one of them was one who had recently outrun Miss Shields, the protective Officer, and made a getaway. He made no effort to catch her. She is said to be related by blood to one of the police.[74]

In Alexandria, as in other training camp communities across the country, the CTCA became increasingly certain of the need to do more than close red-light districts in the battle against vice. In a special report on 20 December 1917, Lieutenant Larremore recounted his meeting with the president of the State Board of Health for Louisiana. Larremore feared that the current policy of social hygiene in Louisiana resulted "in the diseased prostitutes and other undesirables being shunted from one town to another instead of confining her to a place where she would be unable to carry the diseases and to spread them."[75] Larremore hoped that the state board could gain the power and the necessary space to implement a quarantine for venereally diseased prostitutes and undesirables.

In this meeting Larremore signaled a change in emphasis in the antivice work of the CTCA. Finding that success in closing the districts was eliminating neither vice nor venereal disease, the CTCA changed direction in its law enforcement work. The annual report of the CTCA for 1918 described this shift. Noting that the closure of the red-light districts caused prostitutes initially to move to "less convenient and more hazardous places," the report suggested that the resultant law enforcement work only drove the prostitutes to turn to even more clandestine forms of prostitution, forms the CTCA considered more difficult to control. As the CTCA repressed each type of prostitution, prostitutes simply moved to a less easily detected method of soliciting. Recognizing the flexibility and the resilience of prostitution as an institution, the CTCA concluded that ultimately prostitutes themselves, rather than the institution of prostitution, had to become the target of repressive efforts if the CTCA's antivice crusade was ever to succeed. Elimination of prostitution in its more clandestine forms, the report suggested, "lies in the eradication from the field of the prostitute herself, and this is at present the leading feature of municipal activity."[76]

Remaining convinced of the need to eradicate vice from the training camp communities, and indeed from all parts of the nation where troops might pass or visit, the CTCA embarked on a project to eliminate not just prostitution, but the *prostitute* as well. Eager to remove temptation from the training camp communities permanently, the CTCA hoped to develop a system of detention houses and reformatories to house these women and girls during the war.[77] By repressing the individual rather than the institution, the CTCA hoped to control the tenacious problem of illicit sex.

1. Tug-of-war in front of a YMCA tent, Camp Dix, New Jersey. Reformers hoped that healthful activities like athletics would entertain and educate the troops. Courtesy of the National Archives.

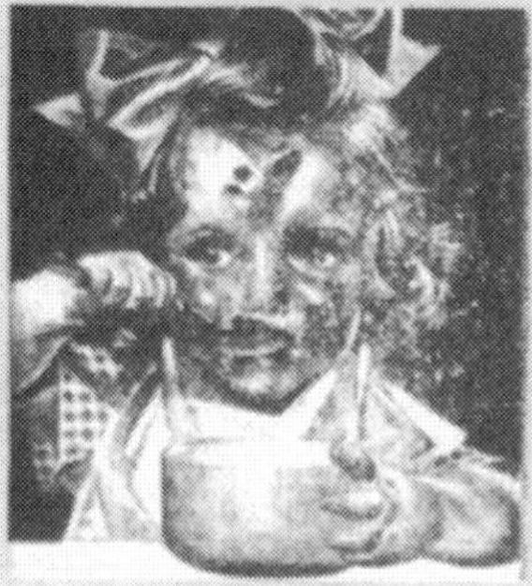

Remember—
Your Future Children
Give 'em a chance
Don't start 'em out with a mortgage
on body or mind

Remember—
Your Father
Your Dad gave YOU the best there was in *him*
He expects you to make good
Don't splash mud on his name

Left: 2. Social hygiene education poster. The CTCA asked soldiers to shoulder new kinds of responsibilities as soldiers and as men. Courtesy of the National Archives.

Right: 3. Social hygiene education poster. Soldiers would be judged not only on their martial expertise, but on their physical and moral health as well. Courtesy of the National Archives.

Remember—
The Folks at Home
Go back to them physically fit
and morally clean
Don't allow a whore to smirch your record

Taking Chances
A real sailor is not
afraid to take a chance
BUT—
If he takes
a foolish
chance—
he may lose
his chance
to get into the
BIG GAME

Left: 4. Social hygiene education poster. The social hygiene education program juxtaposed men's responsibilities to chaste women with the danger posed by fallen women. Courtesy of the National Archives.

Right: 5. Social hygiene education poster. "Real" men kept themselves fit for fighting. Courtesy of the National Archives.

6. Knights of Columbus No. 1 Branch, American Library Association, Camp Kearny Library, California. Soldier clubhouses inside the camps often included libraries, providing men with an opportunity for constructive reading. Courtesy of the National Archives.

7. American Library Association Campaign for Books, Brooklyn, New York. In a massive effort the ALA oversaw libraries in camps throughout the country. Courtesy of the National Archives.

8. American Library Association Campaign for Books, front of public library, New York City. Book and fund-raising drives provided an educational opportunity, introducing civilians to the programs initiated by the CTCA. Courtesy of the National Archives.

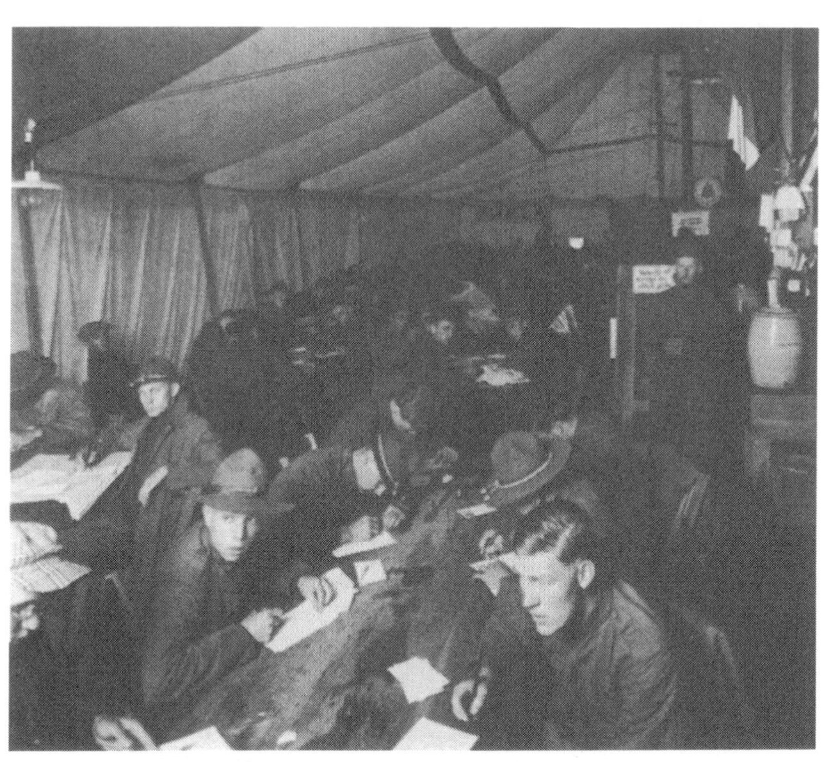

The Jewish Welfare Board
מיר האבען פאר זיי
א היים געבויט

11. Seder, prepared under the auspices of the Jewish Welfare Board. The CTCA's in-camp recreation program sometimes demonstrated a sensitivity to religious differences among the men, making room for a variety of religious observances and traditions. Courtesy of the National Archives.

Facing page:
Top: 9. Inside a YMCA tent, Camp Devens, outside Ayer, Massachusetts. Soldier clubhouses, run by the YMCA, the Knights of Columbus, and the Jewish Welfare Board, provided troops with a morally and physically safe recreational environment inside the camps. Courtesy of the National Archives.
Bottom: 10. "We have built a home for them." Yiddish poster for fund-raising efforts, 1918. Working to acculturate new Americans and seeking to provide recreation for troops of various religious backgrounds, the CTCA included the Knights of Columbus and the Jewish Welfare Board among its affiliated organizations. Courtesy of the National Archives.

COMPANY H
MINSTREL
308 Inf. Co.H Camp Upton

14. Soldiers waiting to get into a Liberty Theater. Liberty Theaters inside the camps allowed the CTCA to present carefully controlled and uplifting entertainment to the troops. Courtesy of the National Archives.

Facing page:
Top: 12. Minstrels at Knights of Columbus Building #2, Camp Zachary, Taylor, Kentucky. Both inside and outside the camp gates, recreation was often segregated, showing little appreciation of the needs of African American troops. Courtesy of the National Archives.
Bottom: 13. "A Wagonload of Minstrels" of Company H, 308th Regiment, Infantry. Minstrel shows, which often included stereotyped representations of African Americans, were common fare for in-camp entertainment. Courtesy of the National Archives.

15. The YWCA Hostess House at Camp Meade, Maryland, "the meeting place of mothers, wives and friends of the men in training." Courtesy of the National Archives.

16. Interior of Hostess House, Camp Fremont, Palo Alto, California. Hostess Houses allowed the CTCA to keep an eye on female visitors to the camps, while also cultivating "proper" relations between men and women. Courtesy of the National Archives.

17. Calisthenics, Camp Dick, Dallas, Texas. Athletics could help develop the "mental, moral and physical manhood" of the men while in camp. Courtesy of the National Archives.

Top: 18. Boxing exhibition, Camp Custer, Michigan. The commission maintained that athletics could promote military expertise as well as providing recreation for the men in camp. Courtesy of the National Archives.
Bottom: 19. Company boxing training, Camp Sherman, Ohio. Training in boxing would facilitate the men's skills as bayonet fighters. Courtesy of the National Archives.

Top: 20. U.S. Marines at the Mare Island Barracks "rehearsing some of the popular war songs." "That it is essential that our soldiers be kept in good spirits is the contention of leading Army and Navy officers. One of the methods employed by the Government is the assignment of singing instructors to the various training camps throughout the country." (This is part of the caption that originally accompanied this photo.) Courtesy of the National Archives.
Bottom: 21. "Victory Sing" in front of Rice Hotel, Houston, Texas. Encouraging soldiers and civilians to enjoy recreation together, the CTCA hoped to overcome the traditional image of the soldier as social pariah and to create a "home away from home" for the man in uniform. Courtesy of the National Archives.

THE GIRLS
LIBERTY LEAGUE
IS THE GIRLS DIVISION

24. Canteen for African American soldiers and sailors in New York City, opened by the National League for Women's Service following requests from African American women. Segregation often resulted in shortages of facilities for African American troops. Courtesy of the National Archives.

Facing page:
Top: 22. Interior view of the Army and Navy Club of the War Camp Community Service of Minneapolis, Minnesota. Out in the communities the War Camp Community Service organized morally and physically safe recreation for the men in uniform, including the establishment of social clubs. Courtesy of the National Archives.
Bottom: 23. Club for African American soldiers, Newark, New Jersey. The social clubs cultivated a taste for middle-class recreation in the company of "upstanding" women. Courtesy of the National Archives.

Top: 25. A War Camp Community Service dance in Mobile, Alabama. "The purpose of the dances is to give men who desire to dance the desire to do so under absolutely desirable conditions." This entailed eliminating working-class styles of dancing from the soldiers' repertoire. Courtesy of the National Archives.
Bottom: 26. The WCCS also sponsored free entertainment for men in the military, including this show at the Casino Theatre in New York. Courtesy of the National Archives.

Top: 27. Social evening of the Young Women's Hebrew Association of New York City for the men in uniform. In addition to the WCCS, other local and national organizations organized recreational opportunities for the men in uniform. Courtesy of the National Archives.
Bottom: 28. Exterior view of the Knights of Columbus "Hut" on Broadway and 46th Street in New York City. In rural outposts and major metropolises alike, the CTCA succeeded in developing new recreational opportunities for the troops. Courtesy of the National Archives.

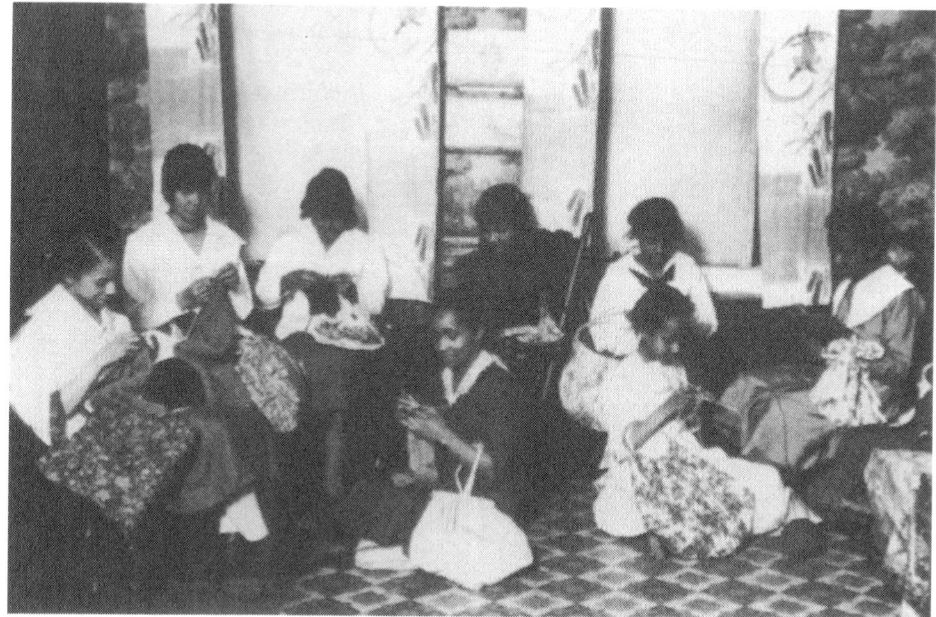

31. Setting up exercises, YMCA school, Camp Travis, Fort Sam Houston, Texas. Courtesy of the National Archives.

Facing page:
Top: 29. Soldiers enjoying the hospitality at an estate on the Hudson River. Although women gained a role in the war through their participation in the CTCA program, the commission often reinforced traditional notions of women's purity and domesticity. Courtesy of the National Archives.
Bottom: 30. Even in their female-segregated recreation program, the CTCA encouraged women and girls to serve the soldiers, in this case by knitting for the troops.

32. Jewish Welfare Board Work. Dancing, Young Men's Hebrew Association, Jewish Welfare Board, New York City. Courtesy of the National Archives.

33. Exercises at Knights of Columbus Building No. 4, Camp Zachary Taylor, Kentucky. Courtesy of the National Archives.

34. Minstrel show at Knights of Columbus Building No. 3, Camp Zachary Taylor, Kentucky. Courtesy of the National Archives.

4-35

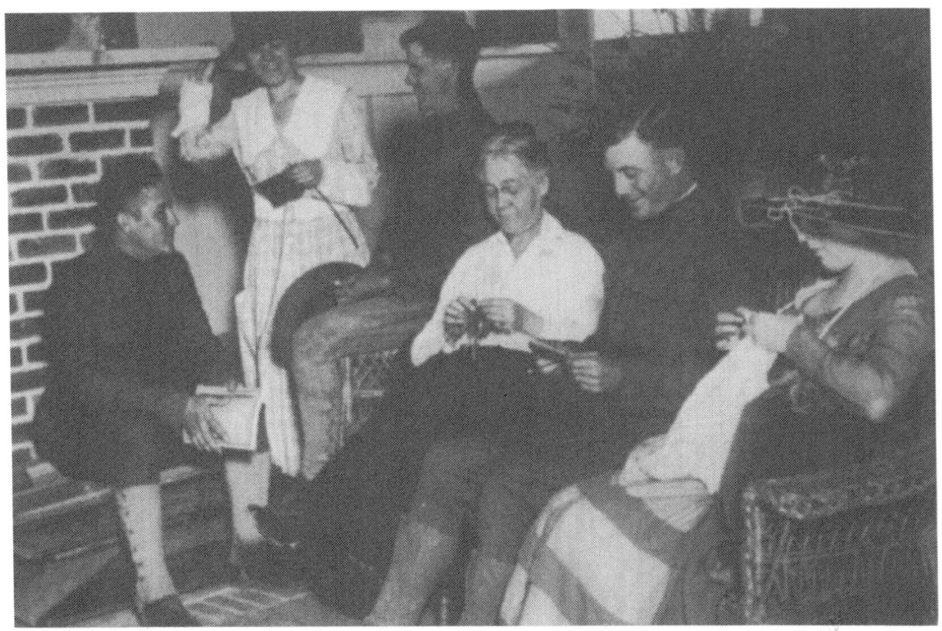

37. "Soldiers stationed at Camp Fremont find 'foster mother' always ready to cheer them at the Hostess House, established by the YWCA." Courtesy of the National Archives.

Facing page:
Top: 35. Football game between Squadron A of Post Field, Oklahoma, and Squadron E of Call Field, Texas. Courtesy of the National Archives.
Bottom: 36. Push Ball, YMCA field day at Camp Devens, Ayer, Massachusetts. Courtesy of the National Archives.

38. "Colored Soldiers' Club" at Battle Creek, Michigan. Courtesy of the National Archives.

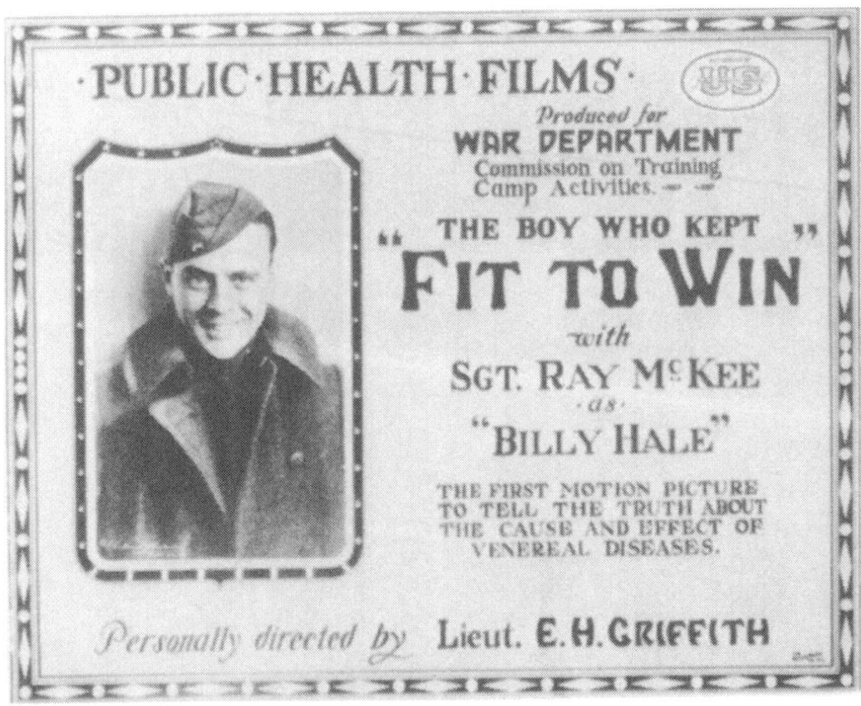

39. The film "Keeping Fit to Fight," renamed "Keeping Fit to Win" after the war, demonstrated the commission's effort to use the most modern methods to eliminate venereal disease. Courtesy of Social Welfare History Archives, University of Minnesota.

By the spring of 1918, though, the CTCA had discovered that prostitutes were not the only individuals standing in the way of the reformers' success. Promiscuous women and girls, like professional prostitutes, threatened the moral well-being of the men in uniform. This problem, as well as its tenacity, had been evident in Alexandria. Much to the chagrin of the CTCA's man there, the federal men were unwilling to arrest women or girls guilty of intercourse with soldiers in a family home. They required that the deed take place in a disorderly house to justify arrest.[78] Yet, to the reformers of the CTCA, changing the location of a sexual rendezvous could not lessen its harmful potential. With the district closed, the importance of suppressing all illicit sex seemed enhanced to the CTCA, as it became increasingly difficult to distinguish between nonprofessional promiscuity and prostitution. Once choosing to attack the individuals breaking the commission's moral codes, rather than the institution of prostitution, the CTCA quickly expanded its campaign to include all promiscuous, or potentially promiscuous, women. In doing so the reformers blurred the lines dividing the foolish, the delinquent, and the criminal female, which were initially fundamental to its programs.

"A Considerable Volume of 'Charity' Intercourse": The Problem of Promiscuity

From the beginning the CTCA acknowledged that there were some women who did not fit neatly into either of the traditional categories describing women. Young women and girls, with still incompletely formed characters, faced a new danger in the man in uniform and at the same time posed an additional threat to that man's purity. Raymond Fosdick described the problem the commission faced, "Briefly, we are confronted with the problem of hundreds of young girls, not yet prostitutes, who seem to have become hysterical at the sight of buttons and uniforms."[79]

In the eyes of the commission these girls really included two distinct types. One group, those targeted by the CTCA's recreation and education programs, were the "silly girls" of the community, innocents who lost control at the sight of a uniform. As one CTCA pamphlet described the problem posed by this girl: "The 'lure of the uniform' is more than a phrase; it is an actuality. Girls often lose their heads in a whirl of emotion brought about by these unusual conditions."[80] This girl was not inherently evil, but she was potentially too emotional to retain control of her behavior. Here was another stereotype—the woman overcome by her feelings. Reformers easily manipulated this image into another version of the depraved woman. Losing their heads, reformers maintained, these girls often became a threat to the soldiers not unlike the practiced prostitute. In an article aptly entitled, in part, "The Girl Problem," one CTCA publicist explained how these girls "consciously or unconsciously, through their method of dressing and their lack of dignity, place temptation in the way of the soldiers."[81]

Another kind of girl posed an even more serious, and more purposeful, threat. According to one CTCA bulletin, this "older and more venturesome" girl was "the girl who has always been 'free' with young men. She goes to camp—alone or with some of her chums—for the sole purpose of 'picking up' acquaintance with soldiers. This kind of girl has not yet committed a crime, but she is on the downward path."[82] To reverse this girl's direction and send her back up the path toward morality, as well as to protect the innocents of the training camp communities, the commission created the Committee on Protective Work for Girls (CPWG) in September 1917.

Maude E. Miner, secretary of the New York Probation and Protective Association, was the first chairwoman of the protective program. Having visited camps in New York and Vermont, in July 1917 Miner had written Fosdick to suggest the need for protective work for girls in the training camp communities. Agreeing with her advice, Fosdick selected her soon after to head the work for the CTCA.[83]

The CTCA maintained a general policy of employing women in the commission's protective work, and under this policy a number of women gained the opportunity to do the work for which they were trained. Some of these women were well known in the fields of penology, social work, and social reform. Historian Barbara Meil Hobson has suggested regarding the CPWG, "The board and regional directories of this protective agency read like a register of social feminists in America."[84]

In each community the CPWG established a local branch responsible for protective and reformative work in that locale. Each branch then established a Protective Bureau, made up of either policewomen or volunteers, to undertake the duties of protective work. The primary responsibility of the protective workers was their scouting and patrol work, which required that these women "go on the streets and in the vicinity of the camp to observe conditions and to follow and warn young girls apparently in danger."[85] Or, as a postwar account described this work, "They patrol the environment of the camp—that is, the woods near-by, or the streets in the town." These workers also patrolled any travel centers unguarded by travelers' aid workers, as well as amusement resorts, including dance halls, amusement parks, movie theaters, and parks.[86]

While patrolling, the protective workers were to engage in their second responsibility—their personal work with the individual girls of the community. Protective workers were to befriend the girls they found on the streets, first warning them of their danger, later visiting them, and when appropriate referring them to other organizations.[87] The CPWG often recommended the employment of local women for this task, "social workers of considerable experience, forceful, tactful, and of splendid physical strength who may previously have established relationships with the young women and girls of the community."[88] Hopefully, the protective workers would be able to save the girls from danger. When the committee's workers discovered girls violating the law, the protective workers were advised to take the girls into custody themselves or to notify the appropriate authorities so that the girls might be detained. Yet the CPWG always maintained that it was not a law enforcement agency. From the beginning it asserted that its role was not to enforce laws against vice or to arrest prostitutes. Although the committee advocated police power for the protective officers, it urged that this power be used only in emergencies.[89]

As a final aspect of their work, the local committees for protective work were encouraged by the national committee to work for the establishment of detention homes in their communities. An alternative to jails, the detention homes would provide a place where girls in trouble for the first time could evade exposure to experienced, and therefore hardened, prostitutes and criminals.

Though some of the work of the CPWG, such as the establishment of detention homes, was clearly repressive, the reformers emphasized the protective and constructive aspects of their work. An article in *Playground* urged regarding protective work "that great emphasis be laid on the preventive and constructive phase of the work." Employing that very logic, the article continued, "Not only shall the girls be warned by the police women and patrols and persuasion be brought to bear when they are found acting foolishly and unwisely but friendly relations should be established." Finally, reasserting that throughout the CTCA program positive means were always preferred to repression, the article argued "that it should be constantly borne in mind that the work of the police women and volunteer patrols is only one phase of the work for girls and should not be over-emphasized to the exclusion of other features of primary importance."[90] Early in the war, then, the CTCA divided its antivice work into two types—protective work for noncriminal girls and the law enforcement work directed at prostitutes and the segregated district. The protective work contained repressive aspects, but its overall tenor was distinct from that of the law enforcement program.

As the war progressed, however, the CTCA found it increasingly difficult to maintain the division between its protective programs and its law enforcement programs. Because soldiers and civilians continued to resist the new behavioral strictures passed by the federal legislature and implemented by the CTCA, the law enforcement programs grew more intricate, more fully staffed, more completely funded, and more repressive, while the focus and funding for protective work dwindled. The CTCA's campaign to eradicate the individual prostitute easily evolved into a broader attack on any woman who seemed to challenge the CTCA's moral codes. Promiscuous girls, no less than prostitutes, posed such a threat.

Although initial discussions of the Committee on Protective Work for Girls emphasized its positive efforts, the committee early understood the important role repressive programs would play in its work. A letter from Roy Smith Wallace, a district director for the CTCA, to Raymond Fosdick in April 1918 made clear the rapid shift undertaken by the commission in its perception of its work with girls. He explained:

> I fear the distinction made . . . between "personal work with girls who need special attention" and "girls who need police treatment" will be very difficult to make in practice. As you know, the girls' protective work started out to be "personal work with girls," and very speedily got to be, because of the urgency of the need of these other girls, work with delinquent girls. Indeed, even when the Protective Workers began work with the girl because she seemed innocent and hopeful, though wild in most cases, it has turned out the girls were really delinquent. I think, therefore, that this distinction . . . will be a very difficult distinction to enforce.[91]

The Committee on Protective Work for Girls, according to Wallace, had discovered a surprising degree of delinquency, or sexual activity, among those girls within its purview. For this reason the committee quickly directed most of its efforts to dealing with the problems of these delinquent girls.

Labeled as *charity girls*, these girls were nonprostitutes who nevertheless engaged in sexual activity with the men in uniform. The term *charity girls* originally referred to young women, generally of the working class, who used sexual relations as barter in the heterosocial world of commercial amusements in the late nineteenth and early twentieth centuries. Unable to afford to entertain themselves, these young women exchanged sexual favors for gifts and evenings out.[92] During the war the term took on additional meaning. Although it might still refer to women using sex as part of an exchange relationship, it also came to refer to any woman who engaged in sexual relations with soldiers free of charge. This problem was particularly troublesome to the CTCA, as it was unaffected by the educational and recreational programs of the WCCS and similarly escaped the attention of the initial antivice efforts of CTCA investigators and local police.

By late 1917 the CTCA was finding it to be a problem both widespread and severe.[93] As one publicist for the CTCA explained regarding protective work, "The original idea was to throw safeguards around young girls as would prevent later delinquency. After six months of purely protective work it was found that the serious problem of the camp cities consisted in the already delinquent women and girls."[94] A report on charity girls in Wrightstown, New Jersey, near Camp Dix, explained the problem:

> In all towns, both large and small, in the vicinity of the camp or accessible to the soldiers by jitney, trolley or train, there still is a considerable volume of "charity" intercourse. There seems to be a psychological feature to this particular evil in that young girls between the ages of 14 and 20 are inordinately susceptible to any man in uniform whether he be an officer or one of lesser rank.[95]

Again suggesting the belief that girls were carried away by the sight of a soldier, this report nevertheless also suggested that the girls had engaged in sexual intercourse prior to the arrival of the troops. This additional point reflected the rising belief among CTCA workers that many girls were not helpless innocents but a threat to the moral and physical health of the soldiers and to themselves. In this sense the CTCA's problem with these charges of the Committee on Protective Work for Girls took on the same characteristics as its problem with prostitutes.

In February 1918 a report on the work of the CTCA's Committee on Protective Work for Girls documented the case histories of fifteen women and girls from South Carolina who had recently been committed first to the National Training School in the District of Columbia and then to the Sherborn Reformatory for Women in Massachusetts. Ranging in age from fifteen to twenty-one, these women were interned as a part of the CTCA's crusade against vice. A number of characteristics appeared repeatedly in their case histories, including low education or mental age, an early entry into the world of work, disrupted or "degenerate" family histories, a long history of "immoral relations with men," often as prostitutes, and repeated arrests for that immorality.[96]

The case of Lois Sarratt was typical. Lois was fifteen years old. She could neither read nor write and had worked as a spooler in the cotton-mills since she was ten years old. She had "been immoral" since the age of eleven and had become a prostitute when she was thirteen. Her mother was a known prostitute and had given birth to Lois illegitimately. In August 1917, while living in the red-light district of Greenville, South Carolina, Lois was arrested for selling liquor to soldiers. Escaping jail, where she was to serve a three-month sentence, she was again arrested and placed in the rescue home, from which she also escaped. When finally picked up and committed, Lois suffered from venereal infection.[97]

Lois exhibited all the characteristics of what the CTCA referred to as a hardened prostitute—a long career in prostitution, a history of repeated arrests, and the resultant venereal disease assumed to infect all prostitutes. Lois, according to the CTCA, was a danger to her community, to the soldiers of Camp Sevier in that community, and finally, to herself. On this basis the CTCA approved of her long-term commitment to a reformatory. Here Lois would receive treatment for both her physical and moral maladies before being permitted to return to her home in South Carolina.

When the CTCA committed Lois Sarratt to the Sherborn Reformatory for Women, it also committed Pauline Richards, a woman of twenty-one. Pauline was from Atlanta, Georgia, where she had a husband. She was arrested in Greenville, South Carolina, where she was found living with a soldier. Her crime, according to the CTCA, was her acceptance of money from the soldier with whom she lived and her infection with both syphilis and gonorrhea. Similarly, Juanita Wright, a twenty-year-old, was arrested in Spartanburg, South Carolina, for living with a soldier. She had no history of prostitution and no venereal diseases.[98] In the arrests of these latter two women one can note the broadening net of the CTCA's law enforcement program, as any violation of its behavioral strictures seemed equally threatening to the commission's success.

"Uprooting Vicious Habits": The Program of Repression

To overcome the problem of promiscuity the Committee on Protective Work for Girls adopted the same essential program earmarked for handling prostitutes, concentrating increasingly on the acquisition of legal provisions and adequate facilities for the quarantine and detention of those girls picked up as charity girls, or delinquents. Maude E. Miner's explanation of the need for this program echoed the decision made regarding prostitutes: "If we are to safeguard the health of soldiers and sailors," she argued, "we must free the communities from the delinquent and the diseased women, who are the greatest menace."[99]

As the work for prostitutes and delinquent girls dovetailed, the commission relied on detention houses, hospitals, and reformatories in its work with both populations. The detention houses would serve essentially as clearinghouses, "where all young girls and women arrested, with the exception of hardened prostitutes and 'repeaters,' can be held while awaiting trial, instead of being held in jail."[100]

Careful study of the inmates of the detention houses, including mental tests, would aid authorities in determining the proper recommendation to be made to the judge in each woman's or girl's case. The chairman of the CTCA suggested:

> With a good house of detention, actively functioning as a clearing house, it will be found that varied treatment should be recommended. There are silly, runaway girls who should be sent home; feeble-minded girls and women who should have permanent custodial care; and, in the majority, untrained, neurotic, irresponsible girls on the verge of drifting into a life of prostitution, who should have industrial training in an institution located

> in the country, where there is abundant opportunity for outdoor work and recreation.[101]

Once a diagnosis was made, reformers argued that long-term internment in venereal hospitals was necessary to ensure the cure of venereal diseases carried by many of the arrested prostitutes.[102] These hospitals were considered a priority both because of the importance of eradicating venereal disease and because of the assumption made by members of the commission that a vast majority of prostitutes were infected with disease.[103]

Curing the physical disease alone, however, was not enough. Concerned with the broader uplift of the society, the CTCA demanded the moral regeneration of its female charges as well as their physical cure. As the chairman of the commission explained, "It has been conclusively proved by cities attempting medical treatment alone that such will not suffice to fit prostitutes for normal, moral living."[104] For those without disease, or cured of disease, long-term detention in a reformatory would serve the purpose of protecting the society from the moral corruption of these criminal women, while also providing the opportunity for their reformation. As one publicist for the CTCA suggested, "It would be impossible to apprehend all the diseased women in the country and lock them up, and even if this were done other prostitutes would doubtless take their places, who would soon become infected. If we are to accomplish anything, we must be able to establish new habits of thought in the minds of these and other women."[105] Believing in the efficacy of environment and education in transforming character, the CTCA anticipated the reformation of its criminal charges.[106]

To secure this rehabilitation, the commission favored long-term commitment on indeterminate sentences, followed by parole. Long stays in reformatories would provide the opportunity for change, placing delinquents and prostitutes in the proper environment until their transformation was complete. Indeterminate sentences secured the long-term commitment and kept troublesome women off the streets indefinitely. At the same time this sort of sentence would encourage the cooperation of those interned.[107]

The character of the reformatories, progressives believed, was integral to the success of the women's and girls' reformation. Reflecting the continuing association of the city with social and moral ills in the minds of

Americans, progressives urged that reformatories be built in the country, where work, education, and leisure could combine to create rehabilitation.[108]

For many inmates work and education overlapped in vocational and prevocational training. Conditions varied from institution to institution, but most inmates engaged in some sort of work for the institution itself. Maintaining the value of this work, one CTCA report argued, "Agricultural work must be developed as a feature of the place for its rehabilitating and economic value. . . . There must be sewing, handwork, and a complete course of training in the domestic work involved in the conduct of a house, including the laundry work. All of the work involved in the upkeep of the institution should be done by the women and girls under direction as far as possible, for this develops a sense of responsibility that nothing else can."[109] According to this argument, through sewing and laundering, gardening and farming, delinquent girls and prostitutes would learn valuable skills, preparing them for a proper life after their release. At the same time involvement in "honest work" would teach them values that would prevent their return to improper behaviors. As another report explained regarding a program of laundering and sewing hospital gowns, "While it may require a stretch of the imagination to apply the term 'prevocational' to this sort of training, it nonetheless has a quite definite value in the plan of uprooting vicious habits by replacing indolence with industry."[110]

It does indeed require a stretch of the imagination to understand laundering and sewing as true vocational training. Most of the work in these institutions trained the women how to survive in an older, anachronistic world, rather than preparing them for entry into the modern, urban, industrial economy. Emphasizing nineteenth-century domesticity, the work programs did little to prepare them for life on the outside.[111] This training did, however, prepare women to fulfill the traditional domestic role, which remained a feature of the CTCA's image of womanhood.

A postwar report on the CTCA's detention houses and reformatories suggested the full day generally followed in the institutions. An average of two and one-fourth hours were spent doing housework, cooking, and laundering, and an additional three and one-half hours were spent on other work. The CTCA also advocated academic schoolwork for the inmates, and this work consumed an average of three hours per day. For what little of the day was left, the CTCA promoted supervised leisure. For instance, as in the training camps, the CTCA emphasized "the humanizing and socializing effect of good music." The recreational period ranged from one to two and one-half hours per day, according to CTCA records.[112]

Keeping the inmates constructively occupied for ten or eleven hours per day, then, the CTCA hoped to instill "lower-class skills and middle-class values."[113] As in other aspects of the CTCA's programs, progressives believed the reformatories would transform marginal, even criminal citizens, into proper Americans. These women might never reach the ranks of crusaders and would not use the training acquired in the reformatories to gain anything other than unskilled, poorly paid work, but reformers believed they would nevertheless be integrated into society with the skills and values appropriate to their class and their gender.

There was one set of inmates, however, that the CTCA and other reformers assumed could never be integrated into the larger society; they warranted segregation even from delinquents and prostitutes. Adhering to the popular progressive belief that many criminals, especially women guilty of sexual immorality, were what they referred to as feebleminded, the CTCA early in the war began efforts to permanently intern in their own institutions all women discovered to be feebleminded.[114]

This concern with feebleminded criminals had its roots in biological interpretations of crime, popular in the late nineteenth and early twentieth centuries. According to these theories women were the natural moral superiors of men unless biologically determined to be criminals. Criminal women, in this view, were particularly depraved, with an excess of male traits and a distinct shortage of feminine attributes.[115]

By World War One many progressives had largely dismissed this strict biological determinism. After the turn of the century new penologists and reformers, especially women, began to explore the environmental causes of crime. At the same time, however, many also accepted a new version of biological determinism, turning to theories that described a new category of innate criminality, defective delinquency. Until after the 1920s "hard-core biological determinism" remained a powerful force in American penology.[116]

According to this argument, made popular in part by the CTCA's own Katherine Bement Davis, there were two types of criminals—"congenital defectives" and those forced into crime by their environment. Congenital defectives, or defective delinquents, were those criminals who had a natural, biologically determined proclivity for crime. In women it was associated with early sexual development and promiscuity.[117] Although those shaped by their environment might be transformed through the reformatory system, progressives believed, defective delinquents could not be reformed, only removed. Operating on this premise, the CTCA wanted to establish routine mental examinations of all women and girls arrested, as well as separate facilities for the permanent institutionalization of those females discovered to be mentally defective.[118]

The CTCA, and progressive reformers generally, always vastly overestimated this problem. One study of one hundred prostitutes discovered ninety-one with mental ages of less than ten. Another suggested that 38 percent of prostitutes under consideration were clinically feebleminded.[119] The reasons for these exaggerated findings are easy to understand. As the historian Ruth Rosen suggests, "Rather than indicating mental deficiency, the label *feeble-minded* instead referred to prostitutes' refusal or failure to conform to middle-class values and behavioral patterns."[120] Given that prostitutes and promiscuous girls were often arrested for precisely that refusal or failure, it is not surprising that reformers would diagnose many of them as feebleminded. Further, arguments of congenital causes for female criminality solved a vexing theoretical problem for many progressives. Biological determinism allowed reformers to retain their belief in women's natural purity, despite the existence of rampant prostitution.[121]

While "congenital defectives" were relegated to permanent incarceration, reformers hoped to transform prostitutes and promiscuous girls into respectable citizens. Ultimately, the CTCA realized, its detention and reformatory program required two essentials to allow it to succeed—laws providing legal justification for the internment of women and financing to provide the proper facilities for such internment.[122]

The CTCA urged cities and states alike to pass legislation legalizing the examination of all arrested persons suspected of being venereal disease carriers.[123] As early as March 1918 the CTCA could count thirty-two states with laws requiring medical inspections of all arrested prostitutes.[124] Eager to standardize local laws pertaining to the arrest, detention, and examination of women, the CTCA eventually published a pamphlet of standard laws that might be used as prototypes for local laws. The pamphlet included laws for the repression of prostitution, for the outlawing of fornication between unmarried persons, for the control of venereal disease, for the removal from office of ineffectual officials, and for the establishment of reformatories. Also provided were an injunction and abatement act and suggestions for a law for the examination and commitment of feebleminded persons. Reflecting again the reformers' ability to view the most repressive acts as inherently constructive, the pamphlet suggested that these laws were "drawn with a view of furnishing legal machinery for the protection of society against both the moral and physical hazards incident to prostitution and also for the rehabilitative treatment of sex offenders themselves."[125]

Aware of the constitutional questions surrounding many of these laws, Attorney General Thomas W. Gregory assisted the CTCA by affirming the legality of the laws. Citing exhaustively from various works on police power, constitutional law, and actual court cases, Gregory was explicit in stating the position of the Department of Justice regarding the constitutionality of examining and quarantining women suspected of being venereally infected. He concluded a memorandum in April 1918:

> The right and, in fact, the duty of those in charge of a prison, or other place of detention, to ascertain the state of health of the inmates and to administer the necessary medical treatment, is surely beyond question. The Department of Justice entertains no doubt upon the right to subject a person convicted of prostitution to a medical examination in order to ascertain whether or not she is afflicted with a communicable disease.[126]

Operating beyond the restraints of conventional civil liberties, the CTCA, with the blessing of the Justice Department, adopted law enforcement routines that were clearly unconstitutional. Women could be arrested on the basis of the flimsiest suspicions regarding their moral character. No suspicion of a specific crime was necessary to warrant arrest, only the suspicion that a woman or girl might have promiscuous tendencies or might be venereally infected, traits considered largely interchangeable by the reformers.[127] Once arrested under section 13, females automatically faced medical examination for venereal disease. If a woman was found to be diseased, prosecution was suspended while the defendant underwent treatment in a venereal hospital.[128] Once recovered, the woman faced prosecution for promiscuity or prostitution, with her conviction commonly resulting in long-term detention. If guilty of no crime other than her disease, a woman was nevertheless detained for the duration of the disease.

When this general policy was applied on the local level, further abrogation of rights often occurred. In Indianapolis, for instance, the state and city boards of health, the police, and the police judge cooperated in the following program:

> Suspected prostitutes are arrested upon suspicion, and if convicted are sent to the State Women's Prison, where they receive treatment. If not convicted they are remanded to jail for a few days, waiting further evidence, and are examined by the physicians of the State Board. If found to be infected these cases are quarantined in one wing of the hospital.[129]

In this plan all arrested women were assumed guilty, and all powers were directed to detaining the woman at all cost, with no regard for her civil liberties.

With growing support for the concept of detention, the CTCA confronted a shortage of facilities. Determined not to be stopped by the shortage, the commission embarked on a drive to gain adequate detention houses and reformatories throughout the nation. By February 1918 the rising preoccupation of the Committee on Protective Work for Girls with detention work was clear. Eager to expand detention facilities, the committee needed money in order to assist states and communities in providing the type of facilities the CTCA and the CPWG desired. Demonstrating executive support for the detention program, in late February President Wilson gave $250,000 from the President's Emergency Fund to the committee to be used as a supplement to state money raised for the development of detention homes and reformatories. The head of the CPWG, Maude Miner, earmarked $225,000 of this money for aid in the construction of additional reformatory facilities and $25,000 for aid in establishing and maintaining detention houses.[130]

"Subordinated to the Interests of the Soldiers": Completing the System of Repression

The new financial arrangements were only a foreshadowing of more extensive changes about to occur. In April 1918 the CTCA underwent a vast reorganization, which carried with it broad implications regarding the commission's plans for work with women and girls. The new organizational scheme placed much greater emphasis on law enforcement, establishing a separate Law Enforcement Division under the supervision of Bascom Johnson, who had long headed the commission's law enforcement work. The division had three subdivisions, including the Section on Vice and Liquor Control, the Section on Women and Girls, and the Section on Reformatories and Detention Homes. In this plan, the Committee on Protective Work for Girls essentially ceased to exist, being replaced by the Section on Protective Work for Girls.[131] This section soon changed its name to the Section on Women and Girls, perhaps because it did so little protective work. (For a chart of the structure and personnel of the CTCA following reorganization, see Appendix E.)

The Section on Women and Girls delineated its work in a way that immediately suggested the new orientation of the work. The bulletin describing the reorganization to the field representatives of the now defunct Committee on Protective Work for Girls indicated regarding the role of the new section:

> It will concern itself with delinquent girls and all girls between the ages of 10 and 21 against whom there has been any definite complaint. The Protective Work Section will also be responsible for work with the so-called charity girl and professional prostitute, whether diseased or not, and with women having venereal disease.[132]

Under the new framework the Section on Women and Girls combined the work with delinquent and charity girls with that for prostitutes. This alteration institutionalized the transition in the commission's work that had been under way over the preceding months.

Not everyone involved in the work with girls approved of these changes, and the reorganization led to the resignation of Maude Miner. Miner had favored "dealing with the girl problem as a whole," uniting a "girls' protective bureau, houses of detention, an industrial division dealing with women employees in the camps, educational work and the training of women workers" under a single division, allowing "all girls and women" to "work together for the girlhood of America in this wartime." In her letter of resignation Miner argued that the separation of the work with women into its various elements based on the CTCA's organizational structure had left the protective work program overtaxed and virtually unfinanced.[133]

Though lodging these concerns, Miner's official letter of resignation was evasive on the specific reasons for her departure. In private correspondence Miner was more open about the forces compelling her to resign. Committed to working for the protection of girls, Miner believed that the CTCA did not share her concerns. In a letter to another reformer she lamented a "change in the organization here" and her own "realization that the protection of girls was not really the thing which was sought by the Commission, but that the entire emphasis was being placed on the protection of the soldier." Explaining her decision to resign, she continued, "I could not be satisfied . . . to see the girl interests entirely subordinated to the interests of the soldier and the only reason for caring for girls in detention homes or reformatories reduced to just that." Completing this private explanation, Miner noted, "This is the true reason about which I have not said very much." Though Miner was quite clear about her reason for leaving the CTCA, she did not articulate this openly in her official letter of resignation, nor had she "said very much" about it. Instead, Miner withdrew quietly to resume her efforts from outside the commission.[134]

Miner was not alone in her opposition to the growing repressiveness of the commission's law enforcement work. The War Department promoted antiprostitution efforts in order to protect the physical and moral health of the soldiers, but many women, like Maude Miner, came to their work with the CTCA with the interests of women foremost in their minds. For these reformers the direction in which the CTCA moved over the course of the war made their participation in its work increasingly uncomfortable. Some critics complained about the government's affirmation of the sexual double standard, which punished women but not men for sexual transgressions. Others felt that the CTCA and its officers penalized working-class women and the unescorted more commonly than other groups of citizens. Still others, particularly feminists, opposed the medical examinations, considering them outrageous and offensive.[135] Though a group of feminists opposing the increasingly repressive nature of the commission's work convened a conference in 1918 in order to "air their grievances," the CTCA's work was unaffected by this meeting, and the commission was able to continue its law enforcement program during the war with remarkably little open opposition.[136]

Following its reorganization the CTCA reported immediate progress in its efforts to facilitate the repression of prostitutes, promiscuous girls, and women infected with venereal disease. A report from the Section on Women and Girls of the Law Enforcement Division for the period from 16 June to 30 June 1918 listed several instances of communities providing the legal mechanism for the medical inspection of girls and women arrested for vagrancy or prostitution and the detention and quarantine of those found to be infected with venereal disease. In Texas, for instance, the state Prohibition Law and Social Hygiene Laws went into effect on 26 June, and in San Diego, "Conditions . . . have greatly improved in the last five months due to a stringent fornication act and to the stringent treatment of venereal diseases."[137]

The same report also documented the establishment of facilities for detention and quarantine. In Columbia, South Carolina, a clinic was established in the city jail and offered to the county for use as well. Greenville, South Carolina, reported purchase of a detention house, while in Louisiana the legislature passed a bill for the establishment of an institution for delinquent girls and the establishment of a venereal disease hospital. In Illinois two detention houses were projected. In Newport News, Virginia, a CTCA worker reported, "All girls of ill fame who are arrested are examined before trial, are held for quarantine after conviction, and serve their sentences after release from quarantine."[138]

Despite these successes other CTCA workers continued to cite problems in their ability to repress sexually active women and girls. The complaints usually focused on the lack of legal authority for the detention of these females and the shortage of facilities in which to hold them. In Illinois interpretations of the federal law prohibiting prostitution near the troops required evidence that women had been inmates of actual houses of prostitution before these women could be detained. A worker in Charlotte, North Carolina, reported, "Diseased girls are being released from prison, as it has not yet been decided how they could be held legally." Similarly, in Montgomery, Alabama, near Camp Sheridan, "Prostitutes are released when declared cured, and as yet it is impossible to secure any cooperation for long-term sentences. Several women have refused to go to the hospital and none of the officials have compelled them." In Deming, New Mexico, the more active efforts of the police to arrest prostitutes and examine them under the new Health Law provided an overflow of internees, halting the activities of the police.[139]

In July 1918 the CTCA received a boost from Congress's passage of the Chamberlain-Kahn Act, as part of the Army Appropriations Act.[140] This act created the new Interdepartmental Social Hygiene Board to direct the program of venereal disease control nationwide and granted $1 million to the War and Navy Departments to be used in a "civilian quarantine and isolation fund."[141]

The board immediately developed a variety of schemes for the provision of facilities for commitment, but its plans were disrupted when, on 26 November 1918, the comptroller of the Treasury ruled that the board had no authority to provide funding for construction, enlargement, or repairs on buildings that were not federal property. Forced to change its plans, the board used its funds to assist states in the maintenance of facilities, rather than for their construction.[142] Under these provisions, only one-fifth of the allotment was spent, and a great deal of construction planned by the board and advocated by the CTCA was abandoned.[143]

Though this setback undoubtedly limited the number of women ultimately detained under the CTCA's program of quarantine and detention, the commission nevertheless succeeded in implementing a broadly repressive program for the detention of prostitutes and promiscuous women and girls. Estimates of the number of women ultimately detained under the CTCA's law enforcement program and the Interdepartmental Social Hygiene Board's activities vary, but they generally suggest a figure around 30,000 women.[144] According to Thomas A. Storey, special consultant to the Interdepartmental Social Hygiene Board, forty-three federally aided detention houses and reformatories in communities near army and navy training camps detained 15,520 infected prostitutes during a twenty-seven month period from 1918 to 1920. These women were detained for an average of seventy days in the detention houses and one year in the reformatories. Further, this figure includes only those women held in federally aided detention houses and reformatories. Thousands more were surely detained in local jails.[145]

The women detained under this program were not necessarily prostitutes; they could be any venereally infected woman or girl or any sexually active female. Only one-third of those women detained during the war were charged with prostitution.[146] The crime for which women were punished was their failure to adhere to the progressive sexual code. Actions, or even tendencies, that strayed from this code were viewed as inherently immoral and illegal. With crime redefined in this way, the sexual act was no longer necessary to convince reformers of a woman's guilt. Guilt could be established on the basis of a woman's choice of amusements or clothing or on the basis of habits of posture or speech.

In this context class again played a substantial role in identifying troublesome women for the reformers. Field-workers of the CTCA often suggested they could easily identify dangerous women. In one instance a report from New Jersey suggested that promiscuous girls were easily identified by the way they danced. "The investigator attended a dance and personally danced with some of the young girls present," the report explained. "The manner of dancing by certain of these girls was so suggestive as to constitute almost positive proof of their indulging in sexual intercourse."[147] Similarly, prostitutes were easily identified, and investigators commented on "women quite obviously professional prostitutes of a very crude type" or "women who appeared to be prostitutes," without suggesting any substantive evidence that this was the case.[148] A report from Chillicothe, Ohio, suggested, "The worst kind of women do not parade the streets as the Girls' Protective League operates under the 'arrest on suspicion' rule, and strangers are not in town long before being picked up."[149] Identified not by any legally proscribed behavior, these women were presumed guilty on the basis of appearance.

Women who failed to exhibit the profile of a pure woman were assumed by the commission to be morally corrupt, the only alternative in the reformers' narrow notions of womanhood. As a result single, working-class women, caught alone on the street, or engaging in what progressive reformers considered suspect recreation, such as improper dancing, drinking, or visiting cafes unchaperoned, faced repression at the hands of the CTCA.

"Giving Jail Sentences to the Women and Fining the Men": The Repressive Program in Historical Perspective

The increasingly harsh measures taken against women were not matched by comparable actions against men involved in breaking the CTCA's moral tenets. Though Raymond Fosdick suggested in a letter in November 1917 that there was "a growing tendency to treat law breakers, whether they are men or women, on a par," this tendency was rarely discernible in practice.[150] A letter to the editor of the *San Diego Sun* pointed out the obvious gender and class discrimination inherent in the work of the CTCA and its field workers:

> So we are told that if an indecent dance is done by a male, it is to be laughed at. If by a female, what then? Are we to say we don't believe it, and so let it go on? If it is in a best hotel, yes? If in a cheap resort, raid it and publish the names? Oh, not if some of our "best" society is there. Our raiders are too honorable for that. Only in case there are found there two poor, foolish working girls; then blazon their names! Paint them in scarlet! And put them behind bars and boast that we are "cleaning up" our city![151]

The CTCA, pledged to eliminate the sexual double standard, instead reinforced that double standard, punishing women, especially working-class women, for illicit sexual activity, without developing comparable punishment for men.

On the local level the actions of police and courts of law punished women far more severely than their male counterparts. Women generally received harsher penalties than those soldiers coconspiring in their criminality. Reports on antivice work often suggested that whereas women were arrested, soldiers were released. For instance a report on Augusta, Georgia, explained:

> The sheriff of the county told me that on a recent raid on a country road he rounded up ten women with as many soldiers. He arrested the women but let the soldiers go free, one of the soldiers being a captain. Lewd women are dealt with severely in the police court and other courts in Augusta. Most generally they are given a work sentence without the alternative of a fine.[152]

In San Antonio citizens complained about the local policy by which the soldiers routinely escaped punishment. In one case an observer noted that "thirty three officers were caught in one raid and allowed to go scot-free, while of course the women were punished."[153] The soldier equivalent of arrest and internment for moral violations was the program of chemical prophylaxis discussed in chapter 2.

The inequity evident in these policies did not escape notice. In a report from San Francisco a local affiliate of the CTCA congratulated the work of a judge, suggesting, "He came through in great shape, giving jail sentences to the women and fining the men."[154] Observing this tendency, however, one citizen wrote to the War Department,

> It is understood that at this crisis the government is taking severe measures to suppress unfortunate women. Judges in San Francisco feel of course that they must support the authorities, though they, like many others regret harsh treatment towards women,—especially when the men go uncondemned and free. I am amongst those who would, sir, be thankful if more humane and equal measures could be taken.[155]

In other instances reports suggested the intention of communities to apply comparable sentences to men and women but their inability to follow through. In Houston, Texas, home of Camp Logan, the state law for quarantining diseased persons included both men and women, but by September 1918 it had not yet been applied to men "on account of the lack of suitable quarters at the farm, and also because men have been more prompt than women in reporting for treatment at the clinic."[156] These cases suggest that it was not necessarily the status as soldiers that prevented men from being punished similarly to women, but rather their gender.

Only rarely were men and women treated in a comparable way. In Detroit all arrested prostitutes were examined for venereal disease. Another regulation held that men found consorting with prostitutes were also considered to have been exposed to contagious disease and were to be detained and examined. In Norfolk, Virginia, too, ordinances required all arrested persons, male and female, to undergo medical examination.[157] Yet these statutes do little to imply a temperance of the attacks on women. Rather, they suggest that in a few instances communities extended the attacks to men as well.

Throughout the war the CTCA did engage in the prosecution of bootlegging, and here its targets were predominantly male. Section 12 of the Draft Act of 1917 gave the secretary of war the power to prohibit liquor in or near training camps, and it established bone-dry prohibition for all members of the American military. Members of the CTCA referred to vice and alcohol as "twin evils" and suggested that these dangers and the resulting venereal diseases constituted the central threats to the welfare of the men in uniform and to the progressives' broader goals.[158]

Throughout the course of the war the CTCA investigated, arrested, and prosecuted bootleggers and other purveyors of alcohol guilty of selling to men in uniform.

Yet, one cannot help but notice the CTCA's overwhelming preoccupation not with the issue of liquor, but with the issue of sexual behavior. Efforts to control alcohol use by the troops were motivated primarily by the desire to halt prostitution and prevent venereal disease among the men in uniform.[159] The antiliquor crusade never employed a network of personnel and plans as intricate as that designed for the eradication of vice.

Having gained soldier prohibition as a federal statute in the Draft Act, the CTCA hoped that strict enforcement of the federal law, with its provisions for heavy fines and imprisonment, would provide sufficient deterrence to soldiers and their civilian suppliers.[160] While encouraging local police and courts to punish bootleggers and providing investigators to uncover those criminals, the CTCA never engaged in an escalation of its crusade against alcohol similar to that in its crusade against vice. Unlike its position with antivice legislation, for instance, in which the CTCA even provided local communities with standard forms of appropriate laws to aid in the fight against prostitution, in the case of prohibition legislation the CTCA kept a distinct distance from local debates.

In many training camp communities heated contests over local prohibition ordinances ensued, with the prohibition forces eager to enlist the support of the CTCA. Though the commission never discouraged local communities from passing bone-dry legislation, it generally avoided any real involvement in local prohibition debates. In the fall of 1917 the city of San Diego, home of Camp Kearny, engaged in a struggle over the issue of local prohibition. The proposed ordinance was a strict one, calling for absolute prohibition, outlawing the presence of alcohol even in private homes. When in late October a citizen of San Diego wrote Secretary of War Baker for assistance in the local election, Chairman Fosdick replied politely,

> The War Department is unable to place itself on record, either as favoring or disapproving a local prohibition ordinance, such as you enclose. This is a matter for the community to decide for itself. At the same time, as the officer in charge of moral conditions in the neighborhood of military camps, I am bound to say that our task is greatly facilitated in dry communities.[161]

The issue of civilian prohibition seems to be one of the few instances in which the CTCA fulfilled its promise of deferring to local preferences. Though liquor continued to be a problem for the CTCA throughout the war, the commission never really changed its tactics for the suppression of alcohol and its purveyors.[162]

One could argue that this imbalance was the logical result of the commission's overarching concern with venereal disease. Because it was illicit sex, and not alcohol, that caused venereal disease, vice, rather than bootlegging, was the appropriate primary target for the commission. Although this argument should not be discounted, it does not explain the increasingly harsh character of the CTCA's attack on women suspected of immoral behavior, a harshness in stark opposition to the CTCA's purported allegiance to the single standard.

It is tempting to dismiss the harshness of the CTCA, of local police, and of the justice system as part of the war effort, as action appropriate to the war emergency. This argument is convenient, too, as it provides justification for the repression of women while men escaped largely unpunished for comparable acts. Yet this argument is too simple and fails to give adequate weight to the distinctly antifemale character of the law enforcement program.

The CTCA's harsh attitude toward what it viewed as immoral women was prompted most obviously by the practical reality of the continuing resistance of soldiers and civilians alike to the sexual code of the CTCA. Despite its early success with the red-lights, the CTCA continued to find prostitution a difficult and widespread problem in the training camp communities. Facing the continued rejection of its sexual code and the resilience and flexibility of the institution of prostitution, the CTCA chose to attack the vulnerable member of that institution, the individual prostitute. Vulnerable for the same reasons of class and gender that had often brought her to prostitution, the prostitute became the target of the CTCA's repressive program.[163]

The character of the attacks on prostitutes and potential prostitutes is also linked to the broad societal concern regarding the sexuality of women. The fallen woman, and even the woman who appeared a potential sexual transgressor, posed a challenge to order in this society. In the early twentieth century changes in the society brought on by industrialization, urbanization, and immigration caused many Americans to doubt the stability of their society. Concerns about manhood and womanhood were a part of those doubts.[164] In this setting the moral aspects of antivice efforts struck at much more than vice alone. Viewing women's purity as one of the bastions of order at a time when chaos seemed ready to overtake them, many Americans saw those who rejected the tenets of civilized morality as threats to society itself. Battling their own anxiety and threatened, even frightened, by the changes in American society, reformers may have attacked female promiscuity and even the appearance of promiscuity as one of the symbolic causes of the disordering of their society.[165]

In the context of war this struggle over female promiscuity took on new dimensions. The CTCA, attempting to use the war to combat this apparent disordering of American society, promoted a particular vision of womanhood that reasserted women's traditional morality. Here again, degenerate women posed a threat to the culture as they failed to adhere to the moral standards contained in that vision.

Further, contemporaries in 1917 and 1918 understood the actions of the CTCA as a necessary part of the war effort and easily justified them on that basis. Throughout their educational materials the CTCA exploited the rhetorical connection between their work and the war cause. With the sexual health of the soldiers raised to the level of public concern, the CTCA's efforts to protect that health became a form of Americanism, a valued part of the national crusade. In sharp contrast, prostitutes and promiscuous girls who endangered that health became subversives in the American imagination.[166] In letters to the War Department civilians referred to female camp followers as "the diseased vultures that hover around the outskirts" of camps and requested that they be "discovered, arrested, and put in detaining camps until the close of the war or for life." One letter writer demanded, "Shoot the lewd women as you would the worst German spy; they do more damage than all the spys *[sic]*. . . . My neighbors are legion who think as I have written."[167] In a nation at war repression of promiscuity became the repression of subversion, and it warranted the use of harsh measures.

Finally, the CTCA's program was strongly repressive precisely because it was allowed to be. Nothing the CTCA advocated was entirely new. Antiprostitution forces had long called for the closure of the vice districts, the arrest and prosecution of prostitutes, and the medical examination, detention, and long-term internment of prostitutes and delinquents alike. The difference, born of war-time circumstances, was that for the first time antiprostitution forces, especially those prioritizing efficiency, were endowed through the CTCA with federal power and broad public support to take any or all of these actions.[168] War-time demands for healthy troops, for the efficient use of American manpower, justified the use of any tactic necessary to ensure success. The CTCA was much harsher than those vice commissions and social hygiene reformers who preceded it simply because it had the power to be. The evolution of the CTCA's program was not inconsistent in any way with progressivism's expressed purposes or with the prewar programs of many reformers; rather, it was a natural extension of progressivism once empowered.

Yet, some members of the progressive coalition, particularly those most concerned with issues of social justice, decried the repressive program of the CTCA. For these reformers the CTCA's greater concern for efficiency than for the well-being of young women disappointed their hopes for the possibilities of the war and alienated them from the work of the commission.

In choosing to undertake their assault on female promiscuity the CTCA reformers revealed a continued adherence to the dichotomous image of woman as either virgin or whore. According to this view, some women warranted immediate inclusion in the commission's work. Others, though, warranted extensive incarceration for their unnatural immorality. Although these women might eventually become crusaders, this would be possible only after lengthy and far-reaching reformation. Penalizing women but not men for sexual adventuring, the CTCA reinforced the nineteenth-century sexual hierarchy and seemingly abandoned the single sexual standard, in the process undercutting their new woman before she had the chance to gain a firm footing.

The CTCA's inability to escape the stereotypes of its time was even more evident in its relations with African American soldiers and civilians. Seemingly unable to imagine these citizens as anything other than potentially criminal, the CTCA often treated African Americans as a marginal or even inherently deviant population. This tendency, indicative of the broader record of progressivism in the realm of race relations, prompted extensive resistance among African American citizens, who defied the CTCA's attempts to relegate them to a position of inferiority in the new national culture.

CHAPTER FIVE

Repression and Resistance: African Americans and the Progressives' National Community

> The Negro entered the world war and fought for a world democracy with the hope that he would enjoy, in common with those for whom he fought, the reasonable fruits of his effort—free speech, free press and protection of life, liberty, property and happiness. He never contemplated that the old regime of discrimination, segregation, proscription, mob law and unequal economic, civil and political rights would be again imposed on him.
>
> —*Atlanta Independent*, 26 July 1919

In late June 1918 Julius Rosenwald of the Council of National Defense, a man nationally known for his philanthropic contributions to African American education, received a letter from Henry J. Dannenbaum, "a leading citizen" of Houston, Texas.[1] The letter expressed Dannenbaum's concern regarding the dismal state of recreational facilities for African American soldiers training in San Antonio. "While in San Antonio last week I visited the Community House, a place on Alamo Plaza for the recreation of soldiers while in the city," Dannenbaum began. "It is a most attractive place and hundreds of Uncle Sam's boys were enjoying its facilities."[2] Dannenbaum's satisfaction at discovering this recreational center was tempered, however, by his realization that it catered to white soldiers only. "But none of his boys of the negro race were there nor are they provided with a similar social center," Dannenbaum continued. "Across the street I saw two negro soldiers, standing on the sidewalk, in the hot sun. I understand that San Antonio now contains ten thousand of the soldiers of that race."[3]

Dannenbaum worried that the experience of this "gross injustice" would embitter the hearts of these African Americans and impair their value as soldiers. "It would be unprofitable to discuss the reasons for this condition, to locate the responsibility," he maintained. "The fact is here, in San Antonio and elsewhere in the South where negro troops are being trained. I don't see how the Government can afford the condition to continue." Determined to promote the development of more equitable conditions, Dannenbaum concluded, "It seems to me either these troops should be encamped in sections where civilians will furnish them the same welfare agencies as are furnished the soldiers of the white race, or the Government should furnish the same." And further, "If neither remedy be possible, can you not possibly interest other wealthy men of your section to furnish the money with which to do the proper thing by these negro soldiers."[4]

Rosenwald was sympathetic to the plight of the African American soldiers described by Dannenbaum. After receiving this letter he forwarded it to Raymond Fosdick, the chairman of the Commission on Training Camp Activities. The commission, charged with responsibility for providing recreational facilities for all soldiers in the new National Army, had promised to fulfill this trust without discrimination on the basis of race.[5] Despite its policy, however, Rosenwald's letter describing the inadequacy of recreational facilities for African American soldiers in San Antonio recounted a situation common in training camp communities in 1917 and 1918. The problem in San Antonio was not an isolated case, but was, rather, representative.

From its beginning the CTCA pledged to institute a program for African American soldiers identical to that provided for white troops. This promise, however, was confounded by the War Department's willingness to adopt a policy of segregation among the troops, a policy that required dual recreational programs. The CTCA, like many Whites in the progressive movement more generally, viewed racial isolation as a shortcut to racial harmony. Acquiescing to the South's demands for segregation, the CTCA shouldered a new responsibility to create a separate but equal recreational program for African American troops.

Until very late in the war, however, the CTCA neglected this responsibility and approached what it viewed as the problem of African American soldiers as it did the problem of the African American community, primarily as a law enforcement issue. The CTCA seemed unable to visualize the same transformation among the African American populace that it hoped to cultivate among white Americans, suggesting many white progressives' inability to incorporate African Americans into their vision of a national community. Instead, embracing false assumptions and stereotypes regarding African Americans, the reformers emphasized repression and control rather than the positive remaking of men and women in their work with the African American community.

Despite the government's failure to provide adequately for the African American troops, African American civilians rushed to provide financing, facilities, and personnel for the furnishing of recreation for the men in arms. At the same time, many in the African American community also criticized the government's willingness to sacrifice African American rights to the cause of social stability. Finding themselves continually frustrated by the government's neglect and discrimination during the war, African Americans expressed opposition to the racism implicit in the CTCA's policy of segregation. In doing so African Americans represented perhaps the most vocal resistance to the cultural nationalism of the CTCA reformers.

Late in the war the CTCA acknowledged the shortcomings of its recreation program for African Americans and attempted to ameliorate the most blatant examples of discrimination. Like many white progressives, however, the CTCA never rejected segregation. Eager to maintain racial peace in the training camps and their communities, the CTCA instead adopted and retained a policy that led only to racial animosity.

"The Race Segregation System Will Be Carefully Observed": Defining a Racial Policy

When African American draftees answered the call to arms in September 1917, they did so in an environment charged with anxiety, hostility, and fear regarding their participation in the armed forces. Years of violence against African Americans had climaxed in the summer of 1917 in a flurry of race riots nationwide. Though racial violence was traditionally associated with the South, the mob violence in the summer of 1917 spread throughout the country like an epidemic, unconcerned with regional distinctions. Riots flared in Chicago, New York, and Newark in the North, in addition to Danville, Lexington, and Waco in the South. It was East St. Louis, Illinois, though, that experienced the worst incident of racial violence that summer. A month of sporadic unrest in that city resulted in a race riot that left nine Whites and a larger number of African Americans dead, as well as over one hundred African Americans injured.[6]

The United States had a long history of racial violence, and so these incidents were notable not so much for their violent character as for their size and prevalence.[7] Large-scale riots signaled an escalating problem of racial animosity, and their appearance throughout the country demonstrated that the problem was national in scope. The great migration of African Americans northward beginning at the turn of the century and growing exponentially in the years after Europe's descent into war had exacerbated racial tensions in both the North and the South. By the summer of 1917 the issue of race relations was a serious problem no longer isolated in the southern states.

With American entry into war the Wilson administration struggled with decisions regarding the use of African American soldiers in the American war effort. The relationship between progressivism and the African American community had always been complex and troubled. In the North the movement had occasionally enlisted African American reformers whose concerns centered on issues relevant to the African American community. The National Association for the Advancement of Colored People, for instance, constituted a classically progressive organization, and individuals like W. E. B. Du Bois and Ida B. Wells employed progressive tactics—education, legal action, and mass organizing—to pursue notably progressive goals such as economic opportunity, political equality, and social justice.[8] Yet the progressive movement was dominated by white Americans who directed their reform energies to helping other white Americans.[9] In the South white progressives had often been aggressively hostile to the interests of African Americans, understanding segregation and the disfranchisement of Blacks as "seminal 'progressive' reform."[10] In his first administration President Wilson had demonstrated his ties to southern progressivism in his efforts to extend segregation to federal offices and bureaus.[11]

When the United States entered the war, African Americans disagreed about the appropriate response to the looming war effort. A few leading voices, including A. Philip Randolph, counseled against support for the war, while others, for instance Rev. Adam Clayton Powell, Sr., argued in favor of a more tempered response to the war effort, encouraging African Americans to exchange their participation for a guarantee of improved conditions. Most, though, including most notably W. E. B. Du Bois, called on African Americans to join with other citizens in support of the war cause. If for some African Americans patriotism recommended that they set aside racial struggles for the war's duration, for many others service in the war effort seemed to hold the promise of immediate economic opportunity and a chance to encourage broader social and political improvements for African Americans after the war.[12]

President Wilson did not fail to understand the importance of cultivating African American support for the war effort. Despite his sympathy with southern progressivism and the potent opposition of white southerners to African American military service, Wilson conceded to the demands of the African American community that their men be given the chance to serve, and he supported the drafting of African American males. As a result the Draft Act of May 1917 called for the registration of black and white men alike.[13]

The decision to enlist African American soldiers raised additional questions for the decision makers in the War Department, in particular questions regarding the encampment and training of these troops. Many white southerners, fearing armed rebellion by African American soldiers, advocated the encampment of black troops in small units, preferably in the North. Though willing to acknowledge southern concerns, the War Department was nevertheless determined that the South should cooperate in the provision of training facilities for African American troops.[14] Before the administration could resolve the issues revolving around the African American soldiers, however, an incident in Houston, Texas, demonstrated the volatility of American race relations.

On the night of 23 August 1917, African American regulars of the 24th Infantry's 3rd Battalion, stationed at Camp Logan outside Houston, Texas, stormed into that city and in an assault lasting only two hours shot and killed sixteen white civilians and injured twelve others. Four black soldiers also died as a result of the riot.[15] This episode was distinctly different from other racial incidents in the summer of 1917. In Houston armed African Americans attacked the white community in a reversal of roles that shocked white America.

Relations between the African American regulars and local police had been strained throughout the month during which the 24th Infantry had been stationed in Houston, largely because of the city's Jim Crow laws. The city of Houston, in an open display of hostility toward the African American troops, had responded to their arrival with a tightening of their segregation strictures. The men of the 24th, unused to such blatant discrimination and unwilling to endure it, violated the restrictions in street cars and theaters. Their resistance led to conflicts with local police and eventually to arrests and beatings of African American soldiers. Finally, on 23 August the anger of the African American troops erupted over an incident that began with a soldier's attempt to prevent the police from beating an African American woman and ended with rumors that another soldier, inquiring after the first soldier's welfare, had been killed by the Houston police.[16]

Although it was clear that the dispute over local Jim Crow laws lay at the center of the hostility between police and soldiers, white observers at the time interpreted this problem very differently. Many southern Whites blamed the hostility on the African American troops, who, they claimed, ignored local standards of behavior and antagonized the white community. As one southern newspaper explained, "Experience has shown that a large percentage of negroes in the army, when let loose with arms and ammunition in a Southern community, especially if they are Northern negroes, will assume an arrogant swagger which is calculated to precipitate trouble."[17] Both angered and frightened by the riot in Houston, white southerners called for the removal of all African American troops from their region.

Many African American newspapers were quick to condemn the murderous acts of the Houston regulars, but many of these same newspapers also maintained that the men were less guilty than those who had provoked them. The *Washington Bee*, while maintaining that guilt lay on both sides, asserted, "In general, however, the attitude of the Southern white man is intensely provocative toward the negro soldier. . . . The negro soldier feels himself a man and expects to be treated like a man. . . . The Southern white man as a rule demands of the negro the attitude of a servant."[18] And further, "These colored soldiers were systematically insulted and harassed by the local police. Individuals were assaulted or arrested on frivolous grounds. They were called 'niggers' and at every turn were hustled and jostled." Noting that the soldiers had "killed a number of the scoundrels who had been systematically annoying them," the paper concluded, "We make no apology for them. True, they violated the civil law. True, they violated the military law, and were for the time in a state of technical mutiny. But there is a higher law."[19] Though widely condemning the attack on Houston, many African Americans sympathized with the plight of the black regulars.

The response of the War Department to the Houston disaster was swift and harsh and demonstrated no similar sympathy.[20] The entire 3rd Battalion was placed under arrest and shipped to New Mexico. An investigation of the incident began immediately. Six weeks later sixty-three members of the battalion were charged with disobedience of orders, aggravated assault, mutiny, and murder. At the conclusion of the largest court-martial ever held, thirteen men were sentenced to death and forty-three to life imprisonment. Three days after the decision, without allowing time for an appeal, the army executed the thirteen men. As a result of subsequent trials, six other soldiers would eventually hang for the incident in Houston. In its unwillingness to consider the complexities of the situation in Houston or to lay the blame more broadly for the tragedy that occurred there, the War Department demonstrated its acceptance of the discriminatory racial policies of the southern states and its unwillingness to promote a change in American race relations.

The Houston riot had not eliminated the policy decisions facing the War Department but had only complicated them. In the wake of the Houston tragedy the War Department convened a conference to consider the issues surrounding African American men in uniform. As a result of the conference, the War Department appointed Emmett J. Scott to serve as a special assistant to the secretary of war. He was to be a "confidential advisor in matters affecting the interests of the 10,000,000 Negroes of the United States, and the part they are to play in connection with the present war."[21] Scott, the former private secretary of Booker T. Washington, was still associated with the Tuskegee Institute at the time of his appointment. Scott's assignment was an important acknowledgement of the needs of African Americans; however, the selection of Scott was a safe move for the War Department, given Scott's well-known moderate stance on racial issues.

The War Department ultimately settled on a policy for the encampment of African American soldiers that distributed black trainees throughout the camps, in the South as well as in the North. This prevented the concentration of African Americans at any one camp and quelled southern fears of large-scale armed revolts by the African American troops. It also forced the southern states to accept their share of African American recruits. The War Department also agreed to the training of one all-black combat division. Many southern whites viewed this decision as a tremendous concession to African Americans, but it did little to change their fundamental status in the army. The majority of African American draftees still served as laborers for the army, and the War Department never questioned the segregation of African American soldiers by unit.

These early decisions regarding the encampment and training of African American troops were consistent with the basic policy the War Department eventually applied to all issues related to race during the war. Early in the war Secretary of War Newton D. Baker expressed his intention to navigate a safe middle course through the difficult issues of American racial policy. "As you know," he began, "it has been my policy to discourage discrimination against persons by reasons of their race. This policy has been adopted not merely as an act of justice to all races that go to make up the American people, but also to safeguard the very institutions which we are now at the greatest sacrifice engaged in defending, and which any racial disorders must endanger." "At the same time," Baker asserted, "there is no intention on the part of the War Department to undertake at this time to settle the so-called race question."[22] Though suggesting his determination to prevent discrimination against any of Uncle Sam's soldiers, Baker nevertheless expressed his own unwillingness to undo the existing racial policy as defined by the southern states.

It was this policy that the War Department applied to all questions regarding African American troops during the course of the war, including the issue of recreation for African American soldiers. Throughout the war the CTCA voiced its adherence to the policy of fairness and nondiscrimination in all of its programs. As the acting chairman of the CTCA explained, "The Commission is just as much interested in the entertainment to be provided for colored soldiers as for white, and we are endeavoring to make a program to fit all races and creeds, without distinction in favor of any."[23] Inside the camps the affiliated organizations were pledged to a nondiscrimination policy. As Raymond Fosdick noted, "Many firesides glow for the boys in the training camps. The Y.M.C.A., the Y.W.C.A., the Knights of Columbus and the Jewish Welfare Board all have 'club rooms' in the camps to which all soldiers regardless of race and creed are welcomed."[24] The War Camp Community Service, responsible for recreation out in the communities near the camps, also adopted a policy that acknowledged the WCCS's responsibility to the African American troops and their civilian neighbors. Describing the work being done in Columbia, South Carolina, for the troops of Camp Jackson, Fosdick assured Baker in a letter in October 1917, "This committee will take up for the colored troops very much the same activities that our main committee on training camp activities is taking up for the white soldiers." And further: "The whole spirit of the work is to provide wholesome leisure time activities for the colored troops in the same general way as we do for the white. These activities will be conducted by the colored people with such assistance from our committee of white people as may be needed."[25]

Yet these assurances of fairness masked a commitment to segregation to which the Commission on Training Camp Activities adhered tenaciously throughout the war. Continuing his letter to the secretary of war, Raymond Fosdick asserted, "The colored soldiers will be kept as far as possible in the colored sections, and the white soldiers in the white section." "In other words," Fosdick concluded, "the race segregation system will be carefully observed."[26] In the training camp communities and inside the camps the CTCA's policy of nondiscrimination and fairness often coexisted with a policy of segregation.

Although the CTCA never adopted a policy strictly requiring segregation in its programs, it advocated such a policy whenever local conditions recommended it. As Secretary of War Baker explained, "As a matter of fact the colored people and the white people in this country have lived together now for a good many years and have established relationships in the several parts of the country which are more or less well organized and acquiesced in."[27] If these relationships could be allowed to continue unmolested, the War Department maintained, the chances of peaceful relations between the races would be enhanced. If the particular relationship involved segregation, the need for racial peace recommended its acceptance.

After the incident in Houston the CTCA was anxious to convince African Americans to accept the unpopular policy of segregation, and a program of persuasion was early adopted by the commission. The War

Camp Community Service, concerned with the relations between soldiers and civilians, undertook the task of acquainting the men in uniform with "the customs, laws and observances of the cities in which they are temporarily living." Suggesting the importance WCCS workers placed on this task, one WCCS publicist topped her list of the activities "which are proving most helpful in War Camp Community Service for colored troops," with "the interpretation to the negroes of the customs and observances of the community of which they are a part."[28] Similarly, describing the progress of the WCCS in its first six months, a report on the work in Alabama noted, "Committees have been organized among the colored citizens to carry out a program for the colored troops to whom a careful explanation of southern customs and of Alabama laws affecting the negro has been given."[29] Determined to solve the problem of race relations by accepting local traditions as defined by white residents, the CTCA intended to convince African American soldiers to accept segregation without protest.

"We Have No Suitable Place": Segregation in the Positive Programs

When the War Department finally called up the first African American draftees in September 1917, the implications of a segregated recreation program were immediately clear. Despite the CTCA's promises of fair and equal treatment, both inside the camp gates and in the neighboring civilian communities, demands for segregated facilities led to a severe shortage of recreational opportunities for African American soldiers.

The CTCA had already begun to develop an extensive in-camp recreation program by the time the African American soldiers reported for duty. The segregation of facilities, however, meant that most of the existing facilities or programs could not serve African American troops. Affiliated organization huts serving white soldiers had to be supplemented by additional huts for African Americans. Athletics had to be separately organized to prevent any interracial meetings on the playing field. The YWCA had to provide separate Hostess Houses to serve the African American soldiers' visitors. Until the CTCA and its affiliates duplicated each of these programs, the African American soldiers in many camps had no recreational opportunities, despite the existence of a comprehensive program of in-camp entertainment.

When the first African American draftees reported to camp, however, the CTCA and its affiliates had not even begun this work. The indecision surrounding the black troops' encampment was in part responsible for the delay. J. S. Tichenor of the YMCA explained on 11 September 1917, "The whole question of Association work with colored troops is to be taken up just as soon as we can get definite information as to the number involved and the special camps to which they will be assigned."[30] The affiliated organizations, as well as the army, hesitated to provide any facilities until the permanent encampment of African American troops at a given cantonment seemed certain. Given the general uncertainty surrounding the placement of the various African American units, this hesitancy was a common problem.[31] In addition to requirements of permanency, the number of African American soldiers residing in a camp also regulated the construction or coordination of recreational facilities, and so the determination to avoid encamping large numbers of African Americans in any single camp also worked against their acquisition of an adequate recreation program.[32]

As a result of these controls on the provision of in-camp recreation, African American soldiers experienced a shortage of facilities inside camps all across the country. The shortage of Hostess Houses to accommodate visitors was perhaps felt most keenly.[33] A chaplain at Camp Sherman, in Chillicothe, Ohio, wrote to Emmett J. Scott in May 1918:

> There are in camp between two thousand and three thousand soldiers of our race. These men are constantly visited by their relatives and friends and we have no place where these visitors might be cared for. . . . We have no suitable place where we might meet our company and guests—in fact, the situation is embarrassing. On the other hand, the white soldiers have ample accommodations and conveniences.[34]

The situation at Camp Sherman was by no means uncommon.[35] Though African American troops first began reporting for service in September 1917, the first Hostess House for African American soldiers did not open until April 1918.[36]

An investigation of eleven training camps made for the Military Intelligence Division discovered a continuing failure to provide adequate accommodations for African American women in the training camps even in late 1918. The report noted,

> Unfortunately, no provision was made at any of the camps for a rest room for colored women. In some of the camps the Y.M.C.A. agents saw the necessity of such accommodations and took it upon themselves to set aside a room in their building for this purpose. Such accommodations, however, were necessarily inadequate. In all camps there are ample rest rooms for white women. . . . Camp Taylor was the only camp at which I found a hostess house and this was a very small building which was not put up for that purpose. In several other camps hostess houses were being constructed. Everywhere I found bitter comment on account of the failure of the government to provide for colored women at the camps while every possible comfort was provided for white women.[37]

YMCA clubs for African American soldiers were similarly segregated and also insufficient. In June 1918 the executive secretary of the CTCA wrote the YMCA regarding the conditions for the ten thousand black soldiers at Camp Johnston in Jacksonville, Florida: "I am informed by Mr. Scott of the War Department, that the colored men are without any recreational activities, and that they are in great need."[38] Again, the situation at Camp Johnston reflected a general tendency to underserve African American men in uniform that was especially pronounced in southern camps, where segregation ruled. As a report for the Military Intelligence Division in December 1918 suggested, "It has been the policy of the Y.M.C.A. to provide one hut for every 3,000 soldiers. The Y.M.C.A. has not been able, in many instances, to reach this standard of equipment for the colored soldiers, while, perhaps in the same camp, reaching a closer approximation to it in the case of the white soldiers." This problem would not have been so severe were it not for the policy of segregation. The report continued, "It is understood that, in general, the Y.M.C.A.s for white soldiers do not promote the use of their facilities by colored soldiers and this is felt by the latter."[39] As an investigator explained more specifically,

> There are only a few camps where regular Y.M.C.A. huts have been available for the use of colored soldiers. In some places where there were several thousand colored soldiers in camp, colored Y.M.C.A. agents have been forced to carry on their work in tents or in mess halls ill adapted for

> this service, while in the same camps as many as six or seven Y.M.C.A. huts were available for white troops.

In this context the intransigence of the Whites-only huts in their refusal to serve the black soldiers was outrageous. This investigator explained, "In some camps where the Y.M.C.A. service was inadequate, colored soldiers were even refused the privilige *[sic]* of buying postage stamps at huts set aside for white troops, and at one camp a sign was displayed on a Y.M.C.A. hut which read: 'Colored soldiers not served here by order of military authorities.' "[40]

The injustice of the segregation system in the recreation program was particularly harsh given the wealth of in-camp recreational opportunities for white soldiers. Noting the disparity in facilities, a chaplain from Hattiesburg, Mississippi, wrote to Emmett J. Scott in April 1918:

> Dear Sir:—this come to let you know about some things at Camp Shelby. Mississippi i was appointed visiting chaplain . . . now in visiting i found the White Soldiers nicely provided for. With Houses fited *[sic]* for Religious Service. But no place for the Colored Soldiers. i am asking you to take it up with the Department and have a place fitted up for the colored Soldiers at Camp Shelby. Miss. for Religious instructions.[41]

The YMCA huts opposed discrimination on the basis of religion and supplied time and space in their huts for the religious observances of non-Protestant troops, but the policy of segregation sometimes prevented their extending similar privileges for the religious observances of African American soldiers.

Similarly, an African American observer noted regarding the service of the YMCA at Camp Lee in Virginia, "The Y.M.C.A. service and accommodation for the colored troops is very good, but very inadequate." Though roughly one-seventh of the troops at Camp Lee were African American, they were granted the use of only one of the twelve YMCA huts in camp. "The full significance of this will not be gotten," the observer explained,

> unless you hold in mind the fact that a Negro soldier at Camp Lee can get absolutely no sort of service from the Y.M.C.A. buildings for the whites, not even a postage stamp or a drink of water. . . . On the other hand, three

> or four hundred white soldiers whose barracks happen to be a little nearer the colored Y.M.C.A. quarters than to any white quarters, are willingly accorded every service and courtesy of the colored building.[42]

The inadequacy of in-camp programs for African American soldiers was particularly acute in the South. As one investigator explained in a report on the "Condition Among Negro Troops at Camp Mills," a camp located in New York, "The Y.M.C.A., the K. of C. and the Y.M.H.A. all welcome the colored soldiers in their buildings." And further, "The Y.M.C.A. shows a different attitude to the colored soldiers in this camp than they do in Southern camps. In the South they set aside a separate building in each camp for the colored soldiers. Here they receive all alike."[43] Though the Knights of Columbus and the Young Men's Hebrew Association were reputed to treat all soldiers equally throughout the camps, the YMCA apparently adapted its policies to match local custom.[44] Throughout the South and in some northern camps this involved segregated soldier huts and resulted in the failure to provide appropriately for African American soldiers.[45]

Certainly there were isolated cases in which the provision of recreational facilities inside the camps was adequate. In some northern camps entertainment and recreation was provided for soldiers without regard to race. At Camp Grant in Illinois, for instance, "all recreational centers inside the camp, such as Liberty Theater, Y.M.C.A., Auditorium, etc. are open to all alike."[46] At Camp Sherman in Ohio the YMCA maintained one hut "devoted entirely to the welfare of the colored soldier" but welcomed African American troops at all of their facilities.

Despite segregation, an occasional southern camp was also able to provide for the African Americans adequately. At Camp Gordon, outside Atlanta, Georgia, for instance, the CTCA prided itself on the extensive recreation program available for African American troops inside the camps. By November 1917 the CTCA's athletic director coordinated a program of baseball, rugby, basketball, volleyball, soccer, quoits, and medicine ball, and the YMCA staff sought to make building number 154, the YMCA hut for African American soldiers, "as home like as possible for the fellows." At the same time three hundred men were enrolled in elementary education through the YMCA, and many had already learned to sign their names and to write "several words." For those already able to read, Atlanta University had provided books for the in-camp library for African American troops.[47] Yet the case of Camp Gordon was the exception, not the rule. In most training camps across the country African American soldiers suffered from a shortage of recreational facilities that was particularly obvious and significant in the context of the broad provision of facilities for white soldiers.[48]

This failure inside the camps only enhanced the CTCA's responsibility in the communities. Having segregated in-camp recreation so that African American soldiers often found recreational opportunities sharply limited, the CTCA unconsciously encouraged African American soldiers to leave camp in pursuit of entertainment—a position counter to the CTCA's purpose of using adequate recreation inside the camps as a way to limit the soldiers' trips to neighboring communities. Unfortunately, by encouraging acceptance of segregation in the communities as well, the CTCA again constricted the recreational opportunities available for African American soldiers.

A variety of problems in the communities themselves complicated the provision of recreation for African American soldiers. First of all, many white citizens greeted the news of the encampment of African Americans soldiers near their communities with open hostility. When the African American officers' training school at Camp Dodge opened in the summer of 1917, for instance, "The people of Des Moines, a few miles north of the camp, protested vigorously when it was announced that the Government intended to establish negro training-quarters so near to their city."[49]

The open hostility ensured the need for segregated recreation, at the same time enhancing the difficulty of raising sufficient funds for a duplicate program for African American soldiers. The small size of the African American community near many northern camps, combined with the hostility of Whites and the insistence on segregation, left African American soldiers with little hope for reasonable recreation.[50] In Des Moines, for instance, "There were not many colored families of their own type to provide pleasant association . . . and although granted equal rights with the white men through the laws of Iowa, the negro soldiers could not comfortably put this theory into practice." Describing more general problems, the WCCS explained further:

> The lack of funds at first offered another obstruction to the immediate provision of adequate recreational facilities. A further lack—that of understanding among both colored and white civilians of the aim of those benefi-

cent activities—hindered the progress of the work in many communities. Occasionally mistrust, sometimes indifference, often inexperience impeded progress.[51]

Reports noting the shortage of recreation for African American soldiers visiting neighboring civilian communities were plentiful. One CTCA worker reported in March 1918, "Very little has been done in Little Rock for the colored soldiers." A report from Newport News, Virginia, that same week suggested, "No recreation is provided for the colored stevedore regiment at Camp Hill." And from Charlotte, North Carolina, a report in April 1918 stated: "There are practically no recreational opportunities for colored people in Charlotte. There is no movie, no YMCA." Or as a report on eleven camp communities suggested regarding WCCS provisions for African American troops in late 1918, "In many instances accommodations were long delayed and have only been recently established."[52]

It appears that the community recreation programs in the North served African American troops considerably more effectively than those in the South.[53] H. S. Braucher, the executive secretary of the WCCS, explained the difficulties of organizing in the South: "In general recreational facilities for colored people in the South are very poor. It has been hard enough to get the leading people in the South to make provision for the municipal recreation centers for the white people, but it has been very nearly impossible to secure any appropriation at all adequate for the colored people."[54] In northern communities, by contrast, the WCCS sometimes succeeded in developing a community recreation program that served African Americans. In some northern cities facilities were open to all without regard to race, making the job of the WCCS significantly easier.[55] New York City, for instance, was heralded for its outstanding provisions for African American troops.[56]

Despite the negligence of the CTCA, the African American community was often active in efforts to coordinate recreation for the black men in uniform, both inside and outside the camp gates. The initiative and enthusiasm of the African American community of Atlanta, for instance, was at least partially responsible for the success of the CTCA program inside Camp Gordon.[57] Similarly, African American citizens of Montgomery, Alabama, were quick to address the needs of their black neighbors at Camp Sheridan in the fall of 1917. As a result of their formation of a Central Committee on Entertainment, by the end of October 1917 African American citizens of Montgomery had organized a vast recreational network for the military men. Inside the camp local clergy had conducted services, and citizens had sent books, magazines, and newspapers for the troops. In Montgomery soldiers had been invited to visit the local churches, with dinner invitations from church members a common occurrence. The central committee had also organized a community chorus including both soldiers and civilians, had planned a trip to the Tuskegee Institute for men from the camp, had opened a rest room for the soldiers in town, and had hosted a "grand public reception" for the men of the 9th Ohio.[58]

The energetic efforts of African American citizens in communities near the training camps could not always guarantee the men a comprehensive recreation program, however. While the CTCA rushed to coordinate the efforts of white civilians and to lend money, personnel, and expertise to local white organizers, rarely did the CTCA reach out to African American activists in a similar manner. The example of the CTCA's indifference in Atlanta, Georgia, demonstrates how the commission's negligence often caused the frustration of sincere efforts on the part of the African American community to provide for the black men in uniform.

Even before the opening of Camp Gordon outside of Atlanta, a committee of African American citizens met and organized what they termed the Colored Committee to coordinate recreation for the future black soldiers of the camp. With the arrival of African American troops this committee worked to send entertainers to the camp and to coordinate a community recreation program for African American soldiers visiting Atlanta. Local citizens responded with enthusiasm, and by August efforts to serve the men in camp began to take shape in Atlanta's African American community. Black churches invited soldiers to supper with their members. A local Social Charity Club changed its aims "from a social nature to welfare work for the colored soldiers." "Hereafter," the club noted, "we will devote our time to the entertaining of those of our loved ones who are now engaged in serving their country, of whom the race is very proud." The local African American newspaper, the *Atlanta Independent*, spearheaded a drive to supply the men in camp with newspapers, and the local African American baseball team, the Atlanta Cubs, opened their 1918 season against an African American team from Camp

Gordon. In the spring of 1918 African American soldiers and civilians joined in a grand parade as part of the War Savings Stamps drive. The parade was led by one thousand African American soldiers from Camp Gordon, who were joined by fifteen thousand African American residents of Atlanta.[59]

Despite this obvious groundswell of activity in the African American community of Atlanta, the CTCA failed to coordinate these efforts into an organized community recreation program and instead thwarted the efforts of the local African American community. The CTCA failed to acknowledge the existing Colored Committee; instead, it formed its own committee of Whites, designated as the Committee on Colored Cooperation. This new committee held no meetings, but the original Colored Committee continued to meet. Finally, in July 1918, the head of the Colored Committee wrote to the chairman of the CTCA to express his disillusionment. "In every way possible," he explained, "it seemed that discouragement was placed in the way of the colored committee. There was no such things as cooperation." He continued: "Whenever an attempt was made by the Colored Committee to do something which they believed to be in line with their wishes it was blotted and eventually stopped. The result is that nothing has been done for Colored Soldiers at Camp Gordon who come into the city of Atlanta."[60] Another report in October outlined the same conditions, noting, "The War Camp Community Service has made practically no provision for the colored soldiers in Atlanta."[61]

Not only was there no effort by the CTCA to organize recreation for African American soldiers in Atlanta, but the soldiers were also excluded from activities to which they surely warranted an invitation. After the city hosted a parade with seven thousand participants that rebuffed the African American community as well as the African American soldiers at Camp Gordon in October 1917, the *Atlanta Independent* queried,

> What would have delighted the soldier boys of Camp Gordon and the officers from Des Moines, Iowa, and the thousands of Negro school children more than to have had an opportunity to have displayed their patriotic spirit and their loyalty to the flag and to have marched in the parade along with their white citizens? Nothing in the world. They would have vied with their white fellow citizens in displaying the martial spirit. But not a single colored person was invited to take part; it was a burning shame and a reflection upon the great city of Atlanta!

Reminding their readers that the African American soldiers were volunteering to fight for their country, the newspaper concluded, "Yet they were snubbed and treated like scullions. . . . They were not wanted—actions spoke louder than words."[62] Though the CTCA was successful inside Camp Gordon, it failed to harness the energy of the African American community of Atlanta, alienating once enthusiastic supporters of its work. Here, as in countless other training camp communities, the CTCA's acceptance of segregated recreation resulted in a desperate shortage of recreational opportunities for African American soldiers.

The CTCA did sponsor occasional events in which Black and White participated together, breaking out of the confines of segregation.[63] All too often, though, African Americans were invited to participate in these events only as entertainers. It was in this stereotyped role that African Americans were most commonly admitted by the CTCA and the white community into the broader recreational life of the training camps and of the local communities.

This tendency was clearly marked in Des Moines, Iowa, home of Camp Dodge, where the African Americans' presence had been greeted initially by cold hostility. The CTCA later boasted of its tremendous success at improving relations between the races by way of community singing, featuring the African American troops. "Community singing and a colored military review at the Drake Stadium through the offices of the War Camp Community Service where the troops were shown in a complimentary light," the WCCS suggested, "helped to solve the difficulty somewhat, for such a dignified public appearance and the splendid singing characteristic of the race, stimulated sympathy and approval in the minds of the citizen spectators."[64] Another report suggested,

> The War Camp Community Service of Des Moines is justly proud of its accomplishment in creating among the citizens of the community a spirit of appreciation of the ability of the colored soldier and the service he is performing for his country. Possibly no one thing has been more helpful in bringing about this feeling than the community sing held at the Stadium of Drake University in July where 12,000 people gathered together. The singing of national hymns and of negro melodies by the colored soldiers will long be remembered.[65]

Casting the African American troops in the role of entertainers, the CTCA welcomed them to a community event. It was in this role, too, that the white people of Des Moines were willing to accept the African American men in uniform as a part of the public life of the community.[66]

Inside the camps, too, African American soldiers often found the acceptance normally denied them in the recreational arena when they arrived as performers. At Camp Logan, for instance, African American troops often entertained the white men in camp. "The ladies of Houston have entered heartily into the plan to provide wholesome entertainment for the men at Camp Logan, and each week parties of musicians, readers and other artists give enjoyable programs at several of the Y.M.C.A. buildings," the *Camp Logan Reveille* explained. "A new feature that has been secured," the article continued, "is the minstrel show from the 15th Division Labor Battalion, composed of negroes. In this organization are a number of clever artists and they put on a show that has been much enjoyed by the white soldiers. These minstrels have already visited several 'Y' buildings and next Friday evening they will be at Building No. 48."[67] At Camp Devens, near Ayer, Massachusetts, too, the soldier paper advertised "negro entertainers" who had performed at Hut 22 the past Friday. "It was those negro boys!" the report exclaimed, "those melody mixers of Dixie Land, that land of moonlight serenades and banjo strumming." And further, "They had a jazz band in that company, and, boys, it's one of those zippy, quippy, rippy kind!"[68] African American soldiers, often excluded from enjoying the facilities of the all-white Y huts, could sometimes gain open access only through the back door as entertainers.

Casting African American troops as entertainers, rather than as soldiers, the CTCA, and much of white America, found a black man in uniform it could accept. As the *Montgomery Emancipator* suggested, "Not only in the war zones abroad, but here in the various military training camps in America, the Negro is singing and laughing his way into the hearts of his white fellow soldiers."[69]

African Americans were aware of the irony inherent in the CTCA's use of the black soldier as entertainer. After an African American band played at an all-white patriotic rally in Baltimore, the *Afro-American* ran an article entitled "Colored People Barred From Patriotic Rally—Though Band Played, The Meeting Was Only For the White People—Colored Patriots Not Admitted." The newspaper suggested, "Much indignation has been expressed among the colored people of the city because all Negroes were excluded from the patriotic rally."[70] The African American community was well aware that the acceptance its soldiers found as entertainers did not lessen the discrimination those same soldiers endured when they stepped off the stage.

African American women and girls shared the neglect faced by the men in uniform, as the CTCA also delayed the establishment of recreation for African American civilians. A report on Charlotte, North Carolina, in April 1918 suggested the CTCA's failure to develop positive programs for African American girls. "It has been reported that there is great need for recreational work among the colored population at Charlotte, North Carolina," the report began. "There are so few recreational facilities that the colored girls are obliged to walk the streets, with a consequence that much prostitution is being carried on by these young men and girls."[71] By summer 1918, however, the CTCA was still discussing the possibilities for positive recreational work with girls, reflecting the continuing absence of any real progress in this program.[72]

From the beginning the CTCA expressed a strong commitment to the provision of protective work for African American girls. In August 1917 H. S. Braucher announced to his field workers the importance of this work: "In cities where there is a large colored population special attention should be given by our workers to our protective work for colored girls. It has been suggested that there ought to be special police women to work among the colored girls."[73] Even this program, with its more repressive tone, remained underdeveloped by the CTCA. As historian John F. Piper notes, "Even the Negro prostitutes faced a serious plight, for few cities had Negro women workers or police women to deal with them."[74]

The commission was no less negligent in providing social hygiene education for African Americans. The CTCA assumed the ignorance of African Americans. This assumption led the commission to two contradictory responses to the issue of the provision of sex education. On the one hand, the CTCA suggested the tremendous importance of educating the African American population about social hygiene.[75] On the other hand, a belief that African Americans might prove ineducable contributed to the commission's sluggish development of a sex education program for them.[76]

The CTCA social hygiene work with African American soldiers moved haltingly until the summer of 1918. A memo from the Social Hygiene Instruction Division in February 1918 announced the intentions of the commission to adapt the educational material for use with African American soldiers.[77] By April 1918, however, little progress was evident.

Though the commission was working on establishing a separate series of lectures on venereal disease for African American soldiers, those lectures remained in the planning stage.[78] Some African American troops did attend lectures on social hygiene, but the program remained disorganized and haphazard.[79] It was not until June 1918 that the plans of the Social Hygiene Division for a separate education program geared to the African American troops began to solidify.[80] Work on a civilian social hygiene education program was similarly slow moving.[81]

The CTCA's failure to provide adequate recreation or sex education for African American men and women is striking, given the commission's powerful commitment to these programs and its broad success in providing them for white troops and civilians. Though the CTCA practiced neglect in providing for African Americans' recreational and educational lives, the reformers were far more aggressive in their law enforcement efforts.

"The Females of This Race Are Unmoral": Stereotypes, Racial Myths, and the Law Enforcement Program

The CTCA always maintained that the provision of healthful recreation and social hygiene education would help to prevent the soldiers' engagement in less savory amusements, such as drinking and prostitution. In the case of African Americans, though, the CTCA had neglected these positive programs. This failure alone might have driven the CTCA to emphasize its law enforcement work with African Americans. The reformers' uncritical acceptance of popular stereotypes of African Americans as sexually immoral and naturally criminal, however, further encouraged the CTCA's reliance on law enforcement in its efforts to control African Americans.

In the years since the Civil War white Americans had struggled to reassert control over the African American community, freed at the conclusion of the war. Racial violence, specifically the rape of black women and the lynching of black men, played a critical role in this attempt. To explain these actions Whites developed myths about African American sexual immorality that, in their minds, served to justify or explain away these atrocities.[82] Rather than combatting these harmful racial stereotypes, the federal reformers only reinforced them.

According to the CTCA, the control of prostitution in several training camp communities was complicated by the high rate of immorality, and the consequent criminality, among African Americans. This criminality, the commission maintained, was especially prominent among the women of the race. "Holding down the social evil to a minimum is complicated in the South," the commission representative in Atlanta, Georgia, suggested, "when you consider the large percentage of our colored population, on account of the well known high percentage of immorality that exists among the colored women."[83] Revealing his own acceptance of stereotypes of African American immorality, another CTCA worker commented regarding the vice situation in Washington, D.C., "Of course, the problem of meeting a situation such as would naturally exist where there are twenty thousand negro women and girls, with little sense of morality dwelling in a rather congested district, is most difficult of solution."[84]

This sort of stereotyping was not limited to the commission's field workers. The CTCA's chairman, Raymond Fosdick, may not have consciously intended to discriminate against African Americans, but his acceptance of stereotypes, alongside his acceptance of segregation, ensured that African American soldiers and civilians would face mistreatment at the hands of the CTCA. Concurring in the difficulty of controlling vice among African Americans, Fosdick suggested regarding the situation in Washington, D.C., "As far as conditions in the city are concerned I believe they are as clean as can be expected in any large center of population in which the negro element so largely predominates."[85]

Not only were African Americans more likely immoral, the commission maintained, but they were also more difficult to control. The executive secretary of the CTCA for Waco, Texas, explained regarding the work still to be done after the closure of the red-light district in Waco: "I believe that when this problem of immoral women is settled we still have the larger problem of the colored women who will persistently hang around the camp and open up opportunity. Ordinary restriction will not control it and it is impossible to provide a force large enough to cover it. . . . I suppose this is a problem common to every camp in the South."[86]

Not all field-workers automatically accepted the stereotype of African Americans as immoral. Alan Johnstone, Jr., in a report on Augusta, Georgia, in 1917, for instance, suggested, "I do not believe that prostitution among the negroes is serious, although several people with whom I talked feared so."[87] Even Johnstone, though rejecting the stereotype, admitted its prevalence.[88]

Evidence now suggests that African American women may have been overrepresented among the prostitute population, though never to the extent suggested by observers in 1917 and 1918. This situation reflected not a natural immorality, as the reformers intimated, but the discriminatory economic conditions to which African American women had long been subjected.[89] A report on conditions in Macon, Georgia, near Camp Wheeler, alluded to this fact: "The illegitimate sexual intercourse of the soldiers with negro women and girls, in and all around Macon, has been and is something frightful. It is done openly and clandestinely," the report began. As a consequence, this report noted, "It is very hard to get a negro female servant in Macon now because they have all apparently gone into this business."[90] Prostitution, it seems, paid better and offered better working conditions than other forms of work available to African American women. Given the particularly difficult economic situation of African American women, their participation in prostitution is hardly surprising. Even with this economic motivation, however, African American women never entered prostitution in the numbers suggested by those assuming the promiscuity of all African American women.

Based on a popular belief in the high rate of venereal disease among African American civilians, black women were twice condemned as criminals by the CTCA. A report from Alexandria, Louisiana, suggested that as many as 70 percent of the African American residents suffered from a venereal disease. Although these statistics were clearly exaggerated, it is important to note the interpretation made of them. The mayor of that town explained, "We have a large negro population and as you well know the female of this race are unmoral."[91] To this observer, African American citizens were infected with venereal disease not because of poor health care, but because of their own immorality. The CTCA was inclined to agree, as demonstrated by their willingness to detain as criminals women infected with a venereal disease. A report on prostitution and liquor traffic in Pensacola, Florida, noted, "The segregation of colored prostitutes is favored on sanitary as well as racial grounds as they are believed to be more generally infected with venereal disease."[92]

The statistics on the rate of venereal disease among African American and white women, though varying, all suggest a fairly small difference in rates between the two groups. A study comparing poor white and poor black civilian men and women in Galveston, Texas, just before the war showed both groups with about a 25 percent to 30 percent infection rate. Another study of female African American patients in a charity hospital in a large southern city suggested that only 16.6 percent of the women were infected. Willing to accept as fact any information that reinforced their stereotypes, though, many members of the CTCA embraced without evidence the rumors of high rates of African American infection and failed to understand the importance of class in determining disease rates.[93]

Reforming efforts directed at prostitution in the early years of the twentieth century had only helped to reinforce these stereotypes. Many cities tolerated vice, but reform efforts commonly pushed vice into a restricted area, usually in the poorer segments of a city. All too often the restriction of vice led to its concentration in African American and ethnic neighborhoods, where "respectable" white citizens soon assumed it belonged.[94] In its "Suggestions for Special Activities for the Reduction of Venereal Diseases Among Colored Soldiers in Cantonments," the CTCA stated: "Policy of Southern Cities is to leave colored part of town wide open and to center in the colored portion much of the vice of the whites. Slums in Southern Cities, [are] always colored slums, although catering largely to white vice. The usual method of cleaning up these Cities is to sweep the dregs into the colored section."[95] As suggested earlier, after the antiprostitution campaign of the war, prostitutes were forced to pursue their trade in safer locations. This often meant retreating to African American neighborhoods, where police were more willing to overlook the newly illegal behavior. As an investigator for the CTCA's Special Committee on the Welfare of Negro Troops noted, efforts by the commission to eradicate prostitution had produced "a scattering of prostitutes to all sections inhabited by colored people."[96]

As a result white reformers viewed African American neighborhoods as an important locus of crime, simply on the basis of the color of the residents. A letter from the CTCA representative in Louisville, Kentucky, to the commanding officer of Camp Taylor regarding the possibility of banning white troops from African American neighborhoods suggested, "You probably feel, as I do, that the white soldier, as a general rule, has no more good reason for being in the negro sections, than in saloons. . . . In view of the extent to which soldiers are affected by negro prostitution and 'bootlegging,' I respectfully ask your careful consideration of the plan."[97] Willing to accept stereotypes of African American criminality, the CTCA ignored its own role in creating the appearance of an African American proclivity for immorality.

Those African American women and girls who faced arrest and detention for their alleged immorality and criminality also faced discriminatory conditions of detention, particularly in the South. According to the reports of Charles Williams of the Hampton Institute, field agent for the Committee on the Welfare of Negro Troops of the General War-Time Commission of the Federal Council of Churches, "With the exception of one makeshift, detention homes were not found anywhere in the South. In most cases girls were placed in jail because there was no other place to put them. Strong opposition to establishing detention homes for colored girls is almost universal in the South."[98] The consequences of this tendency were clear. Williams noted in another context,

> Money appropriated by the Government for the establishment of detention homes in cantonment cities was seldom used for Negro girls. Instead they were usually placed in jail, or sent to the prison farm or the "stockade," the home of the chain gang. . . . The inmates lived in dirt and disease, sleeping on ragged greasy mattresses on concrete floors and eating food prepared in the most unsanitary manner.[99]

Reports from the CTCA's Law Enforcement Division confirmed Williams's perception of the discriminatory conditions of detention. In Louisville, Kentucky, African American women faced detention in the city jail or workhouse, while the majority of white women were quarantined in the City Hospital.[100] The CTCA praised the state of North Carolina for establishing a State Home and Industrial School for Girls and Women, which included "comfortable cottages, healthful woodland, and good farming." In February 1919, however, the CTCA also reported, "Only white girls are there at the present time." Though the report hoped that African American women and girls could eventually be placed there, these plans had been deferred until "later."[101] More likely to face arrest and detention due to the CTCA's acceptance of stereotypes and its failure to develop any positive program for African American women and girls, these females often faced shocking conditions for the duration of their detention.

African American soldiers, like their white counterparts, were to some extent shielded from the full repressive power of the CTCA because of their status as members of the armed forces. This is not to suggest, however, that the CTCA did not make similar judgments regarding their natural promiscuity.[102] The assumption of the immorality of African American men was most obvious in the program of mandatory chemical prophylaxis aimed at many black soldiers. Assuming that all African American troops were engaging in sexual activities during their leave time, some camps required all black soldiers returning from leave to receive prophylactic treatments.[103] An inspector of the prophylaxis station at Camp Hill, for instance, discovered that "all colored men at this station are required to take prophylactic treatment upon returning from pass."[104] The same inspector noted that a similar order had existed at Camp Alexander until April 1919, when the order was rescinded because of complaints.[105]

In a few instances the assumption of African American criminality resulted in even harsher discrimination against African American troops by the military police. A report conducted for the Military Intelligence Division suggested regarding Camp Sevier, in Greenville, South Carolina, "The most unsatisfactory thing about this camp is the treatment which the colored soldiers receive from the military police." The report explained further:

> I can safely say that a colored soldier in this city has no more show, so far as safety or justice is concerned than a jack rabbit. The military police make it their business to interfere with every colored soldier they see on the streets, whether accompanied or unaccompanied by friends. They are cursed at and asked to show their passes, and when the proper credentials are shown they are cursed for having shown them. At night time the military police thrust revolvers into the faces of the colored soldiers and demand of them to show their passes. This is done without any cause or provocation on the part of the soldier.[106]

Though the military police undoubtedly acted without connection to the CTCA in many instances, in some camps and communities the CTCA allied itself with the MPs, relying on their repressive actions to maintain order. In a letter outlining the local CTCA's efforts to enforce complete segregation in Little Rock, the local executive secretary suggested, "We have asked for a heavy white military police in the negro section."[107] The CTCA's assumptions of African American criminality, then, did nothing to encourage the careful provision of recreation and education, but only produced additional discrimination by the commission and by the military.

It is not surprising that a situation such as that created by the CTCA, in which discrimination on the basis of race was institutionalized in a government program, led to heightened racial tensions. The CTCA's acceptance of segregation placed the stamp of federal approval on the racist objections of many local Whites to the visiting African American troops, encouraging further discrimination against those troops. The government's failure to fulfill its promises to the African American soldiers, combined with the white community's continued demands for segregation, also disappointed African American hopes raised by the rhetoric of the war and led some to protest the injustice of the situation. An exploration of the evolution of the CTCA program in Camp Funston, Kansas, demonstrates how the commission's adherence to the policy of segregation, rather than calming race relations there, only increased the likelihood of racial tensions.

"To Avoid Such Conflicts": The Case of Camp Funston

In the fall of 1917 plans were drawn up for the encampment of several thousand African Americans at Camp Funston, a National Army camp attached to Fort Riley, in northeastern Kansas. From the beginning representatives of the CTCA were concerned about the recreational problems certain to evolve with the placement of such a large number of African Americans at the camp. On 10 October 1917 F. B. Barnes, a representative of the CTCA at Camp Funston, wrote to the chairman of the commission, asking that the order to send African American troops there be rescinded. He explained in a telegram: "ACTION OF WAR DEPARTMENT IN SENDING TWELVE THOUSAND NEGRO TROOPS TO CAMP FUNSTON FROM MISSISSIPPI CREATES MORAL AND RECREATIONAL PROBLEMS EXCEEDINGLY DIFFICULT TO SOLVE." The problem, according to Barnes, lay in both the need for segregation and the shortage of available resources for African American recreation. He continued, "CITIES ADJACENT TO CAMP HAVE ONLY SIX AND SEVEN THOUSAND POPULATION WITH SMALL PROPORTION COLORED NEGRO TROOPS WOULD HAVE VERY LIMITED CIVILIAN POPULATION

OF OWN RACE WITH WHOM TO ASSOCIATE." And further, "THE SITUATION WITHIN CAMP EXTREMELY COMPLICATED PROBABLY NECESSARY TO DUPLICATE ALL AMUSEMENT AND RECREATIONAL ACTIVITIES." According to Barnes the arrival of the African American soldiers could only result in rising racial animosity and immorality. Unable to envision any solution to the racial situation at Camp Funston, Barnes urged that the chairman use his "INFLUENCE AND STRONGEST EFFORTS TO HAVE THE ORDER" bringing African American troops to Funston rescinded.[108]

Barnes was correct that the small size of the African American communities in the nearby towns of Manhattan and Junction City would complicate the provision of recreation for the African American men in uniform. A report from the War Camp Community Service in January 1918 explained:

> The planning of activities for the thousands of colored troops at Camp Funston has proved a difficult problem because of the fact that there is practically no colored population to be mobilized in the nearby cities. In the colored district of Junction City it was found there were only 120 families, all working people, whose resources are wholly inadequate to the needs.[109]

Similarly, the town of Manhattan had only 110 African American families.

Though the white community of Manhattan understood the problem the small African American community faced in providing recreation for the men in uniform, they offered no assistance. Instead, the leading white citizens of Manhattan revealed their own resistance to integrated recreation and their willingness to sacrifice elements of the recreation program for white soldiers to prevent it. In a telegram to the chairman of the CTCA, the Manhattan Commercial Club, led by the mayor, the president of the local agricultural college, the county and city attorney, and two city commissioners, declared,

> THE MANHATTAN COMMERCIAL CLUB UNANIMOUSLY VOTED THAT COMPLETION AND ATTEMPT TO USE COMMODIOUS COMMUNITY HOUSE ABOUT TO BE CONSTRUCTED FOR BENEFIT AND RECREATION OF SOLDIERS WOULD BE UNWISE AND UNSAFE IF LARGE QUOTA OF COLORED TROOPS ARE STATIONED AT CAMP FUNSTON. JOINT USE

OF COMMUNITY HOUSE BY WHITE AND COLORED TROOPS IMPOSSIBLE AND COLORED CIVILIAN POPULATION TOO SMALL TO EFFECTIVELY COOPERATE IN ENTERPRISES INTENDED FOR THE BENEFIT AND RECREATION OF COLORED TROOPS.[110]

In the expression of their concerns the leading White citizens of Manhattan revealed their prejudices regarding African Americans. "INFLUX OF LARGE NUMBER OF COLORED TROOPS INTO PARKS, STREETS AND PLACES OF AMUSEMENT OF SMALL CITIES NEAR CAMP FUNSTON WOULD INEVITABLY RESULT IN RACE CONFLICTS WHICH THE LOCAL CIVIL AUTHORITIES WOULD BE UNABLE TO CONTROL," they complained. Perhaps more importantly, the Commercial Club members warned, "THE STATE AGRICULTURAL COLLEGE LOCATED AT MANHATTAN INCLUDES OVER ONE THOUSAND YOUNG WOMEN STUDENTS WHO RESIDE THROUGHOUT THE CITY AND THEIR WELFARE IS GRAVELY THREATENED BY THE PROPOSED ACTION. THE WHOLE MORAL SITUATION OF THE TOWNS AND COUNTY ADJACENT TO THE CAMP WOULD BE GREATLY DISTURBED."[111] In the eyes of these citizens, the arrival of African American troops threatened the racial peace of the region as well as the moral and physical well-being of local white women. F. B. Barnes, the CTCA representative in town, did nothing to dissuade them.

In January 1918 the first African American troops began to arrive at Camp Funston. Approximately twenty-seven hundred black soldiers reported for training that January. Despite the CTCA's early awareness of the difficulties surrounding the provision of recreation, arriving African American troops found a camp and a community largely unprepared to offer them the segregated recreation expected by the white community. In December 1917 the CTCA had decided to reserve the use of one government theater for use by the African American troops. This provision had been prompted, however, by the CTCA's awareness of the African American soldiers' complete exclusion from an amusement zone, then under construction, which already included three theaters for white soldiers. While this Whites-only zone was under construction in December 1917, the CTCA representative at Camp Funston admitted, "no definite plans are complete for any recreation for black troops." Aware that the construction of the government's own theater inside this segregated zone would highlight the shortage of facilities for African Americans, the CTCA chose to grant them the use of one theater.[112]

But a single theater inside the camp did not begin to fill the recreational needs of the African American soldiers stationed at Camp Funston. Most importantly, the problem of providing recreation in the small neighboring communities was severe. A report on the situation in the spring of 1918 confirmed the fears that facilities for African Americans in the towns of Manhattan and Junction City would be slow in coming. "I find no Community House nor Club Room for the convenience of the colored men and their people," the report suggested. "I do not know why this is. . . . The proper party in our department should investigate the conditions at Funston and see if something more cannot be done for the colored troops."[113] The report noted that despite the shortage of recreation, no serious problems seemed to be rising out of this situation. The reason for the peacefulness, however, was clear: "The colored men in and about Army City are well looked after by the military police."[114]

The primary use of the military police to control the African American troops suggests the failure of the CTCA's program in Camp Funston. The CTCA had been charged with responsibility for the recreation and amusement of African American troops both inside and outside the camps. Through the provision of alternative forms of recreation the CTCA had hoped to prevent immorality and criminality among the men in uniform. And yet at Camp Funston, as late as May 1918, the CTCA had to admit that adequate recreational opportunities for African American men did not exist. The CTCA's acceptance of local demands for segregation and its failure to develop a separate recreation program for African Americans had led to a program based primarily in law enforcement.

Ultimately, the shortage of facilities prompted precisely the heightened racial animosity the CTCA had hoped to avoid. In late March 1918 an African American sergeant of the 92nd Division sought to enter a theater in Manhattan, Kansas. The theater manager refused to admit him on the basis of the possible objection of white patrons. Upon hearing of this incident, the white commander of the African American 92nd Division, General Charles C. Ballou, issued what would become his infamous Bulletin No. 35, a document that demonstrates well the consequences of the CTCA's failure adequately to provide for the recreational needs of African American men in uniform. In this document the general cautioned the African American men from going where they were not wanted and suggested the men must give up their legal rights if pursuance of those rights would provoke racial enmity: "It should be well known to all colored officers and men that no useful purpose is served by such acts as will cause the 'color question' to be raised. It is not a question of legal rights, but a question of policy," Ballou began. "To avoid such conflicts," he continued,

> the Division Commander has repeatedly urged that all colored members of his command . . . should refrain from going where their presence will be resented. In spite of this injunction, one of the sergeants of the Medical Department has recently precipitated the precise trouble that should be avoided, and then called on the Division Commander to take sides in a row that should never have occurred had the sergeant placed the general good above his personal pleasure and convenience.[115]

Though conceding the legal right of the African American soldier to attend the theater, Ballou maintained nevertheless that African American soldiers had a responsibility to sacrifice their personal rights for the cause of racial peace. "This sergeant entered a theater, as he undoubtedly had a legal right to do and precipitated trouble by making it possible to allege race discrimination in the seat he was given," Ballou explained. "He is strictly within his legal rights in this matter, and the theater manager is legally wrong. Nevertheless the sergeant is guilty of the GREATER wrong in doing ANYTHING, NO MATTER HOW LEGALLY CORRECT, that will provoke race animosity." Ballou concluded by asserting:

> White men made the Division, and they can break it just as easily if it becomes a troublemaker. All concerned are again enjoined to place the general interest of the Division above personal pride and gratification. Avoid every situation that can give rise to racial ill-will. Attend quietly and faithfully to your duties, and don't go where your presence is not desired.[116]

Ballou's bulletin was in no way inconsistent with the recreational policy outlined by the CTCA, but was rather the logical extension of that policy. It was an extension, however, for which many African Americans had no tolerance. Ballou's bulletin created a storm of protest in the African American community nationwide. The title of an editorial in the *Chicago Defender* suggested the hostility the bulletin evoked: "This Is No Soldier! Ballou Might Have Done a Worse Thing; That's Doubtful." The editorial queried, "General Ballou may be a fighter, but is he a soldier?

Soldiers are made of stuff beyond 'Order 35'." Noting that the business of the hour was the international war, the editorial raged,

> But Ballou, in asking soldiers to surrender to the lawless and lawlessness, in his foolish request to freemen in free states to adopt the shameless customs of slavedrivers and their slaves in the slave states, gives faithful indication that there is at least one general in the great army of the United States who does not believe that the soldiers under him are fit to enjoy the blessings he hopes to give the world by the blood of soldiers under him.[117]

The Baltimore *Afro-American* concurred, exclaiming, "The wording of the order is regarded as a direct slap at the colored people of this country, and especially at the colored officers." And further, "The order is resented among the colored officers and men at the various cantonments."[118] In public meetings across the nation African Americans called for the resignation of General Ballou.[119] Yet General Ballou only articulated the official stance of the War Department, a position shared by the CTCA.

"Trying to Prove the Manhood of Their Race": Resistance to the System of Segregation

General Ballou's bulletin was not the first instance of the institutionalization of discrimination against the African American troops. Neither was the African American community's response to it the first expression of black hostility to the government's acceptance of segregation in recreation, of racial stereotypes, and of the consequent discrimination against the African American men in uniform. Not only did African American civilians sometimes find a voice of protest in their newspapers editors and in their grassroots efforts to take care of the troops, but African American soldiers also often responded to their mistreatment by the army, the local civilians, and the CTCA by openly criticizing and even challenging the system of segregation in recreation. As already noted, troops across the country responded angrily to General Ballou's bulletin. Earlier, in August 1917 in Waco, Texas, members of the 24th Infantry "tore down the jim crow signs in a restaurant, and thereby came into a clash with the police."[120] African American officer candidates at Camp Dodge were similarly resistant to segregation in Des Moines, though these soldiers chose to avoid Des Moines altogether as their way of resisting acceptance of Jim Crow restrictions. According to one CTCA report: "The boys were trying to prove the manhood of their race to the nation, so kept pretty close in camp to avoid any unpleasantness which attempting to attend movies, dances, or other public affairs would produce. They did not wish to have a segregated section reserved for them, as this would start a precedent by negroes—a thing they refuse to do."[121] Forced to choose between segregated recreation in the city and remaining in camp on their leave time, African American officer trainees chose to follow the less offensive option of remaining in camp. In the process they articulated an alternative vision of manhood, based in race pride, which challenged the CTCA's attempt to cast them in an inferior role.

In other cases the anger and frustration of African American soldiers boiled over into more violent clashes with white civilians and local police. In addition to African American violence in Houston discussed earlier, a report by the army released in 1942 listed two other serious incidents involving African American troops. The army did not identify by name either the camps or the communities in which the incidents took place. In both instances hostile relations between local Whites and African American soldiers prompted the soldiers' outbreak. In one case the army described a raid by between nine and fifteen raiders who jumped the wall of a camp and entered the neighboring town, killing one civilian and injuring a policeman. This incident, according to the army, had been prompted by a series of confrontations between the soldiers and civilians. Perhaps most importantly, soldiers resented the system of segregation and the hostile attitude of local residents. A study of African American troops, conducted by the Army War College, reported, "Several incidents occurred between the soldiers and civilians of the town which aggravated an already tense situation." More specifically, "Soldiers were not permitted to drink with white people at the principal bars, though in some cases separate bars were put up for their use, this having an opposite effect to that intended—(the bartender was killed in such a bar)."[122]

In a second case, on 29 July 1917, a group of African American soldiers entered the town neighboring their camp and fired thirty shots. No one was injured. Again, resentment and anger at the system of segregation and its harsh enforcement had prompted the actions of the men in uniform. The night of the incident the troops had endured disparaging remarks from white civilians during their visit to town, and in breaking up the resultant crowd the city police had clubbed an African American soldier. Further, according to the Army War College report,

> The enlisted men resented the Jim Crow laws. They entered a drug store where colored people are not served and insisted on being waited upon. In one instance signs "white" and "colored" in a restaurant were taken down by the men. The regulations segregating white and colored on surface cars were not observed by some of the soldiers. After the colored soldier was clubbed, some of his friends accompanied him back to camp. These men got their rifles and returned to the city.[123]

Emmett J. Scott, though clearly eager to downplay the magnitude of racial incidents during the war, nevertheless reported an incident at Newport News in September 1918, as well as "other affairs of no great seriousness that were reported at Camp Upton, Camp Merritt, Camp Grant, and one or two others." He concluded, "Many minor encounters grew out of the refusal of white soldiers to salute colored officers, and of efforts to draw the colorline in places of recreation and amusement."[124] The anger and frustration of the African American men in uniform, most obvious in these outbursts of violence but undoubtedly present throughout the training camps, were born of the discrimination and mistreatment these soldiers endured.[125]

"To Counteract Some of the Mischievous Impressions": The Limits of the CTCA's Program

The CTCA never acknowledged the injustice inherent in its program. When African American members of a community committee on recreation questioned the inequity of the men's situation in Des Moines, the CTCA prided itself on its ability to dismiss the broad issue of injustice. "A committee of representative, respectable negroes was appointed to work out a program of entertainment for their men and to make a registration of homes suitable for the entertainment of negro visitors—as hotels would not accommodate them," one report explained. "Discussion of the 'injustice' of inequality arose in committee meeting and was promptly squelched by our representative at the camp, Mr. Patin, who said they were not there to discuss any question of justice, but to make pleasant the leisure hours of the soldiers and leave the situation to adjust itself."[126]

The CTCA failed to understand that in order to make the leisure hours of the African American men in uniform truly pleasant, issues of injustice had to be addressed.[127]

Instead, the CTCA chose to deal with the problems produced by segregation and the resultant shortage of facilities without ever challenging the policy of segregation itself or considering the essential injustice of its own stance. The primary cause of racial strife in the training camp communities, according to the WCCS, was the African American soldiers' dissatisfaction and impatience: "The colored soldier's conception of what was his due was, in some cases, apt to be an idea that these rights were long overdue, and he was impatient to hurry along that democracy where the colored man would come into his own," the report explained.[128] Both in Des Moines and later at Camp Funston the War Department made clear its position on the conflict between rights and local tradition, calling on the troops to give up their right to fair treatment in the realm of recreation for the good of the war cause. Further, to counter the rising dissatisfaction of African American troops, the CTCA was willing to use "a definite propaganda which will counteract some of the mischievous impressions that are going around."[129]

Though the CTCA never altered its position on segregation, the commission did eventually begin efforts to mitigate the shortages of recreation its policy had caused. By the summer of 1918 the CTCA conceded that its work for African American soldiers had been inadequate and that attention had to be focused on the development of programs for these troops. The plea from Camp Funston, urging attention to the needs of African American troops, had been echoed by requests from camps all over the country, and in June 1918 the CTCA and its affiliates finally seemed ready to respond.

Suggesting the link between protests and the CTCA's changing position, the minutes of the meeting of the executive committee of the CTCA noted:

> Mr. McBride [acting chairman of the commission] brought to the Commission's attention the importance of the work among colored soldiers. He said that the colored men now numbered about ten per cent of the entire army, that heretofore it had been the custom to attend to the white men first, but that hereafter the white and black must be attended to at the same time, so as to put a stop to the growing feeling among the negroes that they were being neglected.[130]

At the same meeting the CTCA member in charge of the YMCA's work for soldiers in the camps suggested a similar change of heart. The minutes of the meeting continued, "Mr. Tichenor then said that it had been decided at an executive session of the YMCA that white and black soldiers should henceforth be treated alike."[131] The YMCA had always expressed a policy of equal treatment. In June 1918, however, the association was able to posit this as a new position, suggesting its earlier neglect of African American troops. The War Camp Community Service, too, seemed to demonstrate awakened concern for the African American man in uniform.[132] There also appeared to be a rising interest in work with African American women and girls.[133] These late calls for adequate recreation for African American troops by the CTCA and its various affiliates in the summer of 1918 are perhaps the most convincing evidence of the CTCA's general negligence toward those troops.

In July 1918 progress in the community work for African American soldiers finally became discernible. In San Antonio the community recreation worker reported: "Just organizing negro work. One woman worker employed. Churches and lodges at work."[134] In Charlotte, North Carolina, and Spartanburg, South Carolina, money was appropriated for clubs for African American soldiers; in Columbia, South Carolina, a club had already been leased for use. A "fairly strong colored committee" had been organized in Augusta, Georgia, and "considerable work" was being done there.[135] By the time of the armistice in 1918, the CTCA could boast of twenty-three soldier clubs in training camp communities for African American men in uniform, as compared to just seven at the end of June 1918.[136]

The YMCA and YWCA, too, stepped up their work for the men inside the camps. In the same report from November 1918 the YMCA claimed twenty-five soldier huts or buildings and an additional twenty-one tents serving the leisure needs of the African American troops inside the confines of the camps; the YWCA claimed to have built twelve buildings for entertaining female visitors to camp.[137]

These examples demonstrate a more earnest attempt by the CTCA to meet the needs of African American soldiers in the second half of 1918. The provision of these facilities, however, did nothing to alter the existing system of segregated recreation, which had been the initial cause of the shortage of facilities. As long as segregation continued, incidents would occur in which African American soldiers required more facilities than were provided for them and would suffer the shortage because of the policy of segregation.

Through the end of the war shortages of facilities did, indeed, occur. As late as 24 October 1918, the chief of the new Morale Branch of the army, E. L. Munson, wrote to the head of the CTCA, "There seems reason to believe that the matter of stimulation of morale among negro troops should be given special attention, and I am writing to ask that you concentrate to a larger extent, for the present, on this problem." Munson's letter suggests that even with the CTCA's redirected energies beginning in the summer of 1918, its provisions for African American soldiers and civilians continued to lag well behind those made for Whites.[138]

After the armistice the problem of recreational shortages persisted, aggravated by the special circumstances of demobilization. Uncertainty regarding the future residents of the camps, as well as the future of the camps themselves, stalled the development of segregated recreational facilities and threatened the closure of existing facilities.[139]

The CTCA did make some effort to protect the interests of returning African American soldiers during the demobilization period. Aware of the importance of greeting African American soldiers returning from overseas with adequate recreational opportunities, W. Prentice Sanger, executive secretary of the CTCA, urged the bolstering of programs for these soldiers.[140] Shortly after the armistice, too, Secretary of War Newton D. Baker wrote his special assistant, Emmett J. Scott, urging him to remain at his job through the period of demobilization, which he did.[141] As the affiliated organizations began to plan for the closure of recreational facilities, Scott convinced the CTCA to fight for the continued operation of facilities for African American soldiers until all had been demobilized.[142] Similarly, in June 1919 George A. Sloan, an executive officer of the CTCA, asked the YWCA to continue to operate its Hostess Houses for African Americans at Camps Meade and Lee. He explained, "It is the opinion of the District Directors that it is advisable to continue these two colored Hostess Houses for a period of at least two months, or until such a time as the colored troops are being demobilized in these camps, as there is no other place for them to congregate or meet their relatives and friends."[143] While demonstrating the efforts of the CTCA to protect the limited recreational facilities for African Americans during the demobilization period, this statement also suggests the commission's continued adherence to the policy of segregation.

The segregation policy was no less discriminatory during the demobilization period than it had been during the months of the war.[144] At Camp Upton, for instance, the policy of segregation continued to frustrate African American troops, even as they returned home from the war. On 14 February 1919 the commanding officer of Camp Upton released a memorandum to the commanding officer of the all–African American 372nd Infantry urging the troops and their female visitors to use the Hostess House specially set aside for their use and to leave the other Hostess Houses to the white troops and their visitors. It explained, "This applies particularly to Sundays, when in all probability, large number of white women will be in camp to visit the white soldiers, and it is not desirable to have them served and accommodated in the same Hostess House with the families of the colored soldiers if it can possibly be avoided."[145] Though the YWCA was quick to express its disappointment with the memorandum and its assurance that African American men and women had never been turned away from any Hostess House, the memorandum stood.[146]

That the African American community resented this discrimination was clear in letters sent to the War Department and in editorials published in the African American press. George E. Cannon of the National Medical Association wrote Secretary of War Baker, "We have been a forebearing and patient race, but patience is being almost exhausted by such trying conditions as manifested in this." The NAACP concurred, exclaiming, "Probably no more inopportune and inappropriate time could have been chosen for issuing such instructions, when thousands of colored soldiers are returning to America after having made a record in France surpassed by none."[147]

In the demobilization period African Americans found no relief from the discrimination they had endured throughout the war. The CTCA, maintaining its policy of segregation, added insult to injury by denying African American soldiers, returning from the fields of France, equal access to recreational facilities back in the States.

In its relations with African Americans the Commission on Training Camp Activities embodied all of the worst features of the existing racial policies in the United States in the early years of the twentieth century and demonstrated the often hostile relationship between white progressives and the African American community. In the years before the war many white progressives had openly embraced segregation, but many African American reformers had nevertheless found allies within the progressive movement. During the war, though, the CTCA did not challenge the policy of segregation, but accepted it. Only the separation of the races, many white reformers maintained, could possibly protect racial peace within the nation.

Yet a program such as that enacted by the CTCA could neither cultivate racial peace nor encourage the continued acceptance of discrimination by African Americans. Finding the discrimination intolerable, many African American soldiers and civilians responded in protest to the institutionalized racism of the CTCA programs.

There was irony in this turn of events. The CTCA had professed a determination to create crusaders among the American people through the development of the positive programs of recreation and education. These programs would cultivate new habits and values among more marginal Americans, integrating the bulk of the populace into the reformers' vision of a mainstream American culture. Americans would aspire to new standards of manhood and womanhood and in the process become members of a new national community based in a shared social vision.

This vision, however, seemed to hold little promise for African Americans, who found themselves without a place in the white reformers' national community. They were not to be integrated into the national culture in any substantial way, but were to be isolated in the permanent marginalization of segregation. The CTCA reformers, it seemed, could not imagine African Americans as crusaders. As a result they simply ignored the needs of these Americans. As one African American soldier being held with venereal disease lamented from Camp Lee, in Virginia:

> We have waited and have looked for some change in conditions at Camp Lee and it seems to get worse everyday and we as negroes and treated unlike soldiers have grew tired to death of our treatments that we get hear *[sic]*. . . . god in heaven do know that we all have worn out at such as to not have the chance to go to no place but to work and when we are in from work then we are in prison until time to go to work again. . . . from the way that we are being handled here it looks like to me and others . . . that it will be slavery instead of freedom.[148]

Sensitive to the meaning of this treatment, the soldier concluded, "We dont even be looked on as a real man by no one."[149] Though the war was fought for democracy abroad, it was a democracy most white Americans, including the reformers in the War Department, were unwilling to extend to the African American citizens of the United States. Instead, the reformers expected African Americans to simply accept the condition of segregation, and with it the insult and injury it carried.

Many African Americans participated in the war convinced that the vision articulated by the leaders of a war to "make the world safe for democracy" held special meaning for them. As the *Chicago Defender* articulated this optimism:

> Probably out of this great world struggle may come industrial and civil freedom. Already hopeful signs are appearing upon the horizon. Opportunities are opening up to us along avenues that were heretofore closed. The colored soldier who fights side by side with the white American in the titanic struggle now raging across the sea will hardly be begrudged a fair chance when the victorious armies return.[150]

Expecting at least minimal rewards for their patriotic participation in the war, many African Americans reacted with surprise, disappointment, and anger to the nation's failure to grant them their due. Having resisted the reformers' attempts to subject them to a degraded position in the national community during the war, many African Americans entered the postwar period with a renewed and expanded determination to claim political, social, and economic equality.[151] Frustrated in his attempts to bring change through unmitigated cooperation with the progressive war effort, W. E. B. Du Bois articulated this new position:

> By the God of Heaven, we are cowards and jackasses if now that war is over, we do not marshal every ounce of our brain and brawn to fight a sterner, longer, more unbending battle against the forces of hell in our own land.
>
> *We return.*
> *We return from fighting.*
> *We return fighting.*
>
> Make way for Democracy! We saved it in France, and by the Great Jehovah, we will save it in the United States of America, or know the reason why.[152]

This broadened commitment, widely expressed by African Americans, was evident in their response to the race riots of 1919, in their continued migration northward, and in the flourishing of African American culture in the Harlem Renaissance. Unable to envision African Americans embracing their standards of manhood and womanhood, the CTCA reformers inadvertently encouraged the African American community to develop its own reform aspirations based in racial pride. Hoping to prevent a change in race relations, the reformers of the CTCA had contributed to precisely that change.

In addition to the resistance of African Americans to the vision of the CTCA, in the postwar era the CTCA faced increasing opposition from many other groups of Americans. The commission's loss of its intimate association with the war effort, combined with the needs of demobilization, compounded the problems it faced in the period following the war. The CTCA's difficulties in establishing its work on a permanent basis during the demobilization period provides important clues to the postwar disintegration of the progressive movement itself.

CHAPTER SIX

The End of the Crusade: Demobilization and the Legacy of the CTCA

> Permit me to say with all respect sir, that in thus depriving the men of their rights of manhood you are committing the gravest error yet committed by a Secretary of War, in the interest of the good of the service. You ask us to give our lives for our beloved country, which we are only too willing to do—but you deprive us of the privilege of a glass of wine or beer even at our meals—and—most of all you deny us the freedom of our God-given rights of manhood! I have spoken with hundreds of men on these subjects and while they are willing to forego all liquor simply because you request it, they feel that in being denied their sex instincts they are virtually held as slaves—not as freemen. . . . Many of the men are intensely bitter on this subject and hate with all the intensity of their nature, those they feel are responsible for this demoralizing state of affairs under present orders.
>
> —"A Commissioned Officer of Artillery, USA," to Secretary of War Baker, 1 December 1917

In July 1919, with the Commission on Training Camp Activities largely demobilized, Secretary of War Baker sent a letter to the commission's chairman. "Have you ever thought," Baker queried, "about what the Army would have been like if we had not at the very outset taken the steps we did take to keep it clean and contented?" Describing the commission's success and acknowledging Fosdick's contributions, Baker suggested,

> Nobody could have stopped America from building a great army, nor could all the Germans in the world have stopped our army from securing a military victory; but the character of the army that went and of the army that returned is even more significant than its military success. Without your help in the matter I should never have had the faith to try many things which not only were tried, but succeeded.[1]

Reinforcing the notion that the CTCA had triumphed, Baker predicted the long-term significance of the commission's work: "I should be very surprised, as well as disappointed if the work which you have done during this war does not after awhile turn out to be perhaps the most significant thing done by anybody."[2]

Within a few years of the war's conclusion it was clear that Baker had misjudged the CTCA's legacy. During the twenty months of war the progressives in the CTCA wielded unprecedented control over social relations in the training camps and their surrounding communities. In the twenty months following the war, however, the CTCA's programs were assaulted by former adversaries and by former allies. Once restrained by sympathy with the war cause, opponents of the commission articulated, following the armistice, a rising opposition to the CTCA's work. Having dominated the cultural competitions of wartime, in the postwar era the reformers discovered, nevertheless, their failure to convert Americans to their cultural perspective. Struggling to establish their recreational, educational, and law enforcement programs on a permanent basis as they faced their own demobilization, the reformers found few crusaders enlisted to help fight their battles. Despite Baker's optimism the postwar era provided little evidence, either institutional or individual, to suggest a substantial and lasting legacy for the CTCA.

"The Temptation Will Be to Break Training": The Perils of Peacetime and the Plans for Demobilization

On the morning of 11 November 1918 the troops on the front lines of Europe laid down their weapons, signaling the end of a global war that had raged for over four years. Though many soldiers had hesitated to accept the rumors of an imminent cease-fire, the silence that fell over the front at 11:00 A.M. convinced the troops that the war was finally over. In the United States 11 November was scheduled to be the first day of a new round of inductions targeted to add a quarter million soldiers to the National Army. With the announcement of the armistice thousands of draftees headed for training camps found their trains switched to sidings and rerouted back toward home. Another two million men in uniform, already engaged in military training, greeted news of the peace from inside cantonments all across the United States.[3]

Members of the Commission on Training Camp Activities saw in the signing of the armistice the beginning of a new chapter in their work. The reformers in the CTCA had always hoped that the programs they were establishing—in recreation, social hygiene education, and law enforcement—would become a permanent feature of American life after the cessation of hostilities. Though the war emergency had now drawn to a close, in the eyes of the reformers in the War Department, the demobilization period offered challenges in every way equal to those of the war months.

The end of the war, the reformers conceded, had removed the primary motivation for cooperation with their programs. Freed from the responsibilities of the overseas campaign, the soldiers were likely to shed their invisible armor. The chairman of the commission explained, "The army has been keeping itself fit to fight overseas, because there was a fight to wage, but now with the battles all won, the incentive is gone, and the temptation will be to break training just as a foot-ball team breaks training at the end of the season."[4] Reformers feared that civilians, too, might become indifferent toward their duties, bringing a resurgence of the threats of alcohol and prostitution. As Secretary of War Baker suggested, "I am concerned lest the jubilance over the victory now assured and natural relaxation from the strain and effort put forth to attain it should in any way cause the fruits of eighteen months persistent crusading against these twin evils to be slackened or lost."[5]

Though the reformers believed that the armistice made their work more difficult, they also understood their responsibility as unchanged.[6] Indeed, given the natural slackening that follows military victory, many in the commission believed that their obligation was enlarged. "During this period men and women must be guarded by their communities," William H. Zinsser of the Social Hygiene Division cautioned. "The vicious elements will try to take advantage of the national feeling of relaxation and jubilation which peace ushers in. Prostitution and venereal disease must not obtain a new foothold. The war made it possible to take this problem from the darkness into the light. We must keep the limelight of public opinion focused upon it."[7]

During the war the CTCA had linked its programs with the war effort, suggesting that Americans' cooperation with its programs was a necessary sacrifice of wartime. With the armistice, this explanation for the commission's work lost its persuasive power, but it was soon replaced by other justifications more appropriate for a nation no longer at war. Throughout the conflict the commission had articulated its intentions to remake the American populace into a legion of crusaders, better able to act as citizens of the American democracy. This goal weathered the transition to peacetime. E. L. Munson of the Morale Branch of the army, which eventually replaced the CTCA, suggested shortly after the armistice, "With the approach of peace, the morale problem pertaining to our troops changes from one to promote military efficiency in men recently from civil life, to one to promote high ideals of citizenship and civic duty among soldiers shortly to return to the civil community."[8]

In correspondence with its affiliates the CTCA pointed to this purpose—the production of citizens ready and willing to take up their responsibilities in the *civilian* world—as inducement for their continued activity. "We have no longer the inspiration and incentive of the Victory to be achieved," the chairman of the CTCA noted, "but we have the new incentive that lies in the return of these men to civil life better equipped than ever before to take up their economic and social responsibilities."[9] In a letter to mayors and governors the secretary of war concurred: "We are bound as a patriotic necessity to do everything in our power to promote the health and conserve the vitality of the men who are now to be absorbed back into the keen, industrial competition which awaits the nations of the world, ours foremost among the rest."[10] The competition of the postwar world, Baker seemed to suggest, required men as morally and physically fit as those who had fought in the war.

Despite the peace, then, in the eyes of the reformers the CTCA continued to have an important role to play in the development of American men. The recreation program, for instance, while continuing to entertain the men in uniform, could now be used to turn the minds of the soldiers toward their postwar responsibilities. As one district director outlined:

> While emphasis must, therefore, be placed upon making the men have a good time, I suggested that everything possible be brought to bear to make them begin to think of home, and home, not in a sentimental and idealistic way, but in concrete facts, so that instead of its being an absolute change

> from the free-and-easy life to one of responsibility again, some preparation and thought might have been given before the moment of discharge.[11]

The reformers' programs would continue to play a constructive role, shaping the soldiers' attitudes and behaviors to match the nation's changing needs.

E. L. Munson suggested themes for entertainment likely to encourage soldiers to embrace their civic duty and good citizenship, and in the process he revealed the CTCA's continuing preoccupation with social stability. Although noting that the traditional themes of patriotism, democracy, liberty, justice, peace, truth, and honor were all ideals integral to the creation of good citizens, Munson chose to emphasize the importance of "getting a steadying message to the soldiers in camp and out of it, and to the civil population to which they return." He asserted, "It is believed that whenever playwrights can work in the idea of good citizenship, 'don't rock the boat', and other similar steadying features, this should be done."[12] Munson encouraged those entertaining the troops to produce shows highlighting the characters' steadfastness during economic and industrial stress, much as the soldiers had shown steadfastness against the enemy in the war. Anticipating upheavals after the war, and already aware of the unrest in Europe, the CTCA emphasized the importance of creating veterans who would accept their economic responsibilities without questioning the status quo.

With the war at an end, however, the CTCA also faced the challenge of its own dismantling. The reformers in the commission had always hoped that their work could have an influence that would outlast the war, and in shaping their demobilization strategy they implemented this goal. At a meeting in early December the executives of the CTCA decided that the commission would pursue two closely related purposes in the postwar era—the demobilization of the commission and the establishing of its work as a permanent feature of military life.[13]

Once under way, the dismantling of the CTCA was rapid. Plans called for all CTCA executives, district directors, and division heads to be removed by 1 February 1919. By 30 June 1919 the CTCA as a central organizing bureau had ceased to exist, and by November all of the branch work of the CTCA had been transferred or demobilized. As the demobilization process moved forward, the reformers also sought the continuation of their work, seeking to preserve each of their programs in some new form. Though the CTCA was generally successful in finding successors for its work, those agencies and organizations that took over their programs did not always reflect the original intentions of the commission.

"We Will Most Assuredly Withdraw Our Support": The Recreation Program in the Demobilization Period

It was the recreational work that survived most unscathed into the postwar era. During the war the CTCA had been largely triumphant in its attempts to develop carefully circumscribed but plentiful entertainment for the troops both inside and outside the camp gates. Though largely successful in institutionalizing the recreational work after the war, during the demobilization period the CTCA experienced conflicts with both its former allies and its former enemies that foreshadowed the problems that would compromise the survival of its other programs.

Even before the end of the war the army had begun to incorporate the recreational work being done by the CTCA into the regular responsibilities of the military. On 12 April 1918 an informal conference on army morale, including members from the CTCA, the army, and the War Department, discussed the development of a "systematic plan for stimulating and sustaining morale" among the men in uniform. As a result of this and subsequent meetings, on 5 October 1918 the secretary of war created the Morale Branch of the army, within the General Staff.[14]

The new Morale Branch was charged with the "improvement of the efficiency of the soldier through the betterment of morale." To accomplish this the Morale Branch would initiate and administer "plans and measures to stimulate and maintain the morale of troops" and take charge of "the organization, training, coordination and direction of all agencies, military and civil, operating within military zones, in so far as they serve to stimulate and maintain morale of the troops."[15] A morale officer in each camp, under the jurisdiction of the General Staff and the commanding officer of the camp, would oversee the work of the new branch, which would serve as a "sister" to the CTCA, operating on equal footing with the commission.[16]

In the months following its formation, the Morale Branch worked closely with the existing agencies concerned with the morale of the troops, including the CTCA and the affiliated organizations, such as the YMCA, acting largely in the role of supervisor. Because the Morale Branch was not an administrative body, it depended initially on the CTCA and its affiliates to administer the educational and recreational programs for which they had been responsible throughout the war.[17]

Though the army still relied on the CTCA to provide much of the recreation for the troops in the months following the armistice, planning for the demobilization of the commission's recreation workers began immediately. At the meeting in early December 1918 the Executive Committee of the CTCA urged that all commission field workers—including athletic directors, boxing instructors, song leaders, drama directors, and theater managers—be replaced by June 30.

Though moving more slowly in determining the future of the affiliated organizations in the in-camp recreational work, in a letter to the secretary of war on 1 June 1919 the chairman of the CTCA urged that the affiliated organizations, too, be demobilized. "Morale is as important as ammunition and is just as legitimate a charge against the public treasury," he noted. And further,

> I believe the time has come for the Army to take over this whole activity from the field of private enterprise. The experiments of the last two years seem to point irresistibly to this conclusion. Baseballs and books and all the other factors that make for a rounded life are an essential part of the nation's direct responsibility toward its troops.[18]

Ironically, Fosdick's conviction that the army should assume complete responsibility for the in-camp work was fostered, at least in part, by the problems the commission experienced with the affiliated organizations. Throughout the war members of the CTCA complained about the sectarianism of some of the affiliates and the energy and efficiency lost in needless competition between the organizations.[19] These problems continued unabated into the postwar period and helped to convince civilian and military leaders alike of the need to eliminate the affiliates.[20] Certain of the importance of the recreational work and of the unnecessary trouble caused by the continued involvement of civilian organizations, by the end of 1919, with the blessing of the CTCA's leadership, the army had accepted full responsibility for in-camp soldier recreation.[21]

The military also took over the community recreation program, but not before the reformers encountered renewed opposition to their work from civilians outside the formal structures of the CTCA's programs, who vexed the reformers during the demobilization period.[22]

During the war the most significant resistance to the recreation work had come from traditional Americans who worried about Sunday amusements. Wearing the mantle of the war cause, though, the CTCA had been relatively successful in convincing even these Americans to go along with its program. In the months following the end of hostilities, however, the community recreation workers faced a new barrage of criticism aimed at the commission's provision of programs on the Sabbath. As the chairman of the local Law and Order League wrote Secretary of War Baker regarding Sunday recreation at Camp Dodge:

> We wish to call your attention to what the decent people of Iowa term a disgrace—viz that of allowing a football game to be played last Lords Day between Camp Dodge and Camp Pike. In these times when God has been so gracious, as always, it is certainly a most heinous sin to allow anything of this sort. . . . If we as a nation flaunt such things in the face of the Almighty we will have to render an account.[23]

Having survived the war, Sabbatarians maintained, it was the responsibility of the nation to acknowledge its blessings through devout observance of the Sabbath. Those who refused, they argued, courted national disaster.

In Little Rock, Arkansas, the CTCA had fought a particularly grueling battle over the issue of Sunday amusements. By the end of the war, though, Sunday recreation was well established in that town. Reports from the WCCS for February 1919 suggested the city had even begun allowing movies on the Sabbath as part of their contribution to the soldiers' welfare.[24] But in the months following the war the struggle between the CTCA and the Sabbatarians resumed. No longer driven by responsibility to the war cause, Sabbatarians in Little Rock reasserted their commitment to the traditional Sabbath and threatened to break with the CTCA over this issue. One resident complained, "We do not like this sort of position by your representative. . . . Sunday picture shows and Sunday amusements for pay in our city are against the law, and we claim to be law abiding citizens, regardless of our moral convictions on the subject." Though suggesting his essential approval of the commission's work, the citizen continued, "We are large contributors to your work here, and if your leaders persist in this sort of business we will most assuredly withdraw our support."[25]

Although this concern was deeply held by Sabbatarians, it was never sufficiently popular to derail the community recreation work of the commission or its transfer to the military. Like the functions of the in-camp affiliates, the War Camp Community Service, renamed simply Community Service after the war, was eventually incorporated into the Education and Recreation Branch of the army, representing a clear victory for the reformers in the preservation of both the structures and the spirit of the recreation work.[26]

"We Ought Not to Be Wiped Out by Petty Jealousies or Politics": The Struggle for Social Hygiene Education

The structural transition of the social hygiene work was similarly smooth and seemed to suggest further success in the reformers' attempts to perpetuate their work. When the Social Hygiene Division was officially demobilized on 31 March 1919, its work with men in the army had already been transferred to the office of the surgeon general of the army, and the work of its navy section had been adopted by the Bureau of Navigation. The division's work with civilians was adopted by two separate government agencies, the Interdepartmental Social Hygiene Board and the Venereal Disease Division of the United States Public Health Service, as well as by the American Social Hygiene Association, a private organization that had worked with the CTCA throughout the war.[27]

Despite this apparent abundance of organizational strength for the continuation of social hygiene education, the postwar social hygienists suffered a series of challenges and defeats in their efforts to retain a civilian social hygiene program, which documented their declining power in the postwar years. Faced with a shrinking federal bureaucracy and the public reassertion of traditional mores, the sex education and prophylaxis programs, unlike the recreation work, succumbed to internal and external pressures and retreated from the bold advances of wartime.

The Interdepartmental Social Hygiene Board (ISHB) was established by federal law in July 1918 for the purpose of creating a comprehensive program for the prevention, treatment, and control of venereal disease.[28] Recall that during the war the ISHB played an important role in the law enforcement efforts of the CTCA. With the conclusion of hostilities the board was a logical successor to the CTCA in the handling of the social hygiene education work.

But the Interdepartmental Social Hygiene Board's innovative work during the war did nothing to ensure it a secure position as a powerful, or even permanent, government agency. Though the original financial provision for the board was a generous $4 million, its work was early hampered by Treasury Department rulings in November 1918 that narrowly defined the ways in which this money might be spent. One of these rulings, for instance, prevented the board from using the money for its own organization or administration.[29] These early setbacks foreshadowed the long-term outlook for the board. In 1921 Congress refused to provide for the budget of the Interdepartmental Social Hygiene Board. By October 1922 the ISHB had ceased to exist.[30]

In its final days the board had been beleaguered not only by the Treasury Department and the Congress, but also by its supposed allies in the struggle against venereal disease. The ISHB's initial appropriation of $4 million included $200,000 for the creation of a division of venereal diseases within the already existing United States Public Health Service (USPHS).[31] About the same time, on 1 July 1918, the president, by executive order, charged the USPHS with responsibility for the supervision of "all sanitary or public health activities carried on by any executive bureau, agency or office especially created for or concerned in the prosecution of the war."[32] This division was rapidly established and worked alongside the CTCA and the Interdepartmental Social Hygiene Board during the remainder of the war.

The relationship between the USPHS and its allies was never an easy one. The creation of the new division of the USPHS and the service's clear mandate to head all work related to the eradication of venereal disease brought conflict and disagreement to the social hygiene work. Members of the CTCA Social Hygiene Division resented the attempts of the USPHS to establish itself as the primary agency responsible for the battle against venereal disease. William H. Zinsser, head of the CTCA's social hygiene work with civilian men, felt especially threatened by the work of the USPHS and often argued that the USPHS had waited until the work was well established by the commission before stepping in to help. He exclaimed in a letter to Raymond Fosdick in October 1918: "I cannot seem to believe that the War Department . . . will stand, or will be forced to stand on the outside while the Public Health Service takes over all the work which the Surgeon General and the Commission have been doing in outside communities to fight venereal disease. . . . Now that you have made a success of it, we ought not to be wiped out by petty jealousies or politics."[33] The struggle for dominance between the Social Hygiene Division of the CTCA and the Venereal Division of the USPHS did not ease until the end of the larger war, when concessions by the USPHS, followed by the eventual demobilization of the CTCA, finally ended the conflicts between the two agencies.[34]

With the CTCA disbanded and the Interdepartmental Social Hygiene Board dismantled, the USPHS emerged as the sole government agency responsible for civilian social hygiene work. Though it would survive as an institutional entity, the USPHS, like its allies, suffered from a declining national interest in, and support for, social hygiene education. Federal expenditures for fighting venereal disease declined from $4 million in 1920 to just $60,000 in 1926. At the same time moralist forces in the nation, freed from restraints imposed upon them by the issue of efficiency during the war emergency, reasserted their opposition to a social hygiene education program based in public health rather than moral concerns.

During the war many Catholics had been troubled by the social hygiene work of the CTCA, particularly the movie *Fit to Fight*. The National Catholic War Council opposed the movie because, as one leading Catholic explained, "Out of negation nothing can come. Out of fear simply of physically evil consequences nothing can come when the danger of such consequences are *[sic]* removed. Purity is not simply abstinence from sexual indulgence: purity is the moral life of the soul."[35] To the Catholic leadership the CTCA's social hygiene program failed to emphasize the essentially moral issue at the heart of the social hygiene problem. Because of the war emergency, though, Catholics and the CTCA had managed to keep their disagreements private until late in the conflict.[36]

In the fall of 1918, however, the leaders of the National Catholic War Council made their hostility to the social hygiene work public. The extension of the CTCA's work with civilians, obvious in the production of a second film, *The End of the Road*, and the announcement of the CTCA's intention to show both its films to civilian audiences, including young women and girls, had prompted the Catholics' changed position. After the war the CTCA continued to expand its civilian programs, and the Catholic leadership continued "a national campaign against the entire social hygiene project."[37]

The Catholic establishment was not alone in its antagonism to the postwar social hygiene work, and the force of opposition ultimately compelled reformers to temper their programs to meet public approval. In the period following the war other moralists attacked the film *The End of the Road* and expanded the assault to include *Fit to Fight*. By 1922 the USPHS had withdrawn from circulation all of its educational films dealing with the subject of venereal disease. A similar attack on the promotion of chemical prophylaxis as a deterrent to disease prevented the establishment of any broad program of prophylaxis. Though many health officials understood the potential value of the prophylaxis program in their efforts to eradicate venereal disease, popular opposition to a program that many Americans believed encouraged promiscuity blocked the actions of public health officers.[38]

This determination to place morality above health was not isolated in the traditional moralist forces. The social hygiene movement, which had long been divided between moralist and efficiency forces, again exhibited this split personality in the postwar era. The American Social Hygiene Association (ASHA), a close ally of the CTCA during the war and an important successor after, demonstrated the power of the moralist position in its own reassertion of a moral perspective following the war.

With American entry into the war the CTCA had called upon the ASHA, the foremost force in American social hygiene education, to help it plan and carry out its work in that field. Many of the early publications of the CTCA's Social Hygiene Division were actually produced by the ASHA, which agreed with the commission's opposition to prostitution and its advocacy of a program of quarantine for diseased women and long-term internment for sexually promiscuous women and girls.

Yet there was always a difference of approach between the CTCA and the ASHA, which persisted despite their alliance. William H. Zinsser suggested this difference in a letter he penned in March 1919:

> You know that ever since I have been in this work, I have tried to get away as much as possible from the old reform point of view on social hygiene. . . . The very name "social hygiene" was used as camouflage. We threw it to the winds as far as we could, and on this stationery, as on all of our printed pamphlets we issued, wherever social hygiene was used, the words

"venereal diseases," "syphilis," "gonorrhea," etc., were used a hundred times to one of "social hygiene."

Zinsser identified his approach as one "of tackling this subject like business men; of 'selling' the idea to the public; of making it interesting, human, putting in a lot of red-blood and using brass knuckles where necessary." Zinsser maintained the difference between his work and that of the ASHA, declaring, "The army has done during the war a piece of work that . . . would have taken the American Social Hygiene Association a score of years."[39]

With the advent of the armistice and the demobilization of the CTCA, Zinsser worried that the disassembling of the CTCA apparatus would cause the national social hygiene program to revert back to its older emphasis on purity and morality. "When I saw myself going back to the varnish business," he intimated, "I was very much afraid all the work we had started here . . . would go begging, and, to make things worse, go back to the old school and give out unintentionally in all its printed matter the stereotyped expressions of the well-known reformer, pictured in a high hat, frock coat and white tie, and whose every third word was 'purity' with a capital 'P'." Zinsser hoped to avert this disaster and acquired a year's financing to continue publicizing the social hygiene position of the CTCA through the Bureau of Social Hygiene of the Rockefeller Foundation. Suggesting the importance he attached to supplementing the work of the ASHA, Zinsser stated, "We are going to be a part of the American Social Hygiene Association, but an entirely independent part."[40]

At the conclusion of hostilities the CTCA returned to the ASHA the workers it had borrowed during the war.[41] The close ties between the ASHA and the CTCA and the intentions of the ASHA to pick up where the CTCA had left off were obvious in the publications of the ASHA. In a pamphlet entitled *What the War has done to stamp out Venereal Diseases—A Summary and a Summons*, the ASHA documented the accomplishments of the CTCA in battling venereal disease and called upon civilian Americans to follow the lead of the War Department in aggressively carrying on the fight against venereal disease and prostitution in their communities. Like the CTCA, the ASHA argued for the eradication of prostitution, the development of recreational resources in the community, and the quarantine and treatment of persons infected with a venereal disease.[42]

Despite its close ties to the CTCA, as Zinsser had feared, in the postwar era the ASHA opposed the program of chemical prophylaxis promoted by the commission during the war and advocated the return to moralism as the basis for the social hygiene program. The rejection of chemical prophylaxis by the ASHA contributed to the acquiescence of many public health officers to the broader societal abandonment of this practical and scientific approach to venereal disease.[43]

During the 1920s the branch of the social hygiene movement emphasizing the moral aspects of the venereal disease problem resumed its dominance in the movement. These reformers pointed to loosening sexual codes to explain the tremendous increase in venereal disease that occurred during the decade and looked only to the control of sexual habits to counter the epidemic. Public health measures such as the chemical prophylaxis program of the CTCA were increasingly viewed as immoral promoters of promiscuity. Despite medical gains made during the decade, infection rates skyrocketed. The open discussion of venereal diseases cultivated by the CTCA was soon replaced by the old Victorian code of silence.[44]

The decline of the social hygiene forces in the period following the war and the social hygienists' increasing acceptance of a program described in moral terms demonstrated the importance of the war emergency in allowing for the development of the CTCA's sex education and prophylaxis programs. In the postwar period it became obvious that though the nation was now willing to accept some measure of social hygiene education, many Americans still expected that education to be moral in its content. Though the CTCA succeeded in establishing social hygiene education as a concern of the government with a permanent base in a federal agency, this was a somewhat hollow victory. The USPHS limped through the 1920s as a weak successor to the commission it had replaced. It would not be until the late 1930s that the federal government, supported by physicians and public health officials, would again approach the problem of venereal disease as the public health problem that it was.[45]

"The War's Over and Things Are Getting Right Again": The Collapse of the Law Enforcement Program

The Law Enforcement Division, like the other aspects of the CTCA's program, faced demobilization after the war. This work had never operated unopposed, and in the postwar era resistance to the invasive law enforcement program only increased. As a result the reformers were unable to establish a federal program to continue the law enforcement work. Ironically, the power of the moralist perspective in the postwar era, which undercut the social hygiene work, at the same time ensured that other Americans would pick up the effort to control and repress American sexuality.

The conclusion of hostilities brought no change in the attitudes of the Law Enforcement Division regarding the danger posed by sexually promiscuous women and girls. With the loss of what they referred to as the "fit to fight" motive, however, the division anticipated a growing law enforcement problem in the months until the troops could be completely demobilized. To prevent this degeneration, the division, as well as the secretary of war, urged the heightened vigilance of local law enforcement officers.[46]

In many cases local police officers were cooperative and initiated or maintained their antivice and antiliquor efforts at a high pitch.[47] Perhaps most impressively, the red-light districts closed by the commission during the war remained inoperative in the months following the armistice.[48]

Despite this success the commission encountered increasing opposition to its law enforcement work in the months following the cessation of hostilities. Prostitutes, charity girls, and men in uniform had continued to engage in illicit sexual activity throughout the months of war, despite the efforts of local police and the CTCA. After the war ended, these activities persisted, often with declining interference on the part of local law enforcement officers. In Ayer, Massachusetts, near Camp Devens, the CTCA reported, "Woman problem growing." And further, "Ayer has let down upon arrested women, and are giving light sentences. General relaxation in surrounding towns."[49] A similar problem arose near Camp Lewis, where a report on law enforcement efforts in the towns nearby suggested, "This is a transition time between the old officers and the newly elected ones . . . and combined with the end of hostilities and the demobilization the general laxity and uncertainty is becoming quite noticable *[sic]*, producing harder conditions to handle in law enforcement."[50]

The easing of local law enforcement efforts often resulted in a growing problem with prostitution. In Atlanta, for instance, loosened conditions following the end of the war led to the reestablishment of the local vice trade. "Not long after the armistice was signed," one report noted:

> the police department relaxed in their activity, and gradually the condition that existed before the Camp was erected is returning. Many of the hotels are again harboring prostitutes, and porters, bellboys, etc., soliciting for them. They claim "it is all over now" and expect no further police interference. . . . The prostitutes, porters, bellboys and chauffeurs all claim a return of prosperity.[51]

Confirming the link between the end of the war and the loosening conditions, a report ten days later stated,

> The prostitutes are permitted to operate in the various resorts unmolested. Bellboys, porters and hotel employees in general look upon no one with suspicion. All frankly admit that they have nothing to fear, inasmuch as the police have ceased to be interested in their doings. "The war's over and things are getting right again," is the comment heard on all sides.[52]

While in some cities and towns the police only passively resisted the CTCA through their diminished law enforcement efforts, in other cities local officials aggressively protested the CTCA's continued repressive work in their communities. In San Francisco, for instance, the Board of Supervisors refused to recommend the budget proposed by the city health officer. When the CTCA's district director visited the city to investigate the problem, it became clear that the city's resistance to the health officer's work was rooted in hostility toward the law enforcement program carried on during the war. Describing his encounter with one supervisor, the district director reported, "He stated that nobody had the right to come to San Francisco and dictate to the San Francisco people what the social life of the city should be." This same supervisor suggested that he would favor the appropriation if it were indeed a health measure, "but if it had anything to do with the law enforcement work and the raids which had been executed in San Francisco, he would be bitterly opposed to it." A second supervisor, the district director noted, had stated, "it was high time that the police power which had been exercised by the Federal Government during the period of the war should be given back to the state, where it belonged." The district director concluded, "It is my impression . . . that it is their desire to have San Francisco 'wide open.' They . . . made it clear that they felt San Francisco could handle its own social problems."[53] Though the supervisors eventually agreed to make an emergency appropriation later if the anti–venereal disease clinic were threatened with closure, they did not make the appropriation originally requested by the city health officer.

The hostility toward the CTCA's work in San Francisco carried over into the courts. Describing an interview with the U. S. District Court judge in San Francisco, the CTCA district director explained, "His attitude is that the war is over, to all intents and purposes, and that the people feel that the Federal Government should withdraw. He said it is impossible in his court to get a jury to convict any of the women that are brought in now." As a result, the district director concluded, "It looks to me as though the whole Federal Court program here is broken down. There are two distinct effects following this: First of all, there is now no fear of the Federal Courts in the hearts of these women; and secondly, the Moral Squad feel that it is quite useless to work up their cases and make arrests."[54] Though the district in San Francisco remained closed, this success in no way eradicated vice in San Francisco. Instead, despite that limited victory, the reformers endured a resounding defeat in that city as local officials abandoned the CTCA's law enforcement program.

In New Orleans, too, the end of the war brought trouble for the CTCA. The city of New Orleans had promised to keep its red-light district closed, but with the conclusion of the war vice again flourished there. A field officer for the Law Enforcement Division reported distressing conditions in February 1919 and estimated that at least twenty-five hundred prostitutes had returned. "It seems that word has gone out that New Orleans is 'good' and so they are flocking here from far and near," Capt. J. B. Collins reported.[55]

The CTCA's response to the situation in New Orleans reflected the difficulties faced by the commission in the context of its own demobilization. Though William H. Zinsser protested what he saw as the degenerating situation in New Orleans, his superiors in the War Department refused to pursue the issue as diligently as they had during the war. In a letter to the mayor of New Orleans, Secretary of War Baker expressed his disagreement with Zinsser's position and his own refusal to believe that conditions in New Orleans had worsened.[56] As Assistant Secretary of War F. P. Keppel explained to Zinsser in a letter, "The War Department is consciously relaxing its direction and control which it exercised during the days of war, and is endeavoring to stimulate local civilian organizations in carrying on this important phase of the work." Though Keppel thanked Zinsser for his "untiring efforts," which had been "instrumental in revolutionizing public sentiment towards prostitution and all its attending evils," it appeared, at least to Zinsser, that his program in New Orleans had been abandoned by his superiors.[57]

On 31 March 1919 another CTCA worker accused New Orleans of having thirty-five to forty houses of prostitution operating in the old district. When the city's district attorney demanded evidence for this statement, the CTCA's abandonment of its earlier activism in that city was clear in its response. Refusing to dispatch investigators to New Orleans, James H. Buell of the CTCA wrote, "Our immediate purpose is to direct the attention of these agencies to the existence of conditions requiring correction. . . . We feel that the officers of the civil community may then be relied upon as American citizens equally interested in the welfare of their army, and of their own citizens, to initiate such investigation and resultant enforcement of law, as will eliminate the causes of the trouble."[58] Facing its own demobilization, the CTCA was forced to rely on civilian America to continue its law enforcement program, even in cities known to be hostile to its work.

The Law Enforcement Division was scheduled for early dismantling on 31 March 1919.[59] Although the division's work had been critical to the program of the CTCA, in peacetime the invasive work of the division was no longer acceptable. In a bulletin detailing the demobilization plans for the Law Enforcement Division, the director of the division suggested, "As the country returns to the peace basis, it is inevitable that the work of the Law Enforcement Division be passed over gradually to the ordinary civilian law enforcement authorities of the country."[60] Turning to local legislators, local law enforcement agencies, and the Interdepartmental Social Hygiene Board, the War Department hoped to promote a shared responsibility for the work once carried out by the CTCA's Law Enforcement Division.

In its final months the Law Enforcement Division concentrated on a legislative program designed to establish at the state level the apparatus for the continued suppression of vice.[61] To assist the states in their adoption of appropriate legislation, the CTCA published a pamphlet, *Standard Forms of Laws*, which included laws "For The Repression of Prostitution, The Control of Venereal Diseases, The Establishment and Management of Reformatories for Women and Girls, and Suggestions for a Law Relating to Feeble-Minded Persons."[62]

The legislative program began in January 1919 and quickly led to the passage of laws in a number of states.[63] As the CTCA clearly understood, however, these laws would have little impact without their enforcement by local police agencies. Confirming the government's continued interest in the law enforcement program despite the armistice, Secretary of War Baker wrote a letter to the governors and mayors of the country urging their continued cooperation in law enforcement efforts: "I can assure you that the War Department will continue to do its full part in these matters and will relax no vigilance in maintaining the high standard which now prevails." Turning to the mayors and governors for continued aid, Baker stated further, "It is imperative, however, that every agency of law enforcement, state and municipal, should redouble their efforts to enforce all laws against these and allied evils during the demobilizing process."[64] The dismantling of the CTCA and its law enforcement apparatus made this enhanced local attention vital.

With the demobilization of the Law Enforcement Division imminent, the War Department initially turned to the commanding officers of the training camps to play a critical role in the law enforcement work.[65] Because the CTCA was in the hands of the military, this delegation of responsibility was reasonable. By the summer of 1919, however, when the final demobilization of the CTCA was completed, the secretary of war determined that military personnel should no longer interfere in the policing of civilian communities near the training camps.[66]

When the Law Enforcement Division demobilized on 31 March 1919, the majority of the responsibility for the broad-based program of the division passed to the Interdepartmental Social Hygiene Board.[67] The board had cooperated with the CTCA in this work during the war and had been established by Congress for the express purpose of coordinating an anti–venereal disease campaign that included a program of detention, quarantine, and long-term commitment of civilians and that extended beyond the end of the war.[68] As already suggested, however, the board fared poorly in the postwar era and folded by the end of 1922. With the death of the board the national law enforcement work of the CTCA perished as well.

The policing of sexuality did not cease with the departure of the Interdepartmental Social Hygiene Board, however. Though the CTCA was unable to institutionalize its law enforcement work permanently on the national level, the work continued in many cases on the state and local level throughout the 1920s. Many people challenged the sexual code of the CTCA and continued to engage in illicit sex in the postwar era, but many others staunchly opposed the new sexual mores represented by those actions and demanded legislated control of sexuality. The success of the CTCA's legislative campaign is one example of the activism of these moralist forces. In addition the regulation of dance halls, the rise of movie censorship, and the national prohibition amendment all represented the efforts of moralists to stem the tide of changing mores breaking over the nation in the 1920s. Generally controlled by the forces of entrenched tradition, however, these programs rarely represented the position staked out by the CTCA during the war.

The CTCA experienced mixed results in its efforts to perpetuate its programs. Although largely successful in institutionalizing the recreation program, which aroused suspicion only when it operated on Sundays, the reformers were significantly less successful in preserving their social hygiene and law enforcement work. Both programs survived, but they did so in forms so dramatically altered from the war-time campaigns that the agenda of the CTCA was hardly recognizable in their work.

In the context of the CTCA's failure to establish a strong institutional legacy, the importance of its cultural legacy, in the form of changed men and women, grew. Success in the effort to remake the habits and values of the soldiers and civilians would have created a massive corps of crusaders who might have continued the commission's campaigns in the streets of American cities and towns. Here too, however, the commission experienced only marginal success. Though the reformers had succeeded in building the mechanisms to communicate their message to the American people, that message was largely lost on its audience.

"The Tamperers Should Be Told to Mind Their Own Business": The Myth of the Uniformed Crusader

On the evening of 14 November 1917, Cpl. Charles B. Merritt wrote home to his mother and described his camp routine. It was a particularly quiet night, he noted, since most of his friends had "shoved off to town for the evening," while he chose to remain in camp to write a letter. Commenting on his busy schedule, Merritt added, "We don't have time to get lonesome here in the evening. . . . We always have some way to pass away the spare time." He continued, "There is generally something going on in the Y.M.C.A. every eve. On Sunday there is preaching in the morning and evening but by the time I get my washing done and write a few letters I don't have time to do anything."[69]

Over the next four months Corporal Merritt was better able to find time to take advantage of the amusement available for him in camp, and his enthusiasm for the recreation program grew accordingly. He had already begun playing football for Company M by the time of his letter in early November, and he commented enthusiastically the next February, "I am getting to be a regular visitor at the library. I have only missed one night in about the last ten."[70] By March of 1918 Merritt was an outspoken supporter of the Commission on Training Camp Activities' recreation program. Merritt exclaimed to his mother, "The Red Cross and Y.M.C.A. are doing wonders for the soldiers away from home. The Y has been the salvation of many boys."[71]

Merritt's response to the CTCA programs would have heartened the commission reformers. Appreciative of the opportunities for recreation available to him in the training camp, Merritt also seemed to understand the reformative capacity of the recreation and its resultant importance in the lives of the men in uniform. Merritt, it seems, was a convert.

How common, though, was Merritt's response? Was the Commission on Training Camp Activities successful, as Baker suggested, in changing the character of the American fighting man? Though failing to create a meaningful institutional legacy, did the reformers nevertheless leave behind a bequest in the remade habits and values of a generation?

Certainly the CTCA achieved some successes among the men in uniform during World War One. Cpl. Charles B. Merritt was not alone in his enrollment in the CTCA in-camp programs. The U.S. Army Military History Institute has conducted a survey of World War One veterans in the form of a detailed questionnaire regarding their experiences as soldiers. In their responses to these questionnaires veterans proved the importance of the CTCA recreation program in the lives of many soldiers. Responding to the question "What forms of off-duty recreation were common?" soldiers often listed athletic activities, entertainment at the theaters and organizational huts, singing, movies, and dances. It was true, as the commission suggested, that the men looked for entertainment in their free hours, and the CTCA's provision for those recreational needs found ready participants among the troops.[72]

As the commission had hoped, too, the recreation often seemed to serve at least some of the reformers' purposes. Most obviously, the furnishing of recreation helped to fill the unoccupied hours of a soldier's day. Discussing the usefulness of the soldier huts, David Miles Thornton, a soldier at Camp Meade, explained, "They furnish the only places for pleasant recreation. . . . The boys will go to the Y.M.C.A. when they cannot find entertainment elsewhere. It is an invaluable institution in camp and its importance cannot be over-emphasized." And further, "The Y.M.C.A. is the most important factor in camp. It is this institution and this one only that helps to build up the morale of the army. That after all is the foundation stone of the success of an army."[73] Here was another soldier who both appreciated and understood the commission.

Not all soldiers, however, seemed cognizant of the existence of all of this recreation provided for their benefit. Some veterans answering Military History Institute inquiries about their off-duty recreation seemed to have absolutely no awareness of the CTCA program and complained vividly about the conditions in camp. Again in response to the question, "What forms of off-duty recreation were common?" one veteran replied succinctly, "No recreation all work." Another noted, "We did not have any forms of recreation." Still another complained, "No recreation available—just laid around when off duty."[74] These responses were not uncommon, and suggest that the commission's success in providing recreational opportunities for the troops was never complete.

The CTCA had also hoped that the presence of recreational activities within the camps, combined with the new knowledge acquired through the social hygiene program, would limit the soldiers' excursions into local communities. Whether the attractiveness of in-camp activities actually produced soldiers preferring an afternoon or evening in camp to one in town is difficult to discern. Certainly there were soldiers who found sufficient amusement inside the camps to make the more expensive trip to town unnecessary. As Edward F. Allen described this success, "A certain general in a southern cantonment reported that covering a period of three weeks, while seventy per cent. of the men *could* have had leave from the camp, only 30 per cent. availed themselves of the privilege. The meaning of this is clear: that camp was more attractive than the adjacent towns. The boys knew there would be more doing, at less cost."[75]

Yet other observers read the evidence differently and were less convinced about the propensity of the men in uniform to spend their afternoons in camp. Observing the city of Anniston, Alabama, on the day of the first World Series game of 1917 and noting that there was a score board, four movie houses, an opera house, and a dance provided for the men remaining in camp, a worker for a CTCA affiliate concluded, "The streets in the city, were all crowded. This makes me feel conclusively that regardless of what entertainment is furnished at the Post, the men prefer to be in the city during their leisure time."[76] Even Raymond Fosdick acknowledged the tendency of the soldiers to leave camp in their free hours.[77] In their responses to questionnaires veterans, too, made it clear that trips to town were a popular form of recreation.[78]

These trips to town, however, did not necessarily constitute a rejection of the CTCA's purposes. The commission had hoped to reconstitute the relationship between soldier and civilian and restore the reputation of the military man. Proper interactions between upstanding citizens and the men in uniform were permitted, even encouraged, by the commission. The crucial issue remained the soldiers' behavior. What, in other words, did the troops do once in town? What was the nature of their relationship with local civilians, and did it represent a success for the CTCA in its attempts to change the soldiers' behaviors and beliefs?

Though soldiers often completed training in regions far distant from their own, they nevertheless commented frequently on the fine treatment they received from neighboring communities. One editorial in the Camp Wadsworth *Gas Attack* asserted regarding Spartanburg, South Carolina,

> The truth is that we have put real Southern hospitality to the hardest sort of test, and it has stood it splendidly. Our relations with our civilian neighbors are in nearly every case most cordial and pleasant. We have been received into their homes, fed, entertained, and made friends of. A quiet little Southern town has taken pretty good care of 30,000 men, many of them used to big town conveniences.[79]

While this sort of editorial can easily be dismissed as a required courtesy of a newspaper, reports from individual enlisted men supported the paper's contention.[80]

Soldiers described participation in locally sponsored recreation and the development of cordial ties to civilians through that recreation. A soldier from Camp Wadsworth used words that would have thrilled the Spartanburg WCCS:

> I became an associate member of the First Presbyterian Church of Spartanburg, singing in the choir most of the time, and enjoying the fellowship of the good people of the church very much. All of the boys made a number of friends in this way, and we were always invited to Sunday dinner at the various homes of the people of the church. These invitations were heartily welcomed as it was a real touch of home.

This same soldier enjoyed dances with women from a local college, held at a golf club.[81] Other soldiers described their appreciation for the churches and fraternal orders that welcomed their out-of-town members with "the door open wide and the hand of good fellowship extended."[82] Soldiers described auto rides, concerts, Christmas dinners, and group sings, and they recounted simple acts of kindness in sufficient detail to suggest the importance those acts had held.[83] Much of this recreation bore the clear imprint of the commission program, and in this sense the progressives in the CTCA gained an important success.

Other evidence, however, suggests that the traditional experience of the soldier as social pariah persisted. The *Camp Dodger* in November 1917 caught word of a movement afoot in Des Moines "to prevent Camp Dodge soldiers from meeting Des Moines girls." The *Dodger* argued vehemently that men would naturally seek the acquaintance of "good, wholesome girls" and suggested:

> If there is anything which will bring about a condition of lax morality in this field it is just such a wild eyed movement as this. Instead of setting up a bar which will block all opportunity for the men of the 88th becoming acquainted with decent girls in Des Moines, these women should do all in their power to make such introductions easier. Otherwise, the soldiers will have to find acquaintances for themselves. And it is here that the great danger lies.[84]

Similarly, in Spartanburg, South Carolina, a city many soldiers had described as hospitable, a woman brought her nieces to court because "folks were talking because the girls had been seen walking with soldiers." Mortified, the girls denied the action, "as if such an allegation betokened a high crime or misdemeanor." At this point the mayor of Spartanburg interceded for the reputation of the soldiers and encouraged the girls to associate with the troops.[85] Angered by the girls' behavior, though, an article in the Camp Wadsworth *Gas Attack* asserted: "We feel like prolonging Mayor Floyd's advice and saying: 'Young lady, we suspect that there are others like you in the country. We suspect that your attitude is not so much your fault—though it smacks a little of provincialism—as it is the relic of peace times where all good men and true didn't rush to join the armed forces of the nation.' " And further: "To-day it is different. You should realize this, young lady. You should let your mind cope with the problem that civilians who were worth being seen with in the rusty piping times of peace are thrice worth the venture of a promenade in these present days when they have become soldiers in the greatest of all wars."[86] Despite the CTCA's best efforts to polish the reputation of the men in uniform, the fact remained that not every citizen abandoned the old perceptions of the soldier.

The survival of these traditional notions of the troops was likely encouraged by soldiers and civilians who protested, or even rejected altogether, the commission's new moral standards. Some complainants objected to the tight control exerted by the commission. Edith Fosdick Bodley of Louisville wrote Raymond Fosdick in April 1918 to complain that local dances were going to be halted entirely if the regulations forwarded by the chaperones were not tempered. Suggesting that the best citizens of Louisville had sought to welcome the soldiers and that the men in uniform had responded gratefully to the opportunities thus offered, Bodley concluded that the behavior of the chaperones appointed by the local committee was "most disagreeable" and the situation "impossible."[87] Similarly, complaining about "tamperers" who sought to control the dances attended by soldiers in Des Moines, a soldier at Camp Dodge expressed what may have been a common attitude among the men in uniform. Although it is not clear who the intruders were, the actions he attributed to them fit the ascribed behavior of WCCS workers. The soldier asserted: "In Des Moines a king-pin tamperer has forced himself into the public eye during the last week. He proposes to remedy 'conditions at dances attended by soldiers.' That is, he believes that soldiers should not be allowed to dance with girls unless they are given an introduction of the type which embodies everything from ancestors to present 'standing in the community'." Drawing a parallel between this reformer's efforts and Mrs. John D. Rockefeller's plan to organize for "the protection of the working girls in cities near the cantonments," this soldier declared: "Only one thing is to be done. The tamperers should be told to mind their own business and, if they refuse, they should be dealt with the same as other enemies of the service."[88] Anxious to meet women in a freer environment, this soldier opposed the efforts of reformers to control the dance hall.

Social commentator H. L. Mencken added his voice to those who disparaged the work of the commission. "Disappointment now devours the vitals of those optimists who hoped and believed that the entrance of the United States into the war would throw a wet blanket over the uplift," he lamented in September 1917.

> Theoretically it seemed to be very likely. The thing could be proved indeed, by the history of the wars of the past. But actually it has not turned out as the wishbone forecasted. Far from being retired to the rear, there to eat out their great throbbing hearts, the uplifters are more noisily to the front than ever before.

Acknowledging the impact of the war, Mencken concluded: "The only difference is that they now concentrate the stupendous power of their rectitude upon the boys in khaki. A year ago it was the poor working girl, may God defend her! But now it is the fair young soldier."[89]

A more serious challenge to the CTCA came from soldiers and civilians who rejected not only the controls exerted by the commission, but also the moral standards underlying those controls. Many soldiers opposed the restriction on their use of alcohol. Reflecting his attachment to the old style of military camps, a Dr. Hughes complained to his state senator about soldier prohibition:

> It seems that you are sleeping on the porch and that you'r *[sic]* not at all posted on history [of] war and that your ideas seems to be that of a sissy. . . . All the great wars since Washington's time up to now were fought and won by the men of the bone and sinew of this country. All of them drank whiskey and beer and the two greatest nations of the world are today fighting each other England and Germany. Their men are whiskey drinkers and beer drinkers.

Reminding his senator that soldiers had always been drinkers, this citizen claimed that alcohol-free zones and soldier prohibition were unnecessary and even unmasculine.[90] Veterans answering questionnaires also suggested the continuing popularity of alcohol use among the troops. Though there are hundreds of "no" answers to question 14 of the veterans' survey, "Was drinking a problem?" in many instances that reply was followed by a detailed response to the next question, which asked how soldiers procured their alcohol. In some cases, it seems, the enlisted men simply did not consider the use of alcohol a problem.

Despite the CTCA's efforts to the contrary, evidence suggests also that sexual relations with local women remained an important part of many soldiers' recreation. Certainly some men in uniform embraced the moral precepts taught by the CTCA. One soldier acknowledged deep concordance with the advice of the YMCA paper, which urged a clean life. Eager to avoid the trials of a youth in his unit, who was "ruined for life in a social way all because he wanted to be able to talk of a fast life as the older fellows do who have gone thru the mill," he wrote to his mother to reassure her of his convictions and of his fundamental agreement with the advice of the YMCA camp paper. Although sympathetic to the commission's goals, however, this soldier did not attribute his conversion to the CTCA, suggesting that he had reached his moral position "long before joining the army."[91]

Another soldier, though, found the social hygiene material deeply influential. Having attended a lecture entitled "In the Wake of the Huns," a part of which was dedicated to an elucidation of the difference between the honorable wounds of battle and the disgraceful wounds of disease, he wrote, "When I saw that picture drawn before me I almost cried and no better way could reach my heart than the touching appeal he asked us last night."[92] Moved by the commission's message, this doughboy pledged himself to its standards.

Many other soldiers, however, openly rejected the commission's teachings. The continuing difficulties faced by the CTCA's law enforcement program demonstrated the continuing prevalence of illicit relations between soldiers and civilians. In their questionnaire responses veterans confirmed this reality. As one veteran stated succinctly, his off-duty activities included "Wine, women and song."[93] Other veterans recalled a similar collection of pastimes: "I would have to say gambling—liquor and women" and "Some gambled, some drank, some women" were not unusual answers.[94] Illicit sex with women had been the primary concern of the CTCA reformers as they worked to shape the behavior of the men in uniform, and yet these relationships remained common, even if not condoned.

Evidence on venereal disease rates, though, suggests that the CTCA succeeded in lowering infection rates, despite the continued prevalence of sexual adventuring. In the training camps in the United States, rates of venereal disease among white troops ranged from a low of 61.9 per thousand in February 1918 to a high of 167.3 per thousand in July 1918. In France those rates dropped dramatically to 34.64 per thousand. Most importantly in the eyes of some reformers, a study conducted in five of the cantonments in 1918 and 1919 demonstrated that 96 percent of the cases of venereal disease among troops in the stateside cantonments had been contracted by the troops before their enlistment. Overall, venereal disease dropped by 300 percent among the army troops during the war.[95] As the reformers had promised, the men were safer from venereal infection once in uniform than they had been as civilians before the war.[96]

Although the reformers of the CTCA earned a victory over the dangers of venereal disease, however, this achievement cannot be credited to the purity of the men in uniform. Chemical prophylaxis, not the absence of sexual relations, seems more likely to warrant credit for the falling disease rates.

It appears that the CTCA achieved only partial success in its campaign to remake military life. While many soldiers enjoyed the recreational opportunities offered by the commission, and while venereal infection rates dropped, it is clear from the troops' admissions and from the CTCA's law enforcement problems that many Americans continued to participate in the very activities the commission hoped to prevent.

The Legacy of the CTCA: The Decline of Progressivism

With the cessation of hostilities the power of the Commission on Training Camp Activities faded rapidly. Just as the reformers had feared, the national relaxation in peacetime brought a declining commitment to the values of the progressives and a rising resistance to the work of the commission. Further, as the war receded into the past, it became evident that the training of the men in uniform and their civilian counterparts had failed to create a legion of crusaders capable of carrying on the work of the commission. Lacking any wholesale conversion to their perspective, the loss of war-time authority gutted the CTCA reformers' programs and ended their dreams of a nation remade in their own image.

Why were the progressives in the CTCA unsuccessful in fulfilling their long-term goals? On the simplest level one can argue that their hopes for the transformation of a nation were unrealistic, even naive. This conclusion, however, seems to evade the deeper issue of why their plans were unreasonable. One must ask what it was about this particular reform vision that led to its failure. Why were the CTCA reformers, who wielded enormous power and achieved some important successes during the war, unable to transform their war-time strength into lasting changes in American life?

The CTCA reformers set as their ultimate goal the development of a single, shared national culture, based in the habits and values of the white, urban, middle class. Yet, as the CTCA reformers set about homogenizing American culture, they faced a rapidly changing nation and an increasingly diverse population. For the first time in the nation's history, the census of 1920 identified an urban majority in the United States. Though many of those urban Americans continued to live in isolated small towns, the consequences of the population shifts of the late nineteenth and early twentieth centuries were nevertheless dramatic. Increasingly, the culture of the city—with its looser social standards and its anonymity—came to constitute the common culture of the nation. Rural and more traditional Americans, however, did not relinquish their cultural authority without a contest. In the years before World War One, with the nation changing rapidly under the forces of industrialization, immigration, and urbanization, traditionalists challenged the cultural authority of the urban working class and struggled to return the nation to a nineteenth-century morality. Long-term victory for the reformers would have required that they gain broad-based support for their programs, not only among progressives but among this increasingly diverse and contentious American populace.

At odds with the cultural perspectives of both the working class and the rural traditionalists, the CTCA had stepped into this conflict willingly in 1917. The reformers were well aware of the nation's increasing complexity and the resulting cultural disagreements; indeed, it was the sense of cultural chaos that motivated the CTCA in its efforts to cultivate a shared set of habits and values. In shaping their programs, the CTCA activists reacted against what they understood as the growing instability and turmoil of their society.

It was this preoccupation with social stability, in part, that undercut the reformers' other concerns and confounded their efforts to transform American culture. Calling for what they viewed as vast reforms in American society, the reformers were nevertheless culturally conservative, eager to mitigate the social and economic dislocations the war was likely to bring in its wake. The CTCA's conservatism was most obvious in its defense of the social and economic status quo. The CTCA was clearly advocating transformations in training camp culture and in American culture more generally, and yet the commission always intended to control those changes, to ensure that they took only very specific and rather limited forms. As a result, though the reformers allied themselves with the rhetoric of the war and promised to create a more democratic and inclusive nation, they established programs that were instead frequently coercive and often exclusive.

As their fears formed and they contemplated solutions, the CTCA reformers were profoundly affected by their social identities. Middle-class, urban, white Americans, the CTCA reformers surveyed their world from a perspective shaped by that identity and saw in those unlike themselves a threat to the cohesion of their society. Middle-class in outlook, they found in the rising cultural importance of working-class recreation a danger to the morality and efficiency of American life. Urban in origin, they found the particular traditionalism of rural Americans a backward and ultimately inadequate response to the perils of modern life. Born as white Americans, they accepted stereotypes of African American promiscuity and criminality. Seeing cataclysm in difference, the reformers sought sameness in a shared allegiance to their own social and cultural values.

The CTCA hoped to transform the camps and communities into bastions of progressive respectability, peopled by Americans with the habits and values of the white, urban middle class. But the CTCA did not intend to disrupt the traditional boundaries between classes, genders, or racial groups. Instead, the CTCA attempted to construct a reform program that encouraged Americans to adopt the habits and values of the reformers without questioning their own position in the social and economic status quo. Insistent upon a program that cultivated only certain values, the CTCA included among those values an unwavering respect for, and acceptance of, traditional class, gender, and racial roles.

In the program of the commission this essential conservatism carried with it a distinct coerciveness. Though beginning their work with an assertion of their preference for constructive programs and their belief that their goals could be reached through positive persuasion, the progressives' program contained many coercive elements. Much of the coercion was subtle. In the camps and communities, for instance, the CTCA encouraged the development of certain types of recreation, such as athletics, singing, and well-chaperoned dances, pumping federal funds and personnel into programs to cultivate these recreational forms. In promoting these amusements, though, the CTCA was attempting to control the cultural environment of the local community. In the process of developing what they viewed as appropriate recreation, the CTCA often overruled local custom, imposing the progressives' leisure habits with only limited appreciation for the concerns of residents who embraced a different cultural perspective.

In other cases the CTCA's coercion was even less disguised and more blatantly repressive. Inside the camps the CTCA censored camp libraries and carefully controlled the content of any entertainment presented to the troops. Out in the communities the CTCA forced the closure of red-light districts and promoted the arrest, detention, quarantine, and long-term internment of prostitutes and promiscuous girls. In this context Americans whose recreational habits or sexual mores conflicted with the idealized vision of the progressives often found themselves under attack. Similarly, Americans whom the reformers *assumed* would embrace other behavioral standards endured pressure from the commission. African Americans, for instance, faced the CTCA's acceptance of racial segregation, which promoted substantial discrimination.

The progressives of the CTCA moved easily between their positive recreation and education programs, on one hand, and repression, on the other hand, in their efforts to transform Americans into crusaders. Promising Americans a new nation, strengthened by shared values, the commission preferenced only its own perspective. The reformers' unwillingness to accept, or even acknowledge, the existence of legitimate cultural alternatives underlay the attempt at homogenization through cultural nationalism. The dismissal of the habits and values of other cultural groups evident in the CTCA's work, however, undercut the reformers' ability to convert the populace.

Having raised their expectations in response to the reformers' rhetoric, many Americans must have been disappointed by the reality of the commission's work.[97] Soldiers, anticipating increased recreational opportunities, found their entertainment carefully constricted and their most traditional pastimes prohibited. Women, promised a new social equality and an end to the sexual double standard, saw that double standard reinforced as they faced continued subordination in the recreation work and outright repression in the law enforcement program. Working-class Americans, enlisted in a war for democracy, too often found little place for themselves or their civilian counterparts in programs designed to eliminate their cultural influence. Rural Americans, assured of the importance of local preference in shaping recreation, encountered an unwavering War Department that brought unwelcome change to local cultural patterns. African Americans, enlisted in a war for freedom, faced segregation and discrimination in programs more concerned with social stability than social justice. The CTCA progressives were not purposely inconsistent, but they suffered from internal contradictions that were starkly revealed when the reformers gained the power to apply their social theories in the real world. These internal contradictions alienated would-be supporters of the commission's work.

Similar conflicts within the reform coalition itself further hindered the commission's ability to foment deep and lasting change. From the beginning the CTCA represented a variety of progressive types, including especially moral reformers, social justice reformers, and efficiency reformers. In some cases these groups of reformers agreed on the value of the commission's work and shared a commitment to the programs. The provision of recreation for the men in uniform, for instance, easily won the support of all of these reformers. Other aspects of the commission's programs, however, highlighted the differences among the reformers and the inconsistencies inherent in their coalition. Sunday recreation, for instance, seemed crucial to efficiency reformers, whereas moralists worried that breaking the Sabbath was morally destructive to the individual and to the nation. More dramatically, efficiency reformers favored social hygiene education and chemical prophylaxis as a means to prevent manpower losses. To moralists, however, these programs seemed to encourage the very behaviors they were slated to prevent. Similarly, while the efficiency forces developed and implemented the harshly repressive antiprostitution campaign with the blessing of many moralists, social justice reformers recoiled from what they perceived as the unjust and discriminatory punishment of women. And although efficiency reformers favored segregation as a potential route to racial peace, social justice reformers from the African American community recognized the racial slight and the repression inherent in that policy.

Though including the three main wings of the progressive movement, in the implementation of its programs the CTCA represented above all the efficiency reformers. Throughout its program efficiency concerns outweighed social justice and moral concerns in the determination of policy. This choice often cost the commission the support of former allies. During the war internal opposition to the CTCA remained relatively quiet. Maude Miner quit the Committee on Protective Work for Girls without publicizing her reasons for leaving. Catholic leadership maintained silence about their opposition to sex education until late in the war. After the cessation of hostilities, however, opponents of the commission's work were significantly more vocal and often influenced the shape of the CTCA's successors. The social hygiene movement, under the auspices of the USPHS, turned away from public health issues in its rejection of prophylaxis and reemphasized a program based in morality. The law enforcement work was dismantled on the national level and reestablished on the local level, also as part of the moral crusade. African Americans asserted their social justice agenda with new methods and new power following the war. Regaining their claim to legitimate opposition after the war's cessation, opponents of the CTCA redirected the postwar work away from the focus on efficiency. In doing so these reformers signaled the collapse of the progressive coalition.

One must also acknowledge the importance of the war itself in precipitating the decline of the CTCA and its vision. Obviously the commission would not have existed at all without the war. The nature of the CTCA as a war-time agency, though, may provide a final explanation for its limited legacy. During the war the reformers employed in the CTCA brandished extensive federal power. Perhaps a longer war would have provided the CTCA with sufficient opportunity to institutionalize its programs. In World War One, however, its brief exposure to power led only to the alienation of countless Americans, both inside and outside the reform coalition.

The CTCA's defeat in the postwar era was intimately linked to the broader fate of the progressive movement in the years following the war. During the 1920s, though many reformers continued to pursue reforms that could be termed progressive, the progressive movement ceased to function as a powerful reform coalition. Reformers who had once viewed each other as allies no longer worked together as members of a movement, but instead pursued narrower reform agendas in isolation from, or even in competition with, their earlier compatriots. In addition, in the postwar era reformers found the national political atmosphere substantially less hospitable to their efforts. Turning away from the proponents of reform, American voters placed the federal government in the hands of Warren G. Harding, who applied the power of the presidency to the support of big business and a return to "normalcy."[98]

The CTCA was both a cause and a victim of these changes. It seems likely that by the end of the war the contradictions within the progressive movement, made obvious as a result of programs like that of the CTCA, had become overwhelming and intolerable to many members of the movement and helped to prompt the dissolution of the coalition. In the postwar period these reformers would have seen little reason for defending the programs of a commission that had broadly overlooked their concerns or for maintaining a coalition with reformers whose agenda shared so little with their own. The collapse of the progressive movement left reform-minded Americans like those who had worked in the CTCA isolated and largely powerless.

The CTCA reformers were further undermined by the general loss of popular support for reform and for activist government, again a development for which they may bear some responsibility. During the progressive era Americans were broadly supportive of reform and had often called for and accepted a growth in government power. When the United States entered the war, though, Americans experienced an exertion of federal power in their lives to an extent previously unknown. There was much in that experience to discourage continued support for governmental activism. The CTCA, for instance, had often proven invasive, coercive, or even repressive in its use of federal power. This encounter with the controlling side of progressivism likely alienated some Americans from the cause of reform and fostered a renewed suspicion of federal interventionism. The ruptures in the movement caused by unequal access to federal power, complemented by the broader disaffection of the citizenry, ensured the eventual collapse of the progressive reform effort.

Following his service with the Commission on Training Camp Activities, in 1919 Raymond Fosdick traveled to Paris to assume responsibility as an undersecretary general of the new League of Nations. Like Wilson, Fosdick was a strong advocate for international association and saw in the league the world's hope for the future. He wrote the day he departed for

Europe, "It is rather exciting, for there is something new stirring in the world today, and the adventure and hope of it are in the air." The league, he hoped, could rescue the world from the pressures of vindictiveness and repression. "The League stands for disarmament, for peace, for international justice, for the protection of backward peoples, for a better standard of living, for the relief of suffering, for the fight against disease. . . . If the League succeeds it will be because its emphasis has been positive and creative, rather than repressive." As he had suggested regarding the CTCA, Fosdick maintained that the force of positive persuasion would allow the league its proper place in world affairs.

Fosdick's optimism was tempered, though, by his awareness of the horrors of the war and the resulting conditions in Europe, as well as the punitive aspects of the peace. "I confess I am frankly frightened when I see what forces this war has let loose," he explained. "We seem to be faced with a disease which is perhaps too deep to be healed by a peace treaty." The growing opposition to the league at home, spearheaded by Henry Cabot Lodge, and the president's illness constituted a double tragedy that could not be overcome, according to Fosdick.[99]

As Fosdick suggested, the peace treaty and the league went down to defeat in the United States, though they had initially been greeted with broad and enthusiastic public approval. Wilson's loss of the peace, like the CTCA's failure to perpetuate its spirit in the postwar era, reflected transformations afoot in the nation, changes initiated during the war. Though Lodge's highly organized campaign must be credited at least in part with the defeat of the treaty and the league, his ability to mobilize broad opposition must be explained.[100] Wilson's disappointment with the peace reflected, first, the rising isolationism and conservatism of the populace. Weary of war and weary of uplift, many Americans opposed a peace they feared would commit them to further exterior responsibilities. Still others, committed to Wilson's values of self-determination and international cooperation, opposed his peace because of its harshness, suggesting that Wilson had failed to give his ideals life in the treaty. Still others had once supported Wilson but now opposed him out of anger and distrust based in his war-time actions. Having engaged during the war in the harsh repression of many of his former left-wing allies, Wilson had disrupted his reform coalition and robbed himself of important internationalist support after the war.[101]

Wilson's inability to sell the peace reflects the same difficulties faced by the CTCA after the war and provides clues to the broader collapse of the progressive coalition. Always defining the war in progressive terms, the president, and the CTCA too, excited certain expectations about the meaning of the war, a war described as a struggle to "make the world safe for democracy." During the war, however, Americans saw reformers empowered and yet often found their own interests denied, ignored, or even assaulted. By the war's conclusion many Americans had experienced a decidedly undemocratic war at home. Angered or simply disappointed, reformers within the progressive movement looked at one another with hostility. Wearied and often disillusioned, other Americans viewed reform with a newfound distrust. Although activism would persist through the 1920s, the broad-based association of reformers that had defined the spirit of the previous two decades came to an end, ironically eliminated by the progressives' war-time ascent to power.

Epilogue

As we look back at the progressives from the standpoint of the 1990s, they appear at face value hopelessly old-fashioned and helplessly naive. Faced with a diversifying nation and frightened by the apparent chaos it fostered, progressives attempted to stabilize their society by controlling the forces of change. Lampooned even in their own day by the likes of H. L. Mencken, the progressives may seem the inhabitants of a distant time. On closer inspection, though, one cannot help but notice some startling similarities between this faraway world, peopled by the progressives, and our own. As the end of the century approaches, Americans again face rapid social change, fueled by economic restructuring, a diversifying population, and an increasingly global world community.

The consequences of that change have presented Americans with many of the same issues faced by the progressives. Like their predecessors in the second decade of the century, Americans in the 1990s face the mushrooming complexities of a multicultural society. As they recognize the multiple traditions within their society, Americans disagree over the meaning of this condition and over the claim to the title *American.* While some celebrate the richness of a nation based in many cultures, others decry the fragmentation of the society and urge allegiance to a single American culture. The sense of uncertainty in the nation is again enhanced, too, as definitions of masculinity and femininity seem increasingly fluid. Still wrestling with the consequences of the women's movement, the United States faces a reconstruction of gender roles that many find uncomfortable, even distressing. Again, while some celebrate the individual freedom born of less constricting gender definitions, others condemn what they view as the collapse of traditional roles, the traditional family, and ultimately traditional morality. In the midst of these social uncertainties the advent of the AIDS epidemic, like the venereal diseases of the World War One era, has reopened debates about sexual mores and about the role of the government in mandating behavioral codes. Some find in AIDS a public health challenge that must be confronted while individual rights are protected, but others see AIDS as the deserved consequences of a moral scourge.

Given these similarities between the current situation and that of the progressives, their story becomes a valuable one not only for its ability to provide insight into the past, but also for its ability to provide clues about the present. The Commission on Training Camp Activities, headed by progressives dedicated to improving their society and conquering some of its pressing social issues, failed to convert large numbers of Americans to its vision and ultimately faded, forgotten and soon unknown, into the past. Motivated by sincere concern and firm commitments, the reformers of the CTCA were confounded by their own vision and by the methods they used to pursue that vision.

Though the progressives in the CTCA intended to ameliorate cultural conflict through their pursuit of homogeneity based in shared values, their failure to explore the cultural alternatives of their times and to understand and accept the diverse populations of their society crushed the reformers' hopes of a united nation. Today Americans have the opportunity to approach diversity in a new way, embracing it rather than fearing it. Many social commentators caution that multiculturalism will tear the nation apart, breeding a harmful separatism that distances Americans from one another. And yet the attempt to establish a single culture has always asked less powerful groups in American society to abandon their identities in favor of someone else's, and therefore it has cultivated only distrust and alienation, as evidenced in the experience of the CTCA. Allowing Americans to value that which makes them different while cheering that which they share with one another seems to hold a brighter promise for national unity than a false and forced homogeneity. Multicultural education, which encourages respect for differences and appreciation for similarities, may prove a necessary prerequisite to a peaceful future in this country.

Further, this new openness to difference and to change would allow Americans to move beyond the limiting gender definitions that still circumscribe the lives of men and women alike. Many progressives in the World War One era were sincerely committed to a new sexual equality between men and women. Too many others, however, accepted changes in gender roles only at the most superficial level and only if they served to shore up deeper commitments to traditional sex roles. The CTCA advocated public roles for women, but only to ensure that women could exert their domestic and moral force broadly. The contradictions in the commission's approach to gender equality undercut their attempt to establish the single sexual standard and to promote a new partnership among men and women.

Today, the women's movement and economic realities have forced even the most unwilling Americans to encounter a world in which many men and women have chosen to abandon gender stereotypes altogether. Like multiculturalism, the elimination of restrictive gender codes opens up the possibility of heightened understanding between the sexes. Only by moving beyond role definitions that require individuals to conform to arbitrary standards and that encourage continued inequities of power can men and women enjoy real equality and the resulting possibilities for individual and societal growth.

A nation able to appreciate difference within its boundaries and to accept the decline of mandated social roles will, in turn, be far better able to confront the complex of problems it faces. Poverty and unemployment and the plague of violence in our streets, our schools, and our households confront us daily. An attempt to understand the source of these problems, rather than the assumption that they represent the habits of a misguided culture, will be more likely to result in real and lasting improvements in the lives of Americans.

Similarly, a nation able to look at the AIDS epidemic as the public health problem that it is will be better able to establish means for controlling the disease. The rhetoric of moral charges thrown at the victims of AIDS bears a remarkable similarity to the language used to describe soldiers and civilians with venereal disease in the early years of this century. The attempt to shame Americans into new behaviors based in the progressives' value systems, however, was not successful in ending venereal disease and is insensitive and inappropriate in an era of heightened appreciation for differences in sexual orientation. Similarly, calls for quarantines and mandatory AIDS tests are reminiscent of the repressive programs of detention, quarantine, and long-term internment fostered during World War One, programs shocking in their repressiveness and unacceptable in a time of increased concern for the civil rights of the individual. During World War One it was sex education, the use of condoms, and chemical prophylaxis, not moral exhortations or the imprisoning of women, that slowed the venereal disease epidemic. Today, too, it will be needle exchanges and the teaching of safe sex, not discriminatory legislation and condemnations of lifestyle, that will eliminate AIDS.

The Commission on Training Camp Activities attempted to solve the nation's problems by fostering the reformers' own culture at the exclusion of others'. The end results were the progressives' eventual demise as a powerful force in the cultural competitions of the day and the nation's descent into a repressive conservatism evident in the Red Scare, Harding's "normalcy," national prohibition, and the resurgence of the Ku Klux Klan. Today the United States faces many of the same issues that confronted the reformers of the CTCA. This time no war threatens American security or forces the nation's leaders to make hasty decisions based in the exigencies of wartime. The example of the Commission on Training Camp Activities should encourage Americans to approach the nation's problems with an openness, tolerance, and appreciation for difference that can fuel the imagination and lead to real solutions to the nation's vexations.

Appendixes

Appendix A

Songs Included in the Official Army Song Book

"Abide with Me"

"All Hail the Power of Jesus' Name"

"Aloha Oe"

"America"

"America, the Beautiful"

"Annie Laurie"

"Army Trumpet Calls"

"Auld Lang Syne"

"Back Home to Old America"

"Battle Cry of Freedom"

"Battle Hymn of the Republic"

"Believe Me, If All Those Endearing Young Charms"

"Caisson Song"

"Carry Me Back to Old Virginny"

"Coast Artillery Song"

"Columbia, the Gem of the Ocean"

"Come, Thou Almighty King"

"Dixie"

"Drink to Me Only with Thine Eyes"
"Eternal Father, Strong to Save"
"The Flag"
"Garibaldi Hymn"
"Garibaldi Hymn," translation
"Giddy Giddap, Go On, Go On"
"God Save the King"
"Good Morning, Mr. Zip"
"Hip! Hip! Hooray!"
"Holy, Holy, Holy"
"The Home Road"
"How Firm a Foundation"
"In an Old-Fashioned Town"
"Indiana"
"I Need Thee Every Hour"
"Joan of Arc"
"Keep the Home Fires Burning"
"Keep Your Head Down, Fritzie Boy"
"K-K-K-Katy"
"La Brabanconne"
"La Brabanconne," translation
"La Marseillaise"
"La Marseillaise," translation
"Land of Hope and Glory"
"Last Long Mile"
"Lead, Kindly Light"
"Li'l Liza Jane"
"Little Grey Home in the West"
"Loch Lomond"
"Long Boy"
"Lookout Mountain"
"Love's Old Sweet Song"

"Madelon"
"March! March!"
"Men of Harlech"
"Mother Machree"
"My Old Kentucky Home"
"Nearer, My God to Thee"
"O God, Our Help in Ages Past"
"Old Black Joe"
"The Old Oaken Bucket"
"On the Way to France"
"Onward, Christian Soldiers"
"Over There"
"Pack Up Your Troubles in Your Old Kit Bag"
"Prayer of Thanksgiving"
"Rise, Crowned with Light"
"Rock of Ages, Cleft for Me"
"Roll, Jordan, Roll"
"Scots Wha' Hae Wi' Wallace Bled"
"Silver Threads Among the Gold"
"The Son of God Goes Forth to War"
"The Stars and Stripes Forever"
"The Star-Spangled Banner"
"The Sunshine of Your Smile"
"Suwanee River"
"Sweet Adeline"
"Sweet and Low"
"Sweet Genevieve"
"Swing Low, Sweet Chariot"
"There's a Long, Long Trail"
"Tramp, Tramp, Tramp"
"Under the Stars and Stripes"
"When Johnny Comes Marching Home"

"When the Great Red Dawn Is Shining"

"Who Would Not Fight for Freedom?"

"Yaaka Hula Hickey Dula"

The list of songs included in the *Official Army Song Book* is taken from Frances F. Brundage, *Camp Music Division of the War Department Commission on Training Camp Activities*, pamphlet (Washington, D.C., 1919), box 1635, RG 287, National Archives.

Appendix B

Approved Movies as Listed in War Service Bulletin No. 9, Issued 1 July 1918 by the CTCA

This is not a complete list of all movies approved during the war for viewing by the enlisted men. It is simply one example of a bulletin released semimonthly. This list is a compilation of the movie choices selected for use in the camps from a list of appropriate films approved by the National Board of Review.

Name of Film:	*Character of Film:*
Under the Yoke	Spanish-American drama
We Should Worry	Comedy romance
Life Savers	Animated cartoon
Meeting Theda Bara	Animated cartoon
75 Mile Gun	Animated cartoon
The Kid Is Clever	Comedy drama
I'm Man	Patriotic boys' story
Return of O'Garry	Northwestern melodrama
Coming of Faro Nell	Wolfville story
One Dollar Bid	Kentucky story
The Venus Model	Comedy romance
Matching Billy	Farce comedy
The Service Star	Comedy drama

The Widow's Might	Farce comedy
Social Quicksands	Comedy drama
A Man's World	Social morality drama
Opportunity	Farce comedy
Her Spooney Affair	Farce comedy
Ex-Cannibal Carnival	Scenic
The Bravest Way	American-Japanese drama
Hit the Trail Holliday	Comedy drama
Say, Young Fellow	Humorous newspaper story
Firefly of France	War drama
How Could You Jean?	Rural comedy drama
Her Screen Idol	Burlesque
The Kaiser's Shadow	Secret service war story
Sandy	Kentucky romance
Kidder and Ko	Comedy drama
The Voice of Destiny	Detective romance
Little Sister to Everybody	Labor story
The Whirlpool	Crook melodrama
The Safety Curtain	Theatrical romance
Station Content	Problem drama
His Enemy the Law	Western drama
Closin' In	Northwestern mountain story
The Fly God	Western story
The Painted Lily	Romance
The Eagle	Western melodrama
Smashing Through	Western mining drama
The Knockout	Farce comedy
The Soap Girl	Comedy drama
The Girl in His House	Society romance
Boodle and Bandits	Broad comedy

This list of approved films may be found in "War Service Bulletin No. 9," issued 1 July 1918 by the War and Navy Department's Commission on Training Camp Activities, document 34431, entry 393, RG 165, National Archives.

Appendix C

Books and Pamphlets Banned by the War Department

This list of books and pamphlets is taken from appendix 2 of *Books for Sammies: The American Library Association and World War I*, by Arthur P. Young (Pittsburgh: Phi Beta Mu, 1981), 109–113.

America After the War, by an American Jurist (1918)
Balch, Emily G. *Approaches to the Great Settlement* (1918)
Barbusse, Henri. *Under Fire: the Story of a Squad* (1917)
Bennett, J. O'd., et al. *Germany's Just Cause: An Analysis of the Great Crisis by the Leading American Thinkers* (1915)
Berkman, Alexander. *Prison Memoirs of an Anarchist* (1912)
Bierce, Ambrose. *Can Such Things Be?* (1893)
———. *In the Midst of Life: Tales of Soldiers and Civilians* (1898)
[Blackstone, William E.] *Jesus is Coming* (1918)
Boelcke, Herman. *Aviator's Field-Book* (1917)
Burgess, John W. *America's Relations to the Great War* (1916)
———. *The European War of 1914: Its Causes, Purposes, and Probable Results* (1915)
Carson, Capshaw [pseud.]. *A Witness Testifies* (1918)
Chesterton, Gilbert K. *Utopia of Usurers, and other Essays* (1917)
Daniells, Arthur G. *The World in Perplexity* (1918)
———. *The World War: Its Relation to the Eastern Question and Armageddon* (1917)
Delaisi, Francis. *The Inevitable War* (1915)
Dernburg, Bernhard. *Germany and the War: Not a Defense but an Explanation* (1915)
———. *Searchlights on the War* (1915)
Dewitz, Hrolf von. *War's New Weapons: An Expert Analysis in Plain Language of the Weapons and Methods Used in the Present Great War* (1915)

Doty, Madeleine Z. *Short Rations: An American Woman in Germany, 1915–1916* (1917)
Eastman, Max. *Understanding Germany, The Only Way to End War, and other Essays* (1916)
Ewers, Hanns. *Let the Rulers Beware* (Unverified)
———. *Vampire* (Unverified)
Federn, Karl. *The Origin of the War: Facts and Documents* (1915)
Fox, Edward. L. *Behind the Scenes in Warring Germany* (1915)
Frantzius, Friedrich Wilhelm Von. *The Book of Truth and Facts: Facts Which Every American Should Know* (1916)
———. *Germans as Exponents of Culture* (1914)
Free Speech and a Free Press (Unverified)
Freytag-Loringhovern, Hugo Friedrich Philipp Johann. *Deductions from the World War* (1918)
Frobenius, Herman. *German Empire's Hour of Destiny* (1914)
Fullerton, George S. *Germany of To-Day* (1915)
A German Deserter's War Experience (1917)
Glass, Kate Elizabeth (Perkins). *Her Invisible Spirit Mate: A Scientific Novel, and Psychological Lessons on How to Make the World more Beautiful* (1917)
Granger, Albert H. *England's World Empire: Some Reflections upon its Growth and Policy* (1916)
Grasshoff, Richard. *Tragedy of Belgium: An Answer to Professor Wasweiler* (1915)
Harris, Frank. *England or Germany?* (1915)
Hedin, Sven A. *With the German Armies in the West* (1915)
Henderson, Ernest F. *Germany's Fighting Machine: Her Army, Her Navy, Her Airships, and Why She Arrayed Them against the Allied Powers of Europe* (1914)
Howe, Frederic C. *Why War?* (1916)
Hugins, Roland. *Germany Misjudged: An Appeal to International Good Will in the Interest of a Lasting Peace* (1916)
Jeffries, Jouett. *War Diary of an American Woman in the Proclamation of the Holy War, 1914* (1915)
Jones, Rufus M. *A More Excellent Way* (1916)
Jordan, David Starr. *War and Waste: A Series of Discussions of War and War Accessories* (1914)
Kirby, William. *Manual of Camouflage, Concealment, and Cover of Troops* (1917)
———. *Manual of Gas in Attack and Defense* (1918?)
———. *Manual of Grenades and Bombing* (1918?)
Labberton, John H. *Belgium and Germany: A Dutch View* (1916)
Latzko, Adolph A. *Men in War* (1918)
Leadbetter, Charles W. *The Other Side of Death, Scientifically Examined and Carefully Described* (1903)
Leake, W. S. *How to Protect Our Soldiers* (Unverified)
Lincoln, Ignatius T. T. *Revelations of an International Spy* (1916)
McAuley, Mary E. *Germany in War Time: What an American Girl Saw and Heard* (1917)

McCann, Richard M. *War Horror, Its Lesson to America: A Plain Statement of Facts, Not a Controversy* (1915)
McClellan, George B. *The Heel of War* (1916)
McGuire, James K. *The King, The Kaiser, and Irish Freedom* (1915)
———. *What Could Germany Do for Ireland?* (1916)
Mach, Edmund R. *Germany's Point of View* (1915)
——. *What Germany Wants* (1914)
McManus, Seumas. *Ireland's Cause* (1917)
Miller, Kelly. *The Disgrace of Democracy: Open Letter to President Woodrow Wilson* (1917)
Mott, Lawrence. *The Searchlight* (Unverified)
Mucke, Hellmuth Von. *The 'Emden'* (1917)
Munsterberg, Hugo. *The War and America* (1914)
Nearing, Scott. *Open Letter to Profiteers: An Arraignment of Big Business in Its Relation to World War* (1917)
O'Brien, Nora (Connolly). *The Outlook for Religion* (1917)
Reventlow, Ernst von. *The Vampire of the Continent* (1916)
Rohrbach, Paul. *German World Policies* (1915)
Russell, Bertrand R. *Justice in War-time* (1916)
Schrader, Frederick F. *Handbook; Political, Statistical and Sociological, for German Americans and all other Americans who have not Forgotten the History and Traditions of their Country, and who Believe in the Principles of Washington, Jefferson, and Lincoln* (1916)
Skinnider, Margaret. *Doing My Bit for Ireland* (1917)
Souiny-Seydlitz, Leonie. *Russia of Yesterday and Tomorrow* (1917)
Thomas, Norman, ed. *The Conquest of War: Some Studies in a Search for a Christian Order* (1917)
Thompson, Robert J. *England and Germany in the War: Letters to the Department of State* (1915)
Trotsky, Leon. *The Bolsheviki and World Peace* (1918)
Trotsky's Message (Unverified)
Two Thousand Questions and Answers about the War: A Catechism of the Methods of Fighting, Travelling, and Living; of the Armies, Navies and Air Fleets; or the Personalities, Politics, and Geography of the Warring Countries (1918)
Viereck, George S. *Songs of Armageddon and other Poems* (1916)
Wilson, Theordora. *The Last Weapon, a Vision* (1917)
World's Crisis in the Light of Prophecy (no date)

Appendix D

Training Camp and Community Populations

The population figures listed in this appendix were taken from the 1920 census. For this reason they do not reflect the exact populations of the following communities from 1917 to 1919. Nevertheless, they offer a close approximation of the sizes of the communities during World War One. Similarly, figures on troop origins are "approximate numbers received from the States and other sources," listed in *Order of Battle of the United States Land Forces in the World War (1917–1919) Zone of the Interior*, vol. 3, part 1 of 2, by World War I Group, Historical Division, Special Staff United States Army (Washington, D.C.: Government Printing Office, 1949).

Part 1: The Sixteen New National Guard Camps

1. Camp Beauregard, Louisiana

Camp size:	Low: 4,173 (August 1918) High: 24,661 (January 1918)
Troop origins:	Alabama, 157; Arkansas, 300; Canal Zone, 670; Florida, 100; Louisiana, 13,659; Mississippi, 697; other camps: 22,129
Civilian community:	Alexandria, Louisiana located 5 1/2 miles southwest of camp population in 1920: 17,510

2. Camp Bowie, Texas

Camp size:	Low: 4,164 (August 1918) High: 30,417 (May 1918)
Troop origins:	Arkansas, 500; California, 500; Canal Zone, 103; Louisiana, 500; Oklahoma, 3,900; Texas, 6,669; other states, 200; other camps, 13,710
Civilian community:	Fort Worth, Texas located 3 miles south of camp population in 1920: 106,482

3. Camp Cody, New Mexico

Camp size:	Low: 2,559 (December 1918) High: 27,773 (June 1918)
Troop origins:	Colorado, 3,579; Kansas, 1,000; Minnesota, 963; Nebraska, 243; New Mexico, 1,820; Oklahoma, 4,422; Texas, 2,226; other camps, 14,256
Civilian community:	Deming, New Mexico located 3 miles east of camp population in 1920: 3,212

4. Camp Doniphan, Oklahoma (located at site of Fort Sill)

Camp size:	Low: 898 (July 1918) High: 26,789 (December 1917)
Troop origins:	Kansas and Missouri, approx. 3,000; other camps, 30,263
Civilian community:	Near Lawton, Oklahoma population in 1920: 8,930

5. Camp Fremont, California

Camp size:	Low: 4,522 (December 1918) High: 24,085 (June 1918)
Troop origins:	New Mexico, 53; other camps, 25,140
Civilian community:	Palo Alto, California located 2 miles east of camp population in 1920: 5,900

6. Camp Greene, North Carolina

Camp size:	Low: 7,974 (July 1918) High: 41,040 (February 1918)

Troop origins:	No statistics, but troops from Colorado, Idaho, Montana, New Mexico, North Dakota, Oregon, South Dakota, Washington, Washington, D.C., and Wyoming mobilized here
Civilian community:	Charlotte, North Carolina located 2 1/2 miles east of camp population in 1920: 46,338

7. Camp Hancock, Georgia

Camp size:	Low: 11,824 (May 1918) High: 35,148 (October 1918)
Troop origins:	Georgia, 289; Indiana, 534; Michigan, 250; New York, 7,173; Pennsylvania, 5,000; South Carolina, 229; other states, 260; other camps, 32,671
Civilian community:	Augusta adjacent to camp population in 1920: 52,548

8. Camp Kearny, California

Camp size:	Low: 5,109 (September 1917) High: 24,241 (January 1918)
Troop origins:	Arizona, 3,261; California, 5,915; Colorado, 808; Nebraska, 6,000; Utah, 2,139; other camps, 44,226
Civilian community:	San Diego, California located 11 1/2 miles south of camp population in 1920: 74,683

9. Camp Logan, Texas

Camp size:	Low: 3,582 (June 1918) High: 33,346 (December 1917)
Troop origins:	Illinois, 260; Louisiana, 982; New York, 248; Oklahoma, 4,000; Pennsylvania, 123; other camps, 32,292
Civilian community:	Houston, Texas located 1/2 mile east of camp population in 1920: 138,276

10. Camp MacArthur, Texas

Camp size:	Low: 5,859 (September 1917) High: 27,294 (October 1917)

Troop origins: Arkansas, 500; Missouri, 5,600; New Mexico, 400; Texas, 2,006; Wisconsin, 6,000; other camps, 51,462

Civilian community: Waco, Texas
located 1/2 mile southeast of camp
population in 1920: 38,500

11. Camp McClellan, Alabama

Camp size: Low: 5,316 (July 1918)
High: 27,977 (October 1918)

Troop origins: Alabama, 7,638; Georgia, 2,359; Illinois, 3,622; Indiana, 100; Ohio, 1,081; other camps, 24,376

Civilian communities: Anniston, Alabama
located 6 miles south of camp
population in 1920: 17,734
Jacksonville, Alabama
located 6 miles north of camp
population in 1920: 2,395

12. Camp Sevier, South Carolina

Camp size: Low: 7,389 (July 1918)
High: 28,806 (February 1918)

Troop origins: Alabama, 6,800; Kentucky, 7,483; Maryland, 1,000; North Carolina, 1,374; South Carolina, 2,943; Washington, D.C., 1,000; other camps, 39,293

Civilian community: Greenville, South Carolina
located 4 1/2 miles from camp
population in 1920: 23,127

13. Camp Shelby, Mississippi

Camp size: Low: 7,861 (October 1918)
High: 36,284 (August 1918)

Troop origins: Alabama, 2,364; Arkansas, 1,745; Illinois, 4,351; Mississippi, 10,399; Tennessee, 1,100; Wisconsin, 3,543; other states, 650; other camps, 15,182

Civilian community: Hattiesburg, Mississippi
located 10 miles from camp
population in 1920: 13,270

14. Camp Sheridan, Alabama

Camp size:	Low: 10,578 (June 1918) High: 24,568 (December 1917)
Troop origins:	University of Arizona, 137; Indiana, 263; New Mexico Agricultural and Mechanical College, 168; University of Texas, 379; other camps, 29,792
Civilian community:	Montgomery, Alabama located 4 miles south of camp population in 1920: 43,464

15. Camp Wadsworth, South Carolina

Camp size:	Low: 10,966 (December 1918) High: 34,169 (April 1918)
Troop origins:	Delaware, 100; Illinois, 4,000; Maryland, 700; Michigan, 500; Minnesota, 10,000; New Jersey, 800; New York, 25,700; North Carolina, 2,600; Pennsylvania, 9,459; South Carolina, 8,465; Tennessee, 5,500; Virginia, 1,000; other camps, 37,325
Civilian community:	Spartanburg, South Carolina located 3 miles east of camp population in 1920: 22,638

16. Camp Wheeler, Georgia

Camp size:	Low: 4,539 (September 1917) High: 28,960 (July 1918)
Troop origins:	Alabama, 1,500; Georgia, 9,700; Illinois, 12,000; Kentucky, 600; Michigan, 5,000; Mississippi, 400; New York, 3,500; Tennessee, 900; Washington, D.C., 100; other states, 220; other camps, 19,976
Civilian community:	Macon, Georgia located about 6 miles northwest of camp population in 1920: 52,995

Part 2: The Sixteen New National Army Cantonments

1. Camp Custer, Michigan

Camp size:	Low: 8,305 (September 1917) High: 39,412 (October 1918)

Troop origins:	Alabama, 2,023; Illinois, 2,522; Indiana, 3,309; Michigan, 65,976; North Dakota, 3,100; Ohio, 604; Pennsylvania, 5,336; West Virginia, 4,186; Wisconsin, 5,956; other camps, 6,887
Civilian community:	Battle Creek, Michigan located 5 miles north of camp population in 1920: 36,164

2. Camp Devens, Massachusetts

Camp size:	Low: 21,324 (September 1917) High: 48,049 (June 1918)
Troop origins:	Connecticut, 14,470; Florida, 7,570; Maine, 12,599; Massachusetts, 38,184; New Hampshire, 4,191; New York, 8,667; Rhode Island, 2,635; Vermont 3,740; other states, 38; other camps, 16,596
Civilian community:	Ayer, Massachusetts located 1 mile north of camp population in 1920: no listing

3. Camp Dix, New Jersey

Camp size:	Low: 9,013 (September 1917) High: 54,475 (August 1918)
Troop origins:	Delaware, 1,949; Florida, 2,500; Illinois, 2,371; Massachusetts, 4,636; Maryland, 1,768; New Hampshire, 584; New Jersey, 47,642; New York, 31,000; North Carolina, 1,300; Pennsylvania, 3,220; Rhode Island, 849; West Virginia, 200; other states, 1,855; other camps, 48,447
Civilian community:	Wrightstown, New Jersey located 1/2 mile north of camp population in 1920: 270

4. Camp Dodge, Iowa

Camp size:	Low: 15,794 (September 1917) High: 46,491 (July 1918)
Troop origins:	Alabama, 3,403; Illinois, 10,855; Indiana, 3,436; Iowa, 37,111; Minnesota, 21,622; Missouri, 9,246; Montana, 4,000; Nebraska, 7,568; North Dakota, 5,823; Oklahoma, 4,286; South Dakota, 4,000; Tennessee, 2,000; other states, 5,279; other camps, 8,319

Civilian community: Des Moines, Iowa
located 12 miles south of camp
population in 1920: 126,468

5. Camp Funston, Kansas

Camp size: Low: 10,606 (September 1917)
High: 50,550 (October 1918)

Troop origins: Alabama, 1,350; Arizona, 3,452; Colorado, 5,626; Florida, 2,236; Kansas, 29,918; Louisiana, 5,000; Mississippi, 6,043; Missouri, 39,886; Nebraska, 15,554; New Mexico, 2,425; Oklahoma, 500; South Dakota, 10,110; other states, 5,447; other camps, 12,492

Civilian community: Junction City, Kansas
located 4 miles southwest of camp
population in 1920: 7,533

6. Camp Gordon, Georgia

Camp size: Low: 15,063 (December 1918)
High: 47,489 (August 1918)

Troop origins: Alabama, 5,097; Florida, 202; Georgia, 45,401; Illinois, 5,168; Iowa, 6,480; New York, 18,700; Ohio, 9,800; Tennessee, 18,649; other camps, 49,687

Civilian community: Atlanta, Georgia
located about 14 miles from camp
population in 1920: 200,616

7. Camp Grant, Illinois

Camp size: Low: 13,426 (September 1917)
High: 56,238 (October 1918)

Troop origins: Idaho, 1,010; Illinois, 56,115; Indiana, 1,000; Louisiana, 4,318; Mississippi, 3,650; Nebraska, 1,000; North Carolina, 2,000; North Dakota, 2,010; South Dakota, 500; Wisconsin, 27,184; other states, 981; other camps, 26,548

Civilian community: Rockford, Illinois
located about 4 miles north of camp
population in 1920: 65,651

8. Camp Jackson, South Carolina

Camp size: Low: 12,810 (September 1917)
High: 44,242 (July 1918)

Troop origins: Alabama, 1,278; Florida, 6,020; Georgia, 1,152; Illinois, 8,500; Maryland, 16,000; New York, 5,900; North Carolina, 20,528; Ohio, 7,200; South Carolina, 26,598; Tennessee, 2,539; Virginia, 79; other states, 1,154; other camps, 32,721

Civilian community: Columbia, South Carolina
located 7 miles west of camp
population in 1920: 37,524

9. Camp Lee, Virginia

Camp size: Low: 13,155 (September 1917)
High: 57,342 (July 1918)

Troop origins: Pennsylvania, 74,805; Tennessee, 821; Texas, 320; Virginia, 30,339; Washington, D.C., 959; West Virginia, 20,081; other states, 2,070; other camps, 53,670

Civilian community: Petersburg, Virginia
located 3 miles west of camp
population in 1920: 31,012

10. Camp Lewis, Washington

Camp size: Low: 18,784 (September 1917)
High: 44,015 (June 1918)

Troop origins: California, 35,295; Colorado, 1,070; Georgia, 1,000; Idaho, 7,499; Minnesota, 4,714; Montana, 19,668; Nevada, 479; New York, 1,283; North Dakota, 2,230; Oregon, 7,373; South Dakota, 1,848; Utah, 5,621; Washington, 21,054; Wyoming, 3,291; other states, 3,318; other camps, 2,419

Civilian community: Tacoma, Washington
located 17 miles north of camp
population in 1920: 96,965

11. Camp Meade, Maryland

Camp size: Low: 5,708 (September 1917)
High: 47,908 (October 1918)

Troop origins: Connecticut, 1,200; Delaware, 917; Georgia, 500; Maryland, 24,604; Massachusetts, 5,267; New Jersey, 2,006; New York, 4,788; North Carolina, 1,720; Ohio, 1,329; Pennsylvania, 44,153; Rhode Island, 1,593; Tennessee,

2,632; Virginia, 4,000; Washington, D.C., 3,308; West Virginia, 5,945; other states, 320; other camps, 18,157

Civilian community: Baltimore, Maryland
located 18 miles northeast of camp
population in 1920: 733,826

12. Camp Pike, Arkansas

Camp size: Low: 23,049 (September 1917)
High: 54,463 (September 1918)

Troop origins: Alabama, 10,109; Arkansas, 38,734; Iowa, 12,537; Louisiana, 15,733; Mississippi, 13,094; Missouri, 13,035; New Mexico, 1,000; Oklahoma, 7,000; Tennessee, 4,130; other states, 765; other camps, 14,998

Civilian community: Little Rock, Arkansas
located 8 miles southeast of camp
population in 1920: 65,142

13. Camp Sherman, Ohio

Camp size: Low: 12,949 (September 1917)
High: 35,979 (July 1918)

Troop origins: Alabama, 1,000; Indiana, 5,500; Ohio, 83,302; Oklahoma, 1,105; Pennsylvania, 12,173; Tennessee, 5,305; West Virginia, 1,000; other states, 1,140; other camps, 14,057

Civilian community: Chillicothe, Ohio
located 3 miles southeast of camp
population in 1920: 15,831

14. Camp Taylor, Kentucky

Camp size: Low: 14,406 (September 1917)
High: 57,298 (September 1918)

Troop origins: Alabama, 1,994; Illinois, 16,225; Indiana, 36,127; Kentucky, 33,490; Louisiana, 2,879; North Carolina, 1,000; Ohio, 14,210; Tennessee, 1,000; Wisconsin, 5,200; other states, 600; other camps, 11,061

Civilian community: Louisville, Kentucky
located 5 miles northwest of camp
population in 1920: 234,891

15. Camp Travis, Texas

Camp size:	Low: 13,408 (September 1917) High: 37,681 (October 1918)
Troop origins:	Arkansas, 1,500; Colorado, 1,100; Louisiana, 1,975; New Mexico, 748; Oklahoma, 19,816; Texas, 93,792; other states, 593; other camps, 4,827
Civilian community:	San Antonio, Texas adjoined to camp population in 1920: 161,379

16. Camp Upton, New York

Camp size:	Low: 9,834 (September 1917) High: 42,771 (April 1918)
Troop origins:	Connecticut, 6,965; Delaware, 698; Massachusetts, 4,093; New Jersey, 819; New York, 73,604; other states, 2,411; other camps, 32,393
Civilian community:	Yaphank, New York located 5 miles southwest of camp population in 1920: no listing

Appendix E

Commission on Training Camp Activities after 1 April 1918

Chairman: Raymond B. Fosdick
1st Asst. Chairman: Malcom L. McBride
2nd Asst. Chairman: Lee F. Hanmer
Executive Secretary: W. Prentice Sanger
Publicity: John Colter

Executive Committee

Raymond B. Fosdick
Malcom L. McBride
Lee F. Hanmer
Joseph E. Raycroft
E. H. Maling
W. Prentice Sanger

District Directors

1. Ward W. Pickard
2. John P. Myers
3. Henry Hopkins, Jr.
4. Roy Smith Wallace
5. O. B. Towne
6. J. S. Eells

Commissioners

Raymond B. Fosdick
Malcom L. McBride
Lee F. Hanmer
Joseph E. Raycroft
Thomas J. Howells
Joseph Lee
John R. Mott
Charles P. Neill
Brig. Gen. P. E. Pierce
W. Prentice Sanger

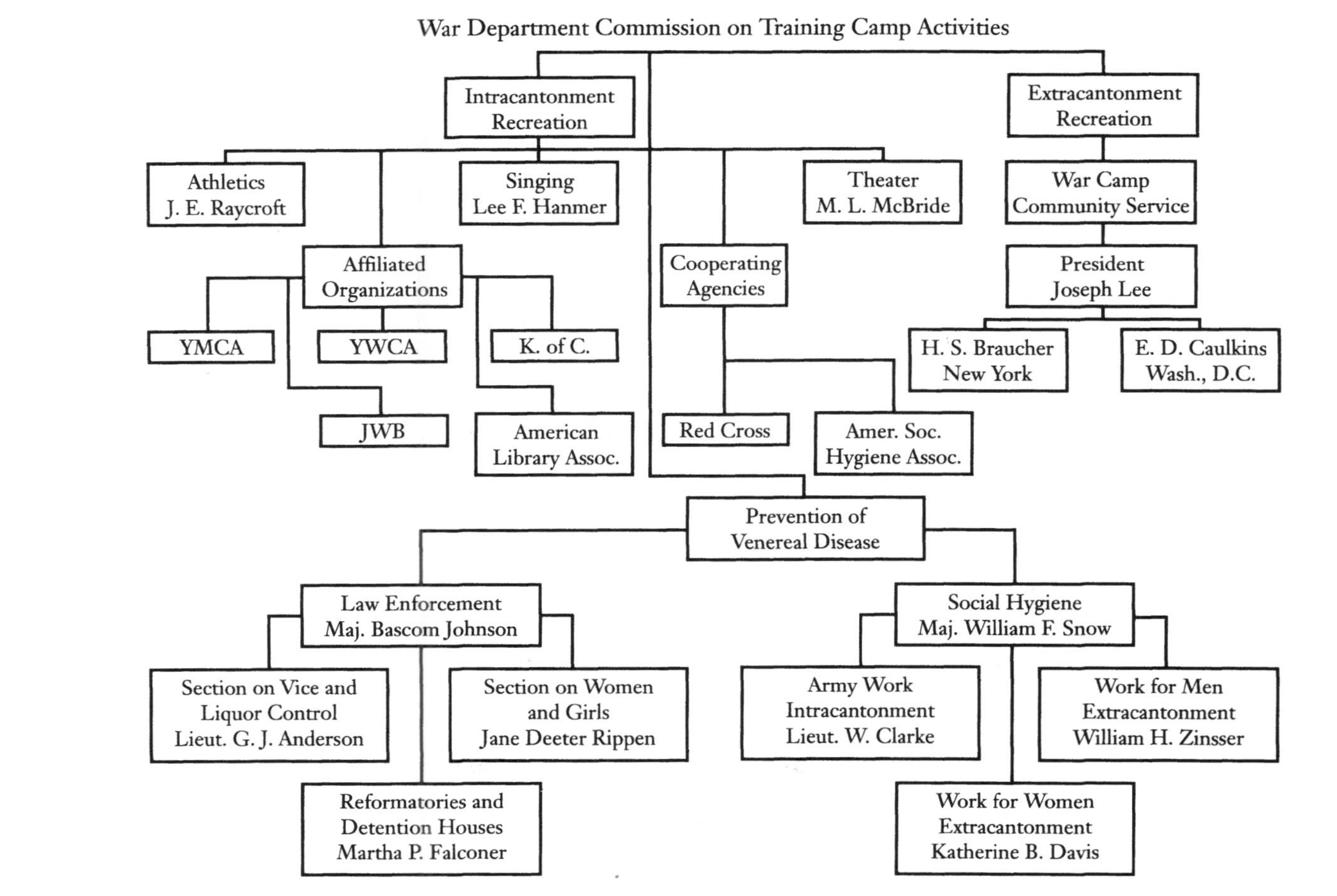
War Department Commission on Training Camp Activities
Intracantonment Recreation
Extracantonment Recreation
Athletics J. E. Raycroft
Singing Lee F. Hanmer
Theater M. L. McBride
War Camp Community Service
Affiliated Organizations
Cooperating Agencies
President Joseph Lee
YMCA
YWCA
K. of C.
H. S. Braucher New York
E. D. Caulkins Wash., D.C.
JWB
American Library Assoc.
Red Cross
Amer. Soc. Hygiene Assoc.
Prevention of Venereal Disease
Law Enforcement Maj. Bascom Johnson
Social Hygiene Maj. William F. Snow
Section on Vice and Liquor Control Lieut. G. J. Anderson
Section on Women and Girls Jane Deeter Rippen
Army Work Intracantonment Lieut. W. Clarke
Work for Men Extracantonment William H. Zinsser
Reformatories and Detention Houses Martha P. Falconer
Work for Women Extracantonment Katherine B. Davis

Notes

PREFACE

1. The CTCA work also included the navy, and military personnel overseas. This book will explore the CTCA inside the United States and will emphasize the commission's work with the army.

NOTES TO CHAPTER ONE

1. Galen W. Morton, of Beardstown, Illinois, to President Wilson, 29 August 1917, doc. 4198, file M, box 5, entry 394, RG 165, National Archives.

2. Marcia Louis Bradley to Secretary Baker, 10 May 1917, doc. 275, file Oregon, box 10, entry 395, RG 165, National Archives.

3. Petition from the Ministerial Association and Christian Endeavor Convention in joint session in Fowler, Illinois, sent by the Presiding Elder of Rock River Conference, U.B. Church, to President Wilson, 29 June 1917, doc. 2937, file A, box 1, entry 394, RG 165, National Archives.

4. Mrs. E. M. Craise, Superintendent of Francis Willard Settlement, Denver, Colorado, to Woodrow Wilson, received by the Commission on Training Camp Activities 29 May 1917, doc. 633, file C, box 1, entry 394, RG 165, National Archives.

5. Rosa Patrick, of Parsons, Kansas, to Secretary Baker, 17 July 1917, doc. 3071, file P, box 6, entry 394, RG 165, National Archives.

6. Charles Royster, *A Revolutionary People at War: The Continental Army and American Character, 1775–1783* (Chapel Hill: University of North Carolina Press, 1979), 70.

7. Royster, *A Revolutionary People at War*, 69–77.

8. Bell Irvin Wiley, *The Life of Johnny Reb: The Common Soldier of the Confederacy* (Baton Rouge: Louisiana State University Press, 1978), 36.

9. For details on the prevalence of vice, drinking, theft, and gambling among Confederate troops, see Wiley, *The Life of Johnny Reb*, 36–58. For information on similar behavior in the Union Army, see Bell Irvin Wiley, *The Life of Billy Yank: The Common Soldier of the Union*

(Baton Rouge: Louisiana State University Press, 1978), 247–274. On vice during the war, see Thomas P. Lowry, *The Story the Soldiers Wouldn't Tell: Sex in the Civil War* (Mechanicsburg, Pa.: Stackpole Books, 1994).

10. Undated letter of J. M. Guess, quoted in *The Life of Johnny Reb*, by Wiley, 58.

11. Anne M. Butler, *Daughters of Joy, Sisters of Misery—Prostitutes in the American West, 1865–1890* (Chicago: University of Illinois Press, 1985), 145, 146.

12. Butler, *Daughters of Joy, Sisters of Misery*, 146.

13. Mrs. Sara D. Hyde to Woodrow Wilson on 8 June 1917, doc. 1298, file A, box 1, entry 394, RG 165, National Archives.

14. Mrs. Elizabeth Heim, of Ross county, Ohio, to Hon. Harry [*sic*] Baker, 28 June 1917, letter file A, box 1, entry 394, RG 165, National Archives.

15. The historian Thomas C. Leonard offers another explanation for the popular condemnation of the training camps, suggesting that the critics of war in the era preceding World War One worked to connect immorality with military service in the public mind. Thomas C. Leonard, *Above the Battle—War-Making in America from Appomattox to Versailles* (New York: Oxford University Press, 1978), 35.

16. Daniel R. Beaver, *Newton D. Baker and the American War Effort, 1917–1919* (Lincoln: University of Nebraska Press, 1966), 4–5.

17. Paul S. Boyer, *Urban Masses and Moral Order in America, 1820–1920* (Cambridge: Harvard University Press, 1978), 220–221, 224; Edward M. Coffman, *The War to End All Wars: The American Military Experience in World War I* (New York: Oxford University Press, 1968), 21; Beaver, *Newton D. Baker and the American War Effort*, 5.

18. Beaver, *Newton D. Baker and the American War Effort*, 1.

19. Allan M. Brandt, *No Magic Bullet: A Social History of Venereal Disease in the United States Since 1880* (New York: Oxford University Press, 1985), 53.

20. Brandt, *No Magic Bullet*, 53.

21. Raymond B. Fosdick, *Chronicle of a Generation: An Autobiography* (New York: Harper, 1958), 122–136.

22. Raymond Fosdick to Honorable Newton D. Baker, Secretary of War, Report on Conditions on the Mexican Border, 10 August 1916, folder 1, box 23, Raymond Blaine Fosdick Papers, Seeley G. Mudd Manuscript Library, Princeton University. Published with permission of Princeton University Libraries.

23. Ibid.; Brandt, *No Magic Bullet*, 53–54. Fosdick's findings were confirmed by a second investigator, Dr. M. J. Exner, employed by the Young Men's Christian Association to carry out a similar project.

24. Fosdick to Baker, Report on Conditions on Mexican Border, 10 August 1916, Fosdick Papers; Brandt, *No Magic Bullet*, 55–56.

25. Brandt, *No Magic Bullet*, 56.

26. For an excellent discussion of the conflicts within progressivism and within individual progressives over the issue of American entry into the war, see David M. Kennedy, *Over Here: The First World War and American Society* (New York: Oxford University Press, 1980), 49–53.

27. Otis Graham, *The Great Campaigns: Reform and War in America, 1900–1928* (Huntington, N.Y.: R. E. Krieger, 1980), 92.

28. Woodrow Wilson, "Speech for Declaration of War against Germany," delivered at joint session of the two houses of Congress, 2 April 1917, reprinted in *Documents of American History*, Henry Steele Commager, ed. (New York: Appleton-Century-Crofts, 1963), 131.

29. Kennedy, *Over Here*, 50–51.

30. John Dewey, "The Social Possibilities of War," in *Characters and Events: Popular*

Essays in Social and Political Philosophy, Joseph Ratner, ed., vol. 2 (New York: H. H. Holt, 1929), 551–560.

31. Kennedy, *Over Here*, 39.

32. Allen F. Davis, "The Flowering of Progressivism," in *The Impact of World War I*, Arthur S. Link, ed. (New York: Harper and Row, 1969), 55.

33. Charles Hirschfeld, "Nationalist Progressivism and World War I," *Mid-America* 45 (July 1963): 141, 145–146.

34. Beaver, *Newton D. Baker and the American War Effort*, 220.

35. Woodrow Wilson, "Special Statement," in *Keeping Our Fighters Fit for War and After*, by Edward Frank Allen with the cooperation of Raymond B. Fosdick (New York: Century, 1918), opening page, no page number.

36. Baker to Fosdick, 18 April 1917, folder 6, box 21, Fosdick Papers.

37. Raymond Fosdick, quoted in *The New Spirit of the New Army: A Message to "Service Flag Homes,"* by Joseph H. Odell (New York: Fleming H. Revell, 1918), 53–56.

38. For decades progressivism confounded historians with its complexity and provoked contentious debates over the nature of progressivism and the existence of a progressive movement. Important landmark works in the historiography of progressivism include Richard Hofstadter, *The Age of Reform: From Bryan to F.D.R* (New York: Vintage Books, 1955); Robert H. Wiebe, *The Search for Order, 1877–1920* (New York: Hill and Wang, 1967); Samuel P. Hays, *Conservation and the Gospel of Efficiency: The Progressive Conservation Movement, 1890–1920* (Cambridge: Harvard University Press, 1959); James Weinstein, *The Corporate Ideal in the Liberal State* (Boston: Beacon Press, 1968); Gabriel Kolko, *The Triumph of Conservatism: A Reinterpretation of American History, 1900–1916* (New York: Free Press, 1963); Arthur S. Link, "What Happened to the Progressive Movement in the 1920's?" *American Historical Review* 64 (1959): 833–851; Peter G. Filene, "An Obituary for 'The Progressive Movement,' " *American Quarterly* 22 (1970): 20–34; John D. Buenker, John C. Burnham, and Robert Crunden, *Progressivism* (Cambridge, Mass.: Schenkman, 1977). For excellent discussions of trends in the historiography of progressivism, see David M. Kennedy, "Overview: The Progressive Era," *The Historian* 37 (1975): 453–458; Daniel T. Rodgers, "In Search of Progressivism," *Reviews in American History* 10 (December 1982): 113–132; Alan Brinkley, "Richard Hofstadter's *Age of Reform:* A Reconsideration," *Reviews in American History* 13 (September 1985): 462–480.

39. Credit for the term "shifting coalitions" goes to John D. Buenker. In a persuasive interpretation of progressivism, Buenker wrote in 1977, "Viewing the [progressive] era as the work of shifting coalitions rather than of a single movement has the potential for reconciling most of the currently conflicting interpretations and of encompassing nearly all of the groups, values and programs that were clearly at work." Buenker, "Essay," in *Progressivism*, by Buenker, Burnham, and Crunden, 31. For somewhat overlapping definitions see also Graham, *The Great Campaigns;* Richard Abrams, "The Failure of Progressivism," in *The Shaping of Twentieth Century America*, 2nd ed., Richard Abrams and Lawrence Levine, eds. (Boston: Little, Brown, 1971); Arthur S. Link, "What Happened to the Progressive Movement in the 1920s?"

40. John C. Burnham, "Essay," in *Progressivism*, by Buenker, Burnham, and Crunden, 16.

41. For excellent overviews of this kind of progressive, see especially Wiebe, *The Search for Order;* Hays, *Conservation and the Gospel of Efficiency*.

42. John Dickinson, *The Building of an Army—A Detailed Account of Legislation, Administration, and Opinion in the United States, 1915–1920* (New York: Century, 1922), 204–206.

43. Allen, *Keeping Our Fighters Fit*, 16–17.

44. Raymond Fosdick, "The War and Navy Departments Commissions on Training Camp Activities," *Annals of the American Academy of Political and Social Science* 79 (September 1918): 142.

45. According to Fosdick, "Our argument had been not primarily one of morals, but of military necessity, for in those pre-penicillin days venereal disease was a far more crippling disability than it is now." Fosdick, *Chronicle of a Generation*, 147.

46. Allen, *Keeping Our Fighters Fit*, 7.

47. Newton D. Baker, "The Call to Free Men," speech given at a tent meeting, Cleveland, Ohio, 17 October 1917, reprinted in *Frontiers of Freedom*, by Newton D. Baker (New York: George H. Doran, 1918), 126.

48. N. D. Baker, "The Call to Free Men," 127.

49. Fosdick, "The War and Navy Departments Commissions on Training Camp Activities," 131.

50. Newton D. Baker, "Problems of the Melting Pot," speech to the Annual Convention of Police Chiefs, 4 December 1917, in *Frontiers of Freedom*, by N. D. Baker, 170–171.

51. Burnham, "Essay," in *Progressivism*, by Buenker, Burnham, and Crunden, 10.

52. Fosdick, "The War and Navy Departments Commissions on Training Camp Activities," 130.

53. N. D. Baker, "The Call to Free Men," 126.

54. N. D. Baker, "Invisible Armor," speech to the National Conference on War Camp Recreation Service, 23 October 1917, reprinted in *Frontiers of Freedom*, by N. D. Baker, 94.

55. Ibid., 94–95.

56. Weldon B. Durham, " 'Big Brother' and the 'Seven Sisters': Camp Life Reforms in World War I," *Military Affairs* 42 (1978): 60.

57. N. D. Baker, "Invisible Armor," 95.

58. Ibid., 96.

59. Ibid., 95.

60. Ibid., 96.

61. Burnham, "Essay," in *Progressivism*, by Buenker, Burnham, and Crunden, 10.

NOTES TO CHAPTER TWO

1. Message from Woodrow Wilson, in *The New Spirit of the New Army—A Message to the "Service Flag Homes,"* by Joseph H. Odell (New York: Fleming H. Revell, 1918), 5.

2. Message from Woodrow Wilson in *The New Spirit of the New Army*, by Odell, 5.

3. Woodrow Wilson, "Special Statement," in *Keeping Our Fighters Fit for War and After*, by Edward F. Allen (New York: Century, 1918), opening page, no page number.

4. Woodrow Wilson, "Special Statement," in *Keeping Our Fighters Fit*, by Allen.

5. Draft of pamphlet, *The Girl You Leave Behind You*, doc. 34991, box 85, entry 393, RG 165, National Archives.

6. Allan Brandt, *No Magic Bullet: A Social History of Venereal Disease in the United States Since 1880* (New York: Oxford University Press, 1985), 69.

7. "Keep Out of the Mire," editorial from *Trench and Camp*, reprinted in *Marching into the Dawn. Editorials from Trench and Camp, The Soldiers' Own Newspaper* (n.p., n.d.), 131–132. In fact, *Trench and Camp* was not exactly the soldiers' own. Published by the YMCA, an organization affiliated with the CTCA, it served to communicate the commission's viewpoint on training camp issues.

8. War Department Commission on Training Camp Activities, *Keeping Fit to Fight*, a

pamphlet produced by the American Social Hygiene Association at the request of and approved by the Surgeon General of the Army, doc. 28201, box 60, entry 393, RG 165, National Archives.

9. Allen, *Keeping Our Fighters Fit*, 42.

10. Fosdick, "The War and Navy Departments Commissions on Training Camp Activities," *Annals of the American Academy of Political and Social Science* 79 (September 1918), 138.

11. War Department Commission on Training Camp Activities, *Keeping Fit to Fight*, National Archives.

12. Allen, *Keeping Our Fighters Fit*, 129.

13. Ibid., 128.

14. As Margaret Marsh suggests, "The concepts of masculine domesticity and 'manliness' were in many ways more complementary than antithetical." The rise of athletics, for instance, may have occurred in conjunction with changes in men's familial relations and role. In this context the competitive athletics would have functioned as "safe outlets" for men's aggressive energies, as part of a fantasy life in which men could continue to act in the traditional masculine roles. Margaret Marsh, "Suburban Men and Masculine Domesticity," in *Meanings for Manhood: Constructions of Masculinity in Victorian America*, Mark C. Carnes and Clyde Griffen, eds. (Chicago: University of Illinois Press, 1990), 122–123.

15. War Department Commission on Training Camp Activities, *Keeping Fit to Fight*, National Archives.

16. Draft of poster, doc. 33308, box 78, entry 393, RG 165, National Archives.

17. Draft of another poster, doc. 33308, box 78, entry 393, RG 165, National Archives.

18. It is important to note that the terms *masculinity* and *manhood*, which will be used interchangeably in this book, are used to describe the social and cultural constructions that Americans have historically applied to maleness.

19. Though men were long the nearly exclusive subject of historical inquiry, it is only recently that historians have begun to investigate the history of manhood. Interestingly, it was the expansion of the discipline's focus to include women that ultimately led to historians' interest in the study of men as men. Historians of women illustrated the danger of generalizing the American story from the experiences of well-known men by documenting the distinctness of women's lives. Their discovery of the vast diversity of American experiences and their development of new methodologies for exploring that diversity encouraged a growing awareness that men, like women, constituted a vast grouping whose experiences could not be understood through a simplistic extrapolation from the lives of well-known men, but which required instead thoughtful and detailed exploration. For a discussion of the evolution of gender studies to include the study of men, see the introduction to *Meanings for Manhood*, Carnes and Griffen, eds., 1–5. See also Joe L. Dubbert, *A Man's Place: Masculinity in Transition* (Englewood Cliffs, N.J.: Prentice-Hall, 1979), 1–12.

20. For examples of the "crisis" approach, see Joe L. Dubbert, "Progressivism and the Masculinity Crisis," in *The American Man*, Elizabeth H. Pleck and Jospeh H. Pleck, eds. (Englewood Cliffs, N.J.: Prentice-Hall, 1980), 303–320; Joe Dubbert, *A Man's Place;* Peter G. Filene, *Him/Her/Self: Sex Roles in Modern America*, 2nd ed. (Baltimore: Johns Hopkins University Press, 1986); E. Anthony Rotundo, "Body and Soul: Changing Ideals of American Middle-Class Manhood, 1770–1920," *Journal of Social History* 16 (1983): 23–38. For a brief critique of this historiographical school, see Clyde Griffen, "Reconstructing Masculinity from the Evangelical Revival to the Waning of Progressivism: A Speculative Synthesis," in *Meanings for Manhood*, Carnes and Griffen, eds., 183–185.

21. The literature on the development of the middle-class ideology of separate spheres and the cult of domesticity is immense. Some of the classic works in this literature include

Kathryn Kish Sklar, *Catharine Beecher: A Study in American Domesticity* (New Haven, Conn.: Yale University Press, 1973); Nancy F. Cott, *Bonds of Womanhood: "Woman's Sphere" in New England, 1780–1835* (New Haven, Conn.: Yale University Press, 1977); Mary P. Ryan, *Cradle of the Middle Class: The Family in Oneida Country, New York, 1790–1865* (New York: Cambridge University Press, 1981).

22. E. Anthony Rotundo, *American Manhood: Transformation in Masculinity from the Revolution to the Modern Era* (New York: Basic Books, 1993), 2–5.

23. Griffen, "Reconstructing Masculinity," 185–187; Donald Yacovone, "Abolitionists and the 'Language of Fraternal Love,' " in *Meanings for Manhood*, Carnes and Griffen, eds., 85–95.

24. Ted Ownby, *Subduing Satan: Religion, Recreation, and Manhood in the Rural South, 1865–1920* (Chapel Hill: University of North Carolina Press, 1990).

25. Peter N. Stearns, *Be A Man! Males in Modern Society* (New York: Holmes and Meier, 1979), 59–78.

26. Rotundo, *American Manhood*, 120. See also Kevin White, *The First Sexual Revolution: The Emergence of Male Heterosexuality in Modern America* (New York: New York University Press, 1993), 2–4.

27. Rotundo, *American Manhood*, 121–122; K. White, *The First Sexual Revolution*, 7.

28. Joseph F. Kett, *Rites of Passage: Adolescence in America 1790 to the Present* (New York: Basic Books, 1977), 27; Charles E. Rosenberg, "Sexuality, Class, and Role in 19th-Century America," in *The American Man*, Elizabeth H. Pleck and Joseph H. Pleck, eds. (Englewood Cliffs, N.J.: Prentice-Hall, 1980), 233–235; David I. Macleod, *Building Character in the American Boy: The Boy Scouts, YMCA, and Their Forerunners, 1870–1920* (Madison: University of Wisconsin Press, 1983), 33–36.

29. Stearns, *Be A Man!* 59–78.

30. Kathy Peiss, *Cheap Amusements: Working Women and Leisure in Turn-of-the-Century New York* (Philadelphia: Temple University Press, 1986), 4; Roy Rosenzweig, *Eight Hours for What We Will: Workers and Leisure in an Industrial City, 1870–1920* (New York: Cambridge University Press, 1983), 38–40.

31. For the development of distinct leisure patterns among the working class, see Rosenzweig, *Eight Hours for What We Will;* Francis G. Couvares, *The Remaking of Pittsburgh—Class and Culture in an Industrializing City, 1877–1919* (New York: State University of New York Press, 1984), chapters 3 and 7; Daniel T. Rodgers, *The Work Ethic in Industrial America, 1850–1920* (Chicago: University of Chicago Press, 1974), chapter 4; Lewis A. Erenberg, *Steppin' Out: New York Nightlife and the Transformation of American Culture, 1890–1930* (Greenwood, Conn.: Greenwood Press, 1981), parts 2 and 3; John T. Cumbler, *Working-Class Community in Industrial America: Work, Leisure, and Struggle in Two Industrial Cities, 1880–1930* (Greenwood, Conn.: Greenwood Press, 1979). For the development of leisure among working-class women and girls, see Peiss, *Cheap Amusements.*

32. Roy Rosenzweig, *Eight Hours for What We Will*, chapter 2; Jon M. Kingsdale, "The 'Poor Man's Club': Social Functions of the Urban Working-Club Saloon," *American Quarterly* 25 (October 1973): 472–489; Peiss, *Cheap Amusements*, 4, 5, 6, 53–55, 108–109; K. White, *The First Sexual Revolution*, chapter 5.

33. My understanding of the meaning of changes in the economy in the lives of middle-class men has been shaped especially by the following discussions of this issue: Jeffrey P. Hantover, "The Boy Scouts and the Validation of Manhood," in *The American Man*, Pleck and Pleck, eds., 288–293; Filene, *Him/Her/Self*, 72–75; Rotundo, *American Manhood*, 248–251; Macleod, *Building Character in the American Boy*, 44–50.

34. Samuel P. Hays, as cited in Hantover, "The Boy Scouts and the Validation of Masculinity," in *The American Man*, Pleck and Pleck, eds., 290.

35. Filene, *Him/Her/Self*, 73.

36. Rotundo, *American Manhood*, 248–249.

37. Hantover, "The Boy Scouts and the Validation of Masculinity," in *The American Man*, Pleck and Pleck, eds., 291.

38. Rotundo, *American Manhood*, 222–227.

39. Sara Evans, *Born for Liberty: A History of Women in America* (New York: Free Press, 1989), 156.

40. Hantover, "The Boy Scouts and the Validation of Masculinity," in *The American Man*, Pleck and Pleck, eds., 292.

41. Macleod, *Building Character in the American Boy*, 46.

42. Rotundo, *American Manhood*, 250.

43. Hantover, "The Boy Scouts and the Validation of Masculinity," in *The American Man*, Pleck and Pleck, eds., 292. Hantover suggests that only one in three men worked in jobs where women constituted more than 5 percent of workers.

44. Evans, *Born for Liberty*, 147.

45. For a thoughtful synthesis of recent work on women's movement into the public sphere between 1865 and 1920, see Evans, *Born for Liberty*, chapters 6 and 7. See also Paula Baker, "The Domestication of Politics: Women and American Political Society, 1780–1920," *American Quarterly* 89 (June 1984): 620–647.

46. Margaret Marsh, "Suburban Men and Masculine Domesticity, 1870–1915," in *Meanings for Manhood*, Carnes and Griffen, eds., 111–127.

47. Evans, *Born for Liberty*, 178.

48. Marsh, "Suburban Men and Masculine Domesticity," in *Meanings for Manhood*, Carnes and Griffen, eds., 112.

49. Rotundo, *American Manhood*, 263.

50. Recall Edward F. Allen's determination that the Hostess House promote an "atmosphere of chivalry." Allen, *Keeping Our Fighters Fit*, 129.

51. Other historians have noted that the changes in male/female relations, often described as the rise of companionate relationships, did not necessarily alter existing power hierarchies between men and women. See for instance Robert L. Griswold, "Divorce and the Legal Redefinition of Victorian Manhood," in *Meanings for Manhood*, Carnes and Griffen, eds., 97, 104; Marsh, "Suburban Men and Masculine Domesticity," in *Meanings for Manhood*, Carnes and Griffen, eds., 126–127; Griffen, "Reconstructing Masculinity," in *Meanings for Manhood*, Carnes and Griffen, eds., 201; Evans, *Born for Liberty*, 177–178.

52. James R. McGovern suggests this tendency in the life of David Graham Phillips. James R. McGovern, "David Graham Phillips and the Virility Impulse of the Progressives," *New England Quarterly* 39 (1966): 351. Joe L. Dubbert makes a comparable argument regarding the life of William Allen White in Dubbert, "Progressivism and the Masculinity Crisis," 313–314. For a broader discussion of this same tendency, see Rotundo, *American Manhood*, 271–274.

The progressives' predecessors, members of the Social Gospel movement, had confronted this exact problem. Identified with a feminized protestantism and devoted to social reforms in a competitive society emphasizing individualism, these reformers sought to define their work in terms that emphasized their masculinity, despite any appearances to the contrary. Susan Curtis, "The Son of Man and God the Father: The Social Gospel and Victorian Masculinity," in *Meanings for Manhood*, Carnes and Griffen, eds., 68, 72, 73, 74, 78.

53. Rotundo, *American Manhood*, 274.

54. Dubbert, "Progressivism and the Masculinity Crisis," 313–314.

55. Odell, *The New Spirit of the New Army*, 94.

56. Newton D. Baker, "Expression versus Suppression," a speech to the National Social Hygiene Association in Washington D.C., 31 January 1918, reprinted in *Frontiers of Freedom*, by Newton D. Baker (New York: George H. Doran, 1918), 236.

57. War Department Commission on Training Camp Activities, *Keeping Fit to Fight*, National Archives.

58. "SYLLABUS OF AN ADDRESS TO ASSIST COMPANY COMMANDERS IN THE INSTRUCTION OF THEIR MEN IN THE KNOWLEDGE OF VENEREAL DISEASES," pp. 4, 6, 7, issued by the Surgeon General, doc. 38401, entry 393, RG 165, National Archives.

59. Walter C. Clarke, "Promotion of Social Hygiene in War Time," *Annals of the American Academy of Political and Social Science* 79 (September 1918): 185, 188.

60. Howard Webster Munder to his father, 12 February 1918, in "Letters and Diary of Bugler Howard Webster Munder," U.S. Army Military History Institute, Carlisle Barracks, Pennsylvania, World War One Research Project, Army Experiences Questionnaire Collection, 28th Division, 55th Infantry Battalion, 109th Infantry Regiment, Company G.

61. Brandt, *No Magic Bullet*, 68–69.

62. Ibid., 7–25. This work is a wonderful exploration not only of venereal disease, but also of the social constructions that surrounded those diseases in American society.

63. Ibid., 31.

64. "Description of Facilities Offered by the Commission on Training Camp Activities—Social Hygiene Division," doc. 25932, box 53, entry 393, RG 165, National Archives. Other information on the elements of the education program comes from Clarke, "Promotion of Social Hygiene in War Time," 181.

65. Annual Report, Commission on Training Camp Activities to the Secretary of War, 1918, p. 10, box 1635, RG 287, National Archives.; Brandt, *No Magic Bullet*, 68.

66. Brandt, *No Magic Bullet*, 110–111. Brandt explains the procedure of medical or chemical prophylaxis.

> Attendants, appointed to each station, administered the treatments. A soldier reporting for the treatment would first urinate. Then, on a specially constructed stool, he would wash his genitals with soap and water followed by bichloride of mercury, while the attendant inspected. The attendant would then inject a solution of protargol into the penis, which the soldier would hold in the urethra for five minutes, then expel. After the injection, calomel ointment would be rubbed on the penis, which would then be wrapped in waxed paper. For the prevention to be effective the soldier could not urinate for four or five hours following the treatment. Brandt, *No Magic Bullet*, 111.

67. One might note that this apparent dilemma persists in arguments against sex education for American youth.

68. *Method of Attack on Venereal Disease*, pamphlet produced by the Surgeon General and the American Social Hygiene Association, August, 1917, letter file S, box 7, entry 394, RG 165, National Archives.

69. War Department Commission on Training Camp Activities, Minutes of Meeting, 26 April 1917, box 57, entry 403, RG 165, National Archives.

70. Allen, *Keeping Our Fighters Fit*, 5–6.

71. Raymond B. Fosdick to Sam L. Olive, President, Georgia State Senate, 28 August 1917, in reply to telegram of Olive to Secretary of War Baker, 22 August 1917, doc. 3798, letter file O, box 6, entry 394, RG 165, National Archives.

72. Raymond B. Fosdick, *Chronicle of a Generation—An Autobiography* (New York: Harper, 1958), 148–149; *War Department Commission on Training Camp Activities*, a pamphlet produced by the War Department (Washington, D.C., 1917), pp. 9–10, box 1635 RG 287, National Archives; Jewish Welfare Board, *Final Report of War Emergency Activities* (New York, 1920), 13.

73. Fosdick to Dr. George A. Coe, 24 May 1917, file F, box 2, entry 394, RG 165, National Archives.

74. Peiss, *Cheap Amusements*, 178–179; Allen F. Davis, *Spearheads for Reform* (New York: Oxford University Press, 1967), 65.

75. Paul Boyer, *Urban Masses and Moral Order in America, 1820–1920* (Cambridge: Harvard University Press, 1978), 222–224, 242–251.

76. Peiss, *Cheap Amusements*, 179. Or as John F. Kasson described the differences between these two styles of recreation, "The contrasting kinds of play, to the minds of a number of reformers, meant the difference between a community and a crowd, perhaps even the difference between civilization and barbarism." John F. Kasson, *Amusing the Million: Coney Island at the Turn of the Century* (New York: Hill and Wang, 1978), 104. See also Rodgers, *The Work Ethic in Industrial America*, 124; Stephen Hardy and Alan G. Ingham, "Games, Structures, and Agency: Historians on the American Play Movement," *Journal of Social History* 17 (Winter 1983): 286.

Given many white progressives' assumptions of a natural promiscuity among African Americans, it is perhaps not surprising that in the eyes of those reformers African Americans appeared a particularly troublesome population. Alan Dawley, *Struggles for Justice: Social Responsibility and the Liberal State* (Cambridge: Harvard University Press, 1991), 43–44, 117–118.

77. Boyer, *Urban Masses and Moral Order*, 242.

78. Ibid., 241. See also Erenberg, *Steppin' Out*, 65; Kasson, *Amusing the Million*, 104.

79. Kasson, *Amusing the Million*, 101.

80. Allen, *Keeping Our Fighters Fit*, 41.

81. Ibid., 53, 55.

82. War Department Commission on Training Camp Activities, *Rules for Boxing* (pamphlet) (Washington, D.C.: Government Printing Office, 1918), 2.

83. Allen, *Keeping Our Fighters Fit*, 62, 63.

84. Ibid., 5–6.

85. Ibid., 42.

86. See for instance Allen, *Keeping Our Fighters Fit*, 51, 54, 63.

87. Allen, *Keeping Our Fighters Fit*, 156–157; *War and Navy Departments Commission on Training Camp Activities* (pamphlet) (Washington, D.C., 1918), p. 17, box 1635, RG 287, National Archives.

88. Fred D. Baldwin, "The American Enlisted Man in World War One," Ph.D. diss., Princeton University, 1964, 117; David M. Kennedy, *Over Here: The First World War and American Society* (New York: Oxford University Press, 1980), 189.

89. Baldwin, "The Enlisted Man in World War One," 117–118.

90. Allen, *Keeping Our Fighters Fit*, 162–163.

91. Ibid., 31; Fosdick, "The War and Navy Departments Commissions on Training Camp Activities," 132; "No Small Job Amusing Men of Cantonment—Y.M.C.A. Report Shows Tremendous Effort Made to Entertain Soldiers," *Camp Dodger*, 14 June 1918, 13; "Many Soldiers Go to the 'Y's," *Camp Dodger*, 31 May 1918.

92. Allen, *Keeping Our Fighters Fit*, 20.

93. Ibid., 21–22.

94. Fosdick, "The War and Navy Departments Commissions on Training Camp Activities," 132, 133.

95. Marshall Bartholomew, secretary, National War Work Council of the YMCA, to other secretaries, 6 May 1918, file Birchard, C.C.B., box 3, entry 399, RG 165, National Archives.

96. Allen, *Keeping Our Fighters Fit*, 79.

97. Ibid., 67, 69, 70, 75; Fosdick, "War and Navy Departments Commissions on Training Camp Activities," 138.

98. The commission suggested "the eight songs required in the soldiers' repertoire: four for patriotism—America, Star-Spangled Banner, Battle Hymn of the Republic, and La Marseillaise; four for American tradition—Old Black Joe, Suwanee River, Old Kentucky Home, and Roll, Jordan, Roll." Frances F. Brundage, *Camp Music Division of the War Department Commission on Training Camp Activities*, War Department Pamphlet, p. 13, box 1635, RG 287, National Archives. It is interesting to note that the commission clearly intended to include the South as an important contributor to American tradition, a tendency common during World War One.

99. Allen, *Keeping Our Fighters Fit*, 82, 83. See also Lee F. Hanmer to Commanding Officer, Camp Beauregard, 17 April 1918, file Camp Beauregard, Louisiana, box 8, entry 399, RG 165, National Archives.

100. Frances F. Brundage, *Camp Music Division of the War Department Commission on Training Camp Activities*, War Department Pamphlet, p. 7, National Archives.

101. Allen, *Keeping Our Fighters Fit*, 26.

102. Ibid., 106; Lee F. Hanmer, member of CTCA in charge of amusements, to Baker, 24 August 1917, in "Camps" file, box 9, entry 399, RG 165, National Archives.

103. *War and Navy Departments Commission on Training Camp Activities* (pamphlet) (Washington, D.C., 1918), box 1635, RG 287, National Archives.

104. Orrin Cocks, motion picture inspector, to Malcolm L. McBride, 20 March 1918, in first Camp Lewis, Washington, file, box 7, entry 399, RG 165, National Archives.

105. Malcolm McBride to E. Dana Caulkins, 28 October 1918, doc. 41223, box 111, entry 393, RG 165, National Archives; "Minutes of Meeting of the War Department Commission on Training Camp Activities," 21 February 1918, box 57, entry 403, RG 165, National Archives.

106. Arthur P. Young, *Books for Sammies: The American Library Association and World War I* (Pittsburgh: Phi Beta Mu, 1981), 13.

107. In July 1918 the War Department began prohibiting certain books in the camp libraries. In July the ALA issued a list of fourteen banned books, recommended by the War Department. In August five more lists would follow. In September the War Department's list of eighty banned books and pamphlets was released and accepted by the ALA. Evidently, toward the end of the war various members of the War Department began to find the banning of books unnecessary, even "absurd." One week after the armistice Baker withdrew the banning recommendations. Young, *Books for Sammies*, 47–55.

108. Young, *Books for Sammies*, 33, 53.

109. Ibid., 52.

110. Allan Brandt makes a similar argument in *No Magic Bullet*, 92.

111. The classic introduction to the "cult of true womanhood" remains Barbara Welter, "The Cult of True Womanhood," *American Quarterly* 18 (1966): 151–174. In this article Welter introduces the four standards of womanhood—piety, purity, domesticity, and submission.

112. Welter, "The Cult of True Womanhood," 152, 154, 157, 158–159, 162–163.

113. On working-class women see Evans, *Born for Liberty*, 99. For a fuller discussion of this topic, see Alice Kessler-Harris, *Out to Work: A History of Wage-Earning Women in the United States* (New York: Oxford University Press, 1982), chapter 3; Christine Stansell, *City of Women: Sex and Class in New York, 1789–1860* (Chicago: University of Illinois Press, 1987). On slave women see Deborah Gray White, *Ar'n't I a Woman* (New York: W. W. Norton, 1985), especially chapter 1.

114. Anne Firor Scott, *Natural Allies: Women's Associations in American History* (Chicago: University of Illinois Press, 1993), 81–82.

115. Catharine Beecher is a classic example of a woman's ability to define domesticity in ways that permitted her a public role. See Sklar, *Catharine Beecher*, especially chapter 11.

116. P. Baker, "The Domestication of Politics," 632–638.

117. *To Girls in Wartime—A Message from the American Government*, leaflet from the Section on Women's Work, Social Hygiene Division, CTCA, doc. 40286, box 108, entry 393, RG 165, National Archives.

118. Ibid.

119. Joseph Lee, "War Camp Community Service," *Annals of the American Academy of Political and Social Science* 79 (September 1918), 193.

120. Ibid., 190.

121. "Committee on Protective Work for Girls," doc. 6211, entry 393, RG 165, National Archives.

122. John Dickinson, *The Building of an Army: A Detailed Account of Legislation, Administration, and Opinion in the United States, 1915–1920* (New York: Century, 1922), 216.

123. Dorothy Ashby, "Building for Lady Visitors at Camp Dodge," *Camp Dodger*, 26 October 1917, 2; Fosdick, "The War and Navy Departments Commissions on Training Camp Activities," 135; "Hostess House is Vital Factor in Camp Life—Utilized For Every Purpose . . .", *Camp Dodger*, 19 July 1918, 5.

124. Allen, *Keeping Our Fighters Fit*, 128.

125. Mary Alden Hopkins, "Why Is A Hostess House?" *World Outlook* 4 (April 1918), 13.

126. Odell, *The New Spirit of the New Army*, 33–34.

127. "Local Federation on Training Camp Meets Wednesday," *Arkansas Democrat*, 16 June 1917, 12.

128. Allen, *Keeping Our Fighters Fit*, 207.

129. Odell, *The New Spirit of the New Army*, 33.

130. Newton D. Baker, "Invisible Armor," speech to the National Conference on War Camp Recreation Service, 23 October 1917, reprinted in *Frontiers of Freedom*, by N. D. Baker, 97.

131. "Six Months of the War Camp Community Service," *Playground* 11 (March 1918): 614.

132. Maj. Granville Fortescue, "Training the New Armies of Liberty—Camp Lee, Virginia's Home for the National Army," *National Geographic Magazine* 32 (November–December 1977): 421.

NOTES TO CHAPTER THREE

1. Newton D. Baker, "Invisible Armor," speech to the National Conference on War Camp Recreation Service, 23 October 1917, reprinted in *Frontiers of Freedom*, by Newton D. Baker (New York: George H. Doran, 1918), 86–87.

2. Ray F. Carter, executive secretary, Tacoma Committee for Recreation of Soldiers, Representative of the CTCA, to E. S. Calkins *[sic]*, 19 September 1917, doc. 5766, file "F," box 2, entry 394, RG 165, National Archives.

3. Report for weeks ending 22 May 1918 and 16 May 1918, from Walter Clarke, Sanitary Corps, to Surgeon General, doc. 32013, box 73, entry 393, RG 165, National Archives.

4. A typical day's headlines in the Camp Lewis paper, *Over-the-Top*, for instance, cited several events for 12 January 1918, including "Soccer Team on Edge for Tomorrow's Game," "Lefty Mails Now in Camp" [Lefty was a pitcher], "Ritchie Fight-Pictures Will Be Shown Here," "Coughlin to be Ritchie's Opponent at Big Smoker" [Ritchie was a boxer], and "Gen. Foltz O.K's Baseball Plans." *Over-the-Top*, 12 January 1918.

5. Commission on Training Camp Activities, *Report of the Chairman on Training Camp Activities to the Secretary of War, 1918*, box 1635, RG 287, National Archives.

6. Arthur P. Young, *Books for Sammies: The American Library Association and World War One* (Pittsburgh: Phi Beta Mu, 1981), 44.

7. Commission on Training Camp Activities, *Report of the Chairman on Training Camp Activities to the Secretary of War, 1918*, 20, National Archives.

8. Edward F. Allen, *Keeping Our Fighters Fit for War and After* (New York: Century, 1918), 26.

9. "Indian Dances and Songs Are Given at 'Y's—Full-blood Sioux Indian Sings and Dances for Men at Camp Dodge," *Camp Dodger*, 15 March 1918, 3; "Y.M.C.A. Has Week of Revival," *Camp Bowie Reconnaissance*, 9 February 1918, 7; "K.C. to Give 363rd Dance," *Over the Top* (Camp Lewis), 13 April 1918, 1; "50 Des Moines Girls Entertained at Hops," *Camp Dodger*, 13 June 1918, 3; "Halloween Party at Hut No. 1," *Trench and Camp* (Camp Beauregard), 15 October 1917, 3.

10. Minutes of Meeting of the War Department Commission on Training Camp Activities, 24 October 1917, box 57, entry 403, RG 165, National Archives.

11. "Interesting Report of Y.M.C.A. Work," *83rd Division News* (Camp Sherman), 27 March 1918, 9; " 'Y' Record at Camp for August," *Trench and Camp* (Camp Pike), 10 September 1918, 8. At times the sheer quantity of productions at the organization huts verged on the incredible. For instance, in March 1918 the YMCA buildings at Camp Dodge in Iowa offered 164 entertainments and 108 movies. In May 89 movies were shown to 31,130 men at Camp Dodge, as well as 294 music and dramatic programs, which were seen by 38,671 soldiers. In one week at Camp Dodge 80,000 feet of film were shown. The YMCA camp secretary figured this would equal 800 miles of movies in one year. "YMCA's Are Very Popular with Soldiers," *Camp Dodger*, 19 April 1918, 1; "No Small Job Amusing Men of Cantonment—Y.M.C.A. Report Shows Tremendous Effort Made to Entertain Soldiers," *Camp Dodger*, 14 June 1918, 13.

12. A. Estelle Paddock, "War Work of Young Women's Christian Association," *Annals of the American Academy of Political and Social Science* 79 (September 1918): 212.

13. William H. Zinsser to Mr. Sanger, 23 August 1918, doc. 37578, box 95, entry 393, RG 165, National Archives.

14. For information on the army program of social hygiene education, see for instance Walter C. Clarke, "The Promotion of Social Hygiene in War Time," *Annals of the American Academy of Political and Social Science* 79 (September 1918): 180–183, 185.

15. Pickard, District Director, S.E. District, to Fosdick, 9 March 1918, doc. 31202, box 71, entry 393, RG 165, National Archives.

16. E. F. Glenn to James Edward Rogers, 30 July 1917, doc. 2989, file Arizona 18, box

3, entry 395, RG 165, National Archives. Later Glenn would write again, making clear his continued appreciation for the work of the CTCA. See E. F. Glenn to Secretary of War, 24 February 1919, doc. 46428, box 132, entry 393, RG 165, National Archives.

17. Allen, *Keeping Our Fighters Fit*, 124–125. See also Major General H. A. Greene, Commanding Officer, Camp Lewis, to Miss Constance Clark, Superintendent, YWCA Hostess House, Camp Lewis, Juen *[sic]* 10, 1918, doc. 33876, box 80, entry 393, RG 165, National Archives.

18. "Congratulations and Obligations," *Tacoma Daily Ledger*, 15 June 1917, 4.

19. "Comprehensive Patriotism," editorial, *Fort Worth Star-Telegram*, 4 August 1917, 4.

20. "Argenta News—Mayor Discusses Capture of Camp," *Arkansas Democrat*, 11 June 1917, 4; "Little Rock and the Cantonment," *Arkansas Democrat*, 11 June 1917, 6; "What Are You Going to Do?" *Arkansas Democrat*, 13 June 1917, 6.

21. Joseph H. Odell, *The New Spirit of the New Army: A Message to "Service Flag" Homes* (New York: Fleming H. Revell, 1918), 99–100.

22. "Big Soldiers' Camp," *Stanford Palo Alto News*, 29 June 1917, 2.

23. "Realty Conditions Affected by Camp," address of George Firmin, general manager of the Little Rock Board of Commerce, to a meeting of the real estate men of the city, reprinted in *Arkansas Democrat*, 11 July 1917, 5.

24. "Expect Business Here to Double within Two Months; Tax Resources," *San Diego Sun*, 25 May 1917, 1.

25. "Trustees Appoint Committee on Camp Matter," *Stanford Palo Alto News*, 27 July 1917, 1.

26. "Our Girls and the Soldiers," editorial, *Fort Worth Star-Telegram*, 17 August 1917, 6.

27. "Imperative That City Raise War Camp Fund," *Arkansas Democrat*, 27 February 1918.

28. Roy L. Thompson, chairman of Little Rock WCCS, to Joseph Lee, 13 June 1918, doc. 33102, box 77, entry 393, RG 165, National Archives. For other examples of the link between local business leaders and the CTCA, see also "War Camp Community Service Has Big Plans for Aiding Soldiers," *Arkansas Democrat*, 6 February 1918, 4; "War Recreation Board Is Doing Much for Men," *Camp Dodger*, 28 December 1917.

29. "The New Fort Worth," editorial, *Fort Worth Star-Telegram*, 20 September 1917, 6.

30. For lists of the achievements in various war camp communities, see "Six Months of War Camp Community Service," *Playground* 11 (March 1918), 563–614; *War Camp Community Service—The Second Six Months, November 1917—May 1918* (New York, 1918); "Community War Recreation Service—Its Meaning—Plan of Work—Accomplishments," *Playground* 11 (October 1917), 349–354; "Accomplishments in Various Cities," *Playground* 11 (October 1917), 363–382; *What New York Did for Fighting Men through New York War Camp Community Service in the World-War of 1917–1918* (New York, 1919).

31. "Six Months of War Camp Community Service," 607. In Little Rock, Arkansas, the community adopted the WCCS position rapidly and by mid-June could advertise extensive recreational opportunities for visiting troops. Though the new National Guard encampment at Camp Pike would not open until late summer, Little Rock entertained soldiers from Fort Logan H. Roots all through the summer of 1917. A sample weekend schedule from June included the following entertainment possibilities:

Friday Night:	Arkansaw Travelers dress parade Military Dansante—street dance

Saturday afternoon:	Amateur Baseball Commercial League Game
	Benefit Tea Dance
	Free Motion Pictures
	YMCA open to soldiers
Saturday evening:	Dance for Officers and Students Training Camp
	"Country Fair" performance
	Musical program and social by City Union of Christian Endeavor
	Smoker—Knights of Columbus club
	Social—Methodist church
Sunday afternoon:	Churches open
	"Take a soldier home to dinner" program
	Public Library open
	Musical by Studio Club
	Navy motion picture and concert
	Band Concert at city park
	Open House—YWCA
	Amateur baseball
	Free movies
Sunday evening:	Band Concert

For this schedule see "Announce Program for the Soldiers," *Arkansas Democrat*, 15 June 1917, 1. This paper printed a schedule each week of the weekend activities planned for the troops.

32. In Norfolk, Virginia, the plan of organization for the local WCCS included thirty-four committees, ranging from the Books and Magazines Committee to the Legal Aid Committee, from the Distinguished Visitors Committee to the Film Service Committee. Montague Gammon, "Plan of Organization of the War Camp Community Service, Norfolk, Virginia," doc. 38326, box 98, entry 393, RG 165, National Archives. The complete list of committees included Executive, Home Hospitality, Service Club, Liberty Theatre, Liberty Sings, Visiting Entertainment, Books and Magazines, School Entertainment, Church Entertainment, Men's Social Club Entertainment, Women's Social Club Entertainment, Newspapers for Sailors, Rooming Bureau, Legal Aid, Athletics, Commercial Relations, Fraternal Entertainment, Entertainment of Our Allies, Girls' Employment, Girls' Activities, Motor Service, Public Comfort Stations, Finance and Budget, Social Entertainment in Armory, Distinguished Visitors, Prep School, Bathing Facilities, Officers' Club and Family Hotel, Film Service, Entertainment for Negroes, Office, Recreation for Industrial Workers, Information, and Union Services.

33. "General War-time Commission of the Churches Survey of National Army Cantonments and National Guard Camps, Nov. 20, 1917," doc. 14594, box 25, entry 393, RG 165, National Archives.

34. "Report on Community Secretaries," excerpt on Camp Shelby, Hattiesburg, Mississippi, doc. 11520, box 16, entry 393, RG 165, National Archives.

35. Report on Hattiesburg and Camp Shelby, "General War-time Commission of the Churches Survey of National Army Cantonments and National Guard Camps, Nov. 20, 1917," doc. 14594, box 25, entry 393, RG 165, National Archives.

36. Memorandum for Mr. Braucher from District Directors Mr. Wallace and Mr. Prickard and one other, 11 January 1918, doc. 31789, box 73, entry 393, RG 165, National Archives.

37. *War Camp Community Service—The Second Six Months*, 43.

38. "Six Months of War Camp Community Service," 587–588.

39. Ibid., 587; *War Camp Community Service—The Second Six Months*, 42.

40. "Statement of the Council of National Defense Relative to RESPONSIBILITY OF CIVIL COMMUNITIES for VENEREAL DISEASE IN THE ARMY," doc. 32726, box 75, entry 393, RG 165, National Archives.

41. "United States Public Health Service—Public Health Protection," edited by Dr. J. G. Townsend, captain, *Pass-In-Review* (Camp Bowie), 9 November 1918, 4.

42. Katherine Bement Davis, "Women's Education in Social Hygiene," *Annals of the American Academy of Political and Social Science* 79 (September 1918): 169; *Your Side of the Fight—"Keeping Them Fit to Work,"* a pamphlet produced by the War Department Commission on Training Camp Activities and the United States Public Health Service (Washington, D.C.: Government Printing Office, no date), at the Hoover Institute on War and Revolution, 12. For additional information on the civilian side of the venereal fight, see Allan Brandt, *No Magic Bullet: A Social History of Venereal Disease in the United States since 1880* (New York: Oxford University Press, 1985), 78–80. Brandt details the creation of the Civilian Committee to Combat Venereal Disease, established by the Council of National Defense. The CCCVD worked alongside the CTCA, dealing with those cities and towns beyond the reach of the CTCA.

43. K. B. Davis, "Women's Education in Social Hygiene," 171.

44. "Activities of the War Camp Community Service—Dancing," *Pass-in-Review*, 31 July 1918, 8.

45. Samuel B. Murray to Fosdick, 19 February 1918, doc. 26834, entry 393, RG 165, National Archives.

46. Fosdick to Samuel B. Murray of Fort Worth, 23 February 1918, doc. 26834, entry 393, RG 165, National Archives.

47. Ray F. Carter to E. S. *[sic]* Calkins, 19 September 1917, doc. 5766, letter file F, box 2, entry 394, RG 165, National Archives.

48. "Community War Recreation Service—Its Meaning—Plan of Work—Accomplishments," 352.

49. Joseph Lee to J. Douglas Swagerty, First Methodist Church, Dallas, 15 May 1918, doc. 28563, entry 393, RG 165, National Archives.

50. See Fosdick to Mr. Jas. A. Armstrong, 29 April 1918, doc. 25767, box 52, entry 393, RG 165, National Archives.

51. Daniel T. Rodgers, *The Work Ethic in Industrial America* (Chicago: University of Chicago Press, 1978), 106, 107.

52. For an insightful account of the tensions between the traditional Sunday and the rise of new amusements, see Martin Paulsson, *The Social Anxieties of Progressive Reform: Atlantic City, 1854–1920* (New York: New York University Press, 1994). See also Rodgers, *The Work Ethic in Industrial America*, 107; Francis G. Couvares, *The Remaking of Pittsburgh: Class and Culture in an Industrializing City, 1877–1919* (Albany: State University of New York Press, 1984), 75–79; Roy Rosenzweig, *Eight Hours for What We Will: Workers and Leisure in an Industrial City, 1870–1920* (New York: Cambridge University Press, 1983), 208.

53. "War Camp Community Service," *Playground* 11 (January 1918), 508.

54. Fosdick to Mr. J. R. Kneebone, City Manager, Beaufort, South Carolina, 24 April 1918, doc. 25843, box 53, entry 393, RG 165, National Archives.

55. Fosdick to the Hon. Robert R. Lawson, 12 September 1918, doc. 38507, box 99, entry 393, RG 165, National Archives.

56. War Camp Community Service, *Keep 'Em Smiling: Handbook of War Camp Community Service* (New York: War Camp Community Service, 1918), 93.

57. Fosdick to Rev. A. R. Holdenby, East Point, Georgia, 4 March 1918, doc. 27495, entry 393, RG 165, National Archives.

58. Fosdick to the Hon. Robert R. Lawson, 12 September 1918, doc. 38507, box 99, entry 393, RG 165, National Archives.

59. Fosdick to Mr. J. R. Kneebone, City Manager, Beaufort, South Carolina, 24 April 1918, doc. 25843, box 53, entry 393, RG 165, National Archives.

60. "God Is Not Mocked," editorial in the *Arkansas Methodist*, quoted in "Entertainment for the Soldiers," *Arkansas Democrat*, 21 July 1917, 4.

61. Communication signed by members of congregation and sent by Rev. W. M. Rader, Beeville, Texas, to Baker, 7 April 1918, doc. 23844, box 48, entry 393, RG 165, National Archives.

62. Ibid.

63. Quotes from "God Is Not Mocked," editorial in the *Arkansas Methodist*, quoted in "Entertainment for the Soldiers," *Arkansas Democrat*, 21 July 1917, 4.

64. C. E. Wilbur, President, Methodist Protestant Ministers Meeting, and E. J. Headley, Secretary, to Baker, 8 May 1918, doc. 28148, box 60, entry 393, RG 165, National Archives.

65. "Relation of the Churches to the Sunday Problem," a confidential report, doc. 41969, box 114, entry 393, RG 165, National Archives.

66. C. W. Pfeiffer, CTCA representative and Executive Secretary of the WCCS Board, Hattiesburg, Mississippi, to E. Dana Calkins, CTCA, 7 March 1918, doc. 21213, box 41, entry 393, RG 165, National Archives.

67. R. Oscar Beckman, Beaufort, South Carolina, to WCCS, New York City, 10 April 1918, doc. 25843, box 53, entry 393, RG 165, National Archives.

68. "Relation of the Churches to the Sunday Problem," confidential report, National Archives.

69. "Movies on Sunday Upheld by Judge," *Arkansas Democrat*, 3 July 1917, 1.

70. Ibid.

71. "Urge Movies for Soldiers Sunday P.M.," editorial quoting statement by members of the CTCA executive committee for Fort Logan, *Arkansas Democrat*, 16 July 1917, 1.

72. "The Sunday Movie Decision," editorial, *Arkansas Democrat*, 3 July 1917, 4.

73. "Sunday Amusements," *Arkansas Democrat*, 18 June 1917, 6.

74. "Sunday Recreation is Championed by Mayor of Argenta," *Arkansas Democrat*, 25 June 1917, 1.

75. "Prominent Leaders of Church Endorse Movies on Sunday," *Arkansas Democrat*, 17 July 1917, 1.

76. "Sunday Amusements," *Arkansas Democrat*, 18 June 1917, 6.

77. "The Sunday Movie Decision," *Arkansas Democrat*, 3 July 1917, 4; "Sunday Amusements," *Arkansas Democrat*, 18 June 1917, 6.

78. "Anti-Movie Logic," *Arkansas Democrat*, 10 July 1917, 6.

79. "Confusing the Issue," *Arkansas Democrat*, 9 July 1917, 4; "Anti-Movie Logic," *Arkansas Democrat* (10 July 1917), 6.

80. "God Is Not Mocked," editorial from *Arkansas Methodist*, broadly quoted in "Entertainment for the Soldiers," *Arkansas Democrat*, 21 July 1917, 4.

81. Editorials from *Arkansas Methodist*, quoted in "Entertainment for the Soldiers," *Arkansas Democrat*, 21 July 1917, 4.

82. Sam H. Campbell, president, Ministerial Alliance, Little Rock, to Baker, 1 August 1917, doc. 4720, file Arkansas—Little Rock, box 4, entry 395, RG 165, National Archives.

83. Ibid.

84. Ibid.

85. S. E. Ryan, of the Scott St. Methodist Episcopal Church, Little Rock, to Fosdick, 1 September 1917, doc. 5682, letter file R, box 7, entry 394, RG 165, National Archives.

86. Ibid.

87. Quotation from the *Arkansas Methodist*, quoted in "Entertainment for the Soldiers," *Arkansas Democrat*, 21 July 1917, 4; "Thanks for the Advertising," *Arkansas Democrat*, 28 July 1917, 6.

88. "Thanks for the Advertising," *Arkansas Democrat*, 28 July 1917, 6; "Sunday Amusements," *Arkansas Democrat*, 17 June 1917, 6; "Myron A. Kessner Going to Atlanta," *Arkansas Democrat*, 18 August 1917, 1.

89. Editorial, *Baptist Advance*, 19 July 1917, quoted in "Anti-Movie Personalities," *Arkansas Democrat*, 24 July 1917, 4.

90. Fosdick to H. S. Braucher, 20 July 1917 and 27 July 1917, doc. 2494, file Alabama 26 (2 of 3), box 2, entry 395, RG 165, National Archives.

91. "Relation of the Churches to the Sunday Problem," Confidential Report, doc. 41969, box 114, entry 393, RG 165, National Archives.

92. Ibid.

93. Fosdick to Joseph H. Odell, 30 March 1918, doc. 43398, box 120, entry 393, RG 165, National Archives.

94. A similar pattern involving apparent victories by Sabbatarians followed by their cooperation in a Sunday recreation program occurred in other training camp communities. For the example in Hattiesburg, Mississippi, see C. W. Pfeiffer, General Secretary, Hattiesburg WCCS, to E. Dana Caulkins, 25 April 1918, doc. 26020, box 53, entry 393, RG 165, National Archives. On Macon, Georgia, see Report on the Sunday Problem in Macon, Georgia, doc. 41969, box 114, entry 393, RG 165, National Archives.

95. Frances Fisher Byers, "Camp Upton—The Melting Pot," *World Outlook* 4 (April 1918), 15. See also David M. Kennedy, *Over Here: The First World War and American Society* (New York: Oxford University Press, 1980), 17–18.

96. Charles F. Welder, "Suggestions for Summer-War Camp Community Service," 27 April 1918, reprinted as War Recreation Bulletin #221, doc. 34813, box 84, entry 393, RG 165, National Archives.

97. War Camp Community Service, *Keep 'Em Smiling*, 96–97.

98. Boston WCCS, *Dances—How to Conduct Them*, box 131, entry 393, RG 165, National Archives.

99. "Report on conditions of prevalence and spread of venereal disease," from Elmore McNeill Mckee of the Sanitary Corps, National Army, to the Surgeon General, 19 October 1917, doc. 10088, file Massachusetts, box 9, entry 395, RG 165, National Archives.

100. Boston WCCS, *Dances—How to Conduct Them*, National Archives.

101. H. S. Braucher, "Policies with Reference to Dance Halls," 27 June 1918, issued as War Recreation Bulletin 441, doc. 37811, box 96, entry 393, RG 165, National Archives.

102. "Would Have to Get Permit Every Day," *Daily Palo Alto Times*, 14 July 1917, 1.

103. "Six Months of War Camp Community Service," 608.

104. *War Camp Community Service—The Second Six Months*, 22.

105. "Dancing Delights Must Be Curtailed," *Camp Dodger*, 20 June 1918, 7.

106. Ray S. Hubbard, "Recreation Plans for Soldiers of Camp—Activities of War Camp Community Service," *Trench and Camp* (Camp Devens), 2 January 1918, 7.

107. "War Camp Community Service Jottings," *Trench and Camp* (Camp Devens), January 30, 1918, 2.

108. Joseph Lee to J. Douglas Swagerty, First Methodist Church, Dallas, 15 May 1918, doc. 28563, entry 393, RG 165, National Archives.

109. War Camp Community Service, *Keep 'Em Smiling*, 62.

110. "Girls Teach Soldiers Here How to Dance," *Camp Dodger*, 12 April 1918.

111. Boston WCCS, *Dances—How to Conduct Them*, National Archives.

112. H. S. Braucher, "Policies with Reference to Dance Halls," 27 June 1918, issued as War Recreation Bulletin 441, doc. 37811, box 96, entry 393, RG 165, National Archives (emphasis mine).

113. Charles F. Welder, "Suggestions for Summer-WCCS," 27 April 1918, reprinted as War Recreation Bulletin 221, doc. 34813, box 84, entry 393, RG 165, National Archives.

114. "Local Community Dances Approved by Commission," *Arkansas Gazette*, 10 August 1917, 4.

115. "War Recreation Board Is Doing Much for Men," *Camp Dodger*, 28 December 1917; Extract from report of R. S. Hubbard, 26 January 1918, reprinted as War Recreation Bulletin 206, 22 May 1918, doc. 32411, box 75, entry 393, RG 165, National Archives; "War Camp Community Service Jottings," *Trench and Camp* (Camp Devens), 9 January 1918, 2.

116. War Camp Community Service, *Keep 'Em Smiling*, 63. The WCCS sometimes limited the attendance of the men in uniform as well. See "War Camp Community Service Jottings," *Trench and Camp* (Camp Devens), 30 January 1918, 2; "In Division Society—The Rock Cliff Club," *Spartanburg Gas Attack* (Camp Wadsworth), 22 December 1917, 16.

117. Robert Bertrand Brown, *War Camp Community Service Calls* (New York, 1919), 33.

118. Ibid., 34.

119. "Dixie Dance Proves to Be Big Success," *Reveille* (Camp Logan), 27 November 1917, 1.

120. A. A. Fisk, "Report from Nogales, Arizona, of the War Commission on Training Camp Activities," reprinted as War Recreation Bulletin #38, doc. 3483, file Arizona 18.1 (2 of 4), box 3, entry 395, RG 165, National Archives.

121. Fosdick to Baker, 17 April 1919, collected in *Letters From the First World War*, box 26, Raymond Blaine Fosdick Papers, Seeley G. Mudd Manuscript Library, Princeton University. Published with permission of Princeton University Libraries.

122. "WCCS Has Big Plans for Aiding Soldiers, "*Arkansas Democrat*, 6 February 1918, 4; *War Camp Community Service—The Second Six Months*, 75; "The Loyal Order of Moose Will Give an Entertainment at Their Hall," *Camp Dodger*, 25 November 1918, 4; "Fraternity Men At Camp Are Registered—College Men From Many States Give Their Affiliations at Hostess House," *Trench and Camp* (Camp Pike), September 1918; "Princeton Men in Camp Logan," *Camp Logan Reveille*, 23 November 1917, 8; "To Cornell Men!" *Gas Attack* (Camp Wadsworth), 26 January 1918, 10; "S.A.E. Fraternity to Entertain Soldiers," *Arkansas Democrat*, 22 June 1917, 12; War Recreation Bulletin #25, doc. 3425, file Arizona 18.1 (2 of 4), box 3, entry 395, RG 165, National Archives; "Big Show For Soldier Elks," *Camp Dodger*, 12 July 1918, 6.

123. "War Camp Community Service," 493.

124. In a similar manner immigrant groups often reached out to members of their own ethnic group. For instance, in Louisville, "The Italian Club is also entertaining and inviting all the Italian soldiers who have difficulty in speaking English to come to their club rooms

on afternoons when they have leave, to meet and chat with people speaking their own tongue." The city also held special parties for Italian soldiers and for Polish soldiers. *War Camp Community Service—The Second Six Months*, 23.

125. Weldon B. Durham, " 'Big Brother' and the 'Seven Sisters': Camp Life Reforms in World War I," *Military Affairs* 42 (1978): 60. Mark C. Carnes explores the meaning of the fraternal organizations and their rituals for middle-class men in "Middle-Class Men and the Solace of Fraternal Ritual," in *Meanings for Manhood: Constructions of Masculinity in Victorian America*, Mark C. Carnes and Clyde Griffen, eds. (Chicago: University of Chicago Press, 1990), 37–52, and in *Secret Ritual and Manhood in Victorian America* (New Haven: Yale University Press, 1989).

126. "War Camp Community Service," 493.

127. It is more difficult to suggest how often the fraternal organizations catered exclusively to their own members and how often they worked for the recreation of the soldiers more broadly. Certainly they sometimes provided entertainment exclusively for their own members. As one calendar for the local Masons of Fort Worth in the Camp Bowie *Reconnaissance* suggested, "All soldiers who are Masons are cordially invited to attend the following meetings and entertainments." "Masonic Calendar," *Reconnaissance* (Camp Bowie), 15 January 1918, 4.

128. *War Camp Community Service—The Second Six Months*, 75.

129. "May Use Golf Links," *Trench and Camp* (Camp Beauregard), 15 October 1917, 2.

130. Athletic Division Bulletin (weekly), 3 September 1918, 8, box 1, entry 399, RG 165, National Archives.

131. E. M. Vail, CTCA representative in San Antonio, "A Community's Opportunity—How One of the Largest Military Centers is Dealing with the Problem of caring for their Soldier Guests," doc. 22112, box 44, entry 393, RG 165, National Archives.

132. Report of Allen Cox, 2 February 1918, on the Sunday problem in Macon, Georgia, with excerpts from reports of representatives, doc. 41969, entry 393, RG 165, National Archives.

133. War Camp Community Service, *Keep 'Em Smiling*, 23–37.

134. Ibid., 16–17, 27–29; *War Camp Community Service—The Second Six Months*, 20; "War Camp Community Service," *Camp Bowie Reconnaissance*, 2 March 1918, 7; Spencer R. Gordon, Syracuse CTCA, to Joseph Lee, 23 July 1917, reprinted as War Recreation Bulletin #30, doc. 3425, file Arizona 18.1 (2 of 4), box 3, entry 395, RG 165, National Archives; Report on Chicago, Little Rock, WCCS in "Extracts from Report—War Recreation Service in Communities Near Training Camps, June, 1917," reprinted as War Recreation Bulletin #14, doc. 2649, letter file P, box 6, entry 394, RG 165, National Archives; "War Camp Community Service," 512; "Six Months of War Camp Community Service," 569; "Women to Sew Buttons and Mend Socks," *Camp Dodger*, 28 September 1917, 4; "Every Soldier to Have a Mother," *Camp Dodger*, 23 November 1917, 9; "W.C.T.U. of Des Moines Act As Hostesses," *Camp Dodger*, 1 February 1918, 2; "Extracts from Report—War Recreation Service in Communities Near Training Camps, June, 1917," reprinted as War Recreation Bulletin #14, National Archives; "Accomplishments in Various Cities," 367.

135. "Monthly Report of Ira W. Jayne, June, 1917," reprinted as War Recreation Bulletin #6, doc. 764, file Arizona 18.1 (2 of 4), box 3, entry 395, RG 165, National Archives.

136. This was precisely the fate met by F. Scott Fitzgerald's Jay Gatsby, who met Daisy while training at Camp Taylor, outside of Louisville. F. Scott Fitzgerald, *The Great Gatsby* (New York: Charles Scribner's, 1953), 75–79, 111–112, 148–152.

NOTES TO CHAPTER FOUR

1. All information on *End of the Road* is taken from the film itself. It is available for viewing at the Motion Picture, Sound, and Video Branch, National Archives.

2. The choice of the name Mary is probably not coincidental.

3. Doc. 33308, box 78, entry 393, RG 165, National Archives.

4. "Work for Girls in Camp Communities," doc. 20329, box 39, entry 393, RG 165, National Archives; Joseph Lee, H. S. Braucher, "Recreation in the Neighborhood of Military Training Camps," confidential, not for publication, doc. 7797, file Alabama 1.3, box 1, entry 395, RG 165, National Archives.

5. Fosdick to Esther B. Means, Executive Secretary, Church Mission of Help, Philadelphia, Pennsylvania, also secretary of Girls Conference, 19 May 1917, doc. 379, letter file M, box 5, entry 394, RG 165, National Archives.

6. "Community War Recreation Service—Its Meaning—Plan of Work—Accomplishments," *Playground* 11 (October 1917): 352.

7. Joseph Lee, "War Camp Community Service," *Annals of the American Academy of Political and Social Science* 79 (September 1918), 193.

8. "News from Division Units—Company L, 105th Gives Dance," *Gas Attack* (Camp Wadsworth), 13 April 1918, 14.

9. "Doughboy Loved Ladies of All Ages, But At Different Times," *Literary Digest* 64 (28 February 1920): 62.

10. "Thousands of Girls Are Awaiting to Adopt Soldiers of Camp Dodge," *Camp Dodger*, 26 October 1917, 1.

11. "Camp Dodge Soldiers Take Advantage of Journal Fighter's Service Bureau," *Camp Dodger*, 9 November 1917, 1.

12. Milton E. Bernet, "The World As I Saw It," U.S. Army Military History Institute, Carlisle Barracks, Pennsylvania, World War One Research Project, Army Experiences Questionnaire Collection, 89th Division, box 3, 314th Supply Train.

13. "Dan Cupid Leads Army of Soldiers to Altar," *Over-the-Top* (Camp Lewis), 5 January 1918, 1. The soldier press was full of stories regarding the marriages of men to women both from their home towns and, frequently, to girls from the training camp communities. For a few examples see "Ruth L. Nuller Weds Oregon Sergeant—Popular Palo Alto Girl Bride of W. R. Bagnall, after Short Romance," and "Miss Smith Will Wed Soldier Engineer—Engagement of Popular Palo Alto Girl to Former Fremont Man Announced," *Stanford Palo Alto News*, 14 September 1917, l; "A Wedding Epidemic," *Camp Dodger*, 26 July 1918, 4; "Weddings Cut Majority of Single Men at Shelby," *Trench and Camp* (Camp Shelby), 4 December 1917, 6.

14. "St. Valentine Complains," *Reveille* (Camp Logan), 22 February 1918, 6.

15. Howard L. Walker to his brother Lynn Walker, February 14, 1918, in the Army Experiences Questionnaire Collection, 83rd Division, 165th Infantry, 323rd Machine Gunners, Company C.

16. Raymond Fosdick, "The War and Navy Departments Commissions on Training Camp Activities," *Annals of the American Academy of Political and Social Sciences* 79 (September 1918), 131.

17. Similarly, section 12 granted the president the power to prohibit liquor in or near training camps and established bone-dry prohibition for all members of the American military. The prohibition program will be discussed below. War Department Commission on Training Camp Activities, *Documents Regarding the Question of Alcohol and Prostitution in the Neighborhood of Military Camps* (1917), 5–6, box 1635, RG 287, National Archives.

18. Commission on Training Camp Activities, *Report of the Chairman of the Commission on Training Camp Activities to the Secretary of War, 1918,* 11, box 1635, RG 287, National Archives.

19. Ruth Rosen, *The Lost Sisterhood: Prostitution in America, 1900–1918* (Baltimore: Johns Hopkins University Press, 1982), 5, 9. For a useful discussion of the pro- and antiregulation arguments, see Leslie Fishbein, "Harlot or Heroine? Changing Views of Prostitution, 1870–1920," *Historian* 43 (1980): 23–35. For a discussion of the class element in the promotion of segregation, see Neil Larry Shumsky, "Tacit Acceptance: Respectable Americans and Segregated Prostitution, 1870–1910," *Journal of Social History* 19 (Summer 1986): 665–679.

20. John Caruthers to Baker, received in the War Department 26 June 1917, doc. 1176, letter file F, box 2, entry 394, RG 165, National Archives. Unfortunately, no home address was included in the letter.

This view would persist in places, becoming an issue again during World War Two. For an excellent study of the Honolulu red-light district, which operated as an unofficial segregated district during much of World War Two, see Beth Bailey and David Farber, "Hotel Street: Prostitution and the Politics of War," *Radical History Review* (1992): 54–77.

21. Mark T. Connelly, *The Response to Prostitution in the Progressive Era* (Chapel Hill: University of North Carolina Press, 1980), 8–9; David J. Pivar, *Purity Crusade: Sexual Morality and Social Control, 1868–1900* (Westport, Conn.: Greenwood Press, 1973), 7; Peter G. Filene, *Him/Her/Self: Sex Roles in Modern America* (Baltimore: Johns Hopkins University Press, 1986), 80–81.

22. Pivar, *Purity Crusade*, 7.

23. For an excellent account of white slave narratives, as well as a broader study of debates over issues surrounding young women's sexuality, see Mary Odem, *Delinquent Daughters: Protecting and Policing Adolescent Female Sexuality in the United States, 1880–1920* (Chapel Hill: University of North Carolina Press, 1995), especially chapters 4–6.

24. Connelly, *The Response to Prostitution*, 115–116, 134.

25. Ibid., 83, 95, 96, 99–101, 103, 113.

26. Ibid., 82; Barbara Meil Hobson, *Uneasy Virtue: The Politics of Prostitution and the American Reform Tradition* (New York: Basic Books, 1987), 150.

27. Fosdick to H. S. Braucher on why policy of segregation will not work, doc. 940, file Alabama 26 (2 of 2), box 2, entry 395, RG 165, National Archives.

28. John Dickinson, *The Building of an Army: A Detailed Account of Legislation, Administration, and Opinion in the United States, 1915–1920* (New York: Century, 1922), 205–206.

29. Commission on Training Camp Activities, *War Department Commission on Training Camp Activities* (pamphlet), 5, box 1635, RG 287, National Archives; Allan M. Brandt, *No Magic Bullet: A Social History of Venereal Disease in the United States since 1880* (New York: Oxford University Press, 1985), 25, 74; Circular letter of William H. Zinsser to Snow, Sanger, Hopkins, and McBride, "RE: COMMUNITY CLEAN-UP BY MAIL," 12 July 1918, doc. 34816, box 84, entry 393, RG 165, National Archives.

30. Commission on Training Camp Activities, *War Department Commission on Training Camp Activities,* pamphlet (1917), 27, National Archives; War and Navy Departments Commissions on Training Camp Activities, *Standard Forms of Laws* (1919), 5, box 1635, RG 287, National Archives.

31. Raymond Fosdick, Preface in War and Navy Departments Commissions on Training Camp Activities, *Standard Forms of Laws,* National Archives.

32. See Charles F. McDermott, Chief of Police, Woburn, Massachusetts, to Fosdick, 9 June 1917, letter file Mc, box 5, entry 394, RG 165, National Archives; J. Elmore Martin, Sheriff of Charleston, South Carolina, to Baker, 22 August 1917, doc. 3571, letter file M, box 5, entry 394, RG 165, National Archives; J. F. Griffen, Sheriff of Polk County, Iowa,

to Baker, 30 August 1917, doc. 4610, file Iowa—Des Moines, box 7, entry 395, RG 165, National Archives; William L. Martin, Attorney General of Alabama, to Baker, 2 July 1917, file Alabama 1.3, box 1, entry 395, RG 165, National Archives; Governor of New Jersey to Baker, 29 May 1917, doc. 594, file New Jersey, box 10, entry 395, RG 165, National Archives; E. L. Phillip, Governor of Wisconsin, to Baker, 31 May 1917, doc. 3145, file Wisconsin, box 10, entry 395, RG 165, National Archives; Governor of Massachusetts to Baker, 18 May 1917, doc. 497, file Massachusetts, box 9, entry 395, RG 165, National Archives; Governor Harding of Iowa to Baker, 4 June 1917, doc. 887, file Iowa, box 7, entry 395, RG 165, National Archives.

33. H. P. Demand, Head of Boy's Work, Interstate YMCA for Arizona, New Mexico, West Texas, to Fosdick, 6 July 1917, doc. 2758, file New Mexico—Deming, box 10, entry 395, RG 165, National Archives.

34. Commission on Training Camp Activities, *War Department Commission on Training Camp Activities*, 26, National Archives. The cities included Deming, New Mexico; El Paso, Waco, San Antonio, Fort Worth, and Houston, Texas; Hattiesburg, Mississippi; Spartanburg, South Carolina; Norfolk and Petersburg, Virginia; Jacksonville, Florida; Alexandria, Louisiana; Savannah, Georgia; Charleston, Columbia, and Greenville, South Carolina; Douglas, Arizona; Louisville, Kentucky; and Montgomery, Alabama.

35. Connelly, *The Response to Prostitution*, 3.

36. John H. Buschemeyer, Mayor of Louisville, to Baker, 2 July 1917, doc. 2770, file Kentucky—Louisville (3 of 4), box 8, entry 395, RG 165, National Archives.

37. Ibid.

38. "Impractical Reform," *Louisville Courier-Journal*, 27 June 1917, 4; "Education vs. Prohibition," *Louisville Courier-Journal*, 17 July 1917, 4.

39. "Education vs. Prohibition," *Louisville Courier-Journal*, 17 July 1917, 4.

40. "Curb on Vice Is Approved—City Official's Efforts Are Indorsed At Meeting," *Louisville Courier-Journal*, 25 August 1917, 2; Henry M. Johnson, President, Men's Federation of Louisville, to Baker, 25 August 1917, doc. 4705, file Kentucky—Louisville (4 of 4), box 8, entry 395, RG 165, National Archives.

41. See, for instance, Alex. T. Wilson to Baker, 23 August 1917, doc. 4115, letter file W, box 9, entry 394, RG 165, National Archives.

42. " 'Redlight' Is Thing of Past—Sorrow and Pathos Predominate On Last Night," *Louisville Courier-Journal*, 1 September 1917, 1.

43. Ibid.

44. Baker to the Governors of all the States and to the Chairmen of the State Councils of Defense, May 26, 1917, reprinted in War Department Commission on Training Camp Activities, *Documents Regarding the Question of Alcohol and Prostitution in the Neighborhood of Military Camps* (1917), 4, box 1635, RG 287, National Archives.

45. The CTCA was also willing to quarantine communities more distantly removed from the camps, if evidence suggested that they were failing to take actions to ensure a clean environment for soldiers. In late 1917 the city of Seattle was put off-limits for the soldiers of Camp Lewis by the commanding officer of the camp, until Seattle conformed to the CTCA's demands. "Hints Bigger Sensation in Seattle Vice," *Tacoma Daily Ledger*, 23 November 1917, 1; John R. Colter to Louis Ludlow, 8 March 1918, doc. 28686, box 62, entry 393, RG 165, National Archives.

46. Clarence A. Perry to Fosdick, 21 May 1917; Clarence A. Perry to William F. Snow, 14 May 1917; Fosdick to Charles A. Perry, 22 May 1917; all in doc. 78, file New Orleans, Louisiana (1 of 4), box 8, entry 395, RG 165, National Archives; Al Rose, *Storyville, New Orleans* (Tuscaloosa: University of Alabama Press, 1974), 167; Bascom Johnson to Fosdick, 27 August 1917, doc. 8508, box 6, entry 393, RG 165, National Archives.

47. Report on New Orleans, Louisiana, Supplementary Report No. 1, 25 September 1917, file New Orleans, Louisiana (1 of 4), box 8, entry 395, RG 165, National Archives; Josephus Daniels, Secretary of the Navy, to Governor Pleasant of Louisiana, 24 September 1917, doc. 6041, file New Orleans, Louisiana (2 of 4), box 8, entry 395, RG 165, National Archives; Brandt, *No Magic Bullet*, 75.

48. Wm. M. Railey, President of the Citizens League of Louisiana, to Fosdick, 6 October 1917, doc. 7634, file New Orleans, Louisiana (2 of 4), box 8, entry 395, RG 165, National Archives; Rose, *Storyville*, 167–168. For a brief but useful account of the closure of Storyville see also Brandt, *No Magic Bullet*, 74–75.

49. Edward F. Allen, *Keeping Our Fighters Fit for War and After* (New York: Century, 1918), 202–203; Commission on Training Camp Activities, *Report of the Chairman on Training Camp Activities* (1918), 11, box 1635, RG 287, National Archives.

50. Brandt, *No Magic Bullet*, 92; Connelly, *The Response to Prostitution*, 149.

51. George J. Anderson, "Making the Camps Safe for the Army," *Annals of the American Academy of Political and Social Science* 79 (September 1918), 149.

52. Commission on Training Camp Activities, *Report of the Chairman on Training Camp Activities* (1918), National Archives.

53. Hilton Howell Railey, "A SURVEY OF MORAL CONDITIONS NEAR FORT LOGAN H. ROOTS, PULASKI COUNTY, ARKANSAS," 20 August 1917, doc. 4816, file Arkansas—Little Rock, box 4, entry 395, RG 165, National Archives.

54. Report on conditions in Atlanta, Georgia, 3 July 1917, 7 to 12 p.m., "Reported by P.K.," doc. 2684, file Atlanta, Georgia (2 of 3), box 6, entry 395, RG 165, National Archives.

55. H. F. Lyman of Cleveland, Ohio, to Baker, 9 June 1917, doc. 1830, letter file L, box 4, entry 393, RG 165, National Archives. For conditions in Chillicothe see "General War-Time Commission of the Churches—Survey of National Army Cantonments and National Guard Camps—November 20, 1917," doc. 14594, box 25, entry 393, RG 165, National Archives; Malcolm McBride to Fosdick, 27 November 1917, doc. 12096, box 17, entry 393, RG 165, National Archives.

56. The report of a visitor to Hattiesburg noted:

> I find here a moral community. . . . To-day I witnessed an unusual scene. I saw more than a dozen "modern Magdalenes" leave town. This came about as a result of the determination of the citizens and city officials not to tolerate any immoral resorts. There will be no "tenderloin" district here when the boys from "up North" arrive. The doors and windows of the houses are closed, and "for keeps," too, the officers tell me. The women were told if they returned they would be "shadowed" by secret service men.

Howard S. Williams, "Hattiesburg Plans Big Welcome for Kentucky and Indiana Boys; Is Healthy, Moral, Pretty City," *Louisville Courier-Journal*, 13 August 1917, 2.

57. Bascom Johnson to Fosdick, 14 June 1917, doc. 1059, file Alabama 16, entry 394, RG 165, National Archives.

58. McHenry Seal, Pastor, Spring Street Baptist Church, East Waco, Texas, to Baker, 26 August 1917, doc. 4141, letter file S, box 7, entry 394, RG 165, National Archives.

59. "The Closing of the Red Light District—The Status of Commericalized *[sic]* Vice in the City of Louisville, Ky., between July 14th and August 27th, 1917," doc. 12249, entry 393, RG 165, National Archives.

60. "Redlight Is Thing of Past," *Louisville Courier-Journal*, 1 September 1917, 2.

61. W. G. Hutton, Sheriff of Pulaski County, Arkansas to Baker, 24 August 1917, doc. 3534, file Arkansas—Miscellaneous, box 4, entry 395, RG 165, National Archives; Bascom Johnson to Louis J. Wilde, Mayor of San Diego, 20 July 1917, doc. 6160, file California—San Diego (1 of 2), box 5, entry 395, RG 165, National Archives.

62. "P.K.," report on Hattiesburg, Mississippi, 27 December 1917, file Mississippi, box 9, entry 395, RG 165, National Archives.

63. Report of 1st Lieut. Edwin K. Piper, Sanitary Corps, USNA, to Bascom Johnson, 18 November 1917, doc. 12540, file Michigan—Battle Creek, box 9, entry 395, RG 165, National Archives.

64. Imogen B. Oakley, corresponding secretary, Civic Club of Philadelphia, to Baker, 6 March 1918, doc. 29319, box 65, entry 393, RG 165, National Archives.

65. "J.S.," Report on Bridgeport, Connecticut, 14 February 1918, file Connecticut, box 5, entry 395, RG 165, National Archives.

66. "General War-Time Commission of the Churches—Survey of National Army Cantonments and National Guard Camps—Nov. 20, 1917," doc. 14594, entry 393, RG 165, National Archives.

67. Letter of Mr. Jacobsen, representative in Alexandria, quoted in George A. Nesbitt, "Assistant," Playground and Recreation Association of America, to Fosdick, 24 August 1917, doc. 3765, letter file P, box 6, entry 394, RG 165, National Archives.

68. Bascom Johnson, "Preliminery *[sic]* Report on Alexandria, September 2–4, 1917," doc. 5911, file Alexandria, Louisiana (4 of 5), box 8, entry 395, RG 165, National Archives. Another visitor to Alexandria in August provided additional information for the CTCA, confirming its concerns regarding conditions there. Suggesting that the red-light district was "ten times worse in bestiality" than the district in Tokyo, the visitor continued, "For bald abandon and brazen shamelessness Alexandria beats Shanghai, and we who have been living in the Orient have repeatedly heard that 'Shanghai is the most immoral city in the world.' " P. L. Gillett to Mr. W. E. Adams, 12 August 1917, doc. 3604, file Alexandria, Louisiana (4 of 5), box 8, entry 395, RG 165, National Archives.

69. G. J. Anderson, "Supplementary Report No. I on Alexandria, La.," doc. 5912, file Alexandria, Louisiana (3 of 5), box 8, entry 395, RG 165, National Archives.; W. W. Whittington, Jr., to Bascom Johnson, 5 September 1917, doc. 5911, file Alexandria, Louisiana (4 of 5), box 8, entry 395, RG 165, National Archives. The law was "Penal Ordinance No. 204," and it was passed on 4 September 1917.

70. G. J. Anderson, "Supplementary Report No 1 on Alexandria, Louisiana, September 22, 1917," doc. 5912, file Alexandria, Louisiana (3 of 5), box 8, entry 395, RG 165, National Archives.

71. Report of Lieutenant Thos. A. Larremore, Sanitary Corps, U.S.A., for week ending 24 November 1917, on Camp Beauregard, Louisiana, file Alexandria, Louisiana (2 of 5), box 8, entry 395, RG 165, National Archives; Reports of Thos. A. Larremore, Sanitary Corps, United States Army, for the weeks ending 1 December 1917, 8 December 1917, 15 December 1917, for eight days ending 23 December 1917, on Camp Beauregard, file Alexandria, Louisiana (1 of 5), box 8, entry 395, RG 165, National Archives.

72. Report of Thos. A. Larremore, Sanitary Corps, National Army, for eight days ending 23 December 1917, Camp Beauregard, National Archives.

73. Ibid.

74. Report of Thos. A. Larremore, Sanitary Corps, USNA, for week ending 14 April 1918, on Camp Beauregard and vicinity, doc. 24961, box 51, entry 393, RG 165, National Archives.

75. Special Report of Lt. Thos. A. Larremore on interview with Dr. Oscar Dowling,

President, State Board of Health, for Major Snow and Mr. Johnson, 20 December 1917, file Alexandria, Louisiana (1 of 5), box 8, entry 395, RG 165, National Archives.

76. Commission on Training Camp Activities, *Report of the Chairman on Training Camp Activities* (1918), 11, box 1635, RG 287, National Archives.

77. Chairman, Committee on Protective Work for Girls, to Baker, 29 January 1918, doc. 18654, box 36, entry 393, RG 165, National Archives; Malcolm L. McBride to Fosdick, 5 February 1918, doc. 20544, box 40, entry 393, RG 165, National Archives; Memorandum of Bascom Johnson to Miss Miner, 4 March 1918, quoting from report of Lieut. C. D. Benson, Sanitary Corps, on Camp Sherman, doc. 20414, box 40, entry 393, RG 165, National Archives.

78. Report of Thos. A. Larremore, Sanitary Corps, National Army, for the week ending 1 December 1917, Camp Beauregard, file Alexandria, Louisiana (1 of 5), box 8, entry 395, RG 165, National Archives.

79. Fosdick to Alfred R. Page, August 1917, doc. 4241, letter file P, box 6, entry 394, RG 165, National Archives.

80. War Department Commission on Training Camp Activities, *Committee on Protective Work for Girls* (pamphlet), 3, box 1635, RG 287, National Archives.

81. "The Girl Problem in the Communities Adjacent to Military Training Camps," *Playground* 11 (October 1917): 382.

82. "A Survey of the Girl Problem at Camp Devens," *Weekly Bulletin*, War Department Commission on Training Camp Activities, Social Hygiene Division, Section on Women's Work, Bulletin #16, 27 August 1918, doc. 48286A, box 108, entry 393, RG 165, National Archives.

83. Maude E. Miner, Secretary of the New York Probation and Protective Association, New York City, to Fosdick, 30 July 1917, doc. 2979, letter file M, box 5, entry 394, RG 165, National Archives; Fosdick to Alfred R. Page, New York City, August, 1917, doc. 4241, letter file P, box 6, entry 394, RG 165, National Archives.

84. Hobson, *Uneasy Virtue*, 171; Brandt, *No Magic Bullet*, 87; Estelle Freedman, *Their Sisters' Keepers: Women's Prison Reform in America, 1830–1930* (Ann Arbor: University of Michigan Press, 1981), 116–117. Maude E. Miner, head of the Committee on Protective Work for Girls, headed the New York Juvenile Probation Department prior to her work with the CTCA. Jane Deeter Rippin, who replaced Miner as the head of the Section on Women and Girls, was a former settlement house worker. Martha P. Falconer, who headed the Section on Reformatories and Detention Houses, was the superintendent of the Pennsylvania State Industrial School for Girls. Katharine Bement Davis, who headed the Social Hygiene work for Women and Girls, was the former superintendent of the New York State Reformatory, as well as the former commissioner of corrections for the city of New York. Her studies in penology were well known.

85. *Committee on Protective Work for Girls*, doc. 6211, entry 393, RG 165, National Archives.

86. Dickinson, *The Building of an Army*, 216.

87. Ibid.

88. "The Girl Problem in Communities Adjacent to Military Camps," 388; Dickinson, *The Building of an Army*, 216.

89. "Report of the Committee on Protective Work for Girls," doc. 25812, box 53, entry 393, RG 165, National Archives.

90. "The Girl Problem in Communities Adjacent to Military Camps," 388.

91. Roy Smith Wallace to Fosdick, 18 April 1918, doc. 24782, box 50, entry 393, RG 165, National Archives.

92. For an excellent discussion of the social and cultural origins and actions of charity girls, see Kathy Peiss, " 'Charity Girls' and City Pleasures: Historical Notes on Working-Class Sexuality, 1880–1920," in *Powers of Desire: The Politics of Sexuality*, by Anne Snitow, Christine Stansell, and Sharon Thompson, eds. (New York: Monthly Review Press, 1983).

93. Reports from all across the nation complained of the problem of charity girls. See letter of Frederick H. Whitin, General Secretary, Committee of Fourteen, to Fosdick, 8 September 1917, doc. 5964, file New Jersey, box 10, entry 395, RG 165, National Archives; Report of "J.S.," 2 October 1917, on Battle Creek, Michigan, doc. 9268, file Michigan—Battle Creek, box 9, entry 395, RG 165, National Archives.

94. Henrietta S. Additon, "Work among Delinquent Women and Girls," *Annals of the American Academy of Political and Social Sciences* 79 (September 1918): 153.

95. C. D. Benson to Fosdick, 1 December 1917, "preliminary survey on vice and liquor traffic conditions in the vicinity of, and affecting, the mobilization camp at Wrightstown, N.J., known as Camp Dix," doc. 13085, file New Jersey, box 10, entry 395, RG 165, National Archives.

96. "Committee on Protective Work for Girls," 20 February 1918, doc. 26908, box 56, entry 393, RG 165, National Archives. This document had a note attached to it, which read, "A brief report for Mr. Fosdick's information. M.E.M. 2/21/18," suggesting that it was written by Maude E. Miner in February 1918.

97. Ibid.

98. Ibid.

99. Ibid.

100. Commission on Training Camp Activities, *Report of the Chairman on Training Camp Activities* (1918), 15, box 1635, RG 287, National Archives.

101. Ibid.

102. Ibid., 11–12.

103. For example, see Bascom Johnson to James Rolph, 13 July 1917, doc. 8454, box 6, entry 393, RG 165, National Archives.

104. Commission on Training Camp Activities, *Report of the Chairman on Training Camp Activities* (1918), 15–16, National Archives.

105. Additon, "Work among Delinquent Women and Girls," 154–155.

106. Commission on Training Camp Activities, *Report of the Chairman on Training Camp Activities* (1918), 16, National Archives.

107. Mary Macey Dietzler, *Detention Houses and Reformatories as Protective Social Agencies in the Campaign of the United States Government Against Venereal Diseases* (Washington, D.C.: Government Printing Office, 1922), 36; Martha P. Falconer, "The Segregation of Delinquent Women and Girls as a War Problem," *Annals of the American Academy of Political and Social Sciences* 79 (September 1918), 165; Copy of letter of Mr. Wallace, sent by Fosdick to Maude E. Miner, 14 February 1918, doc. 20355, box 39, entry 393, RG 165, National Archives; Commission on Training Camp Activities, *Report of the Chairman on Training Camp Activities* (1918), 16, National Archives. For discussions of reformers' beliefs in the efficacy of the indeterminate sentence, see also Anthony M. Platt, *The Child-Savers: The Invention of Delinquency* (Chicago: University of Chicago Press, 1969), 54, 65–67; David J. Rothman, *Conscience and Convenience* (Boston: Little, Brown, 1980).

108. Dietzler, *Detention Houses and Reformatories*, 25.

109. Commission on Training Camp Activities, *Report of the Chairman on Training Camp Activities* (1918), 16, National Archives.

110. Dietzler, *Detention Houses and Reformatories*, 58.

111. Freedman, *Their Sisters' Keepers*, 95; Rosen, *The Lost Sisterhood*, 21.

112. Dietzler, *Detention Houses and Reformatories*, 56–57; Commission on Training Camp Activities, *Report of the Chairman on Training Camp Activities* (1918), 16, National Archives.

113. Platt, *The Child-Savers*, 69.

114. For a very useful discussion of the evolution of progressive thought on the relationship between mental capabilities and crime, see Freedman, *Their Sisters' Keepers*, 16.

115. Ibid., 109–112.

116. Ibid., 111–116.

117. Ibid., 117; Connelly, *The Response to Prostitution*, 41; Hobson, *Uneasy Virtue*, 190–191.

118. Memorandum of Jane D. Rippin to Mr. Sanger, 24 July 1918, doc. 38855, box 101, entry 393, RG 165, National Archives; Commission on Training Camp Activities, *Annual Report of the Commission on Training Camp Activities* (1918), 13–14, box 1635, RG 287, National Archives; Additon, "Work among Delinquent Women and Girls," 156, 157.

119. Brandt, *No Magic Bullet*, 91.

120. Rosen, *The Lost Sisterhood*, 23.

121. Connelly, *The Response to Prostitution*, 43, 152.

122. Falconer, "The Segregation of Delinquent Women and Girls as a War Problem," 161.

123. Brandt, *No Magic Bullet*, 85.

124. Ibid.

125. War and Navy Departments Commissions on Training Camp Activities, *Standard Forms of Laws for the Repression of Prostitution, the Control of Venereal Diseases, the Establishment and Management of Reformatories for Women and Girls, and Suggestions for a Law Relating to Feeble-Minded Persons*, box 1635, RG 287, National Archives.

126. T. W. Gregory, "MEMORANDUM ON THE LEGAL ASPECTS OF THE PROPOSED SYSTEM OF MEDICAL EXAMINATION OF WOMEN CONVICTED UNDER SECTION 13, SELECTIVE SERVICE ACT," 3 April 1918, doc. 27381, box 57, entry 393, RG 165, National Archives.

127. Connelly, *The Response to Prostitution*, 145.

128. T. W. Gregory, Attorney General, Circular No. 812, to all United States Attorneys, 3 April 1918, doc. 27381, box 57, entry 393, RG 165, National Archives.

129. War Department Commission on Training Camp Activities, Weekly Bulletin, Section on Women's Work, Bulletin #17, 3 September 1918, box 5, entry 399, RG 165, National Archives.

130. Thomas A. Storey, "Evaluation of Governmental Aid to Detention Houses and Reformatories," in *Detention Houses and Reformatories*, by Dietzler, 8; Maude E. Miner, "Expenditure of Federal Appropriation," 13 March 1918, doc. 26839, box 55, entry 393, RG 165, National Archives.

131. Commission on Training Camp Activities, *Report of the Chairman on Training Camp Activities* (1918), National Archives; "Bulletin No. 20," from Director, Section on Protective Work for Girls, to Field Representatives, on the Reorganization of Girls Protective Work, 29 April 1918, doc. 34831, box 84, entry 393, RG 165, National Archives.

132. "Bulletin No. 20," from Director, Section on Protective Work for Girls, to Field Representatives, on the Reorganization of Girls Protective Work, 29 April 1918, National Archives.

133. Letter of resignation of Maude E. Miner to Fosdick, 3 April 1918, doc. 26829, box 55, entry 393, RG 165, National Archives. It is important to note that this was a second letter, which included some changes made on the first letter in its presentation to the committee. The first letter can be located in doc. 26056, box 53, entry 393, RG 165,

National Archives. The order of the two letters is a little confusing, as the first letter has the date 9 April, and the second letter the date 3 April. I am fairly certain, however, of the order of the letters, because the one I presume to be second was attached to an additional letter to Fosdick telling him of changes in the letter and asking him to replace the original with this revised version.

134. Maude E. Miner to Mrs. William F. Dummer, April 17, 1918, Schlesinger Library, Radcliffe College, Ethel Sturges Dummer Papers, box 24, folder 378.

135. David J. Pivar, "Cleansing the Nation: The War on Prostitution, 1917–1921," *Prologue* 12 (Spring 1980), 33–40; Brandt, *No Magic Bullet*, 86; Hobson, *Uneasy Virtue*, 178–179.

136. Hobson, *Uneasy Virtue*, 179; Pivar, "Cleansing the Nation," 33–40.

137. Jane Deeter Rippin, "Section on Women and Girls: Report and Personnel Sheet, Based on the reports covering the period from June 16 to June 30, both inclusive," doc. 33441, box 78, entry 393, RG 165, National Archives.

138. Ibid.

139. Ibid.

140. Connelly, *The Response to Prostitution*, 144.

141. These funds were to be used in the same way as those granted earlier by the president, "to aid the states in the establishment and construction of reformatories to care 'for civilian persons whose detention, isolation, quarantine, or commitment to institutions may be found necessary for the protection of military and naval forces of the United States against venereal diseases.'" Brandt, *No Magic Bullet*, 88; "Current Literature—The Chamberlain-Kahn Bill," in the War Department Commission on Training Camp Activities Weekly Bulletin, Section on Women's Work, Social Hygiene Division, Bulletin No. 17 (September 3, 1918), 3, box 5, entry 399, RG 165, National Archives.

This act also granted the United States Public Health Service a large role in the battle against venereal disease, granting $200,000 for the establishment of a division of venereal diseases in the USPHS. Although the USPHS was from this point on an important part of the battle against civilian venereal disease outside the training camp communities, its role will not be considered here. After the division was established, the CTCA and the USPHS cooperated and competed in the anti–venereal disease campaign in the training camp communities, with the CTCA retaining the initiative in those locales. After the war's end the USPHS would remain a fundamental part of the campaign against venereal disease. Chapter 6 will discuss the demobilization of the CTCA's forces. For additional information on the direction the venereal disease campaign takes in the postwar era, see Brandt, *No Magic Bullet*, chapter 4.

142. Dietzler, *Detention Houses and Reformatories*, 25–26.

143. Brandt, *No Magic Bullet*, 88–89.

144. Ibid., chapter 2, n. 118, 89.

145. Storey, "Evaluation of Governmental Aid," in *Detention Houses and Reformatories*, by Dietzler, 3. The War Department claimed to have detained 18,000 women in federally aided institutions during the war, of which Storey's 15,520 were diseased. Hobson, *Uneasy Virtue*, 176; Brandt, *No Magic Bullet*, 89.

146. Hobson, *Uneasy Virtue*, 176.

147. C. D. Benson to Fosdick, 1 December 1917, ". . . preliminary survey on vice traffic conditions in the vicinity of, and affecting, the mobilization camp at Wrightstown, N.J., known as Camp Dix," 1 December 1917, report on Mount Holly, N.J., doc. 13085, file New Jersey, box 10, entry 395, RG 165, National Archives.

148. Bascom Johnson, "Preliminary Report on Moral Conditions Surrounding the Military Camp at Linda Vista and the Naval Training Station at San Diego, California, July

17–19, 1917," doc. 6160, file California—San Diego (1 of 2), box 5, entry 395, RG 165, National Archives.

149. Memorandum from Paul Popenoe, Captain, Sanitary Corps, US Army, to Major Joy, 20 February 1919, quotes report on Camp Sherman, dated 16 January 1919, doc. 46247, box 132, entry 393, RG 165, National Archives.

150. Fosdick to Caroline Heywood, 26 November 1917, doc. 12050, box 17, entry 393, RG 165, National Archives. As late as February 1919 the CTCA still maintained a spoken policy of desiring equal treatment. Memorandum from Director, Section on Vice and Liquor Control, to Henry I. Fox, Louisville, Kentucky, "Subject: Quarantine of venereal disease cases," 14 February 1919, file Civilians, box 15, entry 399, RG 165, National Archives.

151. Letter to the editor of the *San Diego Sun* from "K.E.E.," 13 August 1917, 4. This letter may have been prompted by reports that the city attorney of San Diego refused to release lists of those taken in a raid on the Muskogee Club, because "many daughters of respectable families were gathered in the police dragnet," though the city attorney also contended that those taken might also be used as witnesses in court later. The paper in this instance contended, "Names of witnesses are always made public in 'low brow' raids." "Girls Were Found Amid Gay Scenes," *San Diego Sun*, 11 July 1917.

152. Alan Johnstone, Jr., "Report on Augusta, Georgia," 17 November 1917, file Atlanta, Georgia (1 of 3), box 6, entry 395, RG 165, National Archives.

153. Oswald Garrison Villard to Fosdick, 19 March 1918, doc. 22156, box 44, entry 393, RG 165, National Archives.

154. Allison T. French, Executive Secretary, California Military Welfare Commission, affiliated with the CTCA, to Bascom Johnson, 10 November 1917, doc. 11372, box 15, entry 393, RG 165, National Archives.

155. Caroline Heywood to "Dear Sir," War Department, 6 September 1917, doc. 12050, box 17, entry 393, RG 165, National Archives.

156. War Department Commission on Training Camp Activities, Weekly Bulletin, Section on Women's Work Social Hygiene Division, Bulletin #20, 24 September 1918, box 5, entry 399, RG 165, National Archives.

157. War Department Commission on Training Camp Activities, Weekly Bulletin, Section on Women's Work, Social Hygiene Division, Bulletin #19, 17 September 1918, box 5, entry 399, RG 165, National Archives.

158. War Department Commission on Training Camp Activities, *Smash the Line!* a pamphlet produced by the American Social Hygiene Association and distributed for the War Department Commission on Training Camp Activities, doc. 6157, letter file S, box 7, entry 394, RG 165, National Archives.

159. Commission on Training Camp Activities, *War and Navy Departments Committee on Training Camp Activities* (pamphlet sent to press 1 July 1918), 5, box 1635, RG 287, National Archives; Baker to the Mayors of Cities and Sheriffs of Counties in the Neighborhood of all Military Training Camps, in War Department Commission on Training Camp Activities, *Documents Regarding the Question of Alcohol and Prostitution in the Neighborhood of Military Camps*, box 1635, RG 287, National Archives.

160. Allen, *Keeping Our Fighters Fit*, 203.

161. "Wet-Dry Fight Is Intense," *San Diego Sun*, 23 November 1917, 1; "To Drink Or Not To Drink—That's Burning Question in San Diego," *San Diego Sun*, 7 September 1917, 1; "Keep Liquor from Men in Khaki—Baker," *San Diego Sun*, 20 November 1917, 1; Fosdick to Dr. Fred Baker, San Diego 31 October 1917, doc. 8798, box 7, entry 393, RG 165, National Archives.

162. Examples of the continued problem of bootlegging throughout the nation are

many. See, for instance, reports for Seattle and Tacoma in September 1918. In Seattle, for the week ending 14 September 1918, the report noted 64 arrests and 42 convictions for liquor crimes, with 290 gallons of liquor being seized. The sentence in jail for convictions was 60 days. In Tacoma 84 arrests were made for drunkenness, 10 for drunk and disorderly conduct, and 15 for the possession of liquor. Again, these reports are made with no comment on the need to change tactics. Also, note the short sentence for conviction of a liquor infraction. Report of Lieutenant Robert Newbegin, Sanitary Corps, U.S.A., for the week ending 14 September 1918, on Seattle and Tacoma, file Circular, box 14, entry 399, RG 165, National Archives.

163. Hobson, *Uneasy Virtue*, 161. For a fascinating discussion of one example of prostitutes overcoming this vulnerability and exerting limited control over their circumstances, if only temporarily, see Bailey and Farber, "Hotel Street."

164. This argument regarding the link in the American mind between female behavior and the disordering of society has been made convincingly by a number of historians. See Carroll Smith-Rosenberg, *Disorderly Conduct: Visions of Gender in Victorian America* (New York: Oxford University Press, 1985); Freedman, *Their Sisters' Keepers*, 19–20.

165. Mark T. Connelly makes a similar argument in *The Response to Prostitution*, 6–7.

166. Connelly, *The Response to Prostitution*, 146; Hobson, *Uneasy Virtue*, 165.

167. Marcia Louise Bradley, of Portland, Oregon, to Baker, 10 May 1917, doc. 275, file Oregon, box 10, entry 395, RG 165, National Archives; D. J. Poynter, Albion, Nebraska, to Baker, 6 August 1917, doc. 4082, letter file P, box 6, entry 394, RG 165, National Archives.

168. Connelly, *The Response to Prostitution*, 143, 149.

NOTES TO CHAPTER FIVE

1. Julius Rosenwald to Fosdick, 1 July 1918, doc. 34897, box 84, entry 393, RG 165, National Archives.

2. Ibid.

3. Henry J. Dannenbaum to Julius Rosenwald, Council of National Defense, Houston, Texas, 24 June 1918, doc. 34897, box 84, entry 393, RG 165, National Archives.

4. Ibid.

5. Julius Rosenwald, Council of National Defense, to Fosdick, 1 July 1918, doc. 34897, box 84, entry 393, RG 165, National Archives.

6. Arthur E. Barbeau and Florette Henri, *The Unknown Soldiers: Black American Troops in World War I* (Philadelphia: Temple University Press, 1974), 23; David M. Kennedy, *Over Here: The First World War and American Society* (New York: Oxford University Press, 1980), 281–282. For more detailed information on two of the race riots of the summer of 1917, see Elliot M. Rudwick, *Race Riot at East St. Louis July 2, 1917*, (Carbondale: Southern Illinois University Press, 1964), and Robert V. Haynes, *A Night of Violence: The Houston Riot of 1917* (Baton Rouge: Louisiana State University Press, 1976).

7. It is important to note that lynchings grew during this period as well. Figures vary, but all demonstrate a growing environment of incredible violence and hostility targeting African Americans. Barbeau and Henri, *The Unknown Soldiers*, 21; Kennedy, *Over Here*, 283.

8. Alfreda M. Duster, ed., *Crusade for Justice: The Autobiography of Ida B. Wells* (Chicago: University of Chicago Press, 1970); on W. E. B. Du Bois see David Levering Lewis, *W. E. B. Du Bois: Biography of a Race* (New York: Henry Holt, 1993).

9. Gilbert Osofsky, "Progressivism and the Negro, New York, 1900–1915," *American Quarterly* 16 (Summer 1964): 153–168; Jack Temple Kirby, *Darkness at the Dawning: Race and Reform in the Progressive South* (Philadelphia: Lippincott, 1972), chapter 8.

10. Kirby, *Darkness at the Dawning*, 4. See also John Dittmer, *Black Georgia in the Progressive Era, 1900–1920* (Chicago: University of Illinois Press, 1977), 110.

11. Jane L. Scheiber and Harry N. Scheiber, "The Wilson Administration and the Wartime Mobilization of Black Americans, 1917–1918," *Labor History* 10 (1969): 434.

12. Kennedy, *Over Here*, 29–30, 279–280. For two excellent treatments of the evolution of Du Bois's response to the war, see Mark Ellis, " 'Closing Ranks' and 'Seeking Honors,' " *Journal of American History* 79 (June 1992): 96–99; Lewis, *W. E. B. Du Bois*, 530–580.

13. Barbeau and Henri, *Unknown Soldiers*, 19; Scheiber and Scheiber, "The Wilson Administration and the Wartime Mobilization of Black Americans," 436, 440–441.

This is not to suggest, however, that the draft was applied evenly. According to Arthur Barbeau and Florette Henri, a total of 2,290,527 black men registered for the draft in 1917, making up 9.63 percent of the total number of registered males. Of the African Americans examined under the first draft call of 5 June 1917, 51.65 percent were classified as Class 1. Only 32.53 percent of all Whites examined under the first call were classified as Class 1. Of the African Americans classified as class 1 in the first draft call, 36 percent were inducted into the army, compared with only 24 percent of the Whites so classified. Barbeau and Henri, *Unknown Soldiers*, 36.

14. Barbeau and Henri, *Unknown Soldiers*, 38–39; Kennedy, *Over Here*, 159.

15. Haynes, *A Night of Violence*, 167–168. The figure of seventeen dead was used by Kennedy in *Over Here*, 160.

16. Colonel Robert C. Humber, "Notes on the Employment of Colored Troops," in United States Army War College, Historical Section, *Colored Soldiers in the United States Army*, prepared May 1942, U.S. Army Military History Institute, Carlisle Barracks, Pennsylvania; Barbeau and Henri, *Unknown Soldiers*, 28.

17. "Withdraw All Negro Troops," *Fort Worth Star Telegram*, 25 August 1917, 4.

18. "Now It's Houston," *Washington Bee*, 1 September 1917, 1.

19. "The Houston Riot," *Washington Bee*, 1 September 1917, 4. See also "In the Enemy's Camp," *Chicago Defender*, 1 September 1917, 12; "The Houston Affair," *Atlanta Independent*, 1 September 1917, 4; "The Houston Uprising," *Baltimore Afro-American*, 1 September 1918, 4; "Houston Incident Closed—Not Forgotten," *Afro-American*, 15 December 1917, 4.

20. Haynes, *A Night of Violence*, chapter 1; Barbeau and Henri, *Unknown Soldiers*, chapter 2.

21. Kennedy, *Over Here*, 160; Emmett J. Scott, *Scott's Official History of the American Negro in the World War* (Chicago: Homewood Press, 1919), 40.

22. E. J. Scott, *Scott's Official History*, 103; Copy of the memorandum sent from Baker to Emmett J. Scott, special assistant to the secretary of state, 30 November 1917, reprinted in *Atlanta Independent*, 29 December 1917, 5.

23. Acting Chairman to Lester A. Walton, 12 September 1918, doc. 38771, box 100, entry 393, RG 165, National Archives.

24. Raymond Fosdick, "Teaching Sammy the American for 'Morale,' " *World Outlook* 4 (April 1918), 7.

25. Fosdick to Baker, 10 October 1917, doc. 6589, file Alabama 3, box 1, entry 395, RG 165, National Archives.

26. Ibid.

27. Memorandum of Baker to Special Assistant Emmett J. Scott, 30 November 1917, reprinted in the *Atlanta Independent*, 29 December 1917, 5.

28. Abbie Condit, "War Camp Community Service for Colored Troops," 24 January 1918, doc. 27333, entry 393, RG 165, National Archives.

29. "Six Months of War Camp Community Service," *Playground* 11 (March 1918), 592.

30. J. S. Tichenor to Jasper J. Mayer of the CTCA, 11 September 1917, doc. 4862, file Alabama 36, box 3, entry 395, RG 165, National Archives.

31. Mrs. E. M. Townsend, Chairman, National Hostess House Committee, to Fosdick, 21 August 1918, doc. 40062, box 107, entry 393, RG 165, National Archives; J. S. Moore, Louisville, Kentucky, to George Blandis, Association Executive Secretary, Chicago, 26 November 1918, doc. 44385, entry 393, RG 165, National Archives.

32. J. S. Tichenor to Jasper J. Mayer, of the CTCA, September 11, 1917, doc. 4862, file Alabama 36, box 3, entry 395, RG 165, National Archives; Memorandum from Camp Intelligence Officer, Camp Jackson, to Acting Director, Military Intelligence, Washington, D.C., Subject: QUESTIONNAIRE COVERING CONDITION COLORED TROOPS THIS CAMP, 2 December 1918, doc. 80, subfile 10218–244, Microfilm Publications M1440: Correspondence of the Military Intelligence Division Relating to "Negro Subversion" 1917–1941, National Archives.

33. MEMORANDUM FOR THE DIRECTOR, MILITARY INTELLIGENCE DIVISION, AND THE CHIEF, MORALE BRANCH, EXECUTIVE DIVISION, GENERAL STAFF, from J. E. Cutler, Subject: THE NEGRO IN THE ARMY, 23 December 1918, doc. 10, subfile 10218–279, Microfilm Publications M1440: Correspondence of the Military Intelligence Division Relating to "Negro Subversion" 1917–1941, National Archives.

34. George A. Singleton, Chaplain, 317th Engineers, to Emmett J. Scott, 15 May 1918, doc. 34681, entry 393, RG 165, National Archives.

35. For another example see "Camp Gordon News," *Atlanta Independent*, 17 November 1917, 7.

36. Barbeau and Henri, *Unknown Soldiers*, 41.

37. Memorandum from Major W. H. Loving, P.C., to Chief, Military Morale Section, M.I.D., Subject: Recapitulation of investigation of military camps, 24 November 1918, subfile 10218–280, Microfilm Publication M1440: Correspondence of the Military Intelligence Division Relating to "Negro Subversion" 1917–1941, National Archives.

38. Executive Secretary ("P.S.") to YMCA, 14 June 1918, doc. 32732, entry 393, RG 165, National Archives.

39. MEMORANDUM FOR THE DIRECTOR, MILITARY INTELLIGENCE DIVISION, AND THE CHIEF, MORALE BRANCH, EXECUTIVE DIVISION, GENERAL STAFF, from J. E. Cutler, Subject: THE NEGRO IN THE ARMY, 23 December 1918, doc. 10, National Archives. See also SECRET M.I.3 Bulletin for Intelligence Officers, No. 31, 21 October 1918, "Special Bulletin—The Negro Problem in the Army," subfile 10218–244, Microfilm Publication M1440: Correspondence of the Military Intelligence Division Relating to "Negro Subversion" 1917–1941, National Archives.

40. Memorandum from Major W. H. Loving to Chief, Military Morale Section, M.I.D., Subject: Recapitulation of investigation of military camps, 24 November 1918, National Archives. Loving's investigation included eleven camps, ten of them in the South. In the reports from specific camps, Loving calls special attention to problems in Camp Wheeler, Camp Jackson, Camp Sevier, and Camp Greene. See reports from each of these camps, which are attachments to the memorandum listed above.

Charles H. Williams noted, "In connection with the Y.M.C.A. work several instances were found where discrimination was encouraged and even promoted in conjunction with the military authorities. It is stated, however, that the War Department is working to eliminate that practice." Charles H. Williams, RESUME OF CONDITIONS SURROUNDING NEGRO TROOPS, 5 August 1918, subfile 10218–279, Microfilm Publication M1440: Correspondence of the Military Intelligence Division Relating to "Negro Subversion" 1917–1941, National Archives.

41. S. W. White, Hattiesburg, Mississippi, 18 April 1918, to Emmett J. Scott, Assistant Secretary, War Department, doc. 34031, box 81, entry 393, RG 165, National Archives.

42. "Some Observations on Training of Negro Soldiers," *Afro-American*, 8 March 1918, 1.

43. Memorandum from Major W. H. Loving to Chief, Military Morale Section, Subject: Condition Among Negro Troops at Camp Mills, 8 November 1918, subfile 10218–280, Microfilm Publication M1440, Correspondence of the Military Intelligence Division Relating to "Negro Subversion" 1917–1941, National Archives.

44. Ibid. In a summary report of his visits to eleven camps, including ten in the South, Loving reported, "In all camps the K. of C. displayed the word 'WELCOME', which meant all that the word implied. There was absolutely no discrimination practiced by this organization. The same is true of the Y.M.H.A." Memorandum of Major W. H. Loving to Chief, Military Morale Section, M.I.D., Subject: Recapitulation of investigation of military camps, 24 November 1918, National Archives.

45. Apparently the shortage of adequate YMCA facilities for African American troops translated into a shortage of educational work with them as well. Because the YMCA oversaw much of the educational work for soldiers unable to read and write, their inadequate provision of recreation included inadequate educational efforts. MEMORANDUM FOR THE DIRECTOR, MILITARY INTELLIGENCE DIVISION, AND THE CHIEF, MORALE BRANCH, EXECUTIVE DIVISION, GENERAL STAFF, Subject: THE NEGRO IN THE ARMY, 23 December 1918, National Archives.

African American soldiers also complained that the camp libraries included no works by African American authors and no journals, newspapers, or periodicals published for African Americans. In December 1918 the Morale Branch initiated action to repair this problem. Letter of E. L. Munson, Chief, Morale Branch, to Liaison Officer, CTCA, 5 December 1918, doc. 43728, box 122, entry 393, RG 165, National Archives.

46. Confidential memorandum from Camp Intelligence Officer, Camp Grant, to Director of Military Intelligence, Subject: Questionnaire Concerning Colored Troops, 28 October 1918, doc. 19, subfile 10218–244, Microfilm Publication M1440: Correspondence of the Military Intelligence Division Relating to "Negro Subversion" 1917–1941, National Archives. As part of an exploration of subversion among African American troops, the Military Intelligence Division conducted a survey of intelligence officers in training camps across the country, which investigated everything from the state of relations between African American soldiers and white civilians to the state of recreational facilities for troops inside and outside the camps. Responses to these questions, though doubtless affected by the prevalent racism evident in the military, nevertheless provided invaluable information on the state of recreation for African American troops in late 1918.

47. "Camp Gordon News," *Atlanta Independent*, 17 November 1917, 7.

48. Memo of Malcolm McBride, Acting Chairman, to Mr. Sanger (Executive Secretary, CTCA), 2 July 1918, doc. 34220, box 82, entry 393, RG 165, National Archives.

49. "Training Negroes for Officers," *Literary Digest* 55 (21 July 1917), 50.

50. See the problems of Battle Creek, Michigan, described in "WCCS Program Sheets, February, 1919," report on Battle Creek, doc. 46494, box 133, entry 393, RG 165, National Archives.

51. "Democracy and the Colored Soldier," *Playground* 13 (September 1918), 260–261. The historian Joseph F. Kett has indirectly suggested another problem involved in the WCCS's provision of recreation for black soldiers. According to Kett, Joseph Lee, the head of the American Playground and Recreation Association, the parent organization of the WCCS, was a racist. Joseph F. Kett, *Rites of Passage: Adolescence in America 1790 to the Present* (New York: Basic Books, 1977), 226.

52. EDC (probably E. Dana Caulkins) to H. S. Braucher, 2 March 1918, doc. 21306, box 42, entry 393, RG 165, National Archives; memorandum of "A.M.W." to Braucher, Malcolm McBride, Dr. Raycroft, and others, 4 March 1918, doc. 31316, box 71, entry 393, RG 165, National Archives; Executive Secretary to Braucher, 17 April 1918, doc. 31718, box 72, entry 393, RG 165, National Archives; memorandum from Major W. H. Loving to Chief, Military Morale Section, 24 November 1918, subfile 10218–279, Microfilm Publication M1440: Correspondence of the Military Intelligence Division Relating to "Negro Subversion" 1917–1941, National Archives.

53. A survey of conditions for African American soldiers in the training camps reported, "On the whole the Northern states have made much better provision for the negro than the southern." The report noted further, "Charlotte, N.C., Rockford, Ill., Chillicothe, Ohio, Des Moines, Iowa, and Battle Creek, Mich., seem to have made the best provision for the care of colored soldiers." Of these five cities, four were northern. Charlotte, the only southern city to make the list, had been completely without recreation in April 1918 but had leased a club for African American soldiers by July.

This survey, which compiled statistics regarding WCCS work in various sections of the country, allows some insight into the weakness of the WCCS in the South. In the eastern section five communities had made provisions, and three had not. In the central section, five communities had made provision, and only one had not. In the southeastern section, six had made provisions, and two had not. In the southern section no communities had made provisions, four had not. SUMMARY OF REPLIES TO QUESTIONNAIRE FROM INTELLIGENCE OFFICERS AT THE LARGE TRAINING CAMPS, prepared by Captain L. C. West, subfile 10218–279, Microfilm Publication M1440: Correspondence of the Military Intelligence Division Relating to "Negro Subversion" 1917–1941, National Archives.

54. H. S. Braucher to Prentice Sanger, 22 April 1918, doc. 31718, box 72, entry 393, RG 165, National Archives.

55. In the summary of the questionnaire filled out by intelligence officers at the large training camps, four communities were listed as drawing no color line in places of recreation. Of those four, two were in the central section, one in the eastern section, and one in the southern. SUMMARY OF REPLIES TO QUESTIONNAIRE FROM INTELLIGENCE OFFICERS AT THE LARGE TRAINING CAMPS, prepared by Captain L. C. West, National Archives.

Another investigation of the recreational facilities noted that moving picture theaters in the South were divided into those for Whites and those for Blacks. Theaters in the Southwest and the West were segregated. In the central and northern regions theaters were open to all. Charles H. Williams, RESUME OF CONDITIONS SURROUNDING NEGRO TROOPS, 5 August 1918, National Archives.

56. MEMORANDUM FOR THE DIRECTOR, MILITARY INTELLIGENCE DIVISION, AND THE CHIEF, MORALE BRANCH, EXECUTIVE DIVISION, GENERAL STAFF, from J. E. Cutler, Subject: THE NEGRO IN THE ARMY, 23 December 1918, National Archives.

57. "The Independent for the Colored Soldiers," *Atlanta Independent*, 6 October 1917,

5; "Camp Gordon News," *Atlanta Independent*, 17 November 1917, 7; George E. Cohron, "Camp Gordon News," *Atlanta Independent*, 22 December 1917, 8; "The Social Charity Club Entertains Some of the Colored Soldiers," *Atlanta Independent*, 29 December 1917, 1; "Baseball—Atlanta Cubs vs. Camp Gordon," *Atlanta Independent*, 27 April 1918, 8; "Camp Gordon Athletic Activities," *Atlanta Independent*, 4 May 1918, 8; E. M. Phillips, "League of Bethel A.M.E. Church Visits Camp Gordon," *Atlanta Independent*, 3 August 1918, 5; E. M. Phillips, "The Concert Given at Camp Gordon by the Patriotic League a Success," *Atlanta Independent*, 24 August 1918, 6; "Convalescent Soldiers Enjoy Sunday Outing," *Atlanta Independent*, 12 October 1918, 5.

58. "What Montgomery Is Doing," *Montgomery Emancipator*, 6 October 1917, 2; "News from Camp Sheridan," *Montgomery Emancipator*, 13 October 1917, 3; "First Baptist Church Entertains Soldiers," *Montgomery Emancipator*, 20 October 1917, 3; "Mammoth Chorus of Colored Soldiers and Citizens Organized," *Montgomery Emancipator*, 20 October 1917, 3; "Montgomery Colored Citizens Make Fine Report to War Secretary for Camp Sheridan on Activities in Interest of Race Soldiers," *Montgomery Emancipator*, 13 October 1917, 1; "News of Camp Sheridan, Camp Doings of Company B, Ninth Ohio Battalion," *Montgomery Emancipator*, 20 October 1917, 3; "News from Camp Sheridan," *Montgomery Emancipator*, 27 October 1917, 3.

59. E. M. Phillips, "The Patriotic League of Bethel A.M.E. Church Visits Camp Gordon," *Atlanta Independent*, 3 August 1918, 5; "The Social Charity Club Entertains Some of the Colored Soldiers," *Atlanta Independent*, 29 December 1917, 1; "The Independent for the Colored Soldiers," *Atlanta Independent*, 6 October 1917, 5; "Baseball—Atlanta Cubs vs. Camp Gordon," *Atlanta Independent*, 27 April 1918, 8; B. J. Davis, "A Great Patriotic and Enthusiastic Parade," *Atlanta Independent*, 20 April 1918, 1.

60. Harry H. Pace, secretary of Colored Committee, Atlanta, to Fosdick, July 20, 1918, doc. 35374, entry 393, RG 165, National Archives.

61. Memorandum of Major W. H. Loving to Chief, Military Morale Section, Subject: Conditions Among Negro Troops at Camp Gordon, 4 October 1918, subfile 10218–280, Microfilm Publications M1440: Correspondence of the Military Intelligence Division Relating to "Negro Subversion" 1917–1941, National Archives.

62. "A Parade of Only One Class of American Citizens," *Atlanta Independent*, 27 October 1917, 4.

63. White citizens would sometimes rally to the cause of the black troops. For one example see "Millionaire Opens Home to Soldiers," *Chicago Defender*, 8 December 1917, 1.

64. "Democracy and the Colored Soldier," 261.

65. Abbie Condit, "War Camp Community Service for Colored Troops," 24 January 1918, doc. 27333, entry 393, RG 165, National Archives.

66. "Negro Soldiers Are Making An Enviable Record—Have Mastered the Scientific Art of Handling a Bayonet in a Few Months," *Camp Dodger*, 22 February 1918, 5.

67. "Y Has Good Program Planned for the Week," *Camp Logan Reveille*, 1 November 1918, 3.

68. "Negro Entertainers," *Trench and Camp* (Camp Devens), 14 August 1918, 3. The ability of these men to perform was often assumed by white soldier and civilian alike. As the YMCA's publication, *Trench and Camp*, explained, "The men are, like all plantation negroes especially, exceedingly musical. They have a wonderful sense of harmony." "Happy Negroes Sing at Their Work and Play," *Trench and Camp* (Camp Beauregard), 14 September 1918, 3.

69. "Negro Song and Humor in Military Camp Life," *Montgomery Emancipator*, 4 May 1918, 2.

70. "Colored People Barred From Patriotic Rally," *Afro-American*, 19 April 1918, 1.

71. Executive Secretary (W.P.S., most likely W. P. Sanger), to Mrs. E. M. Townsend, New York City, 17 April 1918, doc. 27305, box 57, entry 393, RG 165, National Archives.

72. H. S. Braucher to E. Dana Caulkins, 10 June 1918, doc. 32279, box 74, entry 393, RG 165, National Archives.

73. H. S. Braucher to Workers, 23 August 1917, reprinted as W.R.B. #48, (doc. 3453), file Arizona 18.1 (2 of 4), box 3, entry 395, RG 165, National Archives.

74. John F. Piper, Jr., *The American Churches in World War One* (Athens: Ohio University Press, 1985), 169.

75. "Suggestions for Special Activities for the Reduction of Venereal Diseases Among Colored Soldiers in Cantonments," stamped at top "Approved B.J.," probably referring to Bascom Johnson, doc. 17463, box 33, entry 393, RG 165, National Archives.

76. Charles E. Miner, 1st Lieutenant, Sanitary Corps, United States National Army, to Walter Clarke, Education Secretary, American Social Hygiene Association, 20 December 1917, doc. 15999, box 29, entry 393, RG 165, National Archives.

77. Memo from Social Hygiene Instruction Division to Dr. John Geraghty, Johns Hopkins Hospital, "Subject: Pictures and Statistics of Venereal Disease Among Negroes," 20 February 1918, doc. 19979, entry 393, RG 165, National Archives.

78. Director, Army Section, Social Hygiene Division, CTCA, to Captain Arthur B. Spingarn, April 17, 1918; Arthur B. Spingarn to Director, Army Section, Social Hygiene Division, 24 April 1918, doc. 25976, box 53, entry 393, RG 165, National Archives. Spingarn was detailed by the surgeon general as special officer in charge of work with black troops and served in that connection as assistant director of the Army Section of the Social Hygiene Division of the CTCA. "Weekly Bulletin," War Department CTCA, Social Hygiene Division, Section on Women's Work, Bulletin #15, 20 August 1918, file "Bulletins—Hygiene Division," box 5, entry 399, RG 165, National Archives.

79. Arthur B. Spingarn, Sanitary Corps, to Social Hygiene Instruction Division, CTCA, "Subject: Lectures to Negro Troops," April 1918, doc. 34352, entry 393, RG 165, National Archives.

80. Communication from Army Section, Social Hygiene Division, to M. J. Exner, "Subject—Lectures on Sex Education and Lectures to Negro Troops," 8 June 1918, doc. 36329, box 89, entry 393, RG 165, National Archives; Major W. A. Sawyer to Lieutenant Royce R. Long, Sanitary Corps, 20 July 1918, doc. 35622, box 87, entry 393, RG 165, National Archives; "Law Enforcement and Public Health Notes," in "Weekly Bulletin," War Department CTCA, Social Hygiene Division, Section on Women's Work, Bulletin #15, 20 August 1918, file Bulletins—Hygiene Division, box 5, entry 399, RG 165, National Archives.

81. Walter Clarke to Charles E. Miner, December 27, 1917, doc. 15999, box 29, entry 393, RG 165, National Archives.

82. For an excellent discussion of the use of sexual stereotypes to justify racial violence see Jacquelyn Dowd Hall, "The Mind That Burns in Each Body: Women, Rape, and Racial Violence," in *Powers of Desire: The Politics of Sexuality*, by Ann Snitow, Christine Stansell, and Sharon Thompson, eds. (New York: Monthly Review Press, 1983), 328–349.

83. V. H. Kriegshaber to Fosdick, 20 July 1917, doc. 2853, file Atlanta, Georgia (3 of 3), box 6, entry 395, RG 165, National Archives.

84. "Executive Secretary," possibly Harold Keats, District War Service Commission, to Reverend Chs. Wood, Rev. Pierce, and Rev. Wilfley, 27 August 1917, doc. 4686, file District of Columbia, entry 395, RG 165, National Archives.

85. Fosdick to Mr. George A. Nesbitt, 14 September 1917, doc. 6092, file District of Columbia, box 5, entry 395, RG 165, National Archives.

86. Wm. B. Kelsey, Executive Secretary, War Department Commission on Training Camp Activities, Waco, Texas, on "Activities in Community Organization," to H. S. Braucher of the WCCS, 11 August 1917, doc. 4159, file Alabama 26 (1 of 2), box 2, entry 395, RG 165, National Archive.

87. Alan Johnstone, Jr., "Report on Augusta, Georgia," 17 November 1917, file Atlanta, Georgia (2 of 3), box 6, entry 395, RG 165, National Archives.

88. The black community was well aware of the existence of stereotypes and had urged their abandonment by the government and the press. See for instance, J. A. Jackson, "The Truth, the Whole Truth, and Nothing but the Truth," *Atlanta Independent*, 1 December 1917, 7; "The Press and the Impression," *Atlanta Independent*, 22 September 1917, 1; "Taking Snap Judgement against the Negro Woman," *Montgomery Emancipator*, 10 May 1919, 4.

89. Ruth Rosen, *The Lost Sisterhood: Prostitution in America, 1900–1918* (Baltimore: Johns Hopkins University Press, 1982), 80, 147–152.

90. Robert C. Newman, report on Macon, Georgia, and Camp Wheeler, 13 November 1917, doc. 14999, file Macon, Georgia (1 of 3), box 6, entry 395, RG 165, National Archives. Quotations in text come from Newman's report of a conversation with the managing editor of the *Macon Telegraph*.

91. Mayor of Alexandria, W. W. Whittington Jr., to Senator Broussard, 3 September 1917, doc. 6014, file Alexandria—Louisiana (5 of 5), box 8, entry 395, RG 165, National Archives.

92. Report regarding Prostitution and Liquor Traffic in Pensacola, Florida, 8, 9, 10 July 1917, doc. 2719, file Florida—Pensacola, box 6, entry 395, RG 165, National Archives.

93. A Johns Hopkins University study suggested a rate of syphilis among Blacks about one-half times that for Whites. There is absolutely no evidence to suggest the rates of 60 percent and 70 percent often attributed to African American women. Barbeau and Henri, *Unknown Soldiers*, 52–53.

94. Barbeau and Henri, *Unknown Soldiers*, 79–80.

95. "Suggestions for Special Activities for the Reduction of Venereal Diseases Among Colored Soldiers in Cantonments," stamped at top "Approved B.J.," most likely Bascom Johnson, doc. 17463, box 33, entry 393, RG 165, National Archives.

96. Charles Williams of the Hampton Institute, hired by the committee as its field secretary, quoted in *The American Churches in World War One*, by Piper, 169. See also memorandum from Major W. H. Loving, P.C., to Chief, Military Morale Section, Washington, D.C., Subject: Conditions Among Negro Troops In Camp Gordon, 4 October 1918, subfile 10218–280, Microfilm Publications M1440: Correspondence of the Military Intelligence Division Relating to "Negro Subversion" 1917–1941, National Archives.

97. Edward H. Griffith, representative of the War Department Commission on Training Camp Activities, to Major General Harry C. Hale, Commanding officer, Camp Taylor, October 30, 1917, subject: "Proposed exclusion of white soldiers from negro sections," and Griffith to Colonel Lindsey, Chief of Police of Louisville, Kentucky, 4 November 1917, doc. 13649, box 22, entry 393, RG 165, National Archives.

98. Williams noted that treatment of black and white girls was more similar in the West. Charles H. Williams, RESUME OF CONDITIONS SURROUNDING NEGRO TROOPS, 5 August 1918, National Archives.

99. Williams, quoted in *The American Churches in World War One*, by Piper, 169.

100. Henry I. Fox to Dr. T. A. Storey, Executive Secretary, Interdepartmental Social Hygiene Board, Report on the City of Louisville, Kentucky, and Camp Zachary Taylor, for the month ending 31 July 1919, file Civilians, box 15, entry 399, RG 165, National Archives.

101. Report on Samarcand, North Carolina, in Martha P. Falconer, "Report of the Section on Reformatories and Houses of Detention," 1 October 1918—1 February 1919, doc. 46405, box 132, entry 393, RG 165, National Archives.

102. Suggesting the popular white stereotype of black male sexuality, one telegram to the CTCA suggested, "FIND SOME OFFICERS STRONGLY OBJECT TO ABOLISHING NEGRO SEGREGATED DISTRICTS ALLEGING DANGER OF RAPE" Telegram, Popenoe (Deming, New Mexico), to CTCA, 15 November 1917, doc. 10780, box 14, entry 393, RG 165, National Archives.

103. Allan Brandt, *No Magic Bullet: A Social History of Venereal Disease in the United States Since 1880* (New York: Oxford University Press, 1985), 116; Barbeau and Henri, *Unknown Soldiers*, 54–55. It is true that black soldiers registered a higher incidence of the venereal diseases than white soldiers. Yet the reasons for this were directly related to discriminatory treatment by local draft boards, which enlisted African American men despite venereal diseases. Barbeau and Henri, *Unknown Soldiers*, 52–53.

104. Memorandum to the Port Inspector, 16 May 1919, Inspection: Prophylactic Station, Camp Hill, by J. Ryan Devereux, file 322.15—Prophylactic Stations, box 2, entry 34A, RG 159, National Archives Branch Depository, Suitland, Md.

105. Memorandum to the Port Inspector, Inspection: Prophylactic Station, Camp Alexander, by J. Ryan Devereux, 16 May 1919, file 322.15—Prophylactic Stations, box 2, entry 34A, RG 159, National Archives Branch Depository, Suitland, Md.

106. Memorandum of Major W. H. Loving to Chief, Military Morale Section, 13 October 1918, Subject: Conditions Among Negro Troops in Camp Sevier, doc. 5, subfile 10218–280, Microfilm Publication M1440: Correspondence of the Military Intelligence Division Relating to "Negro Subversion" 1917–1941, National Archives.

There were also problems at Camp MacArthur, but the military intelligence officer believed these problems were in the process of being eliminated. Memorandum from Camp Intelligence Officer, Camp MacArthur, Texas, to Director, Military Intelligence Division, 22 November 1918, Subject: Entitled "Questionnaire concerning Colored Troops," doc. 76, subfile 10218–244, Microfilm Publication M1440: Correspondence of the Military Intelligence Division Relating to "Negro Subversion" 1917–1941, National Archives.

107. George J. Owen, Executive Secretary, War Service Board, Little Rock, to Fosdick, 10 October 1917, doc. 6532, box 2, entry 393, RG 165, National Archives.

108. Telegram from J. P. Robertson and F. B. Barnes, representative of the CTCA, to Fosdick, 10 October 1917, docs. 7571 and 6726, file Kansas—Ft. Riley, box 7, entry 395, RG 165, National Archives.

109. Abbie Condit, "War Camp Community Service for Colored Troops," 24 January 1918, doc. 27333, entry 393, RG 165, National Archives.

110. Telegram to Fosdick from the Manhattan Commercial Club, doc. 6540, box 2, entry 393, RG 165, National Archives.

111. Ibid.

112. Telegram of Jasper J. Mayer to Willa Jean Mayer, 8 December 1917, doc. 13969, box 23, entry 393, RG 165, National Archives.

113. A Lt. H. H. Attles quoted in memorandum for Mr. Caulkins from T. H., 2 May 1918, doc. 27178, box 56, entry 393, RG 165, National Archives.

114. Ibid. A report as late as November 1918 continued to note the failure of the WCCS in the communities near Camp Funston. Memorandum from Camp Intelligence Officer, Camp Funston, to Director, Military Intelligence Division, Washington, D.C., November 5, 1918, subfile 10218–244, Microfilm Publication M1440: Correspondence of the Military Intelligence Division Relating to "Negro Subversion" 1917–1941, National Archives.

115. General Ballou, Bulletin No. 35, 28 March 1918, reprinted in *Scott's Official History*, by E. J. Scott, 97–98.

116. Ibid. General Ballou had used a similar tactic in Des Moines with the black officer candidates, following an incident at the Empress Theater, in which two African American soldiers refused to sit in the Jim Crow section of the theater. General Ballou quoted in "Rookies Balk at Jim-Crow," *Afro-American*, 14 July 1917, 1.

117. "This is No Soldier! Ballou Might Have Done a Worse Thing; That's Doubtful," *Chicago Defender*, 4 May 1918, 16.

118. "Ballou's Drastic Order Causes Adverse Comment," *Afro-American*, 19 April 1918, 1.

119. E. J. Scott, *Scott's Official History*, 97.

120. "Colored Men in Uniform, Not U.S. Soldiers," *Afro-American*, 4 August 1917, 4.

121. "Activities for Negro Troops," WRB #60, file Arizona 18.1 (3 of 4), box 3, entry 395, RG 165, National Archives.

122. Description of second case in "Notes on the Employment of Colored Troops," by Colonel Robert C. Humber, U.S. Army War College, Historical Section, *Colored Soldiers in the U.S. Army*, prepared September 1942, U.S. Army Military History Institute, Carlisle Barracks, Pennsylvania.

123. Description of final case, 29 July 1917, in "Notes on the Employment of Colored Troops," by Colonel Robert C. Humber.

124. E. J. Scott, *Scott's Official History*, 94–95.

125. This discussion is not meant to suggest that African American troops were always the initiators of violence in conflicts between Whites and Blacks in the camps and their neighboring communities. In some cases, for instance, white soldiers engaged in violence in response to their discovery of desegregated recreational facilities. See letter of Emmett J. Scott from Camp Merritt, 18 August 1918, subfile 10218–209, Microfilm Publication M1440: Correspondence of the Military Intelligence Division Relating to "Negro Subversion" 1917–1941, National Archives; Memorandum from Harold F. Butler, Intelligence Officer, Camp Meade, to Chief, Military Morale Section, Washington, D.C., 13 August 1918, subfile 10218–199, Microfilm Publication M1440: Correspondence of the Military Intelligence Division Relating to "Negro Subversion" 1917–1941, National Archives.

126. "Activities for Negro Troops," WRB #60, file Arizona 18.1 (3 of 4), box 3, entry 395, RG 165, National Archives. For another case see Dennis M. Moore, Memorandum for Major Jason S. Joy, 15 March 1919, and James H. Buell, Memorandum to Mr. Caulkins, 22 March 1919, doc. 47321, entry 393, RG 165, National Archives.

127. Neil A. Wynn makes a similar point about the government's broader effort to "improve the black mood." See Neil A. Wynn, *From Progressivism to Prosperity: World War I and American Society* (New York: Holmes and Meier, 1986), 187.

128. "Democracy and the Colored Soldier," 260. As another way of dismissing the reality and legitimacy of black complaints, the War Department often suggested that it was German propagandists, not loyal black Americans, who were raising the complaints regarding segregation and discrimination. For examples of this tendency, see "Warning Sounded against Racial Trouble in Camps," *Trench and Camp* (Camp Shelby), 24 November 1917, 4; E. J. Scott, *Scott's Official History*, 9. Evidence of the War Department's sincere belief in a German plot to use the African American troops is abundant, most obviously in the broad effort made by the Military Intelligence Division to investigate "negro subversion" during the war. These materials have been collected in a five-roll microfilm collection, Microfilm Publication M1440, Correspondence of the Military Intelligence Division Relating to "Negro Subversion" 1917–1941, National Archives.

129. This statement was written with a focus on the problem at Newport News. Fosdick to Woodrow Wilson, 2 October 1918, doc. 37969, box 97, entry 393, RG 165, National Archives. Fosdick was answering a letter from the president in which he had responded to a memo on the situation at Newport News. Wilson had written, "Thank you for the memorandum about the negro problem as it presents itself at Newport News. The report gives me a great deal of concern. Can you think of any proper means of correcting their impressions?" Rather than seeking means to correct the recreational problems in Newport News, Wilson appeared to want to correct the impressions, not the actual situation. Wilson to Fosdick, 30 September 1918, folder 7, box 22, Raymond Blaine Fosdick Papers, Seeley G. Mudd Manuscript Library, Princeton University. Published with permission of Princeton University Libraries.

130. Minutes of Meeting, War Department Commission on Training Camp Activities, 18 June 1918, box 57, entry 403, RG 165, National Archives. See also E. D. Caulkins to T. S. Settle, Army and Navy Club, Richmond, Virginia, 21 June 1918, doc. 33092, entry 393, RG 165, National Archives.

131. Ibid.

132. For instance, two months earlier, in April 1918, the WCCS took "definite steps to provide recreation and entertainment for colored soldiers at Newport News," a particularly troublesome spot in the government's neglect of African American troops. THE COLORED SOLDIER AND COMMUNITY PROBLEM AT NEWPORT NEWS, AND A BRIEF STATEMENT OF WHAT THE W.C.C.S. IS DOING TO SOLVE IT, doc. 37783, box 96, entry 393, RG 165, National Archives.

133. A report to H. S. Braucher of the WCCS on the recommendations of the Sanitary Corps of the Surgeon General's Office suggested "that colored girls' work be developed in every camp community having a considerable population regardless whether or not there are colored troops at the encampment." EDC (probably E. Dana Caulkins) to Braucher, 3 June 1918, "Regarding interview with Captain Spingarn of the Sanitary Corps of the Surgeon General's Office," doc. 31194, box 71, entry 393, RG 165, National Archives.

134. McBride to Rosenwald, 10 July 1918, includes reference to telegram just received regarding the San Antonio representative of the WCCS, doc. 34697, entry 393, RG 165, National Archives.

135. T. S. Settle, district representative, WCCS, to Emmett Scott, 31 July 1918, doc. 37405, box 94, entry 393, RG 165, National Archives.

136. George A. Nesbitt to E. D. Caulkins, June 21, 1918, doc. 33831, entry 393, RG 165, National Archives. The work appeared to continue to grow in the months following the armistice. See Report on War Camp Community Service for Colored Soldiers and Sailors, April 1919, file 322.97 (5-1-19) to 322.97 (7-17-17), box 704, Central Decimal Files 1917–1925, RG 407, National Archives.

137. "ORGANIZATION CLUBS AND BUILDING FOR COLORED TROOPS PREPARED BY THE COMMISSION ON TRAINING CAMP ACTIVITIES," November 1918, doc. 43447, entry 393, RG 165, National Archives.

138. E. L. Munson, Brigadier General, General Staff, Chief, Morale Branch, to Fosdick, 24 October 1918, doc. 42411, entry 393, RG 165, National Archives.

139. At Camp Greene uncertainty about the permanence of the camp stalled the development of black recreational facilities. W. Prentice Sanger, Executive Secretary, to Mr. Hopkins, November 19, 1918, doc. 42823, box 118, entry 393, RG 165, National Archives.

140. W. P. Sanger, Executive Secretary, to Roy Smith Wallace, 27 November 1918, doc. 43599, box 121, entry 393, RG 165, National Archives; Sanger to Robt. F. Volentine, doc. 43733, box 122, entry 393, RG 165, National Archives.

141. R. W. Thompson, "Emmett J. Scott to Remain at His Post," *Washington Bee*, 28 December 1918, 1.

142. Emmett J. Scott to Assistant Secretary of War F. P. Keppel, 16 June 1919, doc. 51472, entry 393, RG 165, National Archives. Scott's assurance came in a letter from Jason S. Joy, who became one of the executive officers of the CTCA after the military takeover. This takeover, its operation, and its implications, will be discussed in chapter 6. Jason S. Joy to E. Dana Caulkins, doc. 51472, entry 393, RG 165, National Archives.

143. Geo. A. Sloan, Captain, Infantry, US Army, and executive officer of the CTCA, to Katharine Scott, YWCA, 25 June 1919, doc. 50177, entry 393, RG 165, National Archives.

144. The case of the Hostess House for black troops at Camp Pike is a case in point. Having waited until after the armistice to build a much-needed facility, the YWCA and the CTCA soon found the need decreasing and chose to abandon the plans for a building. Emmett J. Scott to Major Joy, 28 February 1919, and Jason S. Joy to Emmett J. Scott, 28 February 1919, doc. 46292, entry 393, RG 165, National Archives; Katharine Scott, Executive Secretary, National Hostess House Committee, to Major Jason S. Joy, Director, CTCA, 21 May 1919, and Jason S. Joy to Katharine Scott, 25 May 1919, doc. 49115, box 144, entry 393, RG 165, National Archives.

145. Memorandum to Commanding Officer, 372nd Infantry, from Edward V. Howard, Adjutant General, Adjutant, by Command of Brigadier General Nicholson, 14 February 1919, doc. 46426, entry 393, RG 165, National Archives.

146. Camp Upton had been regarded by some as a camp free of racial problems. "No Racial Friction at Camp Upton," *Afro-American*, 15 March 1918.

147. George E. Cannon, Chairman, Executive Board, National Medical Association, to Baker, 20 February 1919, doc. 46426, entry 393, RG 165, National Archives; John R. Shillady, Secretary, NAACP, New York, to Baker, 20 February 1919, doc. 46426, entry 393, RG 165, National Archives; "Would Draw Color Line at Camp Upton—Genl. Nicholson's Order Is Resented by Soldiers and Civilians All Over Country," *New York Age*, 1 March 1919, Special Edition, 1.

As during the war, African American soldiers expressed their outrage at the system of segregation in clashes with civilians and military police. At Newport News, Virginia, in May 1919, a near race riot resulted after a struggle between African American troops and military guards led to the accidental shooting of an African American girl. In Bisbee, Arizona, in July 1919, five persons were wounded in a fight between black soldiers and civilians. "Offended Negroes Clash with Military Officers," *Montgomery Emancipator*, 3 May 1919, 1; "Soldiers and Civilians Clash," *Montgomery Emancipator*, 12 July 1919, 1.

148. Letter to the War Department at Washington and to whom it may concern, from Camp Lee, 14 July 1918, doc. 34862, box 84, entry 393, RG 165, National Archives.

149. Ibid.

150. "Our Position in the War," *Chicago Defender*, 18 May 1918, 16.

151. As the *Montgomery Emancipator* responded to pleas for interracial good will in March 1919,

> We cannot drive out darkness, except by turning on light. Neither can we usher in interracial good will until the victory over injustice is gained. The time has come when the Negro masses are demanding their leaders to speak out frankly and fearlessly and ask for the fundamental things that the race is seeking here at home—the things for which Negro soldiers fought and died side by side with their white comrades on the bloody fields of France. Why ask for good will when what we really want is justice, democracy and a man's chance in life?

"Dr. Moton's Open Letter," *Montgomery Emancipator*, 1 March 1919, 2. See also Alan Dawley, *Struggles for Justice: Social Responsibility and the Liberal State* (Cambridge: Harvard University Press, 1991), 230–231.

152. W. E. B. Du Bois, "Returning Soldiers," from *The Crisis* (May 1919), reprinted in *The Selected Writings of W.E.B. Du Bois*, Walter Wilson, ed. (New York: New American Library, 1970), 172.

NOTES TO CHAPTER SIX

1. Baker to Fosdick, 1 July 1919, in folder 12, box 26, Raymond Blaine Fosdick Papers, Seeley G. Mudd Manuscript Library, Princeton University. Published with permission of Princeton University Libraries.

2. Ibid.

3. Dixon Wecter, *When Johnny Comes Marching Home* (Westport, Conn.: Greenwood Press, 1944), 257–259, 304–305.

4. Speech of Fosdick at the Liberty Hut, Washington, D.C., 16 November 1918, as part of the United War Work Campaign, doc. 50114, box 150, entry 393, RG 165, National Archives.

5. "Draft of a letter from the Secretary of War to Governors and Mayors," doc. 42564, box 116, entry 393, RG 165, National Archives.

6. Ibid.

7. "Exhibit 'A'," letter from Social Hygiene Division to communities with whom the Social Hygiene Division had not corresponded during the war, attached to letter of William H. Zinsser to Fosdick, 19 November 1918, doc. 42968, box 118, entry 393, RG 165, National Archives.

8. Memorandum from E. L. Munson, Brigadier General, Chief of the Morale Branch of the Army, to Liaison Officer, CTCA, 19 November 1918, doc. 43133, box 119, entry 393, RG 165, National Archives.

9. Fosdick, 11 November 1918, doc. 43541, box 121, RG 165, National Archives. The letter is not addressed to anyone, but penciled in is the phrase "affil org demob. letter," probably meaning it was a letter about demobilization for the members of the affiliated organizations.

10. Baker, "Draft of a letter from the Secretary of War to Governors and Mayors," doc. 42564, box 116, entry 393, RG 165, National Archives.

11. Director, First District, Report on Camp Devens, Ayer, Massachusetts, 14 February 1919, file Major Elwell, box 18, entry 399, RG 165, National Archives.

12. Memorandum from E. L. Munson, Brigadier General, Chief, Morale Branch, to Liaison Officer, CTCA, 19 November 1918, doc. 43133, box 119, entry 393, RG 165, National Archives.

13. Malcolm L. McBride, Acting Chairman, to Baker, 6 December 1918, doc. 52396, entry 393, RG 165, National Archives.

14. "Report of Informal Conference on Morale," 12 April 1918, doc. 36766, box 91, entry 393, RG 165, National Archives; "Report of 2nd Conference on Control of Morale," 15 May 1918, doc. 50109, box 150, entry 393, RG 165, National Archives; "MEMORANDUM for the Adjutant General of the Army. Subject: Organization of the Morale Branch, General Staff," from the Chief of Staff, 15 October 1918, doc. 43419, box 120, entry 393, RG 165, National Archives.

15. "MEMORANDUM for the Adjutant General of the Army. Subject: Organization of the Morale Branch, General Staff," from the Chief of Staff, 15 October 1918, National Archives.

16. Report of a joint meeting of the Heads of Departments, District Directors, and Supervisors of the Law Enforcement Division and Section on Women and Girls of the Commission on Training Camp Activities, 12–14 March 1919, doc. 44993, file 9, entry 393, RG 165, National Archives.

17. F. P. Keppel, 3rd Assistant Secretary of War, to Major W. R. Burgess, 29 April 1919, doc. 48788, box 143, entry 393, RG 165, National Archives.

18. Fosdick to Baker, 1 June 1919, in the volume *Letters from the First World War*, box 26, Fosdick Papers.

19. For details on the conflict see Nancy K. Bristow, "Creating Crusaders: The Commission on Training Camp Activities and the Progressive Social Vision during World War One," Ph.D. diss., University of California, Berkeley, 1989, 145–161.

20. Minutes of Meeting, War Department Commission on Training Camp Activities, 20 December 1918, box 57, entry 403, RG 165, National Archives; Memorandum of C. Towner to YMCA, 18 April 1919, doc. 48064, box 140, entry 393, RG 165, National Archives; "Memorandum for Mr. Adams," 1 February 1919, file Camp Lewis, Washington (second), box 7, entry 399, RG 165, National Archives; Capt. Harold A. Zillman, "Memorandum for Mr. Caulkins," 1 February 1919, file Camp Lewis, Washington (second), box 7, entry 399, RG 165, National Archives; Memorandum to Secretary Keppel, 17 May 1919, doc. 49264, box 145, entry 393, RG 165, National Archives.

21. Memorandum from the War Department, Office of Chief of Staff, to Adjutant General, 22 September 1919, doc. 52201, entry 393, RG 165, National Archives.

22. For examples of the continuing close and cordial relationship between the WCCS and the CTCA, see Baker to H. S. Braucher, 14 June 1919, doc. 49776, box 146, entry 393, RG 165, National Archives; Fosdick to Braucher, 25 June 1919, doc. 51968, box 159, entry 393, RG 165, National Archives; Joseph Lee to Baker, 30 September 1919, doc. 52406, entry 393, RG 165, National Archives.

23. C. Leighton, Chairman, Law and Order League, Fort Dodge, to Baker, 11 December 1918, doc. 43699, box 122, entry 393, RG 165, National Archives.

24. WCCS Program Sheets, February 1919, report on Little Rock, doc. 46494, box 133, entry 393, RG 165, National Archives.

25. J. B. Dickinson, February 11, 1919, accompanied by letter of Director, Department of Method, to J. B. Dickinson, 17 February 1919, doc. 46250, box 132, entry 393, RG 165, National Archives.

26. Bascom Johnson, "Purpose, Organization, and Functions of Section on Community Cooperation—Camp Activities Division—Education and Recreation Branch, War Plans Division, U.S. Army," doc. 53387, entry 393, RG 165, National Archives.

27. Confidential report of the meeting of the Heads of Departments of the Commission on Training Camp Activities, 9 April 1919, doc. 44993, file 3, entry 393, RG 165, National Archives; Allan M. Brandt, *No Magic Bullet: A Social History of Venereal Disease in the United States Since 1880* (New York: Oxford University Press, 1985), 125.

28. Mary Macey Dietzler, *Detention Houses and Reformatories as Protective Social Agencies in the Campaign of the United States Government against Venereal Diseases* (Washington, D.C.: Government Printing Office, 1922), 11–12. This work was produced under the auspices of the United States Interdepartmental Social Hygiene Board.

29. Dietzler, *Detention Houses and Reformatories*, 17–18.

30. Brandt, *No Magic Bullet*, 123.

31. Dietzler, *Detention Houses and Reformatories*, 12.

32. Rupert Blue, Surgeon General, to Fosdick, 8 November 1918, doc. 50091, box 150, entry 393, RG 165, National Archives.

33. William H. Zinsser to Fosdick, 16 October 1918, doc. 40886, box 110, entry 393, RG 165, National Archives.

34. William H. Zinsser to Fosdick, 13 November 1918, doc. 42598, entry 393, RG 165, National Archives; Baker to William H. Zinsser, 31 March 1919, doc. 47459, box 137, entry 393, RG 165, National Archives.

35. Father Burke, quoted in *The American Churches in World War One*, by John F. Piper, Jr. (Athens: Ohio University Press, 1985), 157.

36. Piper, *The American Churches in World War One*, 156.

37. Ibid., 157.

38. Brandt, *No Magic Bullet*, 123–125.

39. William H. Zinsser to F. P. Keppel, Third Secretary of War, 14 March 1919, doc. 47459, box 137, entry 393, RG 165, National Archives.

40. Ibid.

41. Confidential report of the meeting of the Heads of Departments of the Commission on Training Camp Activities, 9 April 1919, doc. 44993, file 3, entry 393, RG 165, National Archives.

42. American Social Hygiene Association, with the official permission of the War Department Commission on Training Camp Activities, *What the War has done to stamp out Venereal Diseases—A Summary and a Summons*, doc. 50285, box 151, entry 393, RG 165, National Archives.

43. Brandt, *No Magic Bullet*, 124, 135.

44. Ibid., 125–131.

45. For a full discussion of the evolution of the anti–venereal disease campaign in the 1920s and 1930s, see Brandt, *No Magic Bullet*, chapter 4. Despite the decline of the USPHS in the 1920s, Fosdick still maintained that that agency's work furthered the war-time work. See Fosdick, cited in David J. Pivar, "Cleansing the Nation: The War on Prostitution, 1917–1921," *Prologue* 12 (Spring 1980), 36.

46. Telegram of W. P. Sanger to H. S. Braucher, 19 December 1918, doc. 43886, box 123, entry 393, RG 165, National Archives; "Draft of a letter from the Secretary of War to Governors and Mayors," doc. 42564, box 116, entry 393, RG 165, National Archives.

47. Reports on law enforcement in 1919 contain countless references to continuing or new efforts against vice and alcohol being carried out in cities across the country. See Director, Law Enforcement Division, to Director, Commission on Training Camp Activities, Subject: Report for week ending 22 April 1919, dated 22 April 1919, doc. 44993, file 4, box 128, entry 393, RG 165, National Archives; Minutes of Meeting of Heads of Departments of CTCA, 30 April 1919, doc. 44993, file 5, box 128, entry 393, RG 165, National Archives; Director, Law Enforcement Division (DeLo E. Mook), to Executive Officer, CTCA, Report for the week ending 17 May 1919, doc. 44993, file 4, box 128, entry 393, RG 165, National Archives; Report from Capt. Theodore Hall, Army Section, Social Hygiene Division, to W. H. Zinsser, 11 January 1919, doc. 44656, box 126, entry 393, RG 165, National Archives.

48. Report from Director, Law Enforcement Division, to Director, Commission on Training Camp Activities, "Subject: Report for the Week ending February 11th," dated 11 February 1919, doc. 44993, file 2, entry 393, RG 165, National Archives.

49. District Director, First District, Commission on Training Camp Activities District

Director's Report, to Executive Officer, "Subject: Report on Camp Devens," received 5 April 1919, file Major Elwell, box 19, entry 399, RG 165, National Archives.

50. Report of Lieutenant Robert Newbegin, San. Corps, U.S.A., for week ending 28 December 1918, box 14, entry 399, RG 165, National Archives.

51. Vice report on Atlanta, Georgia, 2, 3, 4 July 1919, file Atlanta, Georgia (1 of 3), box 6, entry 395, RG 165, National Archives.

52. Report on Atlanta, Georgia, 14, 15 July 1919, file Atlanta, Georgia (1 of 3), box 6, entry 395, RG 165, National Archives.

53. District Director, 7th District, CTCA, to the Director, CTCA, "Subject: Resume of work accomplished for the week ending May 24, 1919," dated 24 May 1919, doc. 44993, file 7, entry 393, RG 165, National Archives.

54. Ibid.

55. Report of Captain J. B. Collins, February 11, 1919, quoted in letter of William H. Zinsser, Director, Section on Men's Work, Social Hygiene Division, to F. P. Keppel, 3rd Assistant Secretary of War, 24 February 1919, doc. 46661, box 134, entry 393, RG 165, National Archives.

56. "BAKER IS QUOTED IN CONTROVERSY," *Times-Picayune*, 21 February 1919, clipped and included with letter of William H. Zinsser to F. P. Keppel, 24 February 1919, doc. 46661, box entry 393, RG 165, National Archives.

57. F. P. Keppel to W. H. Zinsser, 1 March 1919, doc. 46661, entry 393, RG 165, National Archives.

58. Chandler C. Luzenberg, District Attorney, New Orleans, to Major Joy and James H. Buell, Director, to Chandler C. Luzenberg, 13 May 1919, doc. 48243, box 141, entry 393, RG 165, National Archives. A later report on New Orleans suggested that the local police were at least attempting to provide an appearance of activism in repressing vice. Confidential report on the meeting of the Heads of Departments of the CTCA, 28 May 1919, doc. 44993, file 6, entry 393, RG 165, National Archives.

59. Jason S. Joy to Mr. McBride, 1 March 1919, doc. 47161, box 136, entry 393, RG 165, National Archives.

60. Bulletin No. 73, From DeLo E. Mook, Captain, Sanitary Corps, U.S. Army, Director of the Law Enforcement Division, to the Section on Vice and Liquor Control, "Subject: Future Work of Law Enforcement Division," doc. 46443, box 133, entry 393, RG 165, National Archives.

61. War and Navy Departments, Commissions on Training Camp Activities, *Standard Forms of Laws*, letter of Josephus Daniels, inside front cover, box 1635, RG 287, National Archives.

62. Ibid.

63. A report of the Law Enforcement Division for the week ending 11 February 1919, for instance, suggested the progress being made by listing the states with legislation adopted from *Standard Forms of Laws* pending in their legislatures. According to this report, eleven states had laws for vice repression pending, two states had fornication laws pending, six states had injunction and abatement acts pending, fourteen states had venereal disease control acts pending, three states had laws pending for the removal of officers guilty of nonfeasance or malfeasance in office, and five states had laws pending for the establishment of reformatories or industrial farms for women and girls. "Report for the Week ending February 11th," from the Director, Law Enforcement Division, to the Director, CTCA, 11 February 1919, doc. 44993, file 2, entry 393, RG 165, National Archives.

64. "Draft of a letter from the Secretary of War to Governors and Mayors," doc. 42564,

box 116, entry 393, RG 165, National Archives; Raymond Fosdick, Preface, *Standard Forms of Laws*, box 1635, RG 287, National Archives.

65. F. P. Keppel to Mr. McBride, 1 March 1919, doc. 47161, box 136, entry 393, RG 165, National Archives.

66. Captain Geo. A. Sloan, Infantry, U.S. Army, executive officer, to Major R. W. Milburn, 27 July 1919, doc. 50943, box 154, entry 393, RG 165, National Archives.

67. Memorandum from Jason S. Joy to Keppel, May 17, 1919, doc. 49264, box 145, entry 393, RG 165, National Archives.

68. Dietzler, *Detention Houses and Reformatories*, 11–12.

69. Letter of Corporal Charles B. Merritt to his mother, 14 November 1917, in "The War Letters of Corporal Charles B. Merritt," U.S. Army Military History Institute at the Carlisle Barracks, Pennsylvania, World War One Research Project, Army Experiences Questionnaire Collection, 28th Division, 112th Infantry, Co. M.

70. Letters of Corporal Charles B. Merritt to his mother, 11 November 1917 and 26 February 1918, "The War Letters of Corporal Charles B. Merritt."

71. Letter of Corporal Charles B. Merritt to his mother, 17 March 1918, "The War Letters of Corporal Charles B. Merritt."

72. These questionnaires have been collected and stored by military division at the U.S. Army Military History Institute at the Carlisle Barracks in Carlisle, Pennsylvania. They are an exceptionally useful source and are complemented by many letters and diaries of soldiers returned with the questionnaires. Of particular use for this project were these questions: (10) "What forms of off-duty recreation were common?" (11) "How did you and your comrades get along with civilians in the US?" (13) "What did soldiers use their pay for?" (14) "Was drinking a problem? How was liquor obtained?" and (15) "Was there much gambling?"

73. Letter of David Miles Thornton to the editor of *Daily Journal*, Mechanicsburg, Pennsylvania, 17 November 1917, in "War Letters of David Miles Thornton," U.S. Army Military History Institute at the Carlisle Barracks, Pennsylvania, World War One Research Project, Army Experiences Questionnaire Collection, 79th Division, 316th Infantry, Machine Gun Company.

74. Army Experiences Questionnaire Collection: 1st Lieutenant Charles S. Robinson, 93rd Division, 371st Regiment, Co. E; Private Elmer R. Luberg, 92nd Division, 317th Ammunition Train, Company E; William H. Brooks, 39th Division, 156th Infantry, Company L. It is interesting to note that these first two complaints came from divisions filled with African American soldiers.

75. Edward F. Allen, *Keeping Our Fighters Fit for War and After* (New York: Century, 1918), 103.

76. WRB #112, Extract from report of Joseph S. Keating, Anniston Alabama, for the week ending 6 October 1917, file Alabama 18.1, box 3, entry 395, RG 165, National Archives.

77. Fosdick to Clarence A. Perry, 29 May 1917, doc. 644, file P, box 6, entry 394, RG 165, National Archives.

78. See Army Experiences Questionnaire Collection: Corporal Edward W. Stutsman, 84th Division, 309th Engineers; First Sergeant Eugene A. Moss, 84th Division, 159th Field Artillery Brigade, 327th Field Artillery Regiment, Headquarters Company; Sergeant First Class Chas. H. Blosser, 87th Division, 347th Headquarters; Guy W. Thurston, 88th Division, 175th Infantry Brigade, 350th Infantry.

79. "Southern Hospitality," *Gas Attack* (Camp Wadsworth), February 9, 1918, 4.

80. Walter J. Strauss, "Reminiscences and Diary of a Private in World War I," in the

Army Experiences Questionnaire Collection, 27th Division, 102nd Engineers. For additional praise, particularly of "southern hospitality," see "An Open Letter to the Editor of Pass in Review," *Pass-in-Review* (Camp Bowie), 15 April 1918, 7; W.J.B., 156th Infantry, "A Soldiers' Appreciation," in "Soldiers' Mail box," *Trench and Camp* (Camp Beauregard), 10 August 1918; Richard J. McBride, Sr., "Passing in Review—Memoirs of World War I, 1917—A.E.F.—1919," in the Army Experiences Questionnaire Collection, Richard J. McBride, Sr., 82nd Division, 328th Infantry.

81. J. Walter Strauss, "Reminiscences and Diary of a Private in World War I," in the Army Experiences Questionnaire Collection, 27th Division, 102nd Engineers.

82. "An Open Letter to the Editor of Pass in Review," *Pass-in-Review* (Camp Bowie), 15 April 1918, 7.

83. Letters of Frank Grace to his mother, 28 June and 5 July 1918, Army Experiences Questionnaire Collection, WWI file #119; Letter of Corporal Charles B. Merritt to his mother, 22 February 1918, in "The War Letters of Corporal Charles B. Merritt," in the Army War Experiences Questionnaire Collection, 28th Division, 112th Infantry, Company M; Norman Arthur Dunham, "The War As I Saw It," 3 volume set, in the Army Experiences Questionnaire Collection, 40th Division, Divisional Troops, 115th Engineers; "Their Bit And Their Utmost," *Gas Attack* (Camp Wadsworth), 23 February 1918.

84. "Dangerous Safety," *Camp Dodger*, 9 November 1917, 4.

85. "Young Lady," editorial in *Gas Attack* (Camp Wadsworth), 9 March 1918, 4.

86. Ibid.

87. Edith Fosdick Bodley to Raymond Fosdick, 21 April 1918, doc. 27898, box 59, entry 393, RG 165, National Archives.

88. "Tamperers," editorial, *Camp Dodger*, 18 January 1918, 2.

89. H. L. Mencken, " 'Reformers' Oppose Sanitary Measures against Disease," *Evening Mail*, 18 September 1917, clipped and included in Frederick H. Whitin to Raymond Fosdick, 24 September 1917, doc. 4859, file Alabama 37 (2 of 2), box 3, entry 395, RG 165, National Archives.

90. Dr. Hughes to Senator Cummins, received at the CTCA 12 July 1917, doc. 2182, letter file, box 1, entry 394, RG 165, National Archives.

91. Corporal Charles B. Merritt to his mother, 24 February 1918, in "War Letters of Corporal Charles B. Merritt," Army Experiences Questionnaire Collection, 28th Division, 112th Infantry, Company M.

92. Howard Webster Munder to father, 12 February 1918, in "Letters and Diary of Bugler Howard Webster Munder," in the Army Experiences Questionnaire Collection, 28th Division, 55th Infantry Battalion, 109th Regiment, Company G.

93. Questionnaire of Sergeant Roy Montgomery, Army Experiences Questionnaire Collection, 36th Division, 72nd Battalion, 143rd Regiment, Headquarters Company.

94. Other answers included "Cards and women-gambling," "For myself it was draw poker. For others it was mostly drinking," and "Going to town, and make—'Woopee,' " Questionnaire of Dennis M. Bass, 39th Division, 114th Engineers, Company E; Questionnaire of Corporal Francis M. Hoffman, 28th Division, 53rd Artillery Brigade, 107th Field Artillery Regiment, Battery A; Questionnaire of Corporal William H. Jones, 85th Division, 169th Infantry Battalion, 338th Infantry Regiment. See also the questionnaires of Private Oscar Edward Young, 91st Division, 181st Infantry Battalion, 361st Infantry Regiment, Headquarters Company; Dolumbo M. Caleffie, 87th Division, 347th Regiment Band. All available in the Army Experiences Questionnaire Collection.

95. Neil A. Wynn, *From Progressivism to Prosperity: World War I and American Society* (New York, Holmes and Meier, 1986), 123.

96. Fred D. Baldwin, "The American Enlisted Man in World War One," Ph.D. diss., Princeton University, 1964, 115, 213.

97. Alan Dawley discusses this notion of raised expectations more broadly in his *Struggles for Justice: Social Responsibility and the Liberal State* (Cambridge: Harvard University Press, 1991), 234–235.

98. Arthur S. Link, "What Happened to the Progressive Movement in the 1920s," *American Historical Review* 64 (1959): 833–851; Dawley, *Struggles for Justice*, 239–240.

99. Raymond B. Fosdick, *Chronicle of a Generation: An Autobiography* (New York: Harper, 1958), 189, 198–199, 201–202.

100. For a thoughtful treatment of Lodge's view of the peace see William C. Widenor, *Henry Cabot Lodge and the Search for an American Foreign Policy* (Berkeley: University of California Press, 1980).

101. David M. Kennedy, *Over Here: The First World War and American Society* (New York: Oxford University Press, 1980), 259–260; Dawley, *Struggles for Justice*, 217, 224–228.

Index

28827974R00186

Made in the USA
Lexington, KY
07 January 2014